Dying Words

THE LANGUAGE LIBRARY

Series editor: David Crystal

The Language Library was created in 1952 by Eric Partridge, the great etymologist and lexicographer, who from 1966 to 1976 was assisted by his co-editor Simeon Potter. Together they commissioned volumes on the traditional themes of language study, with particular emphasis on the history of the English language and on the individual linguistic styles of major English authors. In 1977 David Crystal took over as editor, and *The Language Library* now includes titles in many areas of linguistic enquiry.

The most recently published titles in the series include:

Ronald Carter and Walter Nash	*Seeing Through Language*
Florian Coulmas	*The Writing Systems of the World*
David Crystal	*A Dictionary of Linguistics and Phonetics, Sixth Edition*
J. A. Cuddon	*A Dictionary of Literary Terms and Literary Theory, Fourth Edition*
Viv Edwards	*Multilingualism in the English-speaking World*
Nicholas Evans	*Dying Words: Endangered Languages and What They Have to Tell Us*
Amalia E. Gnanadesikan	*The Writing Revolution: Cuneiform to the Internet*
Geoffrey Hughes	*A History of English Words*
Walter Nash	*Jargon*
Roger Shuy	*Language Crimes*
Gunnel Tottie	*An Introduction to American English*
Ronald Wardhaugh	*Investigating Language*
Ronald Wardhaugh	*Proper English: Myths and Misunderstandings about Language*

Dying Words

Endangered Languages and What They Have to Tell Us

Nicholas Evans

WILEY-BLACKWELL

A John Wiley & Sons, Ltd., Publication

This edition first published 2010

Blackwell Publishing was acquired by John Wiley & Sons in February 2007. Blackwell's publishing program has been merged with Wiley's global Scientific, Technical, and Medical business to form Wiley-Blackwell.

Registered Office
John Wiley & Sons Ltd, The Atrium, Southern Gate, Chichester, West Sussex, PO19 8SQ, United Kingdom

Editorial Offices
350 Main Street, Malden, MA 02148-5020, USA
9600 Garsington Road, Oxford, OX4 2DQ, UK
The Atrium, Southern Gate, Chichester, West Sussex, PO19 8SQ, UK

For details of our global editorial offices, for customer services, and for information about how to apply for permission to reuse the copyright material in this book please see our website at www.wiley.com/wiley-blackwell.

Library of Congress Cataloging-in-Publication Data
Evans, Nicholas, 1956–
    Dying words : endangered languages and what they have to tell us / Nicholas Evans.
       p. cm. – (Language library)
    Includes bibliographical references and indexes.
    ISBN 978-0-631-23305-3 (alk. paper) – ISBN 978-0-631-23306-0 (pbk. : alk. paper)
1. Endangered languages.   I. Title.   II. Series.
    P40.5.E53E93 2009
    408.9–dc22
                                                              2008044645

A catalogue record for this book is available from the British Library.

Set in 10/13pt Minion by Graphicraft Limited, Hong Kong
Printed in Singapore by Ho Printing Singapore Pte Ltd

2 2009

for my parents and children,
by blood and by teaching

Contents

Contents

Acknowledgments

My first debt is to the speakers of fragile languages who have welcomed me into their communities and their ways of talking, thinking, and living. †Darwin and May Moodoonuthi adopted me as their tribal son in 1982 and they and the rest of the Bentinck Island community taught me their language as if I were a new child. The community has extended its love and understanding to me and my wife and children ever since, despite the tragically premature deaths of so many of its members. I particularly thank †Darwin Moodoonuthi, †Roland Moodoonuthi, †Arthur Paul, †Alison Dundaman, †Pluto Bentinck, †Dugal Goongarra, †Pat Gabori, †May Moodoonuthi, Netta Loogatha, †Olive Loogatha, Sally Gabori, and Paula Paul. Since 1982 I have had the good fortune to be taught about other Aboriginal languages by †Toby Gangele, †Minnie Alderson, Eddie Hardie, †Big John Dalnga-Dalnga, and †Mick Kubarkku (Mayali, Gun-djeihmi, Kuninjku, and Kune dialects of Bininj Gun-wok), †David Kalbuma, †Alice Boehm, †Jack Chadum, †Peter Mandeberru, Jimmy Weson, and Maggie Tukumba (Dalabon), †Charlie Wardaga (Ilgar), †Mick Yarmirr (Marrku), †Tim Mamitba, †Brian Yambikbik, Joy Williams, Khaki Marrala, Mary Yarmirr, David Minyumak, and Archie Brown (Iwaidja). Each of these people, and many others too numerous to name and thank individually here, is linked in my mind to vivid and powerful moments as, in their own resonant languages, they discussed things I had never attended to or thought about before.

I would also like to thank my teachers and mentors in linguistics for the way they have imbued the field with fascination and insight: Bob Dixon, Bill Foley, Igor Mel'cuk, †Tim Shopen, and Anna Wierzbicka during my initial studies at the Australian National University, and more recently Barry Blake, Melissa Bowerman, Michael Clyne, Grev Corbett, Ken Hale, Lary Hyman, Steve Levinson, Francesca Merlan, Andy Pawley, Frans Plank, Ger Reesink, Dan Slobin, Peter Sutton, and Alan Rumsey. Many of the ideas touched upon here have developed during conversations with my colleagues Felix Ameka, Alan Dench, Janet Fletcher, Cliff Goddard, Nikolaus Himmelmann, Pat McConvell, Tim McNamara, Rachel Nordlinger, Kia Peiros, Lesley Stirling, Nick Thieberger, Jill Wigglesworth, and David Wilkins, my students Isabel Bickerdike, Amanda Brotchie, Nick Enfield, Sebastian Olcher

Fedden, Alice Gaby, Nicole Kruspe, Robyn Loughnane, Aung Si and Ruth Singer, and my fellow fieldworkers Murray Garde, Bruce Birch, Allan Marett, and Linda Barwick.

In putting this book together I have been overwhelmed by the generosity of scholars from around the world who have shared with me their expertise on particular languages or fields, and I thank the following: Abdul-Samad Abdullah (Arabic), Sander Adelaar (Malagasy and Austronesian more generally), Sasha Aikhenvald (Amazonian languages) Linda Barwick (Arnhem Land song language), Roger Blench (various African languages), Marco Boevé (Arammba), Lera Boroditsky (various Whorfian experiments), Matthias Brenzinger (African languages), Penny Brown (Tzeltal), John Colarusso (Ubykh), Grev Corbett (Archi), Robert Debski (Polish), Mark Durie (Acehnese), Domenyk Eades (Arabic), Carlos Fausto (Kuikurú), David Fleck (Matses), Zygmunt Frajzyngier (Chadic), Bruna Franchetto (Kuikurú), Murray Garde (Arnhem Land clans and languages), Andrew Garrett (Yurok), Jost Gippert (Caucasian Albanian), Victor Golla (Pacific Coast Athabaskan), Lucia Golluscio (indigenous languages of Argentina), Colette Grinevald (Mayan, languages of Nicaragua), Tom Güldemann (Taa and Khoisan in general), Alice Harris (Udi), John Haviland (Guugu Yimithirr, Tzotzil), Luise Hercus (Pali and Sanskrit), Jane Hill (Uto-Aztecan), Kenneth Hill (Hopi), Larry Hyman (West African tone languages), Rhys Jones (Welsh), Russell Jones (Welsh), Anthony Jukes (Makassarese), Dagmar Jung (Athabaskan), Jim Kari (Dena'ina), Sotaro Kita (gesture in Japanese and Turkish), Mike Krauss (Eyak), Nicole Kruspe (Ceq Wong), Jon Landaburu (Andoke), Mary Laughren (Wanyi), Steve Levinson (Guugu Yimithirr, Yélî-Dnye), Robyn Loughnane (Oksapmin), Andrej Malchukov (Siberian languages), Yaron Matras (Romani), Peter Matthews (Mayan epigraphy), Patrick McConvell (various Australian), Fresia Mellica Avendaño (Mapudungun), Cristina Messineo (Toba), Mike Miles (Ottoman Turkish Sign Language), Marianne Mithun (Pomo, Iroquoian), Lesley Moore (Mandara Mountains), Valentín Moreno (Toba), Claire Moyse-Faurie (New Caledonian languages), Hiroshi Nakagawa (|Gui), Christfried Naumann (Taa), Irina Nikolaeva (Siberian languages), Miren Lourdes Oñederra (Basque), Mimi Ono (|Gui, and Khoisan generally), Toshiki Osada (Mundari), Nick Ostler (Aztec, Sanskrit and many others), Midori Osumi (New Caledonian languages), Aslı Özyürek (Turkish gesture, Turkish Sign Language), Andy Pawley (Kalam), Maki Purti (Mundari), Valentin Peralta Ramirez (Nahuatl / Aztec), Bob Rankin (Siouan), Richard Rhodes (Algonquian), Malcolm Ross (Oceanic languages), Alan Rumsey (Ku Waru, New Guinea Highlands chanted tales), Geoff Saxe (Oksapmin counting), Wolfgang Schulze (Caucasian Albanian / Udi), Peter Sutton (Cape York languages), McComas Taylor (Sanskrit), Marina Tchoumakina (Archi), Nick Thieberger (Vanuatu languages, digital archiving), Graham Thurgood (Tsat and Chamic), Mauro Tosco (Cushitic), Ed Vajda (Ket and other Yeniseian), Rand Valentine (Ojibwa), Dave Watters (Kusunda), Kevin Windle (Slavic), Tony Woodbury (Yup'ik), Yunji Wu (Chinese), Roberto Zavala (Oluteco, Mixe-Zoquean), Ulrike Zeshan (Turkish Sign Language).

A special thanks to those who arranged for me to visit or meet with speakers of a wide range of languages around the world as I researched this book: Zarina Estrada Fernandez (northern Mexico), Murray Garde (Bunlap Village, Vanuatu), Andrew Garrett (Yurok, northern California), Lucia Golluscio (Argentina), Nicole Kruspe (Pos Iskandar and Bukit Bangkong, Malaysia), the Mayan language organization OKMA and its director Nik't'e

(María Juliana Sis Iboy) in Antigua, Guatemala, Patricia Shaw (Musqueam Community in Vancouver), and especially Roberto Zavala and Valentín Peralta Ramirez for a memorable journey down through Mexico to Guatemala. Not all these stories made it through to the final, pruned manuscript, but they all shaped its spirit.

A number of institutions and programs have given me indispensable support in researching and writing this book: the University of Melbourne, the Australian National University, the Institut für Sprachwissenschaft, Universität Köln, the Alexander von Humboldt-Stiftung, CIESAS (Mexico), OKMA (Guatemala), and the Universidad de Buenos Aires. Two other organizations whose ambitious research programs have enormously expanded my horizons are the Max Planck Institute for Psycholinguistics in Nijmegen, and the Volkswagenstiftung through its DoBeS Program (*Dokumentation Bedrohter Sprachen*) and in particular for its support of the Iwaidja Documentation Program. In this connection, I thank Vera Szoelloesi-Brenig for her wise stewardship of the overall program, and many participants in the DoBeS program, especially Nikolaus Himmelmann, Ulrike Mosel, Hans-Jürgen Sasse, and Peter Wittenberg, for formative discussions.

The process of putting these obscure and disparate materials together into a coherent book directed at a broad readership would have been impossible without the generous support of two one-month residencies in Italy, one in Bellagio sponsored by the Rockefeller Foundation, and a second in Bogliasco sponsored by the Bogliasco Foundation. I thank these two foundations for their wonderfully humanistic way of supporting creative work, and in particular would like to thank Pilar Palacia (Bellagio) and Anna Maria Quaiat, Ivana Folle, and Alessandra Natale (Bogliasco) for their hospitality and friendship, as well as the other residents for their many clarifying discussions.

Publication of this work was assisted by a publication grant from the University of Melbourne, as well as further financial support from the Research School of Pacific and Asian Studies, Australian National University, and I thank both institutions for their generous support.

At various points along the way Amos Teo and Robert Mailhammer checked the text and chased up materials, cartographers Chandra Jayasuriya (University of Melbourne) and Kay Dancey (Cartographic Services, RSPAS, Australian National University) produced the maps, Julie Manley assisted with many of the visuals, and Felicita Carr gave indispensable help in obtaining permissions on getting the final version of a sprawling manuscript together. Without them this book would still be a draft.

A number of people read and commented on drafts of the entire manuscript and I thank them for their perceptive comments and advice: Michael Clyne, Jane Ellen, Lloyd Evans, Penny Johnson, Andrew Solomon, and Nick Thieberger. David Crystal also read the entire manuscript, and gave invaluable writerly advice and support through the many years of this project's gestation: *diolch yn fawr*! I am also grateful to Melissa Bowerman for her careful comments on an earlier version of chapter 8. Two anonymous reviewers for Blackwell also blessed me with incredibly detailed, helpful, and erudite comments.

The staff at Wiley-Blackwell have been a model of supportive professionalism, although my laggardliness has meant the project has needed to be passed through a large number of individuals: I thank Tami Kaplan, Kelly Basner, and Danielle Descoteaux.

Publishing and Copyright Acknowledgments

The author and publisher gratefully acknowledge the permission granted to reproduce the copyright material in this book. The following sources and copyright holders for materials are given in order of appearance in the text.

Text Credits

Fishman, Joshua. 1982. Whorfianism of the third kind: ethnolinguistic diversity as a worldwide societal asset. *Language in Society* 11:1–14. Quote from Fishman (1982:7) reprinted with permission of Cambridge University Press.

Rogers, Henry. 2005. *Writing Systems: A Linguistic Approach*. Oxford: Blackwell Publishing. Material in table 2.1 herein reprinted with permission of the author and Wiley-Blackwell.

Cann, Rebecca. 2000. Talking trees tell tales. *Nature* 405(29/6/00):1008–9. Quote from Cann (2000:1009) reprinted with permission of Macmillan Publishers Ltd.

Levinson, Stephen C. 2003. *Space in Language and Cognition*. Cambridge: Cambridge University Press. Levinson's figure 4.11 (p. 156) reproduced here as figure 8.3 with permission of Cambridge University Press.

Brown, Penelope. 2001. Learning to talk about motion UP and DOWN in Tzeltal: is there a language-specific bias for verb learning? In *Language Acquisition and Conceptual Development*, ed. Melissa Bowerman and Stephen C. Levinson. Cambridge: Cambridge University Press, pp. 512–43. The second half of Brown's figure 17.2 (p. 529) reproduced here as table 8.2 with permission of Cambridge University Press.

Woodbury, Anthony. 1998. Documenting rhetorical, aesthetic and expressive loss in language shift. In *Endangered Languages: Current Issues and Future Prospects*, ed. L. A. Grenoble and L. J. Whaley. Cambridge: Cambridge University Press, pp. 234–60. Quotes from Woodbury (1998:250, 257) reprinted with permission of Cambridge University Press.

Hale, Ken. 1998. On endangered languages and the importance of linguistic diversity. In *Endangered Languages: Current Issues and Future Prospects*, ed. L. A. Grenoble and L. J. Whaley. Cambridge: Cambridge University Press, pp. 192–216. Quote from Hale (1998:211) reprinted with permission of Cambridge University Press.

Other copyright holders are acknowledged in the text, as appropriate.

Figure Credits

Photo in box 1.1 courtesy of Leslie Moore.

Figure 1.4 from Arizona State Museum, University of Arizona, James Manson (photographer), JWM ASM-25114, reproduced with permission of the Arizona State Museum.

Figure 2.1 from Florida Center for Instructional Technology, University of South Florida, http://etc.usf.edu/clipart/25300/25363/sahagun_25363.htm.

Figure 2.2 no. 14, part XI, p. 62 from the Florentine Codex: *General History of the Things of New Spain, Book 10: The People*, translated from the Azetec into English, with notes and illustration, by Charles E. Dibble and Arthur J. O. Anderson (Santa Fe, NM/Salt Lake City: the School of American Research and the University of Utah, 1961), reproduced with permission of the University of Utah Press.

Figure 2.3 from the American Philosophical Society, Franz Boas Papers, Collection 7. Photographs.

Figure 2.4 reproduced with permission of the National Anthropological Archives, Smithsonian Institution (neg. no. 8300).

Figure 2.5 p. 53 in *Handbook of North American Indians, vol. 17: Languages*, ed. Ives Goddard (Washington, DC: Smithsonian Institution, 1996).

Figure 2.6 courtesy Turk Kulturune Hizmet Vakfi.

Figure 3.1 photo courtesy US National Archives, originally from US Marine Corps, No. 69889-B.

Figure 3.2 photo courtesy of Christfried Naumann.

Photo in box 3.1 from Georges Dumézil, *Documents Anatoliens sur les Langues et les Traditions du Caucase, Vol. 2: Textes Oubykhs* (Paris: Institut d'Ethnologie, 1962).

Figure 3.3 p. 104 in Nancy Munn, *Walbiri Iconography: Graphic Representations and Cultural Symbolism in a Central Australian Society* (Ithaca: Cornell University Press, 1973), reprinted with permission.

Photo in box 3.2 by kind permission of Geoff Saxe.

Figure 4.1 photo courtesy of David Fleck.

Figure 5.1 illustration 3b in Alexander Murray, *Sir William Jones 1746-1794: A Commemoration* (Oxford: Oxford University Press, 1998).

Photo in box 5.1 courtesy of Michael Krauss.

Figure 6.4 pp. 77, 96, 218, and 220 in *The Lexicon of Proto-Oceanic: Volume 1, Material Culture*, ed. Malcolm D. Ross, Andrew Pawley, and Meredith Osmond (Canberra: Australian National University, 1998), reprinted with permission. Original spatula drawings p. 226 in Hans Nevermann, *Admiralitäts-Inseln* in *Ergebnisse der Südsee-Expedition 1908–1910*, ed. G. Thilenus, vol. 2 A3 (Hamburg: Friederichsen, De Gruyter & Co, 1934).

Table 6.3 adapted, with permission, from pp. 96–7 in *The Lexicon of Proto-Oceanic: Volume 1, Material Culture*, ed. Malcolm D. Ross, Andrew Pawley, and Meredith Osmond (Canberra: Australian National University, 1998).

Figure 6.6 reproduced with kind permission of H. Werner.

Figure 7.1 British Library Photo 392/29(95). © British Library Board. All rights reserved 392/29(95). Reproduced with permission.

Figure 7.2 p. 6 in Richard Cook, *Tangut (Xīxià) Orthography and Unicode* (2007). Available online at http://unicode.org/~rscook/Xixia/, accessed May 13, 2008.

Figure 7.4 figure 3, pp. 1–16, in Stephen D. Houston and David Stuart, "The *way* glyph: evidence for 'co-essences' among the Classic Maya," *Research Reports on Ancient Maya Writing* 30 (Washington: Center for Maya Research, 1989). Reproduced with permission.

Figure 7.6 frontispiece in George H. Forsyth and Kurt Weitzmann, with Ihor Ševčenko and Fred Anderegg, *The Monastery of Saint Catherine at Mount Sinai: The Church and Fortress of Justinian, Plates* (Ann Arbor: The University of Michigan Press, 1973).

Figure 7.7 adapted, with permission, from Zaza Alexidze and Betty Blair, "The Albanian script: the process – how its secrets were revealed," *Azerbaijan International* 11/3:44–51 (2003). Available online at www.azer.com/aiweb/categories/magazine/ai113_folder/113_articles/113_zaza_secrets_revealed.html, accessed November 11, 2008.

Figure 7.9 drawing by George E. Stuart reproduced from Terrence Kaufman and John Justeson, "Epi-Olmec hieroglyphic writing and texts" (2001). Available online at www.albany.edu/anthro/maldp/papers.htm, accessed October 15, 2008.

Figure 7.11 from Terrence Kaufman and John Justeson, "Epi-Olmec hieroglyphic writing and texts" (2001). Available online at www.albany.edu/anthro/maldp/papers.htm, accessed October 15, 2008, reprinted by permission.

Figures 8.1 and 8.2 photos excerpted from film footage by John Haviland and Steve Levinson, reproduced with permission.

Figure 8.3 p. 156 in Stephen C. Levinson, *Space in Language and Cognition* (Cambridge: Cambridge University Press, 2003), reprinted by permission of Cambridge University Press.

Figure 8.4 photos by kind permission of Daniel Haun.

Figure 8.5 p. 430 in R. Núñez and E. Sweetser, "With the future behind them: Convergent evidence from Aymara language and gesture in the crosslinguistic comparison of spatial construals of time," *Cognitive Science* 30, 3, 401–50 (2006), reprinted by permission of the publisher (Taylor and Francis Ltd, www.tandf.co.uk/journals).

Figure 8.6 p. 436 in R. Núñez and E. Sweetser, "With the future behind them: Convergent evidence from Aymara language and gesture in the crosslinguistic comparison of spatial construals of time," *Cognitive Science* 30, 3, 401–50 (2006), reprinted by permission of the publisher (Taylor and Francis Ltd, www.tandf.co.uk/journals).

Figures 8.7–11 frames extracted from the video files of experiments reported in Sotaro Kita and Aslı Özyürek, "What does cross-linguistic variation in semantic coordination of speech and gesture reveal? Evidence for an interface representation of spatial thinking and speaking," pp. 16–32 from *Journal of Memory and Language* 48 (2003). Reproduced with permission.

Figure 8.12 from Melissa Bowerman, "The tale of 'tight fit': How a semantic category grew up." PowerPoint presentation for talk at "Language and Space" workshop, Lille, May 9, 2007.

Figure 9.2 from Milman Parry Collection, Harvard University.

Figure 9.3 photo courtesy of Don Niles, Institute of Papua New Guinea Studies.

Photo in box 9.1 courtesy of Nicole Kruspe.

Figure 9.4 photo by Mary Moses, reprinted with permission of Tony Woodbury.

Photo in box 10.1 courtesy of Dave Watters.

Photo in box 10.2 courtesy of Cristina Messineo.

Figure 10.1 photo courtesy of Sarah Cutfield.

Figure 10.2 photo courtesy of John Dumbacher.

Photos in box 10.4 top photo courtesy of Mara Santos, lower photo courtesy of Vincent Carelli.

For permission to use the painting "Sweers Island" on the cover of this book, I would like to thank Mornington Island Arts & Crafts and Alcaston Gallery, as well as the Bentinck Island Artists: Sally Gabori, †May Moodoonuthi, Paula Paul, Netta Loogatha, Amy Loogatha, Dawn Naranatjil, and Ethel Thomas.

Prologue

No volverá tu voz a lo que el persa
Dijo en su lengua de aves y de rosas,
Cuando al ocaso, ante la luz dispersa,
Quieras decir inolvidables cosas

You will never recapture what the Persian
Said in his language woven with birds and roses,
When, in the sunset, before the light disperses,
You wish to give words to unforgettable things

(Borges 1972:116–17)[1]

Un vieillard qui meurt est une bibliothèque
qui brûle.

An old person dying is a library burning.

(Amadou Hampaté Bâ, address to UNESCO, 1960)

Pat Gabori, *Kabararrjingathi bulthuku*,[2] is, at the time I write these words, one of eight remaining speakers of Kayardild, the Aboriginal language of Bentinck Island, Queensland, Australia. For this old man, blind for the last four decades, the wider world entered his life late enough that he never saw how you should sit in a car. He sits cross-legged on the car seat facing backwards, as if in a dinghy. Perhaps his blindness has helped him keep more vividly alive the world he grew up in. He loves to talk for hours about sacred places on Bentinck Island, feats of hunting, intricate tribal genealogies, and feuds over women. Sometimes he interrupts his narrative to break into song. His deep knowledge of tribal law made him a key witness in a recent legal challenge to the Australian government, to obtain recognition of traditional sea rights. But fewer and fewer people can understand his stories.

Kayardild was never a large language. At its peak it probably counted no more than 150 speakers, and by the time I was introduced to Pat in 1982 there were fewer than 40 left, all middle-aged or older.

The fate of the language was sealed in the 1940s when missionaries evacuated the entire population of Bentinck Islanders from their ancestral territories, relocating them to the mission on Mornington Island, some 50 km to the northwest. At the time of their relocation the whole population were monolingual Kayardild speakers, but from that day on no new child would master the tribal language. The sibling link, by which one child

Figure 0.1   Pat Gabori, *Kabararrjingathi bulthuku* (photo: Nicholas Evans)

passes on their language to another, was broken during the first years after the relocation, a dark decade from which no baby survived. A dormitory policy separated children from their parents for most of the day, and punished any child heard speaking an Aboriginal language.

Kayardild, which we shall learn more about in this book, challenges many tenets about what a possible human language is. A famous article on the evolution of language by psycholinguists Steve Pinker and Paul Bloom, for example, claimed that "no language uses noun affixes to express tense"[3] (grammatical time). This putative restriction is in line with Noam Chomsky's theory of Universal Grammar, which sees a prior restriction on possible human languages as an essential aid to the language-learning child in narrowing down the set of hypotheses she needs to deduce the grammar underlying her parents' speech.

Well, Kayardild blithely disregards this supposed impossibility, and marks tense on nouns as well as verbs. If you say "he saw (the) turtle," for example, you say *niya kurrijarra bangana*. You mark the past tense on the verb *kurrij* "to see," as *-arra*, but also on the object-noun *banga* "turtle," as *-na*. Putting this into the future, to "he will see (the) turtle," you say *niya kurriju bangawu*, marking futurity on both verb (*-u*) and noun (*-wu*). (Pronounce *a*, *i*, and *u* with their Spanish or Italian values, the *rr* as a trill, the *ng* as in *singer*, and the *j* as in *jump*.)[4]

Kayardild shows us how dangerous it is to talk about "universals" of language on the basis of a narrow sample that ignores the true extent of the world's linguistic diversity.[5] Thinking about it objectively, the Kayardild system isn't so crazy. Tense locates the whole event in time – the participants, as well as the action depicted by the verb. The tense logics developed by logicians in the twentieth century plug whole propositions into their tense operators, including the bits denoted by both verbs and nouns in English. Spreading around the tense-marking, Kayardild-style, shows the "propositional scope" of tense.

But learning Kayardild is not just a matter of mastering a grammar that no human language is supposed to have. It also requires you to think quite differently about the world. Try moving *the eastern page of this book* a bit further *north on your lap*. Probably you will need to do a bit of unfamiliar thinking before you can follow this instruction. But if you spoke Kayardild, most sentences you uttered would refer to the compass points in this way, and you would respond instantly and accurately to this request.

Pat Gabori is in his eighties, and the youngest fluent speakers are in their sixties. So it seems impossible that a single speaker will remain alive when, in 2042, a hundred years will mark the removal of the Kaiadilt people from Bentinck Island. In the space of a lifetime a unique and fascinating tongue will have gone from being the only language of its people, to a silent figment of the past.

Traveling five hundred miles to the northwest we reach Croker Island in Australia's Northern Territory. There, in 2003, I attended the funeral of Charlie Wardaga, my teacher, friend, and classificatory elder brother. It was a chaotic affair. Weeks had passed between his death and the arrival of mourners, songmen, and dancers from many surrounding tribes. All this time his body lay in a wooden European-style coffin, attracting a growing number of flies in the late dry-season heat, under a traditional Aboriginal bough-shade decked with red pennants in a tradition borrowed from those wide-ranging Indonesian seafarers, the Macassans. His bereaved wife waited under the bough-shade while we all came to pay our last respects, grasping a knife lying on the coffin and slashing our heads with it to allay our grief.

Figure 0.2 Charlie Wardaga (photo: Nicholas Evans)

Later, as the men silently dug Charlie's grave pit, the old women had to be restrained from leaping in. Then the searing, daggering traditional music gave way to Christian hymns more conducive to contemplation and acceptance. With this old man's burial we were not just burying a tribal elder pivotal in the life and struggles of this small community. The book and volume of his brain had been the last to hold several languages of the region: Ilgar, which is the language of his own Mangalara clan, but also Garig, Manangkardi, and Marrku, as well as more widely known languages like Iwaidja and Kunwinjku. Although we had managed to transfer a small fraction of this knowledge into a more durable form before he died, as recordings and fieldnotes, our work had begun too late. When I first met him in 1994 he was already an old man suffering from increasing deafness and physical immobility, so that the job had barely begun, and the Manangkardi language, for instance, had been too far down the queue to get much attention.

For his children and other clan members, the loss of such a knowledgeable senior relative took away their last chance of learning their own language and the full tribal knowledge that it communicated: place-names that identify each stretch of beach, formulae for coaxing turtle to the surface, and the evocative lines of the Seagull song cycle, which Charlie himself had sung at other people's funerals. For me, as a linguist, it left a host of unanswered questions. Some of these questions can still be answered for Iwaidja and Mawng, relatively "large" related languages with around two hundred speakers each. But others were crucially dependent on Ilgar or Marrku data.

My sense of despair at what gets lost when such magnificent languages fall silent – both to their own small communities and to the wider world of scholarship – prompted me to write this book. Although my own first-hand experience has mainly been with fragile languages in Aboriginal Australia, similar tragedies are devastating small speech communities right around the world. Language death has occurred throughout human history, but among the world's six thousand or more modern tongues the pace of extinction is quickening, and we are likely to witness the loss of half of the world's six thousand languages by the end of this century.[6] On best current estimates, every two weeks, somewhere in the world, the last speaker of a fading language dies. No one's mind will again travel the thought-paths that its ancestral speakers once blazed. No one will hear its sounds again except from a recording, and no one can go back to check a translation, or ask a new question about how the language works.

Each language has a different story to tell us. Indeed, if we record it properly, each will have its own library shelf loaded with grammars, dictionaries, botanical and zoological encyclopedias, and collections of songs and stories. But language leads a double life, shuttling between "out there" in the community of speakers and "in there" in individual minds that need to know it all in order to use and teach it. So there come moments of history when the whole accumulated edifice of an oral culture rests, invisible and inaudible, in the memory of its last living witness. This book is about everything that is lost when we bury such a person, and about what we can do to bring out as much of their knowledge as possible into a durable form that can be passed on to future generations.

Such is the distinctiveness of many of these languages that, for certain riddles of humanity, just one language holds the key. But we do not know in advance which language holds the answer to which question. And as the science of linguistics becomes more sophisticated, the questions we seek answers to are multiplying.

The task of recording the knowledge hanging on in the minds of Pat Gabori and his counterparts around the world is a formidable one. For each language, the complexity of information we need to map is comparable to that of the human genome. But, unlike the human genome, or the concrete products of human endeavor that archaeologists study, languages perish without physical trace except in the rare cases where a writing system has been developed. As discernible structures, they only exist as fleeting sounds or movements. The classic goal of a descriptive linguist is to distil this knowledge, by a combination of systematic questioning and the recording and transcribing of whatever stories the speaker wishes to tell, into at least a trilogy of grammar, texts, and a dictionary. Increasingly this is supplemented by sound and video recordings that add information about intonation, gesture, and context. Though documentary linguists now go beyond what most investigators aspired to do a hundred years ago, we can still capture just a fraction of the knowledge that any one speaker holds in their heads, and which – once the speaker population dwindles – is at risk of never coming to light because no one thinks to ask about it.

This book is about the full gamut of what we lose when languages die, about why it matters, and about what questions and techniques best shape our response to this looming collapse of human ways of knowing. These questions, I believe, can only be addressed properly if we give the study of fragile languages its rightful place in the grand narrative of human ideas and the forgotten histories of peoples who walked lightly through the world, without consigning their words to stone or parchment. And because we can only meet this challenge through a concerted effort by linguists, the communities themselves, and the lay public, I have tried to write this book in a way that speaks to all these types of reader.

Revolutions in digital technology mean that linguists can now record and analyze more than they ever could, in exquisitely accurate sound and video, and archive these in ways that were unthinkable a generation ago. At the same time, the history of the field shows us that good linguistic description depends as much on the big questions that linguists are asking as it does on the techniques that they bring to their field site.

Tweaking an old axiom, you only hear what you listen for, and you only listen for what you are wondering about. The goal of this book is to take stock of what we should be wondering about as we listen to the dying words of the thousands of languages falling silent around us, across the totality of what Mike Krauss has christened the "logosphere": just as the "biosphere" is the totality of all species of life and all ecological links on earth, the logosphere is the whole vast realm of the world's words, the languages that they build, and the links between them.

Further Reading

Important books covering the topic of language death include Grenoble and Whaley (1998), Crystal (2000), Nettle and Romaine (2000), Dalby (2003), and Harrison (2007); for a French view, see Hagège (2000).

The difficult challenge of what small communities can do to maintain their languages is a topic I decided not to tackle in this book, partly because there were already so many other topics I wanted to cover, but also because it is such an uphill battle, with so few positive achievements, and as much at the mercy of political and economic factors as of purely linguistic ones. Good general accounts of the problem can be found in Bradley and Bradley (2002), Crystal (2000), Hinton and Hale (2001), Grenoble and Whaley (2006), Tsunoda (2005). See also Fellman (1973) for an account of the successful revival of Hebrew pioneered by Eliezer Ben-Yehuda, and Amery (2000) for an upbeat account of the attempts by the Kaurna people of South Australia to revive their language.

A Note on the Presentation of Linguistic Material

One of the themes of this book is that each language contains its own unique set of clues to some of the mysteries of human existence. At the same time, the only way to weave these disparate threads together into a unifying pattern is on the loom of a common language, which in this book is English.

The paradox we face, as writers and readers about other languages, is to give a faithful representation of what we are studying in all its particularity, and at the same time to make it comprehensible to all who speak our language.

The first problem is how to represent unfamiliar sounds. Do we adapt the English alphabet, Berlitz-style, or do we use the technical phonetic symbols that, with their six hundred or so letter-shapes, are capable of accurately representing each known human speech sound to the trained reader? Thus we can use either English *ng* or the special phonetic symbol ŋ to write the sound in the Kayardild word *bangaa/baŋaː* "turtle" (*aː* represents a long *a*, so the whole word is pronounced something like *bung-ah* in English spelling conventions). Or we can write the Kayardild word for "left" as *thaku*, adapting English letters, but we then need to remember that the initial *th*, although it involves putting the tongue between the teeth like in English, is a stop rather than a fricative. It sounds like the *d* in *width* or the *t* in *eighth* – try watching your tongue in the mirror as you say these – and can be represented accurately by the special phonetic symbol t̪, where the little diacritic shows that the tongue is placed between the teeth: thus, *t̪aku*.

Since so many of the languages we will look at have sounds not easily rendered in English, I will sometimes need to use special phonetic symbols, which are spice to the linguist but indigestible to the lay reader. If you are in this latter category, just ignore the phonetic representation. When the point I am making depends on the pronunciation I will give a Berlitz-style rendition, but when it does not you should just work from the gloss and the English translation. Note also that, since some minority languages have developed their own practical orthographies (spelling systems), it is often more appropriate to write words in these rather than in standardized phonetic symbols.

There is a second problem, perhaps a deeper one, as it engages with the inner concepts of the language, not just the outer garment of its pronunciation: how do we show the often unfamiliar packaging of its concepts? In the technical style of linguistics articles we have a solution to this: a traditional three-line treatment that transcribes each language phonetically on one line, then gives an *interlinear gloss* (or just *gloss*) breaking it down into its smallest meaningful parts, then a free translation into English.

Consider the problem of representing what Pat Gabori said in a Native Title hearing when he was asked to take an oath equivalent to "I shall tell the truth, the whole truth, and nothing but the truth." I was interpreting in that hearing, and Pat and I had to confer for a while before he came up with the following formulation, which I will show the way that linguists would write it:

(1) *Ngada maarra junku-ru-thu,*
     I   only   right-FACTITIVE-POTENTIAL
     thaku-ru-nangku.
     left-FACTITIVE-NEGATIVE.POTENTIAL
     Literally: "I will only make things right, I won't make (anything) left."
     Freely: "I will only make things correct, I won't twist or distort anything."

As you can see, the Kayardild version compresses two English sentences into just four words. Additionally, it uses a symmetrical metaphor (right → correct :: left → incorrect) where English only extends one of the terms (right) into the domain of truth and correctness. Setting the sentence out as in (1), by showing the word roots, makes this clear. Additionally, Kayardild can build new "factitive" verbs from adjectives, with the general meaning "to make, cause [some state X]," by adding a word-building (or "derivational") suffix *-ru*. We could, of course, just treat *junkuru-* as a unit meaning "make correct" and *thakuru-* as a unit meaning "make wrong, twist, garble," but then you would lose the logic of how the words are built up. And, finally, Kayardild verbs choose from a large set of suffixes that show tense (when) and polarity (affirmative vs. negative): *-thu* means "will," while *-nangku* means "won't." They are glossed here as POTENTIAL and NEGATIVE.POTENTIAL.

You might ask why we do not simply translate *-ru-* as "make" and *-thu* as "will"? Well, there is a good reason not to do this: the translation would be rough and inaccurate. This is because *-thu* can also mean "can, may, should" – hence the gloss "potential" which aims to capture what is common in these meanings through a more abstract term. Likewise, *-ru-* does not correspond specially well with "make" since it only combines with words denoting states: to say "I made him come down/descend" I would take the word *thulatha* "descend, come down" and add a different suffix, *-(a)rrmatha*, giving *thulathar-rmatha*. This second suffix is used when causing an action rather than a state.

This method of *interlinear glossing*, then, allows us to show faithfully how words sound in the original language, translate them as well as possible into the language I am using to you, and at the same time display the grammatical structure of the original with as little distortion as possible. In general I will use this method to display examples, but in the interests of broader readability sometimes I will change the glosses of the original sources to make them more accessible without betraying the main point of the example.

In addition to the linguistic examples, I have had to decide what to do with the various quotes that pepper this book, from many languages and cultural traditions. In a book on the fragility of languages, this is not out of obscurity. A major cause of language loss is the belief that everything wise and important can be, and has been, said in English. Conversely, it is a great stimulant to the study of other languages to see what they express so succinctly. So in general I have put such quotes first in their original language, followed by a translation (my own unless otherwise indicated). I hope the slightly greater effort this entails for you, the reader, will be rewarded by the treasures you will go on to discover.

Most languages mentioned in the book can be located from at least one map, except for (a) national languages whose location is well-known or deducible from the nation's location, (b) ancient languages whose location is not known precisely, (c) scripts. If there is no explicit mention of the language's location in the text, use the index at the back of the book to locate a relevant map.

Part I

The Library of Babel

Tuhan, jangan kurangi
sedikit pun adat kami.

Oh God, do not trim
a single custom from us.
(Indonesian proverb)

Oh dear white children, casual as birds,
Playing among the ruined languages,
So small beside their large confusing words
So gay against the greater silences ...

(Auden 1966)

In the biblical myth of the Tower of Babel, humans are punished by God for their arrogance in trying to build a tower that would reach heaven. Condemned to speak a babble of mutually incomprehensible languages, they are quarantined from each other's minds. The many languages spoken on this earth have often seemed a curse to rulers, media magnates, and the person in the street. Some economists have even implicated it as a major cause of corruption and instability in modern nations.[1]

The benefits of communicating in a common idiom have led, in many times and places, to campaigns to spread one or another metropolitan standard – Latin in the Roman Empire, French in Napoleonic France, and Mandarin in today's China. Sometimes these are promoted by governments, but increasingly media organizations, aided by satellite TV, are doing the same: arguably Rupert Murdoch's Star Channel is doing more to spread Hindi into remote Indian villages than 60 years of educational campaigning by the Indian government. We live today with an accelerating tempo of language spread for a few world languages – English, Chinese, Spanish, Hindi, Arabic, Portuguese, French, Russian, Indonesian, Swahili. Another couple of dozen national languages are expanding their speaker bases toward an asymptote where all citizens of their countries speak the one language; at the same time they are giving ground themselves in terms of higher education and technological literature to English and the other world languages.

Humankind is regrouping, away from their Babel, some millennia after sustaining their biblical curse.

But many other cultures have regarded language diversity as a boon. In chapter 1 we shall begin by examining some alternative founding myths, widespread in small-scale cultures, that give very positive reasons for why so many languages are spoken on this earth. For the moment, though, let's stick with the Babel version, but with the twist given to it by Jorge Luis Borges. His fabulous Library of Babel contains all possible books written in all possible languages, subject to a limit of 410 pages per tome. It thus contains all possible things sayable about the world, including all that scientists, philosophers, poets, and novelists might express – plus every possible falsehood and piece of uninterpretable nonsense as well. (We can extend his vision a bit by clarifying that all possible writing systems are allowed – Ethiopic, Chinese, phonetic script, written transcriptions of sign languages . . .)

For Borges, the Library of Babel was an apt metaphor because it allowed us to conceive of a near-infinity of stories and ideas by increasing the number of languages they were *written in*, each idiom stamping its great masterpieces with the rhythm and take of a different world-view – Cervantes alongside Shakespeare, the Divine Comedy alongside the Popol Vuh, Lady Murasaki alongside Dostoyevsky, the Rig Veda alongside the Koran. (We can of course expand his idea to include stories *told* or *chanted in* the countless oral cultures of the world and that have yet to be written down – a topic we return to in chapter 9.) As English, Spanish, Mandarin, and Hindi displace thousands of tiny languages in the hearths of small communities, much of this library is now molding away.

Our library will also contain grammars and dictionaries – of the six thousand or so languages spoken now, plus all that have grown and died since humans began to speak. (Of course most of these grammars and dictionaries have still not been written, and those from vanished past languages never can be, but remember that Borges' Library contains all possible books alongside its actual ones!) In this linguistic reference section of the library we can read how, in the words of George Steiner, every language "casts over the sea its own particular net, and with this net it draws to itself riches, depths of insight, and lifeforms which would otherwise remain unrealized."[2] When we browse our way into this wing, we are looking not so much at what is *written in* or *told in* the languages – but what has been *spoken into* them. By this I mean that speakers, in their quest for clarity and vividness, actually create new grammars and new words over time. Ludwig Wittgenstein once offered his famous advice *Wovon man nicht sprechen kann, darüber muss man schweigen* – "whereof you cannot speak, thereof must you remain silent." Fortunately millennia of his predecessors ignored this injunction, in the process forging the languages that we use to communicate today. Untold generations, through their attempts to persuade and to explain, to move and to court, to trick and to exclude, have unwittingly built the vast, intricate edifices that collectively represent humankind's most fundamental achievement, since without it none of the others could be begun. The contents of this wing of the library are also teetering in disrepair.

In this section of the book we broach two topics. In chapter 1 we take stock of the astonishing linguistic diversity that still exists in those parts of the Library of Babel that are still standing, however rickety. We ask where in the world this diversity is found, how it has come to be, and what it means. In chapter 2 we examine the millennially slow dawning of interest in what these languages have to tell us, an indifference that has left huge and aching gaps in what we know about many past and present peoples of the world. By knowing what our predecessors were deaf to, we will be better prepared to open our ears to the many questions we will be raising in the rest of the book.

1

Warramurrungunji's Children

يَا أَيُّهَا النَّاسُ إِنَّا خَلَقْنَاكُمْ مِنْ ذَكَرٍ وَأُنْثَى وَجَعَلْنَاكُمْ شُعُوبًا وَقَبَائِلَ لِتَعَارَفُوا

Oh Mankind, we have created you male and female, and have made you into nations and
tribes that ye may know one another

(Koran 49:13, Pickthal translation)

In the oral traditions of northwestern Arnhem Land, the first human to enter the Australian
continent was a woman, Warramurrungunji, who came out of the Arafura Sea on Croker
Island near the Cobourg Peninsula, having traveled from Macassar in Indonesia. (Her rather
formidable name is pronounced, roughly: *worra-moorrooo-ngoon-gee* [wóramùruŋùɲɟi].)
Her first job was to sort out the right rituals so that the many children she gave birth to
along the way could survive. The hot mounds of sand, over which she and all women there-
after would have to purify themselves
after childbirth, remain in the landscape as
the giant sandhills along Croker Island's
northern coasts. Then she headed inland,
and as she went she put different children
into particular areas, decreeing which
languages should be spoken where. *Ruka
kundangani riki angbaldaharrama! Ruka
nuyi nuwung inyman!* "I am putting you
here, this is the language you should talk!
This is your language!" she would say, in
the Iwaidja version of the story, naming
a different language for each group and
moving on.

Figure 1.1 Tim Mamitba telling the
Warramurrungunji story (photo: Nick Evans)

Language Diversity and Human Destiny

ŋari-waidbaidjun junbalal-ŋuban wuldjamin	Speech of different clans, mingling
daa-walwaljun lilia-woŋa	together . . .
duandja mada-gulgdun-maraŋala dualgindiu	Dua moiety clans, with their special
	distinct tongues.
wulgandarawiŋoi murunuŋdu jujululwiŋoi	People from Blue Mud Bay, clans of
garaŋariwiŋoi garidjalulu mada-gulgdun-	different tongues talking together . . .
maraŋala	
buduruna ŋari-waidbaidjun woŋa ŋari-ŋariun	Words flying over the country, like the
	voices of birds . . .

(Song 2, Rose River Cycle, Berndt 1976:86–7, 197–8)

The Judeo-Christian tradition sees the profusion of tongues after the Tower of Babel as a negative outcome punishing humans for their presumption, and standing in the way of cooperation and progress. But the Warramurrungunji myth reflects a point of view much more common in small speech communities: that having many languages is a good thing because it shows where each person belongs. Laycock quotes a man from the Sepik region of Papua New Guinea saying "it wouldn't be any good if we all talked the same; we like to know where people come from."[1] The Tzotzil oral traditions of the Mexican Chiapas give another twist to this tune: "while the sun was still walking on the earth, people finally learned to speak (Spanish), and all people everywhere understood each other. Later the nations and municipios were divided because they had begun to quarrel. Language was changed so that people would learn to live together peacefully in smaller groups."[2]

I recently drove down the dusty road from Wilyi on the coast near Croker Island, to the inland town of Jabiru (figure 1.2), while working with speakers of Iwaidja, the language in which Tim Mamitba (figure 1.1) had told me the Warramurrungunji story. The 200-kilometer transect follows Warramurrungunji's path, traveling inland and southwards from beach through eucalyptus savannah, stretches of tropical wetlands and lily ponds, and occasional sandstone outcrops whose caves hold vast galleries of rock paintings. It is a timeless landscape rich in wild food – magpie geese, fish, bush fruits, and yams. Its Aboriginal inhabitants can live easily through the year, finding all they need on their own clan countries. The few river crossings do not present geographical barriers. But Warramurrungunji's legacy of linguistic diversity is clearly here. In a few hours on the road we passed through the territories of nine clans and seven languages from four language families, at least as different from each other as Germanic, Slavic, Indo-Aryan and Romance (see table 1.1).

To give a rough idea of how different the languages are at the two ends of this transect, consider the useful sentence "you eat fish." Taking Iwaidja from one end, and Gun-djeihmi from the other, we compare *kunyarrun yab* and *yihngun djenj* – of which only the final *-n* in the two languages, which marks non-past tense in both, is historically relatable. Imagine I had driven from London to Moscow – 15 times as far. The Russian equivalent *ty esh rybku*, although incomprehensible to English ears, contains three cognate elements, at least if we cheat a bit by taking the earlier English version *thou eatest fish*: *ty* (with English *thou*), *e* (with English *eat*) and *-sh* (with the older English suffix *-est* in *eatest*). And if I satisfy

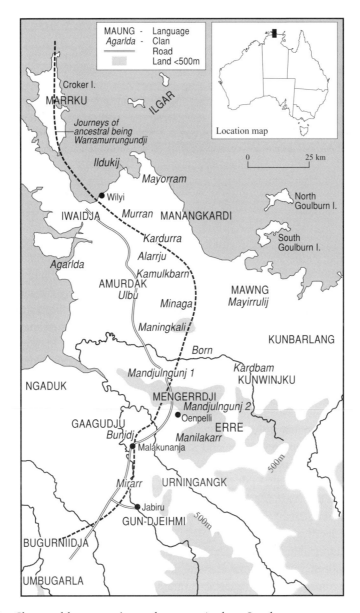

Figure 1.2   Clans and languages in northwestern Arnhem Land

myself with a shorter trip to Berlin – still more than five times the Wilyi–Jabiru trip – we get the almost comprehensible *du ißt (isst) Fisch*, in which every element is cognate.

Some of these languages are now down to just a couple of speakers (Amurdak) or have recently ceased to be spoken (Manangkardi), but others are still being learned by children. Bininj Gun-wok, the largest, now has about 1,600 first-language speakers as members of other groups shift to it. But the average population per language in this region is much smaller, probably less than 500 speakers. And many are even smaller: a recent study by

Table 1.1   Clans and languages along the 200-kilometer track from Wilyi to Jabiru[3]

Clan	Language	Language family
Murran	*Iwaidja*	Iwaidjan; Iwaidjic
Manangkali	*Amurdak*	Iwaidjan; Southern
Minaka	*Manangkardi*	Iwaidjan; Iwaidjic
Born/Kardbam (Alarrju)	*Bininj Gun-wok* *(Kunwinjku dialect)*	Gunwinyguan (Central)
Mandjurlngun	*Bininj Gun-wok* *(Kunwinjku dialect)*	Gunwinyguan (Central)
Bunidj	*Gaagudju*	Gaagudjuan (Isolate)
Mandjurlngun Mengerr	*Mengerrdji*	Giimbiyu
Manilakarr	*Urningangk*	Giimbiyu
Bunidj Gun-djeihmi, Mirarr Gun-djeihmi	*Bininj Gun-wok* *(Gun-djeihmi dialect)*	Gunwinyguan (Central)

Rebecca Green[4] on Gurr-goni, a few hundred kilometers to the east of the Warramurrungunji track, suggests it has been quite stable for as long as anyone remembers, never with more than around 70 speakers.

Each person from this region has one "father language," which they have special rights in, by virtue of the clan membership they get from their father. This vests them with authority and spiritual security as they travel through their ancestral lands. In traveling to places that have not been visited for some time, clan members should call out to the spirits in the local language, to show they belong to the country. Doing this with visitors is the duty and right of a host. It is said that many resources, such as springs, can only be accessed if you address them in the local idiom. For these reasons there are intimate emotional and spiritual links between language and country. Travelers sing songs listing the names of sites as they move through the land, and switch languages as they cross creeks and other clan boundaries. In epics of ancestral travels it is common to flag where the characters have got to simply by switching the language the story is told in – as if the *Odyssey* were told not just in Greek, but in the half a dozen ancient Mediterranean languages Ulysses would have encountered in his travels.

Throughout Aboriginal Australia, speaking the appropriate local language is a kind of passport, marking you – both to local people and to the spirits of the land – as someone known and familiar, with the right to be there. I once went out in a boat with Pat Gabori to map a Kayardild site a few kilometers off shore, in the company of several Kayardild-talkative senior women and a few children who did not know their ancestral language. Pat and the women called out in Kayardild to the spirits and ancestors of the place, identifying themselves and introducing the silent children, and explaining gently that the children's inability to speak Kayardild did not make them strangers – they just hadn't learned the language yet.

A more extreme illustration of this principle comes from a story Pluto Bentinck, another old Kayardild man, related during a Native Title claim. When asked if traditional law included sanctions to be taken against trespassers, he cited an incident during World War II, when a hapless white airman swam ashore on Bentinck Island after his plane crashed in the sea. Pluto told me the man had said *danda ngijinda dulk, ngada warngiida kangka kamburij* ("this is my country, I just speak this one language"), as he struggled ashore without his Berlitz Kayardild phrasebook. When I asked him how he knew what the man had said, when he himself knew no English, Pluto replied: *Marralwarri dangkaa, ngumbanji kangki kamburij!* ("He was an ear-less (crazy) man, he spoke your language!"). Speaking English on Bentinck Island, in Pluto's view, was tantamount to claiming it for English speakers. *Nyingka kabatha birdiya kangki! Ngada yulkaanda mirraya kangki kabath!* he had replied to the man ("You found the wrong words! I've found the right words, since forever"). *Ngada bunjiya balath, karwanguni,* Pluto continued: "And I clubbed him in the back of the neck".[5]

Normal members of Arnhem Land society are highly multilingual, often speaking half a dozen languages by the time they are adults. This is helped by the fact that you have to marry outside your clan, which likely means your wife or husband speaks a different language from you. It also means that your parents each speak a different language, and your grandparents three or four languages between them. The late Charlie Wardaga, my Ilgar teacher, was typical. Knowledge of Ilgar, Manangkardi, Marrku, Iwaidja, and Kunwinjku came to him from his grandparents and parents. Although he lived mostly on lands where Ilgar, Marrku, and Iwaidja were the locally appropriate languages, he married a Kunwinjku-speaking woman from a mainland clan and would regularly speak Kunwinjku with her and her relatives, or when traveling to distant communities as a songman. In this system your clan language is your title deed, establishing your claims to your own country, your spiritual safety and luck in the hunt there. Meanwhile the knowledge of other languages gives you the far-flung network of relatives, spouses actual and potential, ceremonial age-mates and allies, which makes you someone who counts in the greater world. This combination of highly developed multilingualism with strong attachments to small local languages is by no means an Arnhem Land oddity – around the world, it is common in zones of high linguistic diversity, like Nagaland in northeastern India, or the Mandara Mountains of Cameroon (see box 1.1).

Most non-Aboriginal people are astonished when they learn how many demographically tiny languages etch their distinctive local domains across the Australian map. Modern citizens of industrialized countries like Britain or Japan take it for granted that they can use their languages with hundreds of millions of people and that a single language occupies the entire territory of their nation, bar dialect variation, immigrants, and one or two beleaguered minorities like Welsh or Ainu. For speakers of big languages, the question is: why are there so many languages in the world/in Papua New Guinea/in Australia/etc.? The naïve explanation sometimes offered, that they result from mutual isolation in distant valleys and gorges, just does not bear up. In Arnhem Land there are no significant geographical barriers at all. And marriage patterns, in Arnhem Land or the Vaupés region of Amazonia, mean that several languages are spoken on a daily basis inside the one household – hardly a case of mutual isolation.

But maybe we are approaching the problem from the wrong end. Doesn't it make more sense to turn the question round and ask, not why Melanesia, the Amazon, Arnhem Land, the Cameroon, or the Caucasus have so many languages, but rather why Europe or parts of Asia have so few?

Indeed, there are good reasons to believe that our little transect through Arnhem Land is a good representation of how humans have been for most of our past – not just for the 99 percent or so of our history up to 10,000 years ago when we were all hunter-gatherers, but also for much of the time that followed. This is because the dawn of agriculture, although it led to an explosion in human populations, did not automatically lead to the development of much larger societies. Speech communities got a bit bigger but it was rare for them to exceed the few score thousand that could be held together as a homogeneous unit without the panoply of state control that only began with our incorporation into large centralized political entities like the Roman Empire or a modern nation state. Mapping the million or more years of human history onto a 24-hour clock, incorporation into large centralized states did not start for any human society before ten minutes to midnight

---

Box 1.1   The many paths to multilingualism in up-country Cameroon

Jonas courting Gogo in Jilve village in the presence of other villagers (photo: Leslie Moore)

Jonas, the boy in this photo, comes from the village of Jilve in the Mandara region of Cameroon, another region of daunting linguistic diversity, where people speak small "montagnard" languages of the Chadic family, very distantly related to the Semitic languages. Here he is shown courting Gogo, the girl he wants to marry, in her mother's compound, with her girlfriends in attendance. They are speaking primarily in Mada, Gogo's paternal language. Mada is one of eight languages that

(five millennia ago in the Fertile Crescent). For many groups it has only begun to happen in the last seconds.

The island of New Guinea and its Melanesian surrounds, a few hundred kilometers to the north of Warramurrungunji's territory, is a good illustration of a region almost completely made up of Neolithic agricultural societies, with no centralized states until recent colonization by Europeans and Indonesians. Its population of around 10 million people speaks some 1,150 languages – under 10,000 people per language. In the Central Highlands, where the population density is highest thanks to intensive agriculture and pig breeding, elaborate networks of production and ceremonial exchange have gradually bound people together into larger speech communities. The more intensified the system, the more speakers per language. But, even in the most elaborate and intensified highland Papuan communities, the average number of speakers per language rarely exceeds 40,000. And in many other parts of Melanesia languages of that size seem unimaginably large: the nation

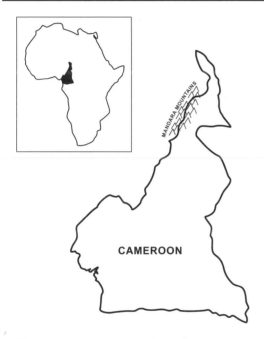

The Mandara mountains, Cameroon

Jonas speaks. Although he began learning Mada in order to court Gogo, the two of them already had two languages in common: Wandala (the local lingua franca) and Wuzlam, the first language of Jonas' father and of Gogo's mother. Prior to this visit, Jonas had prepared a list of topics of conversation and relevant Mada vocabulary, which he had noted on a piece of paper he brought with him but did not consult during the visit.

We know very little about how the impressive levels of multilingualism are acquired in small-scale preliterate societies, but Leslie Moore's pioneering ethnographic work (from which the above vignette is taken) has taught us something about how multilingualism works in Cameroon communities like Jilve. Besides the "normal" acquisition of their mother tongue, children learn French and later English in school, the regional lingua franca Fulfulde from night-time storytelling by their elders, and the languages of neighboring villages through self-instruction of the type we see here. From an early age parents ask their children to memorize messages, in languages they do not yet know, and to go and deliver them orally to people from neighboring villages. Even young children develop a strong metalinguistic awareness, for example using knowledge of cognates in related languages to help them remember new vocabulary.

Figure 1.3   Archi men herding sheep into a *maʔi* or underground sheep fold
(photo: Marina Tchoumakina)

of Vanuatu (total population 195,000), most of whose population are village agriculturalists, counts 105 languages – an average of less than 2,000 speakers per language for the
whole country! Apart from the recently developed national lingua franca, Bislama, its biggest
language (Lenakel) has just 11,500 speakers and only 13 languages have 5,000 speakers
or more.[6]

  We see small languages wherever in the world societies have lain beyond the homo-
genizing reach of great empires. But the situation is most extreme where groups can
maintain themselves self-sufficiently without needing to call on the hospitality of others.
The village cluster of Archib (population 1,237) in the Caucasus is the only place in the
world where the Archi language is spoken – a language whose morphology is so complex
that it has been calculated that a single verb possesses more than 1.5 million inflected forms.
Most of its inhabitants will be born, married, and laid to rest in this one village, basing
their economy on specially adapted mountain sheep, which they tuck up on freezing
winter nights into special underground sheep folds called *maʔi* (see figure 1.3). Or, in
northwestern California, the entire territory of the Chimariko people and their language
consisted of a 20-mile stretch along a narrow canyon of the Trinity River.[7] Until the Gold
Rush, their economic self-sufficiency on this small patch was assured by the rich salmon
stocks in the river.

  There is evidence from many parts of the world that small groups in favored areas did
not simply rely on the drift of time to carry their languages apart from those of their neighbors. In northern Australia the reigning ideology is that each clan should have its own

distinct language variety. This then sanctions the investiture by tribal elders of variant forms as proper to their local languages, driving along a relentless diversification.

Peter Sutton, working on clan identities in the Cape York Peninsula of Australia, reports cases where the fission of clans is rapidly followed by the emergence of new language varieties. In settings where fewer than a hundred people may speak a "clan lect," one or two powerful individuals can readily impose what may have started out as individual idiosyncrasies, and seed the emergence of a new system. In Iwaidja, many forms of nouns and verbs mutate their initial consonants – "his or her arm" is *bawurr*, from the root *mawurr*, for example, whereas the corresponding words in related languages like Charlie Wardaga's language Ilgar keep the original *m*. The mutated forms are based on an obscure "miscellaneous" gender so rare in all the languages of the family that it would never have won out as the standard form by processes of normal change. More likely, at some point in the past, Iwaidja speakers deliberately extended the use of the miscellaneous gender to set their language off from their neighbors, on the "you say tomahto, I say tomato" principle.

In New Guinea language differentiation is sometimes fostered even more deliberately. When we compare the Uisai dialect of Buin (1,500 speakers), on Bougainville Island, with the other dialects of Buin (about 17,000 speakers all up), we see that it has completely flipped over all its gender agreements:[8] all the masculines have become feminine, and all the feminines have become masculine. Because no known mechanism of normal linguistic change could produce this effect, Don Laycock has suggested that "an influential Uisai speaker innovated a linguistic change to differentiate his community from the rest of the Buins." Again we see how much influence a single individual can have in a small speech community. For another Papuan language, Selepet, we actually have a reported instance, witnessed by linguist Ken McElhanon, where one community decided at a meeting to replace the standard Selepet word *bia*, for "no," with the word *bunge*, to differentiate themselves from other Selepet villages.[9]

Although for illustrative purposes we have concentrated on decisions affecting a single word or grammatical feature, this is just the thin end of the wedge. William Thurston studied "esoterogeny" – the engendering of difference and linguistic obscurity – with Anem speakers on the island of New Britain, off the New Guinea mainland. He found that "esoterogenic" languages tend to streamline pronunciation in ways that make the overall structure harder to see, comparable to saying *dja* for *didja* from *did you* in English. They replace clear regular relationships with "suppletive" (totally irregular) ones, reveling in alternations like *good:better* at the expense of the more transparent *big:bigger* style. They have huge numbers of opaque idioms, of the *kick the bucket* type, and entrench prescriptive traditions that limit flexibility of language: "you must speak this way to be a member of our community!" They also elaborate terminology to make subtle distinctions, and speakers take pride in the greater richness of their language than the neighboring language of Lusi in this regard.

During Thurston's research on Anem he found that "some of the boys had devised a competitive word game aimed at exposing one another's ignorance of the name for an obscure vine or bush; in order to keep ahead, boys were asking older people, secretively, for words they could use to try tricking other boys." All these forces conspire to maximize difference between one language and its neighbors – although I should stress that, up till now, we have no more than the sorts of anecdotal evidence reported on here, and systematic studies of the causes and processes of change in small languages are badly needed.

Small-scale societies in such parts of the world are economically self-sufficient, and proudly form the center of their own social universe without needing to defer unduly to more powerful outside groups. Their constructive fostering of variegation – which holds social groupings to a small and manageable size, and keeps outsiders at a suitable distance – is not offset by the need to align their language with large numbers of other people in the world. The great Swiss linguist Ferdinand de Saussure saw language as being pulled in opposite directions by the "spirit of the steeple" – the parochialism of showing which little com-munity you belong to – and the "spirit of wider communication." But, for those small-scale societies able to subsist mostly on their own resources, the force of the steeple is dominant.

Language Diversity through Time and Space

The classic estimate of the world's population on the eve of the Neolithic, ten millennia ago, is 10 million.[10] Combining these figures with a very generous 2,000-speaker maximum for hunter-gatherer languages suggests that, on the eve of agriculture and fixed settlements, there were already from 3,000 to 5,000 languages in the world – roughly the same num-ber as now, even though the population was less than half a percent of its current level. If we assume 1,000 speakers per language, a more realistic figure in my view, the number doubles to between 6,000 and 10,000.[11] Levels of language diversity whose full magnitude we can barely grasp have been with us for a very long time.

Going much further back in time, to the population bottleneck about 150,000 years ago that preceded the long trek out of Africa, Rob Foley estimates from mitochondrial DNA that there were probably between 10,000 and 20,000 women of reproductive age – say 50,000 humans all up, who on the language-size estimates given above would already have been speaking 10–20 distinct languages (and possibly a hundred already if we go with the plaus-ible language population of 500). Already then, at a point when humans went through a population bottleneck probably caused by environmental crises, just before their fortunes turned and they ventured forth across the planet, there were scores of languages. Since our forebears probably began to speak and develop languages long before that,[12] the figure 150,000 years ago is likely to have included tongues that were already quite different from one another.

Let us come back to the emergence of agriculture at the beginning of the Neolithic. As agriculture spread around much of the world from then on, it is likely that the increases in language populations of cultivating groups – perhaps to New Guinea-like levels of around 10,000 – would have been more than offset by the explosion in overall world population, so that the number of languages in the world may have risen to 10,000 or 15,000. However, scholars like Colin Renfrew and Peter Bellwood[13] have argued that the bearers of agricultural expansion would have been just a small number of groups who had made a radical cultural transition. From the hunter-gatherer perspective, agricultural life looks pretty unappealing. In return for the security of regular crop supplies you have to put up with a poorer and less varied diet, monotonous year-round residence in a circumscribed area, and the diseases that come from having so many people living in relatively close quarters, on top of each other's excrement. Most hunter-gatherers would have walked away from the deal. Inexorably, though, the "demic expansion" that agriculturalists could feed from the increased food yields they drew from the land would gradually have squeezed out or assimilated the original populations of hunter-gatherers.

The expansion of these few agriculture-based lineages would have produced what I will call the Renfrew–Bellwood effect: a decrease in deep-level diversity, i.e. in the number of unrelated stocks or deep lineages, as clusters of closely related languages spread outward from the dozen or so foci where agricultural complexes were developed, obliterating the deep-time variability that was there beforehand. If agricultural expansion is old enough, however, there is time for significant new multiplicity to develop, as has happened with the Afro-Asiatic languages stretching from Hausa in Nigeria to Hebrew and Arabic in the Middle East, or the Austric family in Southeast Asia. Each of these families probably goes back to the very dawning of agriculture in their respective regions, and contains languages so different that it has taken many years of work to demonstrate their relatedness – a topic we return to in chapters 5 and 6.

We can see the Renfrew–Bellwood effect clearly in Indonesia where, over most of the archipelago, no linguistic trace remains of the hunter-gatherers who must have occupied its fertile lands until the coming of the Austronesian agriculturalists a few thousand years ago. It is also clear in New Guinea, where the whole fertile highland cordillera along which root-and-pig farmers expanded over the last few millennia is occupied by a single Trans New Guinea family, albeit one with around 400 member languages. New Guinea's most mind-boggling lineage diversity is found in lowland areas like the Sepik and the Trans-Fly region, north and south of the cordillera, where people either practice a much less intensive form of agriculture or mix agriculture, fishing, hunting, and gathering.

We have seen already, though, that even in the densely populated New Guinea Highlands, and even after six to seven thousand years of intense agriculture, there were no really large languages. This is because it was only with the advent of centralized and then industrial-ized state societies that a few languages began to spread to the point where they counted hundreds of thousands and then millions of speakers. Unfortunately, most of these expansionist new societies had no interest in recording anything about the languages of the peoples they subjugated, as we will see in the next chapter. But we can get some idea of what the world was like as the first great empires emerged by looking at the Italian peninsula in the fifth and sixth centuries BC. There, under Greek influence, a number of different civilizations developed their own writing systems in time to leave some record of their languages before they were all sucked into the Latin-speaking vortex of the Romans.

Inscriptions in pre-Roman Italy attest between 12 and 15 distinct languages, quite different from one another, and belonging to between 5 and 10 branches of at least 4 dis-tinct families – 3 branches of Indo-European (Celtic, Italic, and Greek) plus Etruscan, which was non-European. The Romans did not actively try to stamp out other languages – indeed, the retention of other languages by non-Romans favored the policy of *diuide et impera* ("divide and rule"). Umbrians, for example, continued to make inscriptions in their lan-guage for centuries after Roman annexation. But eventually the power and status of Latin prevailed, particularly after all residents of Italy became Roman citizens in the middle of the last century BC. At first other groups would just have used Latin for "outside" purposes, but gradually the centralizing power of Rome "relegated the local speech, just as it did political initiative and concerns, to a secondary, subordinate, and ever retreating position."[14] We do not know exactly when the last speakers of Oscan, Umbrian, Etruscan, and other languages of the peninsula finally passed away, but the elimination of all non-Latin languages from the Italian peninsula is likely to have been almost complete by the time Herod washed his hands of another death in another part of the Roman Empire.[15]

Emerging kingdoms in many parts of the world – in Egypt, Arabia, Persia, Mali, China, Korea, India, Mexico, the Andes – had similar impacts on the smaller peoples in their domains. It was probably in this period – beginning around 2,000 BC – that the first languages with more than a million speakers emerged. Expansionist agricultural–military complexes like the Bantus in the southern half of Africa obliterated vast mosaics of diversity. And then, from 1492, European colonial expansion began to take its toll. Little more than half a century after the Spaniards reached Cuba and Puerto Rico, the Arawakan language Taino would cease to be spoken, although some of its words have survived as loanwords into Spanish (*cacique* "chief") and others passed further into English ("barbecue" < *barbacoa*; "canoe" < *canoa*; "tobacco" < *tabaco*). Thousands of other languages around the world would suffer a similar fate, leading to the accelerating loss of linguistic diversity we see today, and the concomitant dominance of the dozen or so languages with more than a hundred million speakers.

Where the Hotbeds Are

The upshot of what we have been discussing is that language diversity is now distributed very unevenly around the world. On one estimate,[16] 17 countries hold 60 percent of all languages, although these countries make up only 27 percent of the world's population and 9 percent of its land area.[17] Table 1.2 shows two slightly different rankings of the top 25 language-diverse countries – a calculation of sheer number of endemic languages,[18] and an alternative measure showing the number of linguistic lineages, which is a better measure of deep-level language diversity. It also shows the top 25 countries for biological diversity, for reasons we will return to below.

As the preceding discussion should have made clear, the current distribution of languages reflects many influences. The effects of each region's history have been superimposed on original patterns that are likely to have shown even closer parallels between linguistic and biological diversity:

(1)   An original stratum of deep-time language diversity goes back to when all humans were hunter-gatherers. This is visible in regions where people have remained hunter-gatherers until recently. Here there is high language diversity on both measures (i.e. total number of languages and number of independent lineages) except in spread zones such as deserts and other less favored regions that show the effects of repeated recolonization and cultural pressures to extend intercommunicating networks.

Table 1.2   The top 25 megadiverse countries, for endemic species and two measures of language diversity. Left and right columns reprinted with permission from Harmon (1996)

Rank	Endemic languages		Endemic linguistic lineages		Endemic higher vertebrate species	
1	PNG	847	USA	64	Australia	1,346
2	Indonesia	655	PNG	58	Mexico	761
3	Nigeria	376	Indonesia	37	Brazil	725
4	India	309	Brazil	31	Indonesia	673
5	Australia	269	Mexico	24	Madagascar	537
6	Mexico	230	Colombia	24	Philippines	437
7	Cameroon	201	Australia	22	India	373
8	Brazil	185	Peru	21	Peru	332
9	Zaire	158	Russia	17	Colombia	330
10	Philippines	153	Sudan	15	Ecuador	294
11	USA	143	Canada	14	USA	284
12	Vanuatu	105	Bolivia	13	China	256
13	Tanzania	101	Venezuela	11	PNG	203
14	Sudan	97	India	10	Venezuela	186
15	Malaysia	92	China	9	Argentina	168
16	Ethiopia	90	Ethiopia	8	Cuba	152
17	China	77	Chad	8	South Africa	146
18	Peru	75	Argentina	8	Zaire	134
19	Chad	74	Ecuador	8	Sri Lanka	126
20	Russia	71	Nigeria	6	New Zealand	120
21	Solomon Islands	69	Burkina Faso	6	Tanzania	113
22	Nepal	68	Tanzania	5	Japan	112
23	Colombia	55	Cameroon	5	Cameroon	105
24	Ivory Coast	51	Georgia	5	Solomon Islands	101
25	Canada	47	Chile	5	Ethiopia	88
			Laos	5	Somalia	88

(2)   A second stratum results from small-scale agricultural expansion since the end of the Neolithic in some regions, although it was much more recent in some areas. This expansion wiped out hunter-gatherer languages but regrew a more recent pattern of diversification – with more or less lineage density depending on the time-depth of agriculture – leaving a pattern of large numbers of languages groupable into deep-level families like Indo-European or Austronesian.

(3)   The effects of state formation, between 3,000 BC and AD 1,000 depending on the area, produced a steady fall in linguistic diversity. Thus China has a relatively low score, of just 77 endemic languages – fewer than its tiny southern neighbor Laos. This undoubtedly reflects the gradual assimilation of minority populations into the majority Han population over the millennia of centralized state rule, with a shift to speaking Mandarin and other

Chinese varieties. In most countries of Europe, North Africa, and the Middle East the low scores are due to comparable effects over the last two or three millennia.

(4)   Most recently the effects of expansionist colonization by Europeans and the elites of the nation states they created have been to wipe out indigenous linguistic diversity in many of their colonies. In Uruguay, Cuba, Haiti, and all islands of the Caribbean – ironically, the only sea to be named after an indigenous language (Carib) – have the dubious distinction of having completely silenced their indigenous languages.

If we look at countries like Australia, the USA or South Africa, colonized by Europeans in the last few centuries, we get very rapid rates of language death under the impact of English. Comparably rapid rates of language extinction are occurring in much of Brazil under the impact of Portuguese, in Siberia under Russian, in the Sudan under Arabic, throughout Indonesia under Indonesian, and in even quite remote parts of Papua New Guinea under Tok Pisin, the newly developed national lingua franca.

Looking back beyond the recent flattening of multiformity by colonial languages – and the scores in table 1.2 largely bracket this off by giving known numbers of languages at the moment of colonial contact – we can see strong correlations between linguistic and biological diversity. Arizona linguistic anthropologist Doug Harmon first looked at this correlation in an important 1996 study, and since then his findings have been replicated worldwide on a country by country basis,[19] confirmed for Africa at a coarse resolution,[20] and at quite fine resolutions for the Americas[21] using passerine birds as the index of biodiversity and sampling geographical cuts down to squares one degree wide. More recent approaches to this question have used broad ecological areas instead of the rather accidental boundaries given by countries, and again found strong correlations.[22] Ten of the world's top dozen "megadiversity" countries on biological measures also make it into the A-league of the world's top 25 countries for endemic linguistic diversity.[23] Harmon's work also makes it clear where both types of diversity are concentrated: Central and South America, tropical Africa, and South and Southeast Asia across through Indonesia, Melanesia, and Australia to the Western Pacific.

The Wellsprings of Diversity in Language, Culture, and Biology

[Continued loss of biocultural diversity will] staunch the historical flow of being itself, the
evolutionary processes through which the vitality of all life has come down to us through the ages.
(Harmon 2002:xiii)

The arguments for conserving diversity are similar whether we consider the loss of a rare bird or tree species, a body of cultural knowledge that will soon be forgotten, or an endangered language. Since Darwin, we have begun to articulate, at the scientific level, what most cultures have had enshrined in their aesthetics and cosmologies for a long time: that variety is the reservoir of adaptability.

Having a genetically homogenous population of Cavendish bananas is great for maximizing yield and efficiency, but it just takes one new strain of fungus to wipe out the worldwide population. The traditional (agri)cultural practices that were displaced by the technology-driven Green Revolution, with its fertilizers, standardized seeds, and productive new breeds, are increasingly being seen as having strengths that were often overlooked 40 years ago: drought-resilience, disease resistance, lower demands on local water-tables – and, ironically, higher yields if we factor in water consumption rather than just tons of yield per area. The many "land-races" of traditional agriculture around the world are now being genetically archived,[24] so that at least it is possible to draw on their genetic diversity. But we also need all the cultural knowledge that grew up around them. Which variety should be planted in which conditions? What grows best where? Which is resistant to what crop disease? Which are good companion plants? Agriculture, like all technology, only works when artifacts marry know-how, and if we only store seeds without the accompanying knowledge we still have an impoverished picture.

Within the western scholarly and scientific traditions, we can identify two types of attitude to global knowledge. One is universalizing, and sees it as possible to incorporate all knowledge into the world language of the era – Latin, Arabic, French, and English have all had their turn – spoken by a "unified mankind within a single unified realm, subscribing to a universal value system."[25] The other recognizes the strength and richness that comes from distinct traditions that can never be straightforwardly mapped onto a single value system speaking a single world language: "any reduction of language diversity diminishes the adaptational strength of our species because it lowers the pool of knowledge from which we can draw."[26]

Joshua Fishman outlines this alternative view, showing how it has been developed by a succession of thinkers from Vico and Herder to Boas, Sapir, and Whorf:

> the entire world needs a diversity of ethnolinguistic entities for its own salvation, for its greater creativity, for the more certain solution of human problems, for the constant rehumanization of humanity in the face of materialism, for fostering greater esthetic, intellectual, and emotional capacities for humanity as a whole, indeed, for arriving at a higher stage of human functioning . . . the great creative forces that inspire all humanity do not emerge out of universal civilization but out of the individuality of separate ethnic collectivities – most particularly, out of their very own authentic languages. Only if each collectivity contributes its own thread to the tapestry of world history, and only if each is accepted and respected for making its own contribution, can nationalities finally also be ruled by a sense of reciprocity, learning and benefiting from each other's contributions as well. (Fishman 1982:7)

Fishman's wording makes it clear that this is neither a plea for the thousands of particularistic small societies to become mutually isolated museum pieces, nor for a few cute local words to be lifted into a world language like English to form a sort of linguistic theme-park. Rather, it recognizes the deep creative interactions and synthetic insights that come up when we look at one language or culture through the prism of another. A few hundred kilometers east of Warramurrungunji territory, the Yolngu peoples of eastern Arnhem Land, in conceptualizing the value of the bilingual and bicultural schools they are striving to develop on their lands, employ the Yolngu metaphor of *ganma*. This denotes the special mixing that develops when the outgoing freshwater current of a river mingles with the saltwater of the incoming tide.

I will assemble the evidence for the humanistic and scientific value of Warramur-rungunji's bequest as this book unfolds. But to close this chapter, as we have been talking about the relation between linguistic diversity, species diversity, and ecology, let us look at some of the ways in which small languages hold detailed biological and ecological know-ledge, which generations of speakers have gradually discovered and recorded in their languages. These examples will also illustrate the point – developed eloquently in Daniel Nettle and Suzanne Romaine's book *Vanishing Voices* (2000) – that the loss of our linguistic heritage is intimately tied up with the loss of cultures and habitats. The sorts of knowledge and vocabulary I am about to turn to are typically the first things to be lost when speakers of a language are shifted from their traditional lands to a reserve in Oklahoma, a rubber plantation in Malaysia, a ghetto in Ibadan, or pushed into a seden-tary lifestyle where they no longer practice their traditional ecological knowledge.

Words on the Land

> [I]ndividuals draw on cultural resources to structure and accomplish problems with which they engage in everyday socially organized activities.
>
> (Saxe and Esmonde 2005:173)

Small languages and societies have kept their place in the world by being finely tuned to their local ecologies and amassing a rich fund of knowledge about them. Much of this has been carried forward just in their languages. Many aspects of their traditional knowledge are still unknown to western science, and in fact languages are arguably the most impor-tant and distinctive of the "cultural resources" that Saxe and Esmonde are referring to in the above quote.

Consider Seri, spoken by around 500 hunter/gatherer/fisherpeople in Baja California in Mexico. This is most probably an isolate language without known relatives, although some linguists argue it is a southern outpost of the Hokan languages of California. In the course of documenting the Seri lexicon, linguists Edward and Mary Moser were told by Seri speakers about their use of eelgrass (*Zostera marina L.*) as a source of grain, leading to the involvement of ethnobotanist Richard Felger. The resultant research was published in *Science* with the appropriate title "Eelgrass (Zostera marina L.) in the Gulf of Califor-nia: discovery of its nutritional value by the Seri Indians."[27] The authors concluded that this is the only known case of a grain from the sea being harvested as a human food source, and emphasized its considerable potential as a general food resource for humankind, which can be cultivated without fresh water, pesticides, or artificial fertilizer. Despite its potential importance in a world likely to need new crops, this crucial knowledge had been locked up inside the almost impenetrable Seri language, known only to members of the tiny Seri world. Many other words in Seri contain information about the treatment, products, and harvesting of eelgrass. For example, the month of April is called *xnois iháat*

Figure 1.4   A group of Seri people in what outsiders call the "desert," but which they call *heheán* ("place of the plants") (photo: Arizona State Museum)

iizax ("moon of the eelgrass harvest"), and the onset of harvest time is signaled when the black brant bird known as *xnois cacáaso* ("the foreteller of eelgrass seed") dives into the sea to feed on the plant.

All around the world indigenous people transmit, through the words and expressions of their languages, the fruits of millennia of close observation of nature and experimentation with its products. In Arnhem Land there have been a number of cases where the impulse for western natural scientists to recognize new species has come from indigenous traditions of taxonomic naming. The large and striking Oenpelli python, long known to Kunwinjku speakers as *nawaran*, is one such species: it was first incorporated into western scientific taxonomy in 1977 as *Morelia oenpellensis*.[28]

Meanwhile a host of native bees of great economic importance to local Aboriginal people, each with their own honey and wax types, remain unidentified by entomologists. For the time being their English identification in bilingual dictionaries is limited to the inadequate designation *trigona species*.

Traditional cultures also contain detailed knowledge of the healing properties of plants, transmitted in local languages. The recent discovery of a drug, prostarin, effective against HIV-type 1 goes back to a conversation between Samoan tribal healer Epenesa Mauigoa and ethnobotanist Paul Allen Cox about traditional medicinal uses of the stem of a particular tree, *Homalanthus nutans*. The fact that Cox had learned Samoan as a missionary's son was a key fact in enabling this conversation. Comparable curative potentials abound across the immensely variegated world of traditional ethnobotanics, and their full investigation requires the collaboration of traditional healers, ethnobotanists, and linguists.

Vocabularies of indigenous languages often also show the ecological links between particular plant and animal species. Throughout Arnhem Land the spangled grunter fish bears the same name as the native white apple tree, *Syzygium eucalyptoides*, because this fish eats the fruits that fall from this tree into creeks and billabongs:[29] in Kunwinjku both are called *bokorn*. Knowledge of this link is of obvious value to anyone who happens to be out fishing for spangled grunter: look for the tree, and in the water below you are likely to find its fish "mate." The languages of Central Arnhem Land abound in such pairings, making them a veritable fisherman's guide to the area.

As another example of traditional ecological knowledge, consider the Mparntwe Arrernte language of the Alice Springs area, where various types of grub are an important source of food. Mparntwe Arrernte has a special method of naming grubs after the bushes where you can find them: *tnyeme* ("witchetty bush") yields the *tnyematye* ("witchetty grub"), *utnerrenge* ("emu bush") yields the grub known as *utnerrengatye*, and you can work out for yourself the name of the grub found in *thenge*, the ironwood tree.

A host of examples like these lead out into the vast ethnobiological wings of our Library of Babel. But all such knowledge is at great risk, as long as it is only available in little-known languages spoken by just a few hundred people, since a shift to another language can cut off its transmission. Once we go over to calling the *bokorn* fish a "spangled grunter," and the *bokorn* tree a "white apple," our words no longer deliver the ecological link between them.

Further reading

Trigger (1987) and Garde (in press) contain detailed discussions of locally appropriate language uses in Aboriginal speech communities. Feil (1987) gives demographic figures for the New Guinea Highlands showing the correlation between intensification of agriculture and language size. The fascinating multilingual situation in the Amazonian Vaupés is discussed in Jackson (1983) and Aikhenvald (2002). Moore (2004) examines how children become multilingual in upcountry Cameroon, and Thurston (1987, 1992) gives a rare and entertaining watch-it-happen study of the processes and results of "esoterogeny" in New Britain. Sutton (1978) discusses Cape York clan lects, and the origins of Iwaidja mutation are in Evans (1998); Evans (2003a) sets out a model for how ideologies of difference can drive the emergence of clan and other variation. For the situation in pre-Roman Italy see Pulgram (1958), and Robb (1993) on ancient Europe more generally. Ostler (2005) gives a wide-ranging discussion of the fates of languages and past empires in the historical period. On the Taino language of Cuba see Álvarez Nazario (1996).

Collard and Foley (2002) also compare the distribution of biological and linguo-cultural diversity, pointing out the need to take historical forces into account on top of the basic ecological determinants. Maffi (2001, 2005) treat the links between language and biodiversity, while Nettle (1999) is a pioneering essay on the causes of language diversity. The best worldwide listing of the world's languages is Ethnologue (www.ethnologue.com), maintained by the missionary organization Summer Institute of Linguistics; although this is constantly being updated, it is nonetheless far from accurate or consistent.[30] The best current worldwide classification is that by Dryer (2005), and

The World Atlas of Linguistic Structures, in which it appears (Haspelmath et al. 2005), is a mine of information on the geographical distribution of over 140 linguistic features; its information-packed CD, by Hans-Jörg Bibiko, allows you to compile your own maps and tables from a vast database.

On Seri ethnobotany see Felger and Moser (1973, 1985); the latter includes descriptions of how eelgrass seeds are harvested. Arvigo and Balick (1993), Balick and Cox (1996), Cox and Balick (1994), and Sofowora (1982) discuss ethnobotany and traditional herbalism. The Arrernte examples are from Wilkins (1993), and the book this is in (Williams and Baines 1993) contains an interesting collection of papers on the now-burgeoning topic of traditional ecological knowledge. A good discussion of other highly specific indigenous biological knowledge, and a sustained argument linking the loss of linguistic and biological diversity, are in Nettle and Romaine (2000).

2

Four Millennia to Tune In

<table>
<tr>
<td>La mort d'une langue n'est que celle
de la parole.</td>
<td>The death of a language is only the death
of its speech.</td>
</tr>
</table>

(Hagège 2000:45)

Animals, plants, climate, ancient human settlements – all can leave some physical trace after their passing, as fossils, ancient DNA, carbon isotopes in Antarctic ice cores, or archaeological sites. It may take sophisticated science to detect and interpret these remnants, but not to set up the earth's natural archiving processes. Speech, however, is completely evanescent, lasting only as long as the vibrations in the air that transmit it. This makes languages the most fragile of this world's creations. Unless their words are kept alive as oral traditions, they can only survive with the intervention of some form of technology – through writing, sound, or video recording. The means for recording language in an enduring form eluded humans for a long time, and the application of these techniques to all but a handful of powerful tongues is even more recent. In this chapter we look at some key steps along the path to doing this.

An Incident at Mount Bradshaw

<table>
<tr>
<td>Esana eta orbela haizeak eramaten.</td>
<td>Words and dry leaves are carried away by the wind.</td>
</tr>
</table>

(Basque proverb, Gotzon Garate 1998)

The urge to record the world around us is an ancient one. Warramurrungunji's track through western Arnhem Land passes close to the most extensive collection of ancient painted rock galleries in the world, among the sandstone overhangs where her descendants would take shelter. Going back 20,000 years, they vividly bring to life a time of hunting, feasting, love magic, fighting, and sorcery – with superb depictions of hairstyles, weapons, dillybags, and extinct animals like the thylacine.

Over aeons, these artists passed through several artistic styles – abstraction, schematic dynamism, naturalistic realism, and eerie "x-ray paintings" that depict animal anatomy with startling precision. Since these are often painted over one another in the same gallery, we can work out a chronology by finding out what gets painted over what. By studying the changes in subject matter – such as the appearance of barramundi fish and other "estuarine" themes – we can correlate it with major changes in climate and ecology that have occurred during the almost unimaginably long periods they span. Although the Arnhem Land rock artists were more interested in communicating with each other than with us – and in the meantime with whiling away a rainy afternoon in a rock shelter – they ended up bequeathing a vivid picture of how human life unfolded and changed there over millennia.[1]

This picture is almost completely a silent one. But a couple of the dynamic pictures actually attempt to add sound by including the Arnhem Land equivalent of speech balloons, in the form of small bursts spraying from the mouths of people and animals. One was recorded at Mount Bradshaw by George Chaloupka, the pioneer of rock art archaeology in Arnhem Land. From the hunter's hide behind a bunch of grass, he has managed to spear an emu, the force of his throw being shown by the dashed trajectory from the man's hand to the pierced body of the emu. The hunter's headdress and hair-belt, as well as the body and feather coat of the emu, have been carefully depicted by the artist. But what interests us here are the speech bursts in front of the emu and the hunter. We can be pretty sure of what sound the emu is making – emus do not divide up into language groups. But we have no idea what the hunter is saying – whatever languages may have been spoken around Mount Bradshaw when this was painted have now vanished without trace. The gifted painters of this work had not yet found an accurate way to transmute speech into visual symbols.

The Story of A

> The art of writing is one of the ancient arts and crafts in which the science of language has its origin.
>
> (Haas 1969)

It took quite a different set of cultural preoccupations – large-scale trade and government record-keeping – before humans developed ways of *writing* language in an abiding way, in the Middle East, the Indus Valley, China, and Mesoamerica. In each case this was a gradual and painstaking development, and often depended on the symbols being filtered and elaborated by a number of cultures and languages. For the only type of writing flexible enough to allow adaptation and extension to represent all human speech sounds, the alphabet, there was only a single truly independent evolution.[2]

Table 2.1   From ox to *a*, from house to *b*, from eye to *o*[3]

Egyptian hieroglyphic	Sinai script	Early Semitic	Name of letter, illustrating sound in Semitic	Phoenician shape	Early Greek letter	Modern Greek letter
🐂	𓃾	𐤀	ʔaleph "ox"	𐤀	𐌀	A, α
👄	☐	𐤁	beth "house"	𐤁	Β	B, β
👁	👁	O	ʕayin "eye"	O	O	O, o

The Greek alphabet, source of our own Latin alphabet, is a clear example (see table 2.1). The Egyptian hieroglyphs from which it is ultimately derived first represented objects. But the Egyptians and then the Semitic peoples gradually adapted stylized versions of these symbols to represent just the consonants – ʔaleph was "ox," so 𐌀 represented the glottal stop ʔ, beth was "house," so 𐤁 represented *b*, and so on.

The unique grammatical structure of Semitic languages favored this transition, as only the consonants count for the "lexical" part of the word, with the vowels supplying inflectional information – something that, if you know the language, you can usually work out from context. In Arabic, for example, each of the following four words can be written the same, as *ktbt*, with the vowels left out: *katabtu* ("I wrote"), *katabta* ("you (masculine) wrote"), *katabti* ("you (feminine) wrote"), and *katabat* ("she wrote"). Any time this word combines with another word – e.g. if you read *the woman ktbt* – you know it means "the woman wrote" and can work out what the vowels are and where they should go, so not writing them is not a terrible loss. This structural property – found in all the ancient Semitic languages – smoothed the path from symbols originating as pictographs to creating an *abjad* or "consonantory" in which they take on a phonetic value.

The various Semitic peoples had thus made the breakthrough of figuring out how to write consonants individually – by ignoring the vowels, since they do not contribute to word-meaning (as opposed to grammatical meaning). But it was only when their writing system was taken over by the Greeks, a people with an entirely different sort of language, that humankind solved the problem of writing vowels in a reliable way as well. Indeed, some scholars have suggested that the evolution of alphabetic writing was smoothed because the path of transmission led through languages of quite different phonological and grammatical types – a good illustration of how diversity favors certain types of innovation.

Three linguistic differences favored the emergence of an alphabet once a language like Greek came into contact with a Semitic-type consonantal writing system. First, Greek syllables were more complex than Semitic ones, so more information would have been lost if just the initial consonant had been written. This gives correspondingly more advantage in Greek if you write every sound.

Second, differences in Greek vowels make a difference to what the basic word means, not just to the inflectional meaning as in Semitic, so it was harder to figure out written vowel-free passages from context. Say you read a passage about distances in telegraphic English and you read "1 ft; 2 ft": you can work out that the first "ft" represents "foot," and the second "feet," because *oo* and *ee* encode *grammatical* information predictable from whether it is singular (after 1) or plural (after 2). Now you read on, and find a passage about trouble with the *shtng* – you can no longer work out if *oo* is meant (*shooting*) or *ee* (*sheeting*) because here we are dealing with *lexical* information – choices between different dictionary words – and that is not usually deducible from grammatical context. Because of the differences in their grammatical structures, leaving out vowels in Semitic is like the *ft* problem, while leaving them out in Greek is like the *shtng* problem. This made it much more important for Greek to develop a way of showing vowels than it was for the Semitic languages.

Third, Greek happened to lack certain consonants that could start words in Semitic, freeing them up to be redeployed as vowels. With some, as with the ʔ*a* from the first letter (*aleph*), the initial sound was not needed: ʔ denotes the glottal stop that we use in between the two halves of *oh-oh*, which is phonemic in most Semitic languages (i.e. a systematic and contrastive sound) but was not in Greek. So the Greeks just ignored the glottal stop, took over the following vowel sound and used the letter to represent that. With others, the letter was used for a slightly different vowel sound, as with the symbol known as ʕ*ayin*. This got a new job as the *o* (omicron) of the Greek alphabet, after they simply ignored the initial pharyngeal fricative ʕ (a deep growling sound) in the same way as many readers of this book will want to do.

With the advent of writing systems humans became capable, for the first time since the development of speech, of recording their languages in a durable form. Starting from Sumerian around 5,000 years ago, and taking in a growing roll-call of ancient languages – many scores of them by the time of Christ, and close to a hundred by a thousand years ago – these clay tablets, engraved oracle bones, papyruses, and parchments contain our first records of past languages.

Many of these written traditions reflect a sharp curiosity about their own languages. Our first examples of formal second-language teaching come from the Middle East around 2000 BC, in the form of materials for learning Sumerian as a second language. The Greeks, with their philosophical bent, delved into deep questions of meaning and logic. In Alexandria around 100 BC, the Greek scholar Apollonius Dyscolus elaborated the parts of speech that we now use in grammatical parsing.

All these achievements are dwarfed, though, by the Sanskrit linguistic tradition culminating in the famous grammar by Pāṇini, known as the Aṣṭādhyāyī. The elegance and comprehensiveness of its architecture have yet to be surpassed by any grammar of any language, and its ingenious methods of stratifying out use and mention, language and metalanguage, and theorem and metatheorem predate key discoveries in western philosophy by millennia. It anticipates modern computational methods of information compression and algorithmic formulation, honored by the name Panini–Backus form derivation rules for modern programming languages. The Sanskrit grammatical tradition is also the ultimate source of the notion of zero,[4] which, once adopted in the Arabic system of numerals, allowed us to transcend the cumbersome notations of Roman arithmetic. Although writing was already around in India at this time, it was reserved for sacred texts, and Pāṇini's grammar was initially transmitted orally, so that the premium placed by Sanskrit grammarians on brevity and conciseness was partly driven by the limits of human memory. It was only committed to writing much later, gradually accreting further (and much lengthier) written commentaries.

The Sanskrit linguists were concerned to ensure the absolutely correct transmission and perfect pronunciation of sacred ritual and hymnal traditions in the face of language change. The proper study of their language and its application to religious observance, they believed,[5] would avoid the fate of the linguistically slipshod demon who, in endeavoring to procure a son who would slay the god Indra, mispronounced the expression *indra-śatruḥ* ("Indra's slayer") with an accent on the final *uḥ* instead of the *śa*, and instead was given a son who was slain *by* Indra. Getting pronunciation right in ritual language, in the face of the inevitable changes in the spoken form, ensured that, in the words of the first stanza of the later Sanskrit grammarian Bhartṛhari, *anādinidhanaṃ brahma śabdatattvaṃ yad akṣaram* ("The reality is that speech is the imperishable Brahman, without beginning or end").[6]

Among the many achievements of the Indian linguists was their highly developed attention to phonetics. Their detailed descriptions of how each sound was pronounced make us more confident today about how Sanskrit was pronounced than about any other ancient language.[7] At the same time, early Indian linguistics gave us the first sly digs at the "grammarian personality." To those unfortunate enough to socialize with linguists the following Sanskrit formulation will ring all too true: *ardhamātrālāghavena putrotsavam manyante vaiyākaraṇāḥ* ("grammarians rejoice as much over the saving of the length of half a short vowel as over the birth of a son").

What Ovid Did in His Exile

In AD 9 the Roman poet Ovid was exiled from Rome to the remote colony of Thrace near what is now the city of Constanța in Romania, among the tribe known as the Getae. Some years later he is said to have displayed his ability as a linguist by writing a poem eulogizing the emperor Augustus in the language of the Getae. Given his talents as a poet, and the length of time was in exile, he probably learned the language pretty well, however unwelcome the circumstances to learn it in may have been. Modern scholars would love to know something about this language – it would help answer crucial questions about the linguistic transition between Asia Minor and the Balkan Peninsula, and the tribes who lived there in Roman times. But neither Ovid's poem, nor any other records of the language, have come down to us. It was rare enough for Romans to take any interest in the languages of their despised barbarian subjects or neighbors, and even when unusual circumstances and talents overcame their reluctance, as in Ovid's exile, this did not result in any written record: "We deplore the disappearance of the poem, but its loss was inevitable. Who was there to preserve or copy it? No Roman could read it, and of the Getae nobody would bother with it."[8]

We can contrast the linguistically empty legacy of Ovid's exile with another group of exiles much later: the extensive and insightful records of Siberian languages put together in the nineteenth and twentieth centuries by Poles, Germans, and Russians sent to Siberia first under the Tsars and then after the revolution. Outcast scholars like Krejnovich, Dulzon, and Bogoras produced outstanding descriptions of such languages as Ket, Yukaghir, Nivkh, and Chukchi. The curiosity they showed about the peoples around them, and the willingness of even quite oppressive governments to allow the recording and dissemination of their findings, is something quite unattested in the classical world.

Returning to Rome, the indifference to other tongues – except Greek, then the language of sophisticated science and civilization – is shocking. For many centuries the Romans were in contact with the Etruscans just to their north, whom they acknowledged as their cultural mentors in many ways. As I mentioned in the last chapter, it is likely that Etruscan was a non-Indo-European language – and in fact the Greek Dionysius of Halicarnassus, who became interested in the origins of the Etruscans, mentioned that they "agree with no other [nation] either in its language or in its manner of living."[9] A knowledge of Etruscan would thus be of immense value in understanding the much greater levels of lineage diversity that were still present in Europe at the dawn of Roman expansion.

It is not that the Romans were uninterested in the Etruscans. Many leaders intermarried with them, and the emperor Claudius, whose first wife Urgulanilla was Etruscan, even wrote a history of the Etruscans in 20 volumes, though regrettably this has not come down to us. But even though the Etruscans had a long written tradition to which many Romans must have been exposed, and even though the Greeks and Romans wrote geographies that describe peoples from many parts of the ancient world, there is not a single Greek or Latin discussion of any aspect of Etruscan language. Please, just give us a short bilingual word list, we plead with all those dead Roman scholars, or a little parallel text in Etruscan and Latin or Greek! But nothing of the sort exists.[10]

Thanks to a few loanwords and shared place-names, we know how the Etruscan letters are pronounced. And from the contexts in which some inscriptions occur – on family tombs – we can translate small snatches like *Larthal cuclnies Velthurusla* ("of Larth Cuclnie (the son) of Velthur"). These linguistic shards already intrigue us by displaying a rare method of piling up "genitive suffixes," showing the possession of one thing by another (like English *'s*). This is something found elsewhere in the ancient Mediterranean but barely present in the Indo-European languages – *Velthur-us-la* is literally "Velthur's's" – "belonging to (the one) belonging to Velthur." But for most of this tantalizing language, shorn of context and locked up in monolingual isolation, all we can do is pronounce it and wonder what it meant.

A comparable indifference to other languages – unless they be those of a culturally, militarily, or religiously dominant rival group – marked every ancient civilization. The Greeks, so curious in most respects, have bequeathed us practically nothing about the languages they came into contact with: "Only Greek was studied. Foreign words were written as best they could be with the Greek letters, but no scholarly concern was evinced over alien sounds or alien sound systems."[11] Xenophon may well have written his famous advice *hòs àn mathēis, antákouson* ("that you may learn, hear the other side"),[12] but the "other side" was clearly meant to be heard in Greek, not in a barbarian tongue. As new powers emerged they often developed writing systems for their own language, usually adapted from the predecessors they sought to emulate and surpass. But they were never interested in dealing with anyone else's language.

Speaking to Other Hearts and Minds

> The light throws clearer shadows
> objects and feelings
> stand out now
> touchable
> but somehow still forbidding
> What else do I need to do?
> How far is the going yet
> until I am one with you?
>
> (Reesink 1987:xv, with permission of the author)

The idea of learning and committing to writing the languages of other, less militarily powerful peoples did not appear until Christianity, with its early urges to proselytize other peoples in languages they would understand. At first this impulse came from converted rulers who wanted to use translated religious texts as a way of establishing Christianity in their own kingdom. Even before Christianity had become the Roman state religion, the kings of other realms beyond the bounds of the Roman Empire had converted, commissioning scholars to devise writing systems for their languages and embark on translations of the Bible and other religious texts.

At the mountainous northeastern and southeastern extremities of the Christian world, the kingdoms of Georgia, Armenia, and Ethiopia began to produce religious literature, founding new literary traditions in Georgian, Armenian, and Ge'ez, the Ethiopian liturgical language. All these languages are phonetically difficult, bristling with exotic consonants such as the popped sounds known as ejectives. But ingenious new scripts, developed by polyglot priests for their own languages, quickly launched their traditions of religious translation, later to be followed by other forms of literature. The Caucasian systems took off from the Greek alphabet, while Ge'ez was developed from ancient Semitic writing systems of South Arabia. We will return to another forgotten early Christian kingdom and script in chapter 7 – the Caucasian Albanians and the tiny ethnic group near the Caspian Sea who unknowingly kept this "lost" language alive for more than a millennium. The story of its decipherment will bring together letters, monks, and manuscripts from the Caucasus and Ethiopia – two areas that we nowadays think of as belonging to separate worlds – since this language was so complex phonetically that the inventors of its writing system needed to grab letters from both the Caucasus and Ethiopia to get enough shapes to represent all its sounds.

Early Christian monasteries – like their Buddhist counterparts in the east – created an intense matrix of multilingual exchange as they brought together scholars from distant countries with a common focus on the study and interpretation of religious texts.

As it expanded and encountered heathen tribes, Christianity wrestled with the problem of how much of its doctrine could be rendered into other tongues. There was an inevitable tension in this enterprise. Was the goal to win converts from all peoples, by speaking to them simply and comprehensibly in the language of their own hearts? Or to control translations of texts whose theological implications could easily become heretical through careless or unauthorized interpretation? Missionaries like Cyril and his brother Methodius, among the Moravian Slavs in the ninth century who developed the Cyrillic alphabet for their translations into Slavonic, had to reckon with considerable suspicion and resistance from the Church hierarchy in Constantinople. At the same time, the cosmopolitan scholarly community in Constantinople helped them develop a fitting alphabet that would accommodate the many Slavonic sounds unfamiliar to Greek or Roman ears. Cyril and Methodius appear to have been in contact with Constantinople-based Armenian scholars like John the Grammarian and Leon the Philosopher, and to have adapted Armenian symbols to represent some of the sounds of early Slavic.

By the thirteenth century the Catalan scholar Ramon Llull, torn between his fascination for the learning of the Arabic world and his wish to reclaim the Mediterranean for Christianity, was articulating the view that the Church should embrace the study of foreign languages for purposes of conversion. And around 1500 the Dutch scholar Desiderius Erasmus began laying the foundations of humanist scholarship in Europe. His goal was to assure the accuracy of key religious and scholarly texts through disciplined philological study of the languages in which they were written. This activity had been stimulated by the arrival of many Greek classical scholars in Italy and other parts of Europe following the conquest of Byzantium by the Turks.

But the real explosion in missionary-based studies of unknown languages came when the Spaniards and Portuguese embarked on their massive ventures in the Americas, Africa, and Asia, bringing their potent mix of colonial conquest and religious propagation – occasionally leavened with scientific curiosity.

The fateful year 1492 marked three turning points for Spain: the sailing of Columbus and his "discovery" of the Americas, the expulsion of the Jews, and the publication of Antonio de Nebrija's grammar of Spanish, the first grammar of a "modern" European language after 14 centuries of obeisance to Latin and Greek. These three momentous events were curiously linked. The afterglow of Moorish Spain – the continued presence of Muslims and Jews even after the Reconquista – had maintained a multilingual matrix unique in Europe, cross-fertilizing the written traditions of the three monotheistic religions, with Arabic and Hebrew alongside Latin and what since the Renaissance was a revived Greek. In 1492 this gave way to a consolidation of a religiously unified Christian nation, under Queen Isabella's unrelenting hand, further united by the Castilian Spanish that Nebrija's grammar had newly codified. By an ironic lag of history, the scholars traveling with Columbus had grown up in the more polyglot times that had preceded. So probably no European nation could have brought such linguistic sophistication to their encounter with the New World. Columbus' ships included interpreters of Hebrew and Chaldean, prepared to meet descendants of the lost tribes of Israel.

The language policies of Spain in its new colonies were complex and inconstant. Sheer lack of numbers forced the Spaniards to accommodate to the languages they encountered.

In the Yucatan Peninsula in 1542, for example, there were only 8 Spanish priests to 4 million Mayans, so they had no choice but to learn Mayan. The demography in the Aztec territories of Mexico was not much more favorable to the conquerors, and from early on a policy that recognized the Aztec language (also known as Nahuatl) as the administrative language of New Spain was implemented. But there were also many other peoples, often millions strong, with quite different languages of their own, and missionary priests embarked on a massive program of learning the local languages and preparing catechisms, confessionals, dictionaries, grammars, and Bible translations.

The Spanish response to this vast linguistic challenge was unprecedented in world history. They established a printing press in Mexico in 1534, and within 40 years had published grammars of Tarascan, Nahuatl, and the Quechua language of Peru. By 1700, 21 grammars of Amerindian languages had been published, compared to 23 for all European languages by the same date. Four of these Amerindian grammars predated any comparable work on English.

The Spaniards' descriptive work has often been criticized as Latin-centric, and many aspects of these complex languages indeed eluded them. But they also made impressive breakthroughs. These included the devising of new phonetic symbols and the recognition of grammatical processes hitherto unknown to Old-World scholars, such as causatives, applicatives, and noun incorporation, which have all gone on to enrich our general conceptual apparatus for dealing with languages from around the world.

In the feverish profusion of Spanish linguistic work in the New World, one foundational figure stands out, marking the first systematic attempt by any culture in the world to understand, document, and make sense of a thoroughly alien tongue. The priest Fray Bernardino de Sahagún was in charge of the Colegio de Santa Cruz in Tlatelolco, a boarding school whose goal was to enculturate a new generation of Hispanicized and Christianized Mexicans. There he taught an elite group of boys basic Christian doctrine, reading and writing, Latin, rhetoric, logic, and philosophy. In 1533 the Franciscan friars had been instructed "to put the ancient customs of these native Indians, especially those of Mexico, Texcoco and Tlaxcalla, in a book, that there be some memory thereof, that the evil and imponderable might be better refuted and, if there were something good, that it might be recorded even as many things of other gentiles are recorded and remembered."[13] Sahagún's job description nicely captures

Figure 2.1   Fray Bernardino de Sahagún

the ambivalent attitude of the time – most importantly, the willingness to describe and record language, customs, and religious practices. The priests actually organized theological debates, in Nahuatl, with Aztec priests, the better to understand the belief system they wanted to replace. These fascinating debates were written down in majestic verse.

At the same time, there was a dark, destructive side to this engagement. At night-time the friars of the Colegio would organize the schoolboys into mobs who went out to destroy pyramid-temples and disrupt indigenous religious observances. They did all in their power to turn the children against their own parents by emphasizing that under Aztec

Figure 2.2 Page from the Florentine Codex (chapters 26–67)

religion their parents would have given them over for ritual sacrifice.[14] In Sahagún's defense, though, we must emphasize that, while the whole tragic process of colonial expansion and dispossession over the last five centuries has destroyed and dispossessed thousands of traditional cultures and millions of lives in ways comparable to or worse than those of the Spaniards in Mexico, hardly any individuals made the sorts of efforts that Sahagún carried through to at least record everything possible for posterity.

What is most strikingly innovative about Sahagún is how he went about his task. Traveling from place to place with a retinue of scribes and "Latinos," as the young men trained in his school were called, he would ask local chiefs and leaders to show paintings of ancient customs, and to talk about them. Then he would get the young men to write these descriptions down in Nahuatl and work with him on a translation. For the whole duration of the project Sahagún took on no Spanish collaborator, relying entirely on the Mexicans he had educated.

Decades of these collective labors produced the 16-volume masterpiece known as *The General History of the Things of New Spain* or the Florentine Codex (see figure 2.2). This is effectively the world's first ethnography, and also the first exercise in the comprehensive text-gathering now advocated in linguistic documentation – a detailed description of a culture, covering just about every facet of life from food to clothing to festivals to religion to marriage arrangements, throwing in a native account of the conquest of Mexico[15] (book 12). Throughout it is lavishly illustrated and explained by a documentary collective of members of the culture, in their mother tongue. With the immense vocabulary range its encyclopedic dimensions made possible, Sahagún himself regarded it as "a dragnet to bring in all the words of the language with their meaning." Significantly, the Nahuatl version was written first and the translation into Spanish left for later.

As would happen again and again in colonial encounters around the world, the partial official tolerance of indigenous languages and cultures did not last long. Once the Inquisition struck, books like these were seen as describing the works of the devil: "Sahagún said that it was necessary to know the enemy in order to defeat him, but his meticulous recording of remembered rites and practices could as well be seen as encouraging the heathen in their ways."[16] In 1570 Sahagún's work was impounded, and financial support for his scribes was withdrawn. That his book is now often referred to as the Florentine Codex reflects its tenuous survival thanks to a copy or codex, kept in Florence, that escaped the fires of the Inquisition.

Listening to the Word, Listening to the World

Je croye veritablement, que les langages sont le meilleur miroir de l'esprit humain et qu'une analyse exacte de la signification des mots feroit mieux connoistre que toute autre chose les operations de l'entendement.

I am truly convinced that languages are the best mirrors of the human mind, and that a precise analysis of the meaning of words better than anything would show how the mind operates.

(Leibniz, cited in Jankowsky 1995:179; original quote from Leibniz 1887:313)

One effect of the start-again stop-again missionary activity of the Spanish, Portuguese, and other European countries getting onto the colonial bandwagon was to slowly kindle curiosity about the true extent and variety of the world's languages. Travelers and explorers began, for the first time in the world's history, to take an interest in the languages they encountered, and to record them as best they could. Most often their intellectual interests were in tracing "lost tribes" through the evidence of their languages.

By the 1700s, scholars and scientists had begun to comprehend the significance of the world's languages for an understanding of the full history of humankind. Leibniz, for example, overtly broke with the established humanist tradition that only the three divine languages (Hebrew, Greek, and Latin) were worthy of study. Particularly with regard to the question of language relations and origin, he explicitly urged that "the study of language must not be conducted by any other principles but those of the sciences,"[17] and emphasized the need to thoroughly study all modern languages within reach before tackling questions of their historical affinity.

Three enormous encyclopedic works appeared around this time. The first attempts at a global stocktake of the world's linguistic riches, they brought together materials from hundreds of languages in Asia, Africa, Europe, and the Americas. Their titles display their ambitions: *Mithridates oder Allgemeine Sprachkunde* ("Mithridates, or the General Study of Language"), *Idea dell'Universo* ("Idea of the Universe"), *Vocabularia comparativa linguarum totius orbis* ("Comparative Vocabulary of the Languages of the Whole World").

The third of these reveals most about how scientific interest in language diversity was emerging in the eighteenth century. It grew out of an enormous project under the patronage of Empress Catherine II, partly motivated by her astute wish to establish Russian science as a world force. These origins had as one consequence that the transcriptions of many languages contained in it are in Cyrillic – an assertion of scientific nationalism that attracted much criticism from non-Russian scholars at the time. Much of the linguistic data was gathered by the German biologist Peter Simon Pallas, whom Catherine II had put in charge of an expedition from Moscow to Lake Baikal, with the goal of exploring the geography and ethnography of Russia's new Siberian territories. Records from this marathon expedition, which set off in 1768 and only returned in 1772, provide our main source of information for languages of the Yeniseian family like Kott, Assan, and Pumpokol, which fell into disuse by the nineteenth century. The languages of this family were spoken by the only hunter-gatherers in northern Asia, and we will see in chapter 6 how valuable Catherine's sponsorship of this eighteenth-century Siberian research was, since it supplies crucial information in new research linking them to the Athabaskan languages of North America.[18]

The questions that mainly interested these scholars were the historical relationships between languages and evolutionary questions of how languages developed from one type into another. But two other types of concern gradually emerged alongside these, focusing on the different worldviews embodied in different languages and on how widely the full spectrum of human linguistic possibilities can range. The first concern, in particular, was initially linked to the quest of emerging European nations for their own authentic traditions of language, philosophy, and literature – particularly in the case of the Germans and the Slav nations – and the Romantic rebellion against French enlightenment views of universal knowledge, coincidentally expressed in French. The eighteenth-century German philosopher Johann Gottfried Herder defended the advantages of his mother tongue but at the same time extolled the general values of cultural particularity to any people:

> Let us, therefore, be German, not because German is superior to all other nationalities, but because we are Germans and cannot well be anything else and because we can contribute to humanity at large only by being German.[19]
>
> Let us contribute to the honor of our nationality – and learn incessantly from and with others – so that together we can seek the truth and cultivate the garden of the common good.[20]

A few decades later his compatriot William von Humboldt (1767–1835) – diplomat, architect of the Prussian university system, and avid student of languages ranging from Aztec to the sacred Javanese language Kawi – developed a more profound argument for the value of the world's languages: "Comprehensive recognition of the objective world, however, is not obtainable by one language alone. The sum total of all cognitive processes enacted in all existing languages at all times of human history constitutes the sum total of all 'world recognition' accessible to man."[21] This is no drifting and facile relativism, but sets out an immense challenge to philological scholarship: that of gradually drawing nearer to reality through the sensitive and far-reaching study of the different vantage points that each language can give us on the world, through the legacy of what has been forged by each people's distinctive attempt to grasp reality, blazing their own thought-paths down through the millennia. For Humboldt this resulted from the perpetual interplay between the *energeia*, or activity of speech, and the *ergon*, or completed work of language, a vital insight that has reappeared in modern studies of how language structure emerges from use.

Humboldt's most important successors were responsible for the second great wave of linguistic fieldwork in the New World after Sahagún, as they transplanted his ideas to North America and applied them to the study of its languages and cultures.

Franz Boas (born in 1858) originally trained as a physicist in Germany. He was drawn into geography, ethnology, and anthropology through his fieldwork among Eskimo tribes on Baffin Island in the Canadian Arctic, and after emigrating to the USA in 1886 he began fieldwork in British Columbia with the Kwakiutl and other peoples of the Pacific Northwest. He went on to teach anthropology at Columbia University in New York, laying down the integrated "four-field" conception of anthropology – cultural anthropology, physical anthropology, linguistics, and archaeology – which was to bring so many benefits through its emphasis on the cultural matrix of linguistic fieldwork.

Boas made explicit many of the tenets that have become axiomatic in the best descriptive work: the importance of describing each language and each culture on their own terms rather than importing inappropriate European models, the need to discover the inner design of each language inductively through the study of texts, and the scientific responsibility to produce as undistorted a record as possible by setting grammar alongside a comprehensive dictionary and text collection – the so-called Boasian trilogy. Appropriately for someone whose doctoral thesis investigated the chameleon-like color of seawater, he also promoted the technique of participant observation – of understanding a culture and

Figures 2.3 and 2.4   Ambient light and the color of seawater: Franz Boas as anthropology professor (left) and as Kwakiutl ceremonial dancer (right)

language by striving to become a normal participant within it – and took this seriously himself in his own linguistic and anthropological studies (see figures 2.3 and 2.4).

Boas' demanding and inspiring teaching attracted many brilliant students, among them another German Jewish émigré, Edward Sapir (1884–1939). More centered on language than Boas, Sapir was a consummate unraveler of grammatical intricacies, producing masterpieces of description like his grammar of the Oregon language Takelma. But his interests in poetry, psychology, music, and anthropology made him careful to avoid the fate of "the man who is in charge of grammar and is called a grammarian [who] is regarded by all plain men as a frigid and dehumanised pedant."[22] One of the few linguists able to communicate the significance of seemingly obscure grammatical facts to a general audience, he realized that "It is peculiarly important that linguists, who are often accused, and accused justly, of failure to look beyond the pretty patterns of their subject matter, should become aware of what their science may mean for the interpretation of human conduct in general."[23]

Sapir in his turn was to teach, and have a profound influence on Benjamin Lee Whorf (1897–1941), another great North American thinker about what Amerindian languages can bring to the table of world knowledge. Between them they further articulated and grounded Humboldt's grand quest of listening to what the manifold voices of the world's languages have to tell us about the relation of our concepts to reality. Their deep knowledge of Amerindian languages unveiled far more surprising and compelling examples than Humboldt could supply from the library of his country estate in Prussia. But this story deserves a whole chapter to itself, and we will defer it until chapter 8.

Glyphs, Wax Cylinders, and Videos

> The language
> eternal
> through the speech
> extinct
>
> ("Rilke at Glacier Bay", Dauenhauer 1980)

The gradual unfolding of linguistic interest that I have sketched above resulted from an amalgam of developments in politics, religion, and the general history of ideas. From our position today, it is easy for us to underestimate it as simply a technology-free flowering of ideas, like the growth of pure mathematics, occurring almost automatically once enough people turned their minds to it in the right intellectual climate. How much could be achieved by a well-trained modern-day linguist catapulted back to the time of Socrates, like Mark Twain's Connecticut Yankee in King Arthur's court? Could they not simply begin to transcribe and analyze the languages of the Etruscans and other people around them, duly equipped with pen and parchment or at least stylus and tablet?

This is not a crazy scenario. Just think of how much could be accomplished by Pāṇini on his own language, without even writing his grammar down, or by Sahagún on a language that was about as remote from his own as a language can be, with writing and drawing but not much more in the way of technology. There are still eminent field-linguists like Bob Dixon, with major fieldwork achievements under their belts, who advocate something not too different from this. In his acceptance speech on being conferred with the prestigious Bloomfield award for his grammar of the Amazonian language Jarawara, he gave the following advice to aspiring field-linguists:

> A word addressed to junior colleagues who think that it will improve their work to immerse it in the latest electronic technology. Don't. Because it won't. I worked on the Jarawara grammar as I did on previous grammars of Dyirbal, or Yidiñ, of Boumaa Fijian (and of English). I used pencil, pen and spiral-bound notebooks, plus a couple of good-quality tape recorders. No video camera (to have employed one would have compromised my role in the community). No lap-top. No shoebox or anything else of that nature. (Dixon 2006, with permission)

It is certainly the case that linguists are in many senses their own laboratories, counting a hard-won fluency in the language under description as their most valuable analytical asset. And fluency is acquired above all simply by going, childlike, down the long, humiliating, vivid and comical road of talking to the people whose language you are trying to learn.

However, it is important to balance this view with a due appreciation of the role of technology. Writing itself, of course, is a type of technology parallel in many ways to the development of mathematical symbols, musical notation, or perspective in art. Materially simple, these were all advanced by pioneers who attended carefully to the possibilities of their chosen domain, and developed representations that simultaneously help us to think about phenomena more rigorously and – especially in the case of musical notation – train us to perceive and organize finer discriminations than we may otherwise have made.

The International Phonetic Alphabet (IPA), which any well-trained modern linguist has mastered, contains around 170 standardized symbols. Since this includes over 50 diacritic markers that can be recombined with other symbols, the total number of sounds it can represent runs to the thousands. In principle, this enables a fieldworker to transcribe the sounds of any of the world's languages in such a way that another trained investigator who has never heard the language could read back a close replication of the original pronunciation. This eliminates the uncertainties that dog many early transcriptions of little-known languages – such as unsatisfactory early transcriptions of the complex click types found in the Khoisan languages of southern Africa, which are sometimes almost useless for modern purposes. Problems like this arose either because the investigators missed crucial distinctions unfamiliar in their own language, or because they used symbols of unknown or ambiguous sound value. Of course, every now and then a new sound is encountered and a new symbol (or variant) needs to be developed, accompanied by an explicit description of how it is made, but we now have most of the world's sounds covered.

However, there is much that phonetic transcriptions do not capture, both in the realm of sound and in the non-verbal elements of speech, such as gesture and sign. Starting with sound, the first problem has to do with replicability. If I do not hear clicks or tones very well and mine are the only transcriptions of a now-extinct language, you cannot go back and produce your own, better, analysis.

The second problem has to do with pace and naturalness. Investigators like Boas, Sapir, and John Peabody Harrington were all first-rate linguists devoted to writing down extensive textual materials in as faithful a transcription as possible. Harrington himself wrote nearly a million pages of fieldnotes on some 90 languages around California. Boas and Sapir extended their reach by collaborating with native speakers trained in transcription – their Lakhota-speaking colleague Mary Deloria, for example, collected Lakhota stories throughout the 1930s from various native speakers, then retold them in her own words, and Boas paid Tsimshian speaker Henry Tate 15 cents a page (later raised to 20 cents!) to write down extensive text collections.[24] But, although they sometimes could use sound-recorders (see below), they mostly had to work with speakers who dictated to them at a rate slow enough to transcribe, in the process losing much of the verve and rapidly improvised riffs of a master storyteller. As Boas put it: "The slowness of dictation that is necessary for recording texts makes it difficult for the narrator to employ that freedom of diction that belongs to the well-told tale, and consequently an unnatural simplicity of syntax prevails in most of the dictated texts."[25] Speakers also tend to normalize their speech when dictating, eliminating the non-standard forms and abbreviations that so often provide a clue to the future course of language change, something we have only begun to realize now that we have access to good sound-recordings of naturalistic speech.

The third problem has to do with analysis: while a good natural phonetician can work out a lot about new sounds from careful listening and imitation, there are often residual problems that can only be solved by spectral analysis of good recordings. Finally, there are prosodic elements in language, such as its intonational melody, which are very difficult to transcribe faithfully on the run at the same time as writing down the segments.

Figure 2.5   Hidatsa speaker Margaret Haven (left) and Crow speaker Henrietta Pretty On Top (right) being recorded in 1953 by Carl Voegelin

Sound-recording technology has gone through half a dozen revolutions since Bell's invention of the phonograph around 1900 first allowed mechanical recordings of speakers onto acetate or wax cylinders. Some far-sighted investigators began applying this technology quite early. Thanks to Alfred Kroeber's early deployment of wax cylinders, for example, we can still hear the voice of Ishi, the famed last speaker of Yahi, who came out of the Californian mountains and lived out his final years in the Hearst Museum in San Francisco during the years of World War I.

The earliest recordings were expensive, which led many early investigators to limit their use to "high" materials like ritual songs, consigning the humbler phenomena of prosaic speech to their written fieldnotes. They also required bulky equipment – although Kroeber managed to transport recording equipment and wax cylinders upriver to Yurok-speaking villages in northern California by canoe. And their limited frequency range (200–2,000 Hz) skipped infor-mation crucial to distinguishing some types of sibilant sounds.

A parade of technological advances saw acetate and wax cylinders giving way after World War I to wire recorders (80–8,000 Hz range) and aluminium-disk recorders. These were still cumbersome by modern standards, but in principle transportable with the right team: Harrington inveigled his teenage neighbor Jack Marr into carrying his "150-pound 'portable' aluminium disc recording machine over mountains and across rope bridges" in his expeditions recording Californ-ian languages.[26] Reel-to-reel recorders appeared after World War II, using tapes enabled by improvements in plastic technology. They in turn gave way to tape cassettes, and on to the range of digital recording devices in normal use today. Each technological advance saw improvements in recording fidelity, portability, and data compression. When ethnomusicologists Parry and Lord undertook their epic record-ings in Yugoslavia in the 1930s (see chapter 9), they needed a half-ton collection of 3,500 twelve-inch aluminium disks. Today this could all be comfortably accommodated on a small external memory.

Before we pass from sound-recordings to visual recordings, it is worth emphasizing that we often need to go beyond acoustic records if we are to truly understand even the sound systems of the world's languages. Speech transmission is a three-stage process: the initial articulation by the speaker, its acoustic transmission through the air, and its perception and neural decoding by the hearer. Sound-recordings only capture the middle step of this process. Yet it is important to understand articulation as well, and this requires much more complex recording devices like electropalatographs and instruments that measure airflow through the nose and oral tracts. For some of these, speakers need to visit dentists beforehand in order to have special false palates made, and the insertion of tubes through the nose and throat is not an inviting procedure. Yet the scientific payoffs of this kind of study can be significant – ranging from an understanding of the complex articulatory movements needed to produce Khoisan-style clicks, to the subtle accommodatory streamlinings of coarticulated movements that can help us understand why certain sound changes occur in some languages but not others. The intrusive nature of this sort of investigation makes it unlikely that it will ever be part of the repertoire of ordinary field-linguistic techniques, but for some questions it is indispensable.

To close our overview of the role of technology we turn from sound to vision, and ask what we lose when the gestures and facial expressions that accompany speech are filtered out by just recording the sound dimension.

To start with, we know that over 10 percent of speech sounds are in fact "heard" with our eyes. Experiments by psychologists have revealed phenomena like the McGurk Effect, where subjects watch film in which the sound track makes one sound (e.g. *ba*) while the screen shows a speaker producing another (e.g. *ga*). Watching one of these (you can do this on http://www.youtube.com/watch?v=aFPtc8BVdJk) you will have the eerie experience of suddenly moving from hearing *ba* (if you shut your eyes) to hearing the audiovisually fused compromise sound *da* (when you open them and look at the speaker), then hearing *ba* again if you shut your eyes and screen out the visual cues. This sort of experiment helps explain why even quite experienced linguists can make embarrassing basic transcription mistakes, like mixing up *mu* and *ngu* [ŋu], when working off a sound-recording alone.

Next, any full study of speech needs to factor in the contributions of gesture by the hands, facial expressions, and eye contact. One reason is that such gesture is a central part of the feedback system that speakers use to check whether their hearers are following them and that allows us to "gain the floor" with the right fine-grained millisecond timing. Another is that by studying gesture we can gain independent evidence about how speakers structure concepts like time, giving another window into thought from that which language provides.

Another way filmed gesture is important is in revealing speakers' tracking of spatial information as they talk. When Pat Gabori or any other Kayardild speaker talks, their speech is replete with spatial identifications using the points of the compass. Despite having been blind for four decades, Pat consistently orients almost every utterance to the exact layout of the compass. *Jirrkarayiwath* ("Move a bit to the north!"), he says to get you to squeeze over two inches on the car seat. Or, in referring to an uncle of yours who is sitting most easterly on the bench, or living on the east side of the settlement: *Daamija ngumbanda riya kakuju!* ("Ask your east uncle"). Or, telling you how to get into a light plane: *Rayinda munkiriliij!* ("Squeeze yourself in arse-first from the south!").

It is one thing for a field-linguist to report – as I can affirm at first hand – that learning to speak a language like Kayardild requires you to reprogram your mind so as to pay constant attention to the points of the compass. But establishing how people think is much harder than recording how they speak, and we will see in chapter 8 how video recordings of the gestures used by speakers of Kayardild-style languages can reveal much about how they are thinking, independently of speech.

The third major use of film is in the study of sign languages, since it was effectively impossible to analyze fast-moving dynamic signs until film made it possible to record, replay, and compare tokens. An explosion of work since the 1960s has revealed the existence of over 120 sign languages around the world, and just like spoken languages they display major structural variation that we are only just beginning to be aware of. Indeed, we are only just beginning to get basic descriptive information on many village-based sign languages in places like Ghana and Bali, where a significant proportion of the non-deaf population can sign owing to the widespread presence of congenital deafness, so that most families have deaf family members.

Sign languages are destined to play an ever more central role in linguistic theorizing. By dissociating mind from modality, they allow us to see which design features of language are molded to human cognition more generally, and which are simply adaptations to the medium of speech with its inability to deal with parallel channels and three-dimensional representations. They are also vital to our understanding of how language evolved, as the timing and distribution of labor between spoken and signed elements in the course of linguistic evolution is still far from clear. The very recent genesis of many sign languages, often just in the last few decades as nationally established deaf schools gather a quorum of deaf people together for the first time, has allowed scholars to study the incredibly rapid evolution of language systems in real time.[27] I want to close the chapter with one more example of a lost language from the past, this time a sign language, employed in the sixteenth-century Ottoman court in Istanbul.

In 1554 the Flemish nobleman Oghier Ghislain de Busbecq, a visitor to the Ottoman court, reported that "mutes" – most of them deaf – were "a favourite kind of servant among the Turks." The Turkish term *dilsiz* "tongueless" was widely used for this category of servant. There were many reasons why *dilsiz* were favored in the Ottoman court. Being deaf and mute, there was no danger if they were privy to confidential court business: no enemy could bribe or torture them to reveal secrets they had not heard, and could not tell. Deaf servants were therefore actively recruited by the court and, with so many gathered in one place, a system of sign language developed among them. In 1599 another visitor to the Ottoman court, the English organ-builder Thomas Dallam, wrote the following:

> The thirde hundrethe weare Dum men, that could nether heare nore speake, and theye weare likwyse in gouns of riche Clothe of gould and Cordivan buskins; . . . I did moste of all wonder at those dumb men, for they lett me understande by theire perfitt sins [i.e. signs] all thinges that they had sene the presente dow by its motions. (cited in Miles 2000, quoted with permission)

Other witnesses attested to the full expressivity of this Ottoman Sign Language, such as the diplomat Ottaviano Bon:

> And this is worthie the observation, that in the Serraglio, both the King and others can reason and discourse of any thing as well and as distinctly, alla mutesca, by nods and signes,

as they can with words: a thing well befitting the gravitie of the better sort of Turkes, who care not for much babling. The same is also used amongst the Sultanaes, and other the Kings Women: for with them likewise there are divers dumbe women, both old and young. And this hath beene an ancient custome in the Serraglio: wherefore they get as many Mutes as they can possibly find: and chiefly for this one reason; that they hold it not a thing befitting the Grand Signior. Neither stands it with his greatnesse, to speake to any about him familiarly: but he may in that manner more tractably and domestically jest and sport with the Mutes, than with other that are about him. (cited in Bon 1996)

As Bon's description indicates, it was not only deaf people who used the sign language. It was considered so unseemly to disturb the Sultan's tranquillity with the noise of talking, that many courtiers learned and used sign. Mike Miles, from whose fascinating history of mutes in the Ottoman court the above account is drawn, portrays several centuries of unbroken transmission and elaboration of Ottoman Sign Language among a community of both deaf and hearing people, with the code acquiring high status thanks to its use by the sultan and its active cultivation as a second language by courtiers.

Despite this long and illustrious history, and the many mentions of its use by various visitors to the Ottoman court, we have only scanty and inadequate visual records – about the best we have is the odd illustration like figure 2.6 – and no detailed verbal descrip-

tions of individual signs. Our first photographic record depicts signing by two deaf and mute attendants at the Sublime Porte, published in 1917.[28] Yet again we see a missed opportunity, this time primarily due to lack of technology rather than intellectual indifference.

This loss is particularly frustrating for our understanding of sign languages because it is likely that Ottoman Sign Language would have been the world's oldest-growth sign language with a large signing community, and would accordingly have had the most time to develop a complex linguistic profile. This is important because, if we only look at sign languages of recent genesis, we do not know whether features we find – or do not find – are essential characteristics of sign language, or are merely characteristic of new-growth languages. If we just looked at pidgin and creole spoken languages, for example, we might conclude that spoken languages could never have complex systems of inflection, large consonant inventories, or tones, since these

Figure 2.6 A *dilsiz*, or deaf attendant, signing at the Ottoman court (photo: courtesy of Mike Miles)

are confined to old-growth languages that have had millennia to develop grammatical complexity.

Intriguingly, modern-day Turkish Sign Language (Türk İşaret Dili) displays a number of features unique among sign languages, including highly schematized ways of marking negation and a remarkably large proportion of arbitrary (i.e. completely non-pantomimic) signs.[29] It is tempting to regard these elaborations as the heritage of the unique five-hundred-year history of sign language in Turkey.

This hypothesis rests on the fragile assumption that modern Turkish Sign Language is in fact a direct descendant of what was used in the now extinct conditions of the Ottoman court. There have been enough disruptions to educational policy over the last turbulent century in Turkey to render this assumption tenuous. Nonetheless, the timing of modern deaf schools in Turkey permits the merest whisker of a connection:

> Deaf servants were definitely still around at court at the beginning of the 20th century. At the same time, a number of modern schools for the deaf were beginning their classes. Any inter-action at all between the last generation of deaf court servants and the first generation of deaf school children would have been sufficient to ensure at least some continuity of the sign lan-guage. (Zeshan 2002:243, with permission of Harrasowitz Verlag)

But without either historical records of Ottoman Sign Language or recordings from those last deaf court servants, this fascinating hypothesis remains hanging.

Further reading

Good surveys of the evolution of writing systems are Coulmas (1989, 1996) and Rogers (2005). Robins (1979) has chapters on the Greek and Roman grammatical traditions, while Staal (1988), Kiparsky (1995), and Cardona (2000) are useful places to start on Pāṇini and the Sanskrit linguistic tradition.

There is a great deal of material on the Spanish linguistic encounter with the New World. Good summary accounts in English are the opening section of Suarez (1983) and Gray (1999, 2000). Various editions of Sahagún's masterpiece exist, with the translation by Dibble and Anderson (see Sahagún 1950–82) being the most accessible.

On the period of great language collections see Jankowsky (1995), Morpurgo Davies (1998), and Urness (1967) on Peter Pallas. The linguistic history of exiles in Siberia has yet to receive the treat-ment it deserves, although some information can be found in Ashnin et al. (2002).

Sources on Boas, Sapir, and Whorf are numerous and accessible. All three wrote beautifully them-selves, making them appealing primary sources. See particularly Boas (1911), Sapir (1921) and the collection of his works gathered in Mandelbaum (1949), and Whorf (1956). Darnell (1990) is another good source on Sapir, as are Hinton (1994) and Laird (1975) on Harrington.

Pullum and Ladusaw's (1996) handbook on the International Phonetic Alphabet gives the his-tory and origins of each symbol – as well as a detailed phonetic description. Miles (2000) gives a history of Ottoman Turkish Sign Language, and Zeshan (2002) discusses modern Turkish Sign Language and its possible relation to the Ottoman system.

Part II

A Great Feast of Languages

Eine allgemeine Grammatik ist so wenig　　　　A universal grammar is no more
denkbar, als eine allgemeine Form der　　　　conceivable than a universal form of
Staatsverfassungen und der Religionen,　　　　political Constitution or of religion, a
oder eine allgemeine Pflanzen- und Thierform.　　or than universal plant or animal form.

(Steinthal 1861; English translation by Jespersen 1924:48)

There is nothing to beat actuality, present or past, for clinching possibility.
Whatever is or has been actual is obviously possible.

(Dennett 1995:105)

One of the most exciting things about linguistic fieldwork is the way it continuously pushes out the bounds of preconceived possibility, by stumbling upon "unimaginable" languages – those that would never have been thought possible. It is a peculiar fact about linguistics that practically none of the astonishing typological features eventually discovered empirically have been anticipated through prior deduction. This is in marked contrast to the physical sciences where, for example, mathematicians had anticipated the possible existence of the Einsteinian universe by playing speculatively with non-Euclidean geometry, or chemistry, where the existence of a large number of elements was deduced by Mendeleev before they were discovered. Linguistics is much more like the life sciences where the discovery of strange and unimagined new species constantly makes us revise our ideas of what is biologically possible.[1]

But how different, in fact, can languages be? At the universalizing end are scholars who assert that differences in how languages are built are superficial and minor:

One comes almost to believe that the norms of syntax are indestructible, so persistently do they reappear in unexpected places. (Alphonso Smith, quoted in Jespersen 1924:48)

Amid infinite diversity, all languages are, as it were, cut from the same pattern. (Greenberg et al. 1963:xv)

At the relativist end are those who struggle to find anything significant that all languages have in common:

[L]anguages . . . differ . . . without limit and in unpredictable ways. (Joos 1957:96)

Much hangs on these questions, including the teaching of languages, speech technologies, military security, and – for philosophers and psychologists – our conception of the human mind. Early in his career Noam Chomsky pointed out that, since children learn their mother tongue extraordinarily fast from often chaotic input, their task would be greatly facilitated if they did not just come to it with a blank-slate mind but instead brought a highly specific set of neurally wired hypotheses about "Universal Grammar" to the task. This corrals the possible grammars the child has to choose between as they listen to their parents and siblings talk.

Chomsky's theory of Universal Grammar has been hugely influential, but is it correct? If we take "universals" in their strongest sense, as designating properties that all languages must have, the haul of clear and empirically impeccable universals after decades of searching is pitiful. Consider "parts of speech" – the sets of similarly profiled words that determine what can be combined with what, and that are the fundament for all grammatical rules. The jury is still out on whether all languages at least distinguish nouns and verbs, but there are certainly languages without prepositions, adjectives, articles, or adverbs. Even if a language does have nouns and verbs, we cannot know in advance what words will go into what category. "Paternal aunt" can be expressed by a verb in Ilgar, "know" is an adjective in Kayardild, and "love" is a mere suffix in Tiriyó. And things are equally fluid just about anywhere we look – in the sound system, in where the boundaries of concepts are established, in the architecture of grammar, and in which categories a language forces its speakers to attend to constantly.

How many languages do we need to look at before we can know what is a possible language? Well, some very smart mathematicians like Gauss and Riemann conjectured that, however far you count, a number always had more prime numbers below it than its own logarithmic value – and this works beautifully up to any number you can find in a prime number table. But since Littlewood's theorem in 1914 we know that this rule does not keep going forever. In fact, as long as you're willing to wait till 6.62×10^{1165} for the show to start, if you stick around you'll see the log value of N and the number of primes below N race past each other an infinite number of times.[2]

Languages are a bit like this. It's easy to keep a little posse of universals alive provided you only take a few languages into account, but at some point the 51st or 2018th language you examine fails to conform. Of course it is also interesting to see what is common rather than universal, so that finding an odd exception – say a language like Kayardild that marks tense on nouns as well as verbs – does not stop you saying "typically, languages don't do this." But if you happen to be a child growing up learning that language, this information isn't much help. Your job is to learn your parents' language, whether it's typical or not, and your mind must be capable of learning it, not ruling it out in advance. When it comes to universals, then, every language counts.

There is another way to view our Galapagos of tongues: as thousands of natural experiments in how humans can develop intricate functioning linguistic systems, through use, but without conscious planning. From this perspective, unusual languages kill two scientific birds with one stone: they don't just show what is learnable and usable, but they also show what human institutions can evolve as an unplanned outcome of use.

Alton (Pete) Becker, who has written perceptively about his own struggles to get inside Southeast Asian languages like Javanese and Burmese, has described the experience of learning a very different language in situ as "like watching a clearer and clearer picture gradually emerge while a photograph develops in a chemical bath. A vast picture, infinitely detailed, and even now it is still developing."[3] To me this is only half right, since it neglects two crucial aids to getting a good "language photograph." First, there is the incremental growth in concepts that linguists have developed in order to make sense of how a broad range of languages work: these concepts train us to see patterns more quickly. And, second, while doing fieldwork there is the restless probing and formulation of hypotheses to make sense of what we hear our teachers say.

These dialogic explorations can suddenly turn an utterance that speakers take for granted into a Eureka moment for the linguist. In the next two chapters we'll get a feel for these aids. In chapter 3, we will look at the three dimensions on which languages can vary – their sounds, their meanings, and their grammars. In chapter 4, we will focus on one particular task that all languages face – helping speakers keep track of their social universe – and see just how widely languages differ in which aspects of interpersonal reality their grammars force speakers to single out for careful attention.

3

A Galapagos of Tongues

Linguistic theory will never be moved ahead as far by answers to questions we already know enough to ask as it will by discoveries of the unexpected.

(Mithun 2001:45)

The Unbroken Code

During World War II the world's top mathematicians, logicians and linguists were recruited to develop and break codes on both Allied and Axis sides. Initially, the Japanese cryptographers cracked Allied encipherments almost as fast as they could be invented. But the American military then deployed their most successful code of the war. Navajo servicemen communicated military plans to each other by walkie-talkie, in their own language – which had been further adapted for military use by naming plane types after birds, marine corps units after clans, and using objects and animals to stand for letters in case any new word, such as a place-name, needed spelling out. Japanese soldiers listening in on their Allied attackers in the islands of the Pacific would hear a "strange language, gurgling."[1] But their top cryptographers never succeeded in cracking the Navajo code.

It helped, of course, that the Japanese didn't know which language it was, and that special disguised vocabulary was being used. But the main point is that a language that is structurally very different from your own can present such formidable problems of understanding that it takes a talented and well-trained adult years and sometimes decades of exposure to make sense of what children learn effortlessly in the first years of their lives.

Language learners of any age face a *triple mapping problem*.[2] First, they need to map the continuous flux of possible human sounds (or signs, in a sign language) into a structured set of discrete elements – *phonemes*, or language-specific contrasting signals. Second, they need to find the world's joints and carve them into the concepts named by words and *morphemes* – the smallest bits of meaning paired to form. And, third, they need to work out the system

Figure 3.1 Navajo code-talkers Cpt. Henry Bake Jr (left) and Pfc. George H. Kirk (right) operating a portable radio set in the Bougainville Island jungle, December 1943[3]

of mediating structures – the grammar – that expresses complex meanings through assemblages of spoken forms, and deciphers heard forms back into meaning. Let's begin with the sound problem, because that is what we meet first when we encounter a new language.

Sounds Off

> In the hideous, snapping, barking dialect that passes for speech along the [Rossel Island] coast . . . [n]oises like sneezes, snarls and the preliminary stages of choking – impossible to reproduce on paper – represented the names of villages, people and things.
>
> (Grimshaw 1912:191–2)

The first problem confronting our Japanese code-breakers listening to Navajo was to get past the "strange, gurgling" barrier of unfamiliar sounds.

New languages sound more than passing strange. When the Irish–Australian travel writer Beatrice Grimshaw, who penned the above quote, landed on Rossel Island off the New Guinea coast, her novelist's ears were stumped by the sounds of the Yélî-Dnye language.

It is now known to have the largest phoneme inventory in the southwestern Pacific, including many sounds not found in any other human language.[4] But to children learning it, it is the most natural-sounding language in the world.

By the time we reach adulthood, though, our ability to pronounce the sounds of other tongues has atrophied so badly that it is almost impossible to pick up another language in adulthood without having an accent, light or heavy according to how good our ear is. There are well over 1,500 possible speech sounds, all of which can be learned perfectly by any human child. Yet no language selects more than 10 percent of them for use in its phoneme inventory. In tuning in to the small fraction of possible human speech sounds used in our own language we simultaneously turn off our sensitivity to the other 90 percent. If we are lucky enough to grow up multilingual we bag a slightly bigger fraction.

It appears to be a human universal – from which only the odd breed of phoneticians is partially exempt – that the sound of other languages is strange and comical. A Japanese colleague of mine works with the |Gui language of Botswana, whose huge number of click sounds present almost insurmountable pronunciation problems for most non-|Gui. She discovered that they in their turn found her own name – the seemingly straightforward *Mimmi* – almost unpronounceable.

In many languages the names for one's neighbors' tongues are derogatory. In Russian, German is *nemetsky*: "dumb [person's] language," or originally "in a mute, dumb way." And in the Aboriginal language Guugu Yimithirr, the neighboring Gugu Yalanji language is *Guugu Diirrurru* ("mumbling talk"). Conversely, it is normal to call your own language by reassuringly flattering terms like "proper talk." Kayardild, for example, literally means "strong language."

Many anthropologists have suggested that the restless phonological reshaping of languages cashes in on our evolutionarily determined decline in plasticity with age, by making sure that insiders in our group – whose goals are most likely to coincide with ours, and to whom we are therefore most ready to extend our trust – can readily be distinguished from outsiders as soon as they open their mouths. The famous Biblical incident below was probably not the first time, and certainly not the last, that phonetic differences have been placed at the service of group definition (in the original Hebrew, the relevant S(h)ibboleth words have been bolded):[5]

וַיִּלְכֹּד גִּלְעָד אֶת־מַעְבְּרוֹת הַיַּרְדֵּן, לְאֶפְרָיִם; וְהָיָה כִּי יֹאמְרוּ פְּלִיטֵי אֶפְרַיִם "אֶעֱבֹרָה!", וַיֹּאמְרוּ לוֹ אַנְשֵׁי־גִלְעָד "הַאֶפְרָתִי אַתָּה?", וַיֹּאמֶר "לֹא!". וַיֹּאמְרוּ לוֹ "אֱמָר־נָא **שִׁבֹּלֶת!**", וַיֹּאמֶר "**סִבֹּלֶת**", וְלֹא יָכִין לְדַבֵּר כֵּן, וַיֹּאחֲזוּ אוֹתוֹ, וַיִּשְׁחָטוּהוּ אֶל־מַעְבְּרוֹת הַיַּרְדֵּן; וַיִּפֹּל בָּעֵת הַהִיא, מֵאֶפְרַיִם, אַרְבָּעִים וּשְׁנַיִם, אָלֶף.

And the Gileadites took the passages of Jordan before the Ephraimites: and it was so, that when those Ephraimites which were escaped said, Let me go over; that the men of Gilead said unto him, Art thou an Ephraimite? If he said, Nay; then said they unto him, Say now Shibboleth: and he said Sibboleth: for he could not frame to pronounce it right. Then they took him, and slew him at the passages of Jordan: and there fell at that time of the Ephraimites forty and two thousand. (Judges 12:5–6, King James Version)

Box 3.1   Ubykh: too many consonants, not enough speakers

Ubykh is a language of the northwestern Caucasus – that famed region of fiercely independent groups. But a succession of military defeats drove the remaining Ubykhs into exile in Turkey, and Ubykh families switched to speaking Turkish and the languages of larger exiled Caucasian communities like Circassian and Abaza.

During 1930, a scattering of Ubykh elders at Samsun in Turkey would gather each evening, arriving on horseback at the hour of prayer, supping in the garden, sleeping in the landing and returning to their fields before dawn. They were there to work with French Caucasologist George Dumézil, who scoured the villages of the Black Sea coast to bring these few speakers together. Despite the difficult conditions he was working under, Dumézil managed to crack the formidable sound system of Ubykh, whose 81 distinct consonant phonemes include sounds not known in any other language.[6]

The complexity of Ubykh does not stop with the sound system – there are more than 20 verb prefixes delineating spatial relationships, and a polysynthetic grammar that builds one-word verbal expressions like *aqhjazbacr'aghawdætwaaylafaq'ayt'madaqh*
("if only you had not been able to make him take it all out from under me again for them").

Dumézil began his work at the eleventh hour, but thanks to his resourcefulness in locating outstanding teachers among the handful of speakers still alive in 1930, he recorded enough to produce a grammar, texts, and dictionary of this awesomely complex language on the basis of what could be coaxed out of their memories into his field notebook. Somehow the language managed to hang on until October 7, 1992 when its last fluent speaker – who had taught Dumézil – passed away in his sleep. He had prepared the inscription he wanted on his grave: "This is the grave of Tevfik Esenç. He was the last person able to speak the language they called Ubykh."

Tevfik Esenç, the last speaker of Ubykh, aged 57 (Dumézil, 1962)

Figure 3.2   Speakers of !Xóõ (also known as Taa), gathered together for a storytelling competition at Pos 17, Namibia[7] (photo: Christfried Naumann)

But the full potential for languages to vary their sound patterns puts this little *s* vs. *sh* contrast in the shade. Most obviously, this can involve the number of phonemes (contrastive sounds), which can be as low as 10 in the Amazon language Pirahã and 11 in the Papuan language Rotokas. For many years the world-record holder for the most consonants was the Caucasian language Ubykh (see box 3.1), with 82 consonants. But it has now been eclipsed by the reigning champion, !Xóõ or, more pronounceably, Taa (see figure 3.2), which is spoken by about 4,000 people in Botswana and Namibia, and which has somewhere between 84 and 159 consonant phonemes depending on the analysis.[8] English comes in middling at 40–45 depending on the analysis, and Navajo around 50.

Even when two languages have systems of roughly similar size, the actual sounds they contain can draw on very different phonic dimensions for their contrasts. Kayardild has a "long flat" sound system with lots of points of articulation – different ways of touching different parts of the tongue to different parts of the teeth, gums, and roof of the mouth. It has distinct nasal sounds at each of them, but no fricatives like *s*, *z*, *sh*, *f*, or *v*. English scrimps on nasals and points of articulation but then splurges in the fricative department.

Apart from their basic sets of consonants and vowels, languages may play all sorts of "suprasegmentals" over the top, like tone or different types of voice quality. Sometimes, like in Chinese or Navajo, each tone is anchored to a particular vowel. But in other languages, tones "float" unattached and are only detectable through the influence they have on other tones when words combine. In the Bangangte dialect of Bamileke in Cameroon, for example, there is no audible word for "of." Within a phrase like "thing of child" (for "child's thing") it lurks as a "floating high tone" between "thing" and "child." This ghostly connective only makes its presence felt by bumping down the tone of the following word.

As knowledge of languages like this has proliferated, linguists have gradually abandoned their old "segmental" view of sound systems that treated phonemes like beads on a one-string necklace. Instead, we now have a more polyphonic conception in which the equivalent of different voices – one for the tone and one for the consonants and vowels[9] – can each go their own way, although tied together by a shared set of rhythmic organisers like beats and bar lines.

Syllables are the beats *par excellence*. They play a central part as rhythmic units, as well as in determining things like where stress should go, or what form of an affix to select, not to mention scanning words to poetry and song (see chapter 9). But the way they are organized, too, differs greatly from one language to another. Some languages restrict syllables to the single sequence Consonant + Vowel (CV), as in *ma*. Others permit complex "onsets" and "codas" such as in the English one-syllable word *strengths* (/strɛŋθs/), which has three consonants (*str*) in its onset and three more (*ngths* = ŋθs) in its coda. Georgian allows even more complex consonant clusters, as in the word *gvbrdɣvnis* ("he's plucking us") with its eight-consonant onset. And some languages, like Nuxálk (aka Bella Coola) in British Columbia, permit all sorts of consonants to form the nucleus of the syllable, as in a word like *xłp'x̌ʷłtłpłłskʷc'* ("he had a bunchberry plant" – I won't even try to tell you how to pronounce this one).

One of the jobs children face in making sense of the spray of sounds they hear is deciding how to divide up the string of sounds they hear into syllables. Say you are a baby hearing a sequence like *amadaba* – where do you make the syllable snips?

For a long time linguists believed there was a universal rule – the Maximal Onset Principle – favoring cuts that would give syllables a nice consonantal attack. Cuts yielding CV (consonant–vowel) syllables like *ma* would thus be preferred to cuts producing VC syllables like *am*. For *amadaba* this would give the syllabification *a-ma-da-ba*, whatever language the baby is learning. If this rule really was universal, it would greatly simplify the baby's task of learning her language because, whatever else she had to grapple with in her language's sound system, she could at least begin by just wading in with strong assumptions about how to divide the string of sounds into syllables.

This "universal CV-syllable" hypothesis survived for many years, even as descriptions of more and more languages came in. But in the 1990s Gavan Breen and Rob Pensalfini showed that at least one language, Arrernte from Central Australia, did things the other way round, preferring VC syllables:[10] it would syllabify the little stretch above as *am-ad-ab-a*, in defiance of the Maximal Onset Principle. If children really went into the task of language-learning hard-wired to make CV-syllable cuts, they should not be able to learn Arrernte.[11] Just as with Gauss' prime number conjecture (see p. 46), most universals look nice while the number of languages they are checked against is small. But once enough languages are brought into the picture, they almost invariably stumble upon counter-examples.

It is also worth pointing out that the Arrernte analysis took a long time to figure out: decades of work were needed before linguists could assemble a decisive proof. This is because the key evidence rested on the conjunction of a number of particular and unusual conditions, including a way of organizing the phonology so that lip-rounding was primarily linked to consonants rather than vowels, and a particular language-game played by children called Rabbit Talk, which freights syllables from the back to the front of the word, so that *it.ir.em* becomes *ir.em.it*, for example. This enables phonologists to identify syllable boundaries with surgical precision. Falsification of the universal CV-syllable preference thus required a lot of sensitive and ingenious work in getting a description that fitted the language's logic, as well as attention to such seemingly marginal concerns as children's language games. Most important was the tenacity of Arrernte speakers in maintaining their language in the face of English: Arrernte is the only Aboriginal language to survive today in an urban setting.

Let us make our discussion of sound systems a bit more concrete by getting back to Navajo. Unlike English or Japanese,[12] each syllable in Navajo can independently choose a high or a low tone to make meaning distinctions. It has a host of laterals (*l*-like sounds) like the "lateral fricative" ɬ (written ł in the Navajo alphabet), which is a sort of wet hissing *l*-sound, ejective sounds like *t'* made by building up pressure and popping the sound out, and velar fricatives like ɣ (written *gh* in Navajo) close to the sound you make when gargling. The various unfamiliar features can then be combined to make even more exotic sounds, like the "ejective lateral affricate" tɬ' (written **tł'** in the Navajo alphabet), made by twinning a *t* and our new friend ɬ, then giving the whole assemblage a popped release. All up, over a third of the consonant sounds of Navajo are unfamiliar to English or Japanese speakers.

Before moving on from sounds to other types of difference, I want to stress another even more fundamental problem that the Japanese code-breakers faced. Despite what I have said above about the disadvantages adults face in learning other sound systems, it is still possible to learn new sounds, especially with phonetic training. However, the key to figuring the sound system of another language is being corrected when you don't produce the right sound. Somehow this seems to happen most commonly when you inadvertently produce an obscenity or absurdity in the process by getting the wrong member of a "minimal pair" – two words differing in just one phoneme, like English *pat* vs. *bat*.

To illustrate this, consider the different patterning of two pairs of sounds in English and Kayardild. We can transcribe endless hours of English without needing to pay attention to the exact type of *r*-sound. Is it a Scottish-style trill (written r in the phonetic alphabet), or the "approximant" found in most varieties of English (written ɹ in the phonetic alphabet)? Whether you pronounce *very* as *veri* or *veɹi* makes no difference to the word's meaning. At most it serves to identify your regional accent or perhaps class. Nor do we need to notice whether the *d* in *width* is pronounced as a *d* as in *bid*, a *t* as in *wit*, or – most likely – an "interdental" t̪ where your tongue goes between your teeth in readiness for the *th* that follows.

If you try speaking Kayardild with this level of English carelessness about distinguishing *r* and ɹ, or *t* and t̪, you can get into trouble very quickly. Say you want to take an innocent farewell from someone fishing on the beach, like "I'll see you tomorrow; I won't come back to the beach this evening." In Kayardild this should be rendered as *ngada balmbiwu kuṛiju ngumbanju, bikurdawu ṭaanangku ngarnku*. If, as an English-speaker, you don't take care to distinguish the *r* and *ɹ*, and the *t* and *ṭ*, you may well end saying *ngada balmbiwu kuɹiju ngumbanju, bikurdawu taanangku ngarnku* – "I'll bathe you tomorrow; I won't have sex with you on the beach this evening." The gales of laughter and subsequent ridicule that generally greet this kind of delicate phonetic mistake are the linguist's best friend in discovering minimal pairs and drawing their attention to the importance of the relevant phonetic contrasts from that moment on.

If you only hear a language without interacting with speakers, you never get this sort of feedback. Sometimes I have had the discouraging task of trying to transcribe tapes of a language that is no longer spoken. It is practically impossible, because you have no mental model of the language's sounds to funnel your transcriptional attempts into. The contribution of the social matrix to learning sound distinctions is paramount, and it is thus almost impossible to work out a phonological system in a vacuum such as was faced by the Japanese code-breakers.

Knowing the Giving from the Gift

O body swayed to music, O brightening glance,
How can we know the dancer from the dance?

(Yeats 1983:217)

Among all the countless things and classes that there are, most are miscellaneous, gerrymandered, ill-demarcated. Only an elite minority are carved at the joints, so that their boundaries are established by objective sameness and difference in nature.

(Lewis 1984:227)

Once you get past the strange sounds of Navajo the next challenge is to confront an unfamiliar way of carving up the world's phenomena into concepts. To make it even worse, in Navajo the elements we might expect to correspond to *lexemes* – i.e. dictionary words – are hashed and diced and interleaved with bits of grammatical information. If we think of the lexemes as meat, and the grammatical information as onions and capsicums, a Navajo word is like a long shish kebab where the bits have been placed in turns on a skewer – making the use of a Navajo dictionary a very time-consuming process.

The Navajo division of the world into named units also follows very different lines from English. Imagine describing a Christmas scene where different people are giving each other presents. Penny is giving Margaret a ball, Lloyd is giving Dylan a backpack, Catherine is giving John some mittens, Luke is giving Myfanwy a bracelet, and Olwen is giving Freya some marbles. In English we can use the same verb "give" for each individual act, and just vary the names of the presents. But if we translate this description into Navajo, each giving event will need to be described with a different verb. The word written *'ą́* means "give a solid roundish object (e.g. a ball)," *yį́* means "give a load, pack or burden, e.g. a backpack," *lá* means "give a slender flexible object, e.g. rope or mittens," *tą́* means "give a slender stiff object, like an arrow or bracelet," and *jaa'* means "give certain types of plural object, e.g. marbles." (There are plenty more of these "give verbs," and you also get similar proliferations with other verbs like "sit" or "be," but you get the idea).

Because the Navajo verbs are so specific, you may not need to actually mention the given object at all, whereas in English you have to. If you think this is a strange way to do things, try miming these scenes out with no props. You should be able to do it OK, because the actual physical movements of your arms will give a sufficient clue. This shows that, in describing acts of giving, English goes for a generic level description in terms of transfer of possession, leaving the job of naming the transferred object to a noun phrase like "some marbles." Navajo, by contrast, gives a much more detailed physical description of the activity, and this renders the naming of the given object unnecessary much of the time.

Another example of this same principle comes from words for the hopping of macropods (i.e. kangaroos and wallabies) in several Aboriginal languages of Arnhem Land. English loads all the descriptive work onto the noun – *the kangaroo hops, the wallaby hops, the wallaroo hops*, etc. But in Kunwinjku there are different verbs to describe the hopping of these various macropods – *kamawudme* for the hopping of the male antilopine wallaby, *kadjalwahme* for the hopping of the corresponding female, *kanjedjme* for the hopping of the wallaroo, *kamurlbardme* for the hopping of the black wallaroo, and *kalurlhlurlme* for the hopping of the agile wallaby. This focus on identifying macropods by the peculiarities of their gait – which is the main way you can actually identify them from a distance when hunting – is particularly interesting in the light of recent work on computer-vision programs able to identify macropod species, which had far more success doing this on the basis of their movement than their static appearance. The decision about whether to concentrate on describing the dancer or the dance, in other words, may be made quite differently according to the language.

The philosopher Willard Quine once wrote that "Uncritical semantics is the myth of a museum in which the exhibits are meanings and the words are labels."[13] An example like the Navajo "giving" verbs shows what he meant: different languages do not simply select the same entities as their exhibits and then put labels on. Rather, the process of bandying around labels can create quite different exhibits. This brings us to the second reason why very different languages are hard for cryptographers to crack. Say you have two parallel texts, one in English and one in Navajo, and are trying to identify the word "give" in the other language. You can't just go through the text you are trying to crack looking for the word that comes up each time English "give" does, because there IS NO single corresponding unit. Instead, you have to break the representation of reality right down to a very elementary level and start rebuilding from there. Let us look at four ways languages prepare very different "meaning exhibits."

First, they may package larger or smaller clusters of experience together in a single word. Examples are words like Dalabon *karddulunghno* ("smell of rain and ground at beginning of wet season"), Ket (Siberian) átẽtlʌŋō:ks ("single tree of one species growing in an otherwise pure stand of another species"),[14] and Mundari (India) *rawadawa*, which denotes the sensation of realizing that you can get away with doing something wicked because no-one is there to witness it. In the other direction, languages may break complex concepts we take for granted down into sequences of much simpler ones. In the Papuan language Kalam "gather (e.g. firewood)" is broken down into "go hit get come put," and "massage" is broken up into the nine subcomponents *pk wyk d ap tan d ap yap g*, literally "strike rub hold come ascend hold come descend do."[15]

Second, languages may actually segment the boundaries of events or objects in different ways. Consider our bodies, where the boundaries between parts seem obvious and nature-given. But languages are like fashion-designers, chalking the lines of the favored cut in different places. They may group the leg together with the foot, as in Russian *noga*. Or they may mark off the upper lines of the leg differently: the Solomon Islands language Savosavo "leg" category begins at the hip joint (and encompasses the foot), whereas in the Indonesian language Tidore *yohu*, roughly "leg," cuts off three-quarters of the way up the thigh.

Third, languages may treat the roles played by event-participants in rather different ways. English and other European languages like to put humans or animals in the driver's seat, even when the real first cause lies elsewhere. But many languages in Australia and Papua New Guinea are quite happy with depicting a causal sequence that doesn't put humans or animals in the center-stage position. In Mawng, if you want to describe a female turtle trying to lay eggs on ground that is too hard for her to dig a hole, you say *kinyngarajpun jita manpiri*, literally "it (the ground) frustrated-the-egg-laying-attempts-of the female turtle." It seems possible that the different castings you glimpse behind this wording reflects a profoundly different cosmology, in which humans (and turtles!) are less the master of the natural world than they are portrayed to be in European languages. But tackling this question scientifically would take us too far afield here.

Fourth, languages may display different patterns for linking meanings together with the same form, suggesting distinct patterns of connection. This sharing of related meanings by the same form is generally known as polysemy ("many-signifying") in western linguistics, but there are also many oral traditions that share linguists' fascination with finding the nature of the semantic link. Aboriginal languages of the Yolngu group use the more poetic term *likan* ("elbow; fork between two tree branches") to suggest the pivoting of two meaningful limb-parts on a single formal joint, and the discussion of deep semantic linkages, particularly of metaphors extending from the secular to the spiritual world, is an important part of Yolngu ritual training. The sung epics of Rossel Island include a special type of rhyme where adjacent lines of their poetry have to reuse the same word but with a different meaning.

As we move from one language to another, particularly if we traverse wide cultural chasms, many of our familiar links get left behind. English-speakers take it for granted that "I see" can also mean "I understand," but this assumption does not work in many languages of the world. In Kayardild, for example, you extend "I hear" instead. To take another and more puzzling Kayardild example of unexpected meaning connections, the word *jara* extends from "foot" to "footprint" – intuitive enough – but then takes in "rain" as well. This latter link is not at all obvious to English speakers. But if you think about the practice of tracking in hunter-gatherer life, you will appreciate that at end of the dry season the ground looks like a smudgy blackboard overwritten by dozens of teachers. Rain cleanses the ground for new tracks, and it is this that underlies the phrase *jara barjija* ("(new) tracks are falling"). The same connection crops up in other forms elsewhere in Australia, such as the use of the same sign for "track" and "rain" in Warlpiri women's body-painting designs:

One way of dealing with all this variation is to postulate a small stock of "semantic atoms," which can then simply be clustered together into different molecules in different languages. Anna Wierzbicka has been an advocate of this approach, and has proposed around 70 such "semantic primitives" like "this," "me," "now," "want," "think," "know," or "inside," purportedly found in every language. But the proposed primitives run into problems as well. "Want," for example, cannot be freely translated into Kayardild.[16] "Think" and "know" do not map straightforwardly onto the mental verbs of Dalabon: there is a verb *bengkan* that means variously "know" or "remember" according to context, but also "think" in the stable sense of holding an opinion, or contemplating over a long period, while another verb *bengdi* is used for thinking in the sense of having a sudden thought, but also for realizing something or having a flash of inspiration.[17]

The medieval philosopher Thomas Aquinas wrote that *nomina debent naturae rerum congruere* – names should fit with nature. There are certainly parts of language where this formulation is defensible: Brent Berlin and other ethnobiologists have shown that languages do tend to all make the cuts between natural species in the same way, following the lines laid down by nature – provided they are interested enough in the species to have a distinct name for it.[18]

Figure 3.3 The polysemous sign "track/rain" in Warlpiri[19]

But the Aquinas view has resurfaced recently among generative linguists and philosophers, from Jerry Fodor to Stephen Pinker, in a more far-reaching form. They postulate that humans think in a language-independent "mentalese," which is then translated straightforwardly into English, Japanese, Dalabon, or Navajo. Confronted with problems like those we have just seen, though, the question to ask is: what exactly are the concepts that are used in "mentalese"? Is the "give" in mentalese the English "give" or the Navajo one, is the "leg" the English or the Savosavo one, is the "think" the English or the Dalabon one? Only a vanishingly small group of entities are carved at the same joints across different languages, as suggested by the epigraph to this section. Once we take a broad sample of the world's tongues into account, it is clear that even quite basic concepts just do not line up across languages. Their semantic diversity suggests that Edward Sapir was closer to the mark than Aquinas, Fodor, or Pinker when he wrote that "Inasmuch as languages differ very widely in their systematization of fundamental concepts, they tend to be only loosely equivalent to each other as symbolic devices."[20]

There are many interpretations of how far this view affects the intercompatibility of meaning across different languages. At its most radical, it suggests the impossibility of any translation across incommensurable systems. There are many reasons to reject this as implausible. Most obviously, by careful and sometimes long-winded definition we are able to characterize, in our own language, the meanings found prepackaged and compacted in other languages, as with the definitions I gave you above. On this view there may be several roads to the same expressive Rome, although some routes are longer and windier than others.

An example where this "multicompositional" view holds is number systems. The number systems of all languages refer to the same set of integers. Although there are certainly languages with a single word for "one and a half," like Russian *poltora*, I do not know of any language that counts like "one-and-a-quarter, two-and-a-half, three-and-three-quarters." Nonetheless, there is enormous variation in which higher numbers are unitized into one-word elements, and more generally in what number is taken as the base.

Box 3.2   Counting in Oksapmin

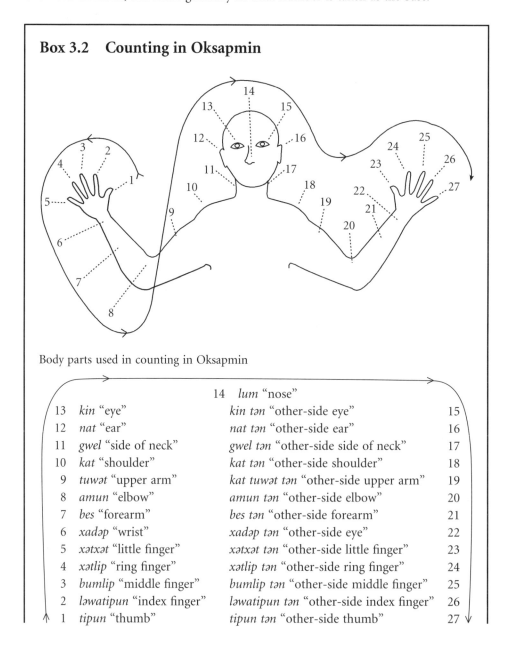

Body parts used in counting in Oksapmin

		14	*lum* "nose"	
13	*kin* "eye"	*kin tən* "other-side eye"	15
12	*nat* "ear"	*nat tən* "other-side ear"	16
11	*gwel* "side of neck"	*gwel tən* "other-side side of neck"	17
10	*kat* "shoulder"	*kat tən* "other-side shoulder"	18
9	*tuwət* "upper arm"	*kat tuwət tən* "other-side upper arm"	19
8	*amun* "elbow"	*amun tən* "other-side elbow"	20
7	*bes* "forearm"	*bes tən* "other-side forearm"	21
6	*xadəp* "wrist"	*xadəp tən* "other-side eye"	22
5	*xətxət* "little finger"	*xətxət tən* "other-side little finger"	23
4	*xətlip* "ring finger"	*xətlip tən* "other-side ring finger"	24
3	*bumlip* "middle finger"	*bumlip tən* "other-side middle finger"	25
2	*ləwatipun* "index finger"	*ləwatipun tən* "other-side index finger"	26
1	*tipun* "thumb"	*tipun tən* "other-side thumb"	27

Oksapmin is a Highlands Papuan language spoken in Sandaun province of Papua New Guinea. Its counting system involves counting up 13 steps from thumb to nose, reaching 14 on the nose, then going back down the other side to reach 27 on the opposite-side thumb. On the completion of the cycle it is customary to raise both fists and exclaim *tit fu*! To say "then he didn't come for eight nights," for example, you say *jɔxɔ amunxe dik jox napingoplio*, literally "then elbow's time (he) didn't come." Although children today are still learning Oksapmin (along with Tok Pisin and English), the 27-base number system is falling out of use, with an English-style system being used for monetary transactions but older speakers still using the traditional system in contexts like counting string bags.

An Oksapmin woman exclaiming *tit fu!* on reaching the count of 27 (photo by kind permission of Geoff Saxe)

Japanese, for example, has a unit word *man* 万 for the number 10,000 = 10^4. There are other units for squares or cubes of 万, such as *oku* (億) for $(10^4)^2 = 10^8 = 100,000,000$ – i.e. 1,0000,0000, following Japanese logic. Hindi and other Indian languages have a unit *lakh*, meaning 100,000. (The Sanskrit word lakṣa, from which *lakh* derives, comes from the same root as the German word *lachs* "salmon" and its Yiddish and now English counterpart *lox*; the extension to 100,000 was based on a metaphor of huge numbers of swarming salmon.) But despite the different packaging in English, Japanese, and Hindi, any higher number can be expressed equally precisely. Whether we take our base as one *thousand* (1,000), 万 (10,000) or *lakh* (100,000), we can still represent the same 700,000: as 700 thousands, 70 万, or 7 *lakhs*.

The same point can be made more dramatically if we look at languages whose number systems are built on non-decimal bases. Mathematically there is no compelling reason why our familiar base 10 has any advantage over known alternatives like quinary (base 5), base 20 as in Mayan languages, or base 60 systems like Sumerian. Each of these systems appears to have evolved from different counting routines – fingers of one hand (base 5), or both hands (base 10), fingers plus toes (base 20), or more complicated routines that check off various parts of the body after the *digits* (fingers and toes) are used up. Box 3.2 illustrates a 27-value counting routine from another Papuan language, Oksapmin (although in this case there is no evidence that the 27-valued counting cycle actually worked as a base for higher numbers).

A number of southern Papuan languages have *senary* systems based on powers of 6. Thus in Kanum the value 200 would be expressed as *swabra ptae ynaoaemy ntamnao*, literally "five thirtysix two threesix", i.e. $(5 \times 6^2) + (2 + (3 \times 6))$ and Arammba (see table 3.1) has a range of simple terms for the first six powers of 6.[21]

It is certainly the case that in each system some numbers are psychologically "easier" and others "harder" in the sense of having simpler or more complicated names, leading

Table 3.1 Some senary-power numerals in Arammba

Arammba term	Value	As power of 6
nimbo	6	6^1
feté	36	6^2
tarumba	216	6^3
ndamno	1,296	6^4
wermeke	7,776	6^5
wi	46,656	6^6

to quicker or slower mental manipulation. But, such speed bumps aside, all these systems are equally able to express all integers: the various number systems just discussed are *notational variants* depicting the same reality.

A deep question is whether we are still just dealing with notational variants when we leave the clean neat world of numbers for the murkier waters of event descriptions – is it possible that the isomorphism of conceptual boundaries goes all the way down?

Consider how we describe motion events, where we need to describe the *path* followed, the *figure* (what moves), and the *manner* (the way it moves), plus the *cause* if I am causing something to move. Brilliant work by Len Talmy has shown that languages differ in which of these three elements they build their motion descriptions up from.[22]

Manner-dominant languages like English prefer to first choose a verb to describe the *manner* (say, *run*), then add a preposition giving the *path*, and are generally indifferent to the figure: "John ran into the building," where "ran" gives the manner and "into" the path.

Path-dominant systems like Spanish start by choosing a verb denoting the *path*, e.g. *entrar* ("enter"), and only if needed add a phrase specifying the *manner*: *Juan entró en el edificio (corriendo)* is literally "Juan entered the building (running)." (Notice in passing that, by using the French loanword "enter" instead of the Germanic "run into," we can replicate the Romance structure in our English translation.)

Figure-dominant languages take the pattern found in a few English sentences like "it's snowing in through the window": the verb specifies the moving object rather than the manner or path. Unlike English, where this is a very minor pattern, figure-dominant languages use this type for most verbs in their lexicon. Languages that do this include Navajo – which is why the "give" verbs we saw earlier in this chapter include information about the moving object – and also Atsugewi, a wonderful language of Northern California that has lost the last of its speakers in the last couple of decades.

To describe motion events in Atsugewi you begin by choosing a root to denote the "figure," like -caq- for slimy, lumpish objects (e.g. toads or cow droppings), -swal- for limp linear objects suspended by one end (e.g. a shirt on a clothesline, a hanging dead rabbit, or a flaccid penis), or -st'aq- for runny icky material (e.g. mud, manure, rotten tomatoes, guts, or chewed gum). Then you add a locative suffix giving the location, like -ik ("on the ground"), -ict ("into liquid"), or -cis ("into fire"), plus a prefix giving the cause for the motion or state, e.g. uh- ("from gravity acting on it / from the object's own weight"), ca- ("from the wind"), or cu- ("from a linear object acting axially upon it"). Figure 3.4 illustrates the make-up of one of these verbs diagrammatically. Finally, you wrap it all up with some inflectional material specifying the agent and patient, and the mood, such as ʔw- . . . . . a ("it (factual)") or s'w- . . . . a ("I acting upon him, her, or it (factual)").

Now we're ready to make some event-descriptions in Atsugewi. I'll start by giving you rather weird-sounding literal translations, phrased to follow the morpheme structures just given: ʔwuhst'aq'ika ("runny icky material is located on the ground from its own weight

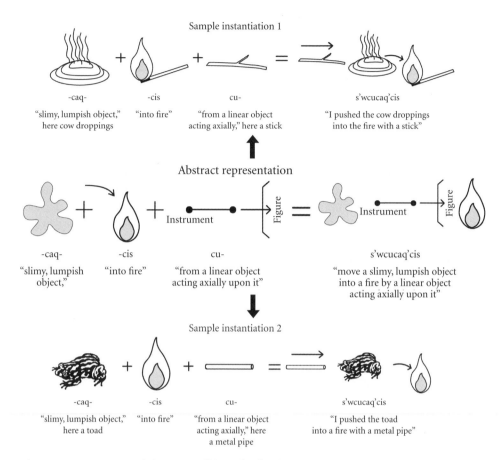

Figure 3.4   How to push lumpy stuff into the fire in Atsugewi

acting on it"), *ʔwcast'aq'ic'ta* ("runny icky material moved into liquid from the wind blowing on it"), or *s'wcust'aq'cis* – see if you can work this one out for yourself.[23]

How well do these meanings line up with English? The translations just given are certainly comprehensible, but are hardly everyday utterances. We are more likely to say things like "guts are lying on the ground" – something we could translate into good Atsugewi as *ʔwuhstaqika* – or "the guts blew into the creek," which we could back-translate into Atsugewi as *ʔwuhstaqicta*. We can thus designate the same situation by our English cast of phrase and the Atsugewi one. But the exact range of situations these phrases describe is different, since *ʔwuhstaqicta*, for example, could also be used of situations where manure gets blown into the creek, or rotten tomatoes get blown into a pond, neither of which could be described as "the guts blew into the creek."

Rather than both semantic roads leading to the same denotational Rome, which is what we saw with numerals, here we have a situation more like where Abraham and Ibrahim both set out for the same Holy City, with Abraham ending up at the Wailing Wall, and Ibrahim at the Al-aqsa Mosque. Do they both end up in the same place? Yes, you may answer – both ended up in Jerusalem. No, you may also answer: Abraham ended up in

Israel, and Ibrahim in Palestine. Depending on the mapping units you are using, your answer will be different.

This means that one of the most important parts of a linguist's job is to map out the full range of contexts in which each word or affix can be used, since the translation you are given the first time you hear it may be quite skewed. In Dalabon there is a verbal prefix *molkkûnh-* (pronounced very roughly as *molk-ken*). The first time I heard it was from my first Dalabon teacher, the late David Kalbuma, in the combination *molkkûnhbon*. He was using it to describe some fundamentalist proselytizers who were "sneaking around," as he put it, on clan lands without permission. Since *bon* means "go," I concluded it meant something like "sneakily."

The second time I heard it was when another of my Dalabon teachers, the late Alice Boehm, who by then was quite old and infirm, took leave of me sadly at the end of a field trip by saying *kardû ngahmolkkûndoniyan bo* ("I might *molkkûn*-die"), which she translated as "I might die suddenly." So I thought *molkkûnh-* must have a second meaning, "suddenly."

The third time I heard the prefix was from the woman who was to become my main Dalabon teacher, Maggie Tukumba. I had turned up late one night with my friend Murray Garde, not having had a chance to notify her when we would arrive – telephone connections to Weemol, the small community she lives in, had not yet been put in. The next morning she reproached us with the following: *dehmolkkûnbong dabangh nahda, mak yilabengkey*, i.e. "you two *molkkûn*-arrived here unannounced yesterday, we didn't know about it."

The true meaning of *molkkûn-* didn't strike me until the fourth time I heard it, this time from the late Dalabon artist and songman Peter Maneberru. On that trip I happened to be investigating the exact use of words like "under" and "inside," using a collection of cartoon-like sketches, and had shown him a sketch of an underground water source beneath a rock. He always liked to give more elaborate and interesting responses than just simple descriptions, and came up with the following. Imagine there are some people camping thirsty in the rock country, he said, who hadn't been able to find a spring. If the water in the picture was right under where they were sleeping, you might say: *kahmolkkûnkolhyu*, literally "it-molkkûn-water-lies."

What unites all these uses is the idea of something happening or being the case without a crucial person knowing about it: the clan owner not being notified of the fundamentalist's visit, old Alice Boehm dying without me (in this case) being informed in time to come to her funeral,[24] Murray and I turning up without letting Maggie Tukumba know, or a hidden spring lying beneath a rock, its presence unsuspected by the thirsty travelers above. Once you get enough examples, it is clear that the first, contextual translations – "sneakily," "suddenly," or "unannounced" – are tangential to the core meaning of this word, and an invariant meaning gradually emerges as you collect more examples.

In this case it even turns out that there is a pretty good English translation – "unbeknown" or "unbeknownst" – although none of my Dalabon teachers would have known this rather literary word, and in fact most of our conversations about meaning took place either in another Aboriginal language, Kunwinjku, or in a creolized form of English shorn of most of its lexical niceties. In any case, translations like "water lies there unbeknownst" or "you arrived last night unbeknownst" sound stilted and unnatural. One reason they feel odd is that English prefers to specify who it is that remains in ignorance (e.g. *unbeknown to me, unbeknown to his mother*), whereas Dalabon always leaves it implicit who is left in the dark. My slow, haphazard gropings toward working out the meaning of *molkkûnh* are typical of the way linguistic fieldwork proceeds. And *molkkûnh* is just one of the many thousands of entries in the Dalabon vocabulary, each presenting its own semantic mapping problem, to the child and linguist alike.

The Great Chain of Being

> Who can act upon whom or who can control whom is of basic interest and concern to Navajos and is one of the dominant perspectives in the Navajo world view.
>
> (Witherspoon 1977:75)

I mentioned that there is a third dimension of the mapping problem: the grammar, whose job is to be a broker between sound and meaning. One key part of meaning, which any language has to convey, is the issue of who is doing what to whom. In English we mainly do this by word order – "the man chased the turtle" tells us something very different from "the turtle chased the man."

Other languages do this by tagging words with "case suffixes" that say who is doing what, regardless of the order of words.

In Kayardild I could translate the first scenario with any of the following six orderings. (When I was first learning Kayardild, and did not understand something, my teachers used to just repeat it, working through the permutations, hoping one of them would hit the spot for me.)

(1) a. *dangkaa durrwaaja bangaya*
   b. *bangaya durrwaaja dangkaa*
   c. *dangkaa bangaya durrwaaja*
   d. *durrwaaja bangaya dangkaa*
   e. *durrwaaja dangkaa bangaya*
   f. *durrwaaja bangaya dangkaa*

The great flexibility of word order here is possible because the final *-a* suffix after *dangka* ("man") identifies him as the doer of the action, and the *-ya* suffix after *banga* ("turtle") identifies it as the one the action is being done to. If the turtle is chasing the man, as you can work out, I say *dangkaya durrwaaja bangaa* or any of the other five orders, as long as "turtle" gets *-a* and "man" gets *-ya*.

Ilgar keeps track of this information in another way, by having markers on the verb tracking the subject and the object. For example, I can put the words *ayan* ("sees"), *wurduwajba* ("woman"), and *arrkbi* ("man") together in any order, just like in Kayardild, to express either "the man sees the woman" or "the woman sees the man." But what determines the interpretation is the prefix you put on the verb *ayan*: *ying-* means "she acting upon him," while *iny-* means "he acting upon her." Thus *wurduwajba **ying**ayan arrkbi* and *arrkbi **ying**ayan wurduwajba*, plus the four other possible orders, all mean "the woman sees the man," and *wurduwajba **inyayan** arrkbi* and *arrkbi **inyayan** wurduwajba*, plus the four other possible orders, all mean "the man sees the woman." It is thus the form of the verbal prefix that sums up who is doing what to whom in the sentence, again leaving the words free to roam in any order.

Navajo also uses prefixes on the verb, but the logic of how they work is rather different. See if you can work out what is going on from the following examples; we use the * to indicate that a sentence is ungrammatical.[25]

(2)	a.	*Diné ashkii yiztał.*	The man kicked the boy.	*Ashkii diné biztał.*
	b.	*Ashkii diné yiztał.*	The boy kicked the man.	*Dine ashkii biztał.*
	c.	*Ashkii łééchąąʔį yiztał.*	The boy kicked the dog.	**Łééchąąʔį ashkii biztał.*
	d.	**Dóola diné yizgoh.*	The bull gored the man.	*Diné dóola bizgoh.*
	e.	*Dóola shash yizgoh.*	The bull gored the bear.	*Shash doola bizgoh.*

Looking at these, you can readily work out that the verb (kicked, gored) goes last. You can also work out that it is possible to put the agent (kicker or gorer) and the patient (kickee and goree) in either order: you use the prefix *yi-* if the agent comes first (as in the first column), and the prefix *bi-* if the patient comes first (as in the third column). So, to work out who is doing what to whom, you have to combine the information from the word order with the information from the prefix.

But (2c) and (2d) also show that sometimes you are not free to vary the order. When the agent and patient are on different "levels," as it were – humans being higher on the chain of being than animals – you always have to put the human before the animal, and then use the prefix appropriate to which way the action is going. Note also that it is perfectly alright, once you know what is being talked about, to leave out the words referring to "man," "bull," or whatever. In a story about a man and a bull, at a certain point you could just say *bizgoh* and it would be clear from the choice of prefix that this meant "it gored him."

So far, so good. But if we look at some more examples we see that we are not just dealing with a two-tiered human vs. animal distinction:

(3)	a.	*Shash mósí yishxash.*	The bear bit the cat.	**Mósí shash bishxash.*
	b.	**Mósí shash yishxash.*	The cat bit the bear.	*Shash mósí bishxash.*
	c.	*Mósí tązhii yinoołchééł.* the turkey.	The cat is chasing	*Tązhii mósí binoołchééł.*
	d.	*Mósí naʔazízí yinoołchééł.*	The cat is chasing the gopher.	**Naʔazízí mósí binoołchééł.*
	e.	*Naʔazízí wóláchííí yinoołchééł.*	The gopher is chasing the ant.	**Wóláchííí naʔazízí binoołchééł.*

Comparing these sentences, you should be able to work out there are several "levels" of animals – bears are higher than cats, which are equal to turkeys but higher than gophers, which in turn are higher than ants. Whenever one entity is higher than another on this great chain of being, it must come first in the sentence; the *yi-* vs. *bi-* contrast is then used to keep track of who is doing what to whom. To speak and understand even simple sentences like these in Navajo, then, you have to know where each animal and other entity sit on the many-runged ladder of being – and in this way Navajo grammar is closely interwoven with Navajo cosmology.

This quick tour of Navajo has, I hope, given you some glimpse into why it posed such a challenge to Japanese code-breakers. Whichever angle you come at the language from – the sound system, the grammar, the vocabulary, the partitioning of meaning between objects and events in its giving verbs – it contradicts assumptions you will make as a Japanese or English speaker about how a language is organized. You need to break things down to very basic elements and start again if you are to finally understand what is going on.

Let us return to the problem the child faces in learning a new language – and remembering that she has to be equally ready to pick up English, Japanese, Kayardild, or Navajo is a good way of reminding ourselves of the challenge she faces. From the flux of sounds in her parents' speech she has to work out what the significant units are and which phonetic features to pay attention to. For example the different *t* sounds in *t̲ake* and *s̲teak* (the first an "aspirated" *tʰ*, the second an unaspirated *t*) do not make a difference to meaning in English, but do in Navajo, and are therefore written with different letters, *t* and *d* respectively, in the Navajo orthography. So children learning Navajo have to cut up the sound-world they hear into different groupings from English-learning children. They also have to work out how the concept-world is cut, as we saw with giving verbs: they are not just looking at bits of the world and seeing what the labels are for predetermined groupings, but at the same time have to work out what the grouping principles are.

The difficulties of having to simultaneously solve the sound-grouping and meaning-grouping problems can be illustrated by putting yourself in the shoes of someone transcribing Kayardild for the first time. On day one you write down the word *char* for "foot," and a few days later you write the word *jar* for "track, footprint." These look like two words, each pairing a different pronunciation with a different meaning. But later you realize that, at the beginnings of words, there is no difference between a *j* and a *ch*, so that "run," for example, can be pronounced either *ja-wij* or *cha-wij*. When you go back over your recordings you realize that in fact "foot" is pronounced *jar* sometimes, and *char* others, and the same goes for "track, footprint." There is, then, a single word *jar*, with a variant pronunciation *char*, taking in a meaning range that includes both the foot and the prints or tracks it leaves.

The initial false start in this example comes from assuming an English cut on the sound system, plus an English cut on the division of the world into entities – we do not say "there's a foot there" when we look at a footprint (though "Look! A foot!" sounds better). Children avoid this mistake by not jumping to conclusions on either the sound or the meaning fronts. By integrating the variant pronunciations, and the varying things that they hear their caregivers refer to by roughly similar names, they gradually zero in on the correct sound-meaning pairing.

But even getting the sounds and the meanings sorted is not enough: children have to work out the grammar too. When I was in high school having to learn poetry I remember getting frustrated by Alexander Pope's line in *An Essay on Man*: "All forms that perish other forms supply." Were the "forms that perish" supplying the "other forms," I wondered, or the other way round? This is rather artificial English, for poetic reasons, but there are languages with every possible word order in their ordinary grammar, so that kids learning basic sentences face the same problem I did with the Pope poem, but much earlier. There are languages where the normal order is subject–object–verb, like Japanese, Hindi, or Quechua, and also (more rarely) languages where the normal order is object–subject–verb, like Urubú in Brazil, where you say *pako xuaa u'u*, literally "banana John ate," for "John ate a banana." So if you are a child learning a language and you hear people say the equivalent of "the child the father loves" – and even if you have worked out what the sounds are and what the individual words mean – you still cannot jump to conclusions about what the sentence means as a whole. You need to figure out the grammar as well, including the basic order of words but many other things besides.

These are the reasons any new language presents a "third-order mapping problem" – you need to learn what sound contrasts to pay attention to, what the conceptual groupings are, and what the grammar is that maps sounds onto meanings and back again. Each of these is a daunting task in itself; solving all three simultaneously is something no supercomputer or crack cryptographer has yet come near achieving, although relaxed and smiling 4-year-olds have the best part of it pretty well stitched up.

Further reading

On the Navajo code-talkers see Paul (1973) and the website at www.nmai.si.edu/education/codetalkers/; on the Navajo language see Frishberg (1972), Hale (1973b), and Faltz (1998). Enfield et al. (2006) surveys how different languages divide up the body into named parts. Georges Dumézil's brief but moving account of his fieldwork in Turkey is in the preface to his classic *La Langue des Oubykhs* (1931); you can hear Tevfik Esenç speaking Ubykh on: www.youtube.com/watch?v=vRj-8oCmnkU. Another useful Ubykh website is at www.circassianworld.com/tevfikesench.html.

Keen (1994) discusses the importance of the *likan* concept in Yolngu cosmology, and Evans (2004) looks at Iwaidja and Mawng verbs, which line up participants in quite a different way from English. Anna Wierzbicka and Cliff Goddard have outlined the case for universal "semantic primitives" in numerous publications (see e.g. Goddard and Wierzbicka 2002). Berlin (1992), in its synthesis of wide-ranging ethnobiological work, mounts the most convincing case for parallel concepts across a range of languages, although confined to biological species. Comrie (2005) surveys endangered numeral systems, while Saxe and Esmonde (2005) discuss historical changes to the Oksapmin number system (although I have taken the actual forms given here from Robyn Loughnane's linguistic description of the Lower Oksapmin dialect). Discussion of Atsugewi and the typology of motion–event descriptions can be found in Talmy (1972, 1985, 2000).

4

Your Mind in Mine:
Social Cognition in Grammar

Kolik jazyků znáš, tolikrát jsi člověkem.   For each language you know, you are a
new person.[1]

(Czech proverb)

So far I have been approaching the structural diversity of languages by examining each part of the system in turn – sounds, meaning, grammar. In this chapter I want to give you a different angle on how much languages can vary, fleshing out the insight of the Czech proverb above by showing why it feels so different to be "inside" different languages.

One of the most insightful discussions about what translation means is by the Spanish philosopher Ortega y Gasset:

> *Cada pueblo calla unas cosas para poder decir otras. Porque todo sería indecible. De aquí la enorme dificultad de la traducción: en ella se trata de decir en un idioma precisamente lo que este idioma tiende a silenciar. Pero, a la vez, se entrevé lo que traducir puede tener de magnífica empresa: la revelación de los secretos mutuos que pueblos y épocas se guardan recíprocamente y tanto contribuyen a su dispersión y hostilidad; en suma, una audaz integración de la Humanidad.*[2]
>
> (Each people leaves some things unsaid in order to be able to say others. Because everything would be unsayable. From this follows the enormous difficulty of translation, which sets out to say in a language precisely what that language tends to remain silent about. But at the same time, it can be seen that translation can be a magnificent enterprise: to reveal the secrets that peoples and times keep from one another, and that contribute so much to their separation and hostility – in sum, an audacious integration of humanity.)[3]

The different grammatical choices made by different languages – in what to say and what to be silent about, in Ortega y Gasset's terms – give very different priorities about what to attend to in the world. We could illustrate this with just about any of the Kantian dimensions of experience – space, time, causality. But I will focus instead on another that, although less explored, is perhaps even more culturally malleable: how we keep track of our social universe and the psychology of its personae.

Languages differ not so much in what you *can* say as in what you *must* say.[4] From the thousands of things we can attend to in the world around us, each language makes a different selection of what gets front-seat treatment as so-called *grammatical categories*, which speakers and hearers need to keep constant track of. Using another of Ortega y Gasset's insights, each language is "exuberant" in some respects, going into loving detail about particular aspects of reality that you need to attend to and encode in most utterances, and "deficient" in others, allowing you to slack off and pay them no mind unless you feel like it. More than anything else, this is what gives each language its own distinct psychological cast, because to speak it you have to attend constantly to facets of the world that other languages let you ignore. We will pursue this language-and-thought angle more in chapter 8, since to demonstrate it convincingly we will need to bring in psychological experiments as well as linguistic facts. For now, though, I would like to concentrate on developing a preliminary "audacious integration" of what the pooled expertise of the world's grammars has to tell us about one domain of reality: psychosocial cognition.

It is increasingly clear that our ability to construct and participate in a shared mental world, to coordinate our attention and our goals, and to keep track of who knows, feels and wants what, lies at the heart of being human. It is this intense sociality that powered our quantum leap out of the company of all other animal species by enabling us to build that constantly evolving shared world we call culture. This achievement rests on an ability to keep constant tabs on the social and psychological consequences of what happens around us. But, although this skill is universal at a generic level, different grammars bring very different aspects of social cognition to the fore. By integrating what the world's languages are collectively sensitive to, we can come up with a much richer picture of human social cognition than any one language alone would give us.

It helps to start by imagining what a language would be like whose grammar makes NO reference to social context. This grammar would happily enable statements like "monkeys throw coconuts" or "all men are mortal," which imply nothing about the social context around. And it is exactly because of their stark social unanchoredness that sentences of this type crop up at the beginning of logic courses. But it doesn't take long for information about our social world to creep in. Once I say "a monkey threw my coconut," or "the prisoner must die," individual social agents have been drawn in, anchoring the event to the here-and-now of you and me communicating – what is generally known as the "speech act."

The "a" in "a monkey" marks its referent either as not previously known to you, and to be identified by me later ("and in fact, it was that monkey that escaped from the zoo"), or as something whose identity is unimportant or unknowable: "I don't know which monkey, though," I could go on to say. "The" in "the prisoner" shows I am confident you will be able to identify who I am talking about – a confidence that depends on me closely monitoring how far you are following my thoughts and previous statements. "My" in "my coconut" indicates not only that one of the participants happens to be the speaker or writer – me! – but also that I am aware of a particular relationship between that participant and the coconut, perhaps of ownership (I bought it this morning) or perhaps merely of interest (I have been looking at it greedily on the fruitstand). And "must" indicates a relation between the still-just-imagined event of the prisoner dying, and my wishes and powers to influence what other people around me do, by issuing an order or stipulation. If I shift to a question – "must the prisoner die?" – there is still a relationship of ordering or stipulation between the speech act and the described event of the prisoner dying, but now it is primarily you rather than me who is being linked "deontically" to the event. ("Deontic" modification is framing a statement with desires or moral requirements like "may," "must," or "ought.") Either I am inquiring about something you know but I do not – whether the prisoner's death is necessary – or I am seeking to influence you by asking a rhetorical question and implying that I do not want the event to happen.

Explorations like this, of the meaning of such categories as definiteness ("the" vs. "a"), possession ("my," "your" . . .) and "mood" ("can," "must," "may" etc.), have long been a staple for philosophers and linguists trying to work out how meaning can be represented and how inferences can be drawn. As such they underpin other enterprises like the representation of information in automatic translation systems, or reasoning algorithms in artificial intelligence. They are categories that are central in English and other European languages. But, once we look at other languages, we start to see the elaboration of rather different categories.

Take the phrase "my coconut." If you try to translate this into many Oceanic languages – say Paamese,[5] a language of Vanuatu – you realize that English has not yet given enough information, that its grammar is deficient with regard to the general domain of possessive relations, whereas Paamese is exuberant in the sense of paying attention to much more detailed distinctions. What exactly are you trying to say, a Paamese speaker would insist? My coconut, whose flesh I am about to eat – OK, say *ani aak*. My coconut, whose juice I wish to drink? In that case, say *ani emak*. My coconut, that is growing on my land? In that case, say *ani esak*. My coconut, that I plan to use for some other purpose (perhaps sitting on it)? In that case, say *ani onak*. Between *ani* ("coconut") and the suffix *-k* ("my"), as you can see, we need to insert an element setting out the intended use the "possessor" will put the object to. Devices like these are generally called "possessive classifiers" by linguists, because they classify the type of possession relation. But another way of seeing them is that they signal a mix of socially recognized ownership types and intentions. Indeed, the late Terry Crowley, who wrote a fine grammar of Paamese, argues that the grammar is classifying types of social control, not just possession.[6]

And by Oceanic standards Paamese is still at the kindergarten level when it comes to possessive classification. The New Caledonian language Tinrin[7] distinguishes, for example, between "my (body part)," "my (burnable object)," "my (thing, to plant)," "my (fruit)," "my (meat)," "my (chewable or suckable object, like sugar cane)," "my (cannibalistically eaten human flesh)," and various others. It is impossible to say just "your X," or "my X" without deciding which of these types of possession is involved.

Projection of intentions, in fact, is a key part of our ability for "social intelligence," as any good poker player or military strategist knows, and working out just how much intention-attribution goes on in our primate cousins is a hot topic in tracing the evolution of hominid social reasoning. At the most complex level, this ability allows us to invest just about any sign with a rich attribution of meaning, by enabling us to guess at the communicative intentions of our interlocutor. Say I am in a room with you, and you point to the window. According to the context, this may variously mean "could you open the window?," "could you close the window?," "isn't it a beautiful window?," "what about we try escaping through the window?," "oh no, what if they come in through the window?," "see, they did decide to put in that tasteless window they were talking about after all," or "look, it's snowing outside." My job as hearer is to work out which of these you mean. Human empathy is well-developed enough that we excel at this sort of mind-reading game, and the philosopher Grice made this ability the corner of his fundamental theory of "implicature," which explains how we are regularly able to mean more than we are able to say. With words, as with window-pointing, we can rely on our interlocutors to top up what we have actually said with additional interpretation based on their informed reasoning about what they think we are intending to convey. This ability has been central in enabling humans to evolve ever more expressive languages by growing new signs – in the sense of constantly developing new words that can say more than we could before.

For now, though, let us think about how intentions are depicted. A common way of doing this in English is to use the preposition "for": "she's going to the cash-machine **for** money"; "he cut the branch **for** a slingshot"; "he's waiting **for** his appointment letter"; "they're searching **for** a unicorn"; "she moved around the ballroom looking **for** a dance partner"; "he planned a surprise party **for** his wife." Suppose you are a cartoonist trying to draw one of the above scenes, or an actor trying to mime them out: how do you convey these intentions to your reader? It's pretty hard, because intentions are not visible, leaving aside a few crude physical indicators of thirst or desire. So you might resort to a thought balloon in your cartoon. But when we watch people doing things, we don't see thought balloons – we rely on detailed knowledge of how they behave, partly rooted in a carefully acquired set of shared cultural routines. The use of the same word *for* in English makes us forget that we are using very different heuristics to work out what the person we are watching is planning to do in each case.

If we translate comparable sentences into Kayardild, we find that every one of these situations needs to be represented by a different case suffix on the word or phrase denoting the goal or intention – see table 4.1. (Case suffixes, remember from the last chapter, are obligatory markers allowing you to work out the role of each object or person talked about in a sentence.) One of the ways you need to reprogram your mind if you learn Kayardild is to pay careful attention to the different ways people go about achieving their goals, and to break down the ways we impute intention into a nuanced set of subtypes.

Close to intention is volition: whether people are consciously in control of the actions they carry out. We humans can attach great importance to volition – our decisions about whether an action was carried out on purpose or not may make the difference between a finding of murder and manslaughter, or, more mundanely, between deciding whether a cough outside the door is simply a passer-by with a cold, or a polite person indicating their presence unobtrusively. But English does not force us to indicate this difference in every utterance: if I say "I coughed" I could be reporting an accidental or a deliberate cough. Of course I could add "on purpose" or "despite my efforts not to" to make this clear, but the point is that the grammar lets you off the hook.

Some languages require their speakers to report every action as volitional or otherwise. Newari, a Nepalese language closely related to Tibetan, is one.[8] Newari verbs take a long

Table 4.1 "For" and intention heuristics in Kayardild

Suffix	Meaning	Example	Translation
-marutha	for the benefit of	*Ngada waaja wangarra ngumbanmarutha.*	I sing a song for you.
-janiija	in order to find, of something that is wanted and must be actively sought	*Niya kalajalaja makujaniija.*	He's going around looking for a woman.
-marra	to use for, of something that can be transformed from something else	*Niya kalatha jari thungali wangalmarr.*	He cut the tree root for a boomerang.
-iiwatha	in order to find, of something that can predictably be found at a given place	*Makuwalada warraja bijurriiwatha.*	The women are going for cockleshells (e.g. to a sandbank known to contain them).
-mariija	for, of something that can only be obtained by waiting	*Makuwalada diija balungka wirrinmariija.*	The women are sitting there in the west waiting for their pension money (which arrives at the post office on a known day).
-kuru	for, of something that is an intention in someone's mind but may not actually exist	*Dangkawalada janijanija Barrindindiwuru.*	The men looked everywhere for Barrindindi (a mythical monster).

final *-ā* (shown by the macron over the *a*) if reporting a volitional action, such as *jī jyā yānā* ("I worked"). But they take a short final *a* if reporting a non-volitional action, such as *jī thula* ("I realized, understood") – since realizing, like remembering, is something over which we have no conscious control. Some verbs, like "meet," can occur with either suffix, depending on whether the action is deliberate or not. Say I meet my friend Manoj. If our meeting was planned, I would say *jī mānaj nāpalānā*, with a long final vowel, but if our meeting was by chance, I would say *jī mānaj nāpalāta*, with the short vowel and the substitution of *t* for *n* just before it.

Since every verb has to be marked for the volitionality contrast, and determining whether the actions of others are carried out on purpose can keep a judge and jury going for many years, you might wonder how Newari speakers manage to apply this to other people's actions. The answer is that the volitionality contrast only comes into play when recounting your own actions, or when questioning those of your interlocutor, who can vouch for their own directly, as in *chā a:pwa twan-ā lā?* ("Did you drink too much (of your own volition)?"). Elsewhere the *-a* form is used, so a better definition of the contrast would be that *-ā* means "volitional, and knowable as such by introspection" while *-a* means "not certifiable by introspection as volitional."

In fact many languages force their speakers to hold back on what mental and emotional states they can attribute to others. Japanese and Korean, for example, both ration the reporting of "private predicates" attributing inner sensations and feelings like "want," "(feel) cold," or "(feel) lonely" to those who can experience them directly.

English is insensitive to this. It is fine to say both "I want to drink water" and "he wants to drink water," "I am cold" and "he is cold," "I am lonely" and "she is lonely." There is no problem in translating the "I" versions of these into Japanese, e.g. *mizu ga nomitai*, literally "water drink-desirable," for "I want to drink water," *samui desu*, literally "cold is" for "I (feel) cold," and *sabishii desu*, literally "lonely is" for "I feel lonely." But I cannot make comparable assertions about other people, since I can never be 100 percent sure what they are wanting or feeling. Rather, I have to use a more circumspect construction closer in its meaning to English "is acting" or "appears to be," e.g. *kare wa mizu o nomita**gatteiru*** ("he evidently wants to drink"), *kare wa samu**gatteiru*** ("he appears to be cold"), or *kare wa sabishi**sooda*** ("he seems to be lonely"). Korean is similar, and also extends the "privacy" condition to verbs like "like." And it skews the translation of statements about people's presumed future actions through the "presumptive" form *kalkeeyyo*, which, used of myself, means "I will go, am going to go," but used of someone else means "he will presumably go, is sure to go." This recognizes the fact that we can be more certain about our own future actions than those of others.

In the examples so far, the question of evidentiary grounding has been restricted to the difference between what can be known subjectively and what is "external" and evident to everyone. But some languages insist on more careful attention to evidence for *all* statements that are made, specifying whether the speaker knows about it from doing it themselves, seeing it, detecting it by some other sense, from hearsay, from inference, or by other means – typically by a grammatical marker on the verb.

Take Eastern Pomo,[9] for example, now spoken by just a few old people in northern California. To translate English "it burned," you have to choose between four suffixed forms of the verb: *pʰa·békʰ-**ink'e*** if you felt the sensation yourself, *pʰa·bék-**a*** if you have other direct evidence for it, *pʰa·bék-**ine*** if you saw circumstantial evidence and are inferring that it happened, and *pʰa·békʰ-·**le*** if you are basing your statement on hearsay. It is possible to translate these back into English versions that have the precision of the Eastern Pomo versions: respectively "I felt it burn me," "I saw it burn," "it must have burned," "they reckon it burned." But the point is that in English we don't *have to* do this – we can get away with being sloppy about the grounds for our statements and just say "it burned" for all four situations. In Eastern Pomo, on the other hand, you *must* specify your source of information for all statements made, so speakers are forced to weigh up their evidence carefully every time they say anything. In fact, a study by Martha Hardman[10] of another language with a well-developed evidential system, Aymara in Bolivia, found that a great deal of effort by children's caregivers goes into teaching them the exact conditions under which it is valid to use the different evidential forms, so as to ensure they are scrupulous and accurate reporters of information.

Well-developed evidential systems are found in many parts of the world – Turkey and the Caucasus, the Himalayas, highland New Guinea, and much of the Americas – and over the last couple of decades linguists have been mapping out the evidential systems across these languages. Gradually they have elaborated a robust cross-linguistic framework or *typo-logy* showing what contrasts are made – e.g. which types of sensory evidence are distinguished? what is considered the most reliable evidence? – and whether one evidential can be stacked up on another. Returning to Eastern Pomo, there are examples of storytellers inflecting a verb for BOTH the non-visual and the hearsay evidentials in a story where the speaker attributes to oral tradition the report of an auditory perception by the old man of someone else walking out.

(1) bà-xa-khí   xówaqa-nk'e-e.
     then-they.say-he   outwards.move-NON.VISUAL.SENSORY-HEARSAY
     "Then he started to walk out, it is said (the old man villain, who is blind, heard the hero start to walk out)."[11]

Our cross-linguistic understanding of evidentials was starting to settle into a comfortable form when linguist David Fleck began investigating evidentials in Matses, a Panoan language in Amazonia along the Brazilian–Peruvian border, and discovered a whole new unimagined dimension to evidentiality.[12] Fleck had started out as a zoologist, and Matses people had invited him to conduct research on the animals in the jungle around their village. As he tried to learn the language and discovered he had bitten off more than he could chew without the right analytic teeth, he decided to switch to linguistics. When he told zoologist colleagues about his change, many of them asked him if he thought there would really be enough material for a doctoral thesis – "a primitive language, maybe enough for a Master's." The Peruvian soldiers who gave him a lift out to Matses territory had a different story – "an impossible language, nothing in it makes sense." And the Matses themselves told him: "you're lucky to be working on our language: it's nice and straightforward."

The astounding thing about Matses is that it can locate both the reported event and the weighing up of evidence separately in time, with independent yardsticks for each. Say a hunter is returning to his

Figure 4.1 A Matses hunter returning with freshly hunted peccary[13] (photo: David Fleck)

village from the jungle, and reports that white-lipped peccaries (*shëktenamë* in Matses) passed by a particular location, on the basis of inference from seeing their track. The verb for "pass by" is *kuen*, and the end of the word takes a suffix meaning "it/they," which is *şh* or *k* according to conditions we needn't worry about here. Now comes the wild part: depending on how much time elapsed between the event and the detection of the evidence, the speaker chooses the suffix *ak* (a short time period), *nëdak* (a long time period), or *ampik* (a very long time period). And depending on how long passed between the detection of the evidence and the report, the speaker chooses *o* (short time period), *onda* (a long time period), or *denne* (a very long time period). The time-to-detection suffix comes first, then the time-to-report suffix. This gives sentences like:

(2)　*shëktenamë kuenakoşh.* White-lipped peccaries (evidently) passed by. (Fresh tracks were discovered a short time ago.)

(3)　*shëktenamë kuenakondaşh.* White-lipped peccaries (evidently) passed by. (Fresh tracks were discovered a long time ago.)

(4)　*shëktenamë kuennëdakoşh.* White-lipped peccaries (evidently) passed by. (Old tracks were discovered a short time ago.)

(5)　*shëktenamë kuenakdennek.* White-lipped peccaries (evidently) passed by. (Fresh tracks were discovered a very long time ago.)

Like many empirical discoveries, the possibility of a system like this is obvious after the fact: if Matses did not exist, some philosopher of language would have had to invent it. And now that we know about the Matses system, we can go on to make sure that representational logics developed for evidential systems, and cognitive models of social reasoning more generally, do not simply classify evidential judgments by type, but locate them in time as well. But the point is that, to my knowledge, no linguist or philosopher HAD actually postulated such a system. There are many more things in the languages of this earth than have yet been dreamed of in our philosophy.

Reviewing the points we have touched on in our quick tour of what different languages elaborate in the domain of social cognition, we can put forward the following overall model of what any language has to enable its speakers to do (see figure 4.2).

First, as shown on the top left of the figure, a language needs to keep a running file on all social agents – people in one's social universe – and the relations between them (e.g. of kinship, clan membership etc.). Sometimes it has to triangulate between more than one of these relationships at the same time, as in Kunwinjku, where the special system called Kun-derbi[14] locates kin from two perspectives at once. Say grandmother Ann is talking with her granddaughter Valda about Mary, who is Ann's daughter and Valda's mother. Ann would refer to Mary as *al-garrng* ("the one who is my daughter and your mother, you being my daughter's daughter"), while Valda would refer to her as *al-doingu* ("the one who is your daughter and my mother, you being my mother's mother"). Here the relations between three people (a, b, and c) are simultaneously specified, and at the same

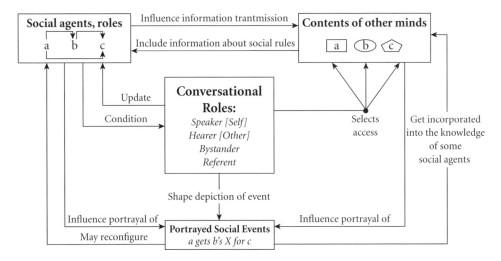

Figure 4.2   A generic model for social cognition in grammar

time linked to the particular conversational roles of speaker, hearer, and referent. A number of Aboriginal languages have systems like this, and their speakers regard the correct use of them, with the ability to take twin perspectives that it requires (plus the encyclopedic knowledge of how everyone in the community is related to everyone else) as the ultimate in courtly refined language.

Passing to the second component in our model, each person in our social universe carries their own set of desires, beliefs, thoughts, and information. Ideally the speaker wants to keep track of all of these so as to predict other people's behavior and interactions. As we saw above, though, many languages are scrupulous in reminding us of the boundaries to how far we can reasonably go in imputing "private" feelings and intentions to others. In the top right of the model, then, are files on what each person, as far as the speaker knows, has in their minds and feelings.

Third, most events that get talked about have some sort of socially relevant component, such as projected intention or change of possession, and the grammar has to allow these components to be depicted in event-descriptions, as shown in the bottom component.

Finally, the act of speech lies at the center of the whole model, as it is speech acts that enable the reliable updating and transmission of such information. A special feature of conversation is its careful training of joint attention, combined with turn-taking between speaker and hearer roles, which permits me as hearer to become privy to your descriptions of your inner feelings. These features enable the intense building of empathy that gives us our best information about where others' minds are at. At the same time, the various types of social relationship impact on conversation and shape the way utterances are framed, something that many languages index grammatically through various types of politeness or respect markers.

To round this chapter off, let us put together some of these themes by seeing how all the socially relevant dimensions of experience we have touched on go into building a single inflected word in Dalabon, a language that makes you attend to rather different social categories from what English grammar directs you to. (As you can see, Dalabon is a polysynthetic language, like Ubykh, which condenses into a single word what would take a sentence in English.) Here is the word:

(6) *Wekemarnûmolkkûndokan.*
"I'm afraid that the two of them, who are in odd-numbered generations with respect to one another, might go, with consequences for someone else, and without a key person knowing about it; by choosing the form of words I do, I hereby indicate that one of those carrying out the action is a mother-in-law of mine or equivalently respected relative."

To speak Dalabon and use words like this, you need to build them up in the following way. First start with the basic meaning, "go." In Dalabon, this is normally *bon*[15] – but when talking about your mother-in-law or comparable high-respect relatives, you have to use a special polite form of this word, *dokan*. So your first job is to check out the kinship relation you bear to the person you are talking about.

Next you put on the prefix *molkkûn-* ("unbeknownst"), which we discussed in the last chapter – in this context it would denote that the action is being carried out surreptitiously, without letting someone know who should have known about it. So you need to know not just what the two people are doing, but whether they are keeping the right people informed about it. Then you add *marnû-*, which means "for someone's benefit / to someone's disadvantage" or "on someone's behalf" – representing the event as having some effect, positive or negative according to the context, on a third party.

Then you need to specify whether two or more than two people are going, and if there were just two, what kinship relationship holds between them. The word I gave you would be appropriate for talking about a mother–daughter or uncle–nephew team, for example, but to talk about two sisters or a grandmother–granddaughter pair you would replace *ke-* with *barra-*. Finally, you add the "apprehensive" prefix *ke-*, to depict the situation as undesirable. I have translated this here with "I'm afraid that . . . might." But in another context, such as advising a more competent person to make sure the two do not go, or that they let the right people know that they are going, a better translation might be "so that they don't end up" or, in more old-fashioned English, "lest."

I have used this word because it illustrates how far grammars can bring us away from our socially disconnected "monkeys eat bananas" scenario. To plan, utter, or decode the single Dalabon word *wekemarnûmolkkûndokan* we need to bring in all four elements of the model I gave above. Starting at the conversational nexus, I locate the event, in the set of possible worlds, as not corresponding to the here and now, and indicate something of my own attitudes by specifying it as undesirable. Moving to the depicted event, by using the prefix *marnû-* I indicate that this event will have broader social ramifications, bringing benefit or misfortune to others. Now looking at the consequences for the society of minds whose contents we are all engaged in trying to keep track of, by using the prefix *molkkûn-* I depict the event as being unbeknown to someone whom it concerns – perhaps the owner of the clan lands they were on, or the recipient of their planned trophy. As for the modeling of social relationships, I refer to kinship relations in two places: the prefix *ke-* keeps track of the "odd-numbered-generation" relationship between the hunters, while the use of *bonghmû* instead of the more normal *bon* for the verb root "go" keeps track of my own in-law relationship to someone else present in the conversation.

Intricate as it is, this one-word example only scratches the surface of how languages use their grammars to construct and update their speakers' ever-unfolding dossier of the social universe they move in. Ngalakan, a language next door to Dalabon, has a special "compassion" prefix, which goes on the verb to indicate the speaker's sympathy for someone in the described event. Languages of the Amazon or the New Guinea Highlands would force me to be scrupulous about what grounds I am asserting this on, specifying my source of evidence. Tibetan,[16] or the Ecuadorian language Tsafiki, would have me specifying whether the information being reported is new to me or something I have known for a while, while others like Andoke[17] in Colombia require me to decide whether what I am reporting is something you are likely to have been aware about yourself, or is evident just to me. Although all languages require us to assess the social significance of what we recount and to position the news and the way we present it with respect to ourselves and our conversation partners, the exact demands they make on our minds as we speak, and the way our mental dossiers on our social universe get updated in each conversational move, vary drastically from language to language. With each new grammar we examine, our composite model of how humans are able to reason about the world becomes richer.

To speak Kayardild you need to discriminate many types of intention. To speak Dalabon you have to pay constant attention to the kinship relations between all people in your social world. To speak Japanese or Korean, you must pay close attention to the boundary between what is knowable by introspection and what is knowable by external observation. To speak Newari you need to keep track of volitionality. To speak Eastern Pomo or Matses you must carefully weigh and specify your information source for each statement. Of course English-speakers, as well, can learn to do all these things, and particularly need to do so if they want to function as genealogists (kinship!), psychologists (private predicates!), judges (volitionality!), or well-footnoted academics or journalists (give your sources!) – or, more generally, as empathetic, sensitive, socially switched-on people who are scrupulous about what they say.

How far Kayardild, Dalabon, Newari, Japanese, Korean, Eastern Pomo, or Matses bring this awareness on sooner or more routinely than English does is the sort of Whorfian question that needs a coordination of linguistic and psychological methods of the type to be outlined in part IV, and there has not as yet been significant research in this area.

But what is clear, just from looking at these languages in the detail that we have, is that you cannot speak them without paying constant attention to the particular sets of categories that they force their speakers not to stay silent about. For each of these languages, the speaking cultures that gradually shaped them over millennia must have made these distinctions often enough in past talk by their speakers for them to become installed in their core grammatical apparatus. The occurrence of distinctions like this in a given language thus provides *an existence proof on the learnability and usability of the respective categories* – a proof that not just psychologists, judges, and genealogists, but all normally functioning members of a speech community, can readily learn these distinctions and incorporate them into more or less permanent attentional scanning. And they also provide *an existence proof on evolvability*: that the words and structures that these grammatical categories derive from can be used often enough for them to evolve into grammatical markers.

A child coming into the world has to have a mind capable of figuring out all of these grammars, and of learning to attend routinely to any of these categories in the course of acquiring their mother tongue. And, as Ortega y Gasset intimated, to map the whole set of human possibilities we need to engage on a bold and vast integration of what the cumulative sensitivities of the world's languages can tell us.

Further reading

Besides Ortega y Gasset's own work, a fine discussion of this problem informed by his position is Becker (1995), with an interesting discussion of Burmese. On the centrality of social cognition to human culture see Goody (1995), Tomasello (1999a, 1999b), and Enfield and Levinson (2006). On evidentiality see Aikhenvald (2004) and the collection of papers in Chafe and Nichols (1986); on the role of inferencing power in building the signs of language see Keller (1994, 1998). Enfield (2002) and Evans (2003b) contain discussions of the mechanisms by which cultural emphases shape grammars over time.

Part III

Faint Tracks in an Ancient Wordscape: Languages and Deep World History

Na:-bí hi:li na:-bí wowa:ci na-mu. My language is my life (history).
(Arizona Tewa saying, as quoted and translated in Kroskrity 1998)

During the merciless slaughters of World War I, the young Czech professor Bedřich Hrosný was drafted into the Austro-Hungarian military. He was lucky enough to come under the command of the easy-going Viennese Lieutenant Kammergruber, who allowed him to spend time in Istanbul examining cuneiform Hittite material in the form of a large quantity of clay tablets found by Hugo Winckler near Boğaz Köy in Turkey. Although these were written in the cuneiform script used to write Akkadian, they represented a different and unknown language.

A decisive moment came when Hrosný encountered a passage reading *nu ninda an ezzatteni wadar – ma ekutteni*. From a Sumerian ideogram adjoining *ninda* in the text he deduced it meant "bread," and the parallelism in the text suggested the form "bread X-ing, Y Z-ing." Knowing the Old High German form *ezzan*, corresponding to English *eat*, and the tantalizing resemblance of the *-tteni* endings to the participial forms of old Indo-European languages like Latin and Sanskrit, he guessed the formula might mean "now you will eat bread, further you will drink water." There in that one line were echoes of the English words "now" (*nu*), "water" (*wadar*), and "eat" (*ezza*). Elsewhere, he found more distant traces of the English *-in'* participle – the castigated English pronunciations like "I'm comin' over" with a so-called "dropped *g*" are in fact bastions of linguistic conservatism.

By 1915 Hrosný had demonstrated that the language written on these tablets was related to our own. Thanks to information in his decipherment, we know it to be the language of the Hittite Empire, which lasted in various guises from 1750 to 1180 BC in Anatolia. Hittite forms part of the great Indo-European family to which English, Lieutenant Kammergruber's German, and Hrosný's own Czech all belong. In fact, Hittite is the most distantly related language within the Indo-European family – Bengali, Armenian, and Russian are all closer to English than Hittite is. Since Indo-European is, at present, the largest grouping including English that all scholars would accept, Hittite is thus the most distant language known to be related to English.

In addition to the many shared grammatical similarities that formed the real meat of the proof, this language from 3,500 years ago contained numerous recognizable words. Some we have just seen, such as *wadar* ("water") and *ezzan* ("eat" – *essen* in German, *jíst* in Czech). Others included *genu* ("knee"; the Latin-derived word "genuflect" preserves the original pronunciation better than does English "knee," especially since we stopped pronouncing the *k*), and *arrash* ("arse" – *Arsch* in German).

No scholars in Hrozný's time had believed that the great civilizations of the Middle East included Indo-European speaking groups, but the Hittite evidence proved irrefutable. The small sound changes that English, German, and Czech have accreted over the years cannot conceal the kinship of these homely Hittite words to those in our modern languages – words to which their equivalents among their Akkadian contemporaries, or the Turkish speakers living in Boğaz Köy today, bear no resemblance whatsoever. The Akkadian words, on the other hand, resemble those in other Semitic languages such as Hebrew, Ge'ez (the ancient language of Ethiopia), and Arabic. In the table below, "cognate" (i.e. historically related) words are grouped by similar shadings.

Indo-European				Semitic				Turkic
English	German	Czech	Hittite	Akkadian	Hebrew	Ge'ez	Arabic	Turkish
water	Wasser	voda	wadar	mû	mayim	māy	mā?	su
knee	Knie	koleno	genu	birku	berek	bərk	rukbat	diz
arse	Arsch	prdel	arrash	šapūlu	šippūl	–	sāfilat	kıç

The words, sounds, and grammars of each language carry innumerable clues about the past histories of their speakers, reaching back for millennia. In general this process of conservation is not deliberate. Even where a culture preserves ancient forms of a language, as with Biblical Hebrew among Jews or Ge'ez among Ethiopian Christians, the goal is to preserve special religious texts, rather than information about the past in general. No one tells their children to keep saying "arse" so as to maintain that precious information about links to our long-lost Hittite relatives. Our unconsciousness of the historical evidence that languages offer is in fact an advantage to science, since attempts to rewrite history for ideological purposes generally leave this part of the record alone: "The great advantage that linguistics offers . . . is the fact that, on the whole, the categories . . . always remain unconscious . . . for this reason the processes which lead to their formation can be followed without the misleading and disturbing factors of secondary explanations, which are so common in ethnology."[1]

In this part of the book we examine how linguistic evidence can help us understand deep world history – by which I mean that part of our history that preceded written records. In chapter 5 I will show the range of reconstructive techniques we can use to reach back into earlier times. In chapter 6 we will dine on the fruits of these techniques, entering past mental worlds, following ancient migrations and uncovering unsuspected links between far-flung populations. In the process, we will anchor some of these reconstructed languages to the dateable and localizable physical evidence, by matching the ancient words that our techniques have restored to ancient objects and crops in archaeological sites. We close this section, in chapter 7, by showing how data from modern languages can unlock hitherto-undeciphered writing systems, and in that sense reopen forgotten shelves of the Library of Babel to written history as well.

5

Sprung from Some Common Source

> Language is an archaeological vehicle, full of the remnants of dead and living pasts, lost and buried civilizations and technologies. The language we speak is a whole palimpsest of human effort and history.
>
> (Russel Hoban, quoted in Haffenden 1985:138)

Speakers of languages around the world notice the sorts of similarities that Hrosný picked up between Hittite and other Indo-European languages, when they compare their own languages to others. Sometimes this is due to mere chance. My first linguistics professor, Bob Dixon, told how the last speaker of Mbabaram, after making him wait years before agreeing to start linguistic work, finally broke the drought by saying: "I'll tell you our word for 'dog': *dog*."[1] As it turned out this was pure historical fluke, and the Mbabaram word derived from a much less similar word in its ancestral language, via the stages *gudaga* > *gudwaga* > *udwoga* > *dwog(a)* > *dwog* > *dog*. Words may also be similar because of the limited set of sounds used by early infants, such as the well-known use of words like *mama* for "mother" and *papa* for "father" right around the world. We should not exaggerate this, though: *mama* means "father" in Georgian and Pitjantjatjara and, although Pitjantjatjara does indeed have a word *papa*, it means "dog."

At other times the similarities are due to the passing of words from one language to another. Linguists call this "borrowing." This is a rather inappropriate term, since the word rarely comes back to the lender and when it does it has usually changed during its sojourn abroad. English "borrowed" the chivalrous French word *fleurter*, literally "to flower," changing its sound to *flirt* and its meaning to what we now know, before giving it back to French as *flirter* – although some modern French purists prefer to reclaim it as a French word unsullied by its centuries across the Channel, respelling it as *fleurter*.

Borrowing can make languages look more alike than their pedigree warrants, and speakers often patriotically claim the new word for their own language. This happened when a Bangladeshi acquaintance told me of his excitement at finding that Germans, too, used the Bangla word *Kindergarten*. I have also heard Italians tell me of their surprise to find that their word for persimmon, *cachi* (pronounced *cacky*), has found its way into Japanese – in fact, the word came into Italian as a loan from Japanese *kaki*.

Figure 5.1   Sir William "Oriental" Jones[2]

Facts like these mean we have to be cautious about reading too much into a few words in common across languages. You thus have every right to be skeptical about whether the Hittite words *wadar, nu, ezzan,* and *arrash* that I cited above are a conclusive proof of relationship. Taken alone, they are not – it is not impossible that these few shared words could be due to chance, or borrowing. But the logic I will now outline gives a more sophisticated and convincing set of diagnostics for language relatedness.

Although people have speculated about language relationships for a long time, and many peoples have the general sense that linguistic similarity is an index of past relatedness between groups, a conceptual block prevented them from developing a scientific method for approaching language change. This was the idea that some language still spoken would be the oldest and original language, from which the others derive. I once drank from an ancient and grotty coffee mug bearing the proud label "Welsh – Europe's oldest language" – and indigenous languages are often described as "ancient." But in fact this makes no sense.

Apart from "new-growth" languages derived from pidgins, language-mixing, or the recent genesis of sign languages in some parts of the world, all languages are equally old. All derive, by an unbroken chain of tiny incremental changes, from the earliest human tongues. At most, "ancient" in this context can mean "archaic," as some languages change more slowly than others. Italian has changed much less from its ancestor Latin than French has, Arabic is closer to its Semitic ancestor than Hebrew is, and Icelandic is much more like Old Norse than Norwegian is.

The breakthrough from the above mental block came from Sir William Jones (1746–1794), a British judge who in addition to the then-standard classical education in Latin and Greek had steeped himself in the study of Chinese and Old Persian – whence his nicknames "Oriental Jones" or "Asiatick Jones." As a judge in Calcutta, where legal transactions under the British Raj were often delegated to the preexisting Hindu system, he decided to teach himself Sanskrit the better to check on the arguments of law being put forward. In his famous address to the Royal Asiatic Society in 1786 he stated:

> The Sanscrit language, whatever be its antiquity, is of a wonderful structure; more perfect than the Greek, more copious than the Latin, and more exquisitely refined than either, yet bearing to both of them a stronger affinity, both in the roots of verbs and in the forms of grammar, than could possibly have been produced by accident; so strong indeed, that no philologer could examine them all three, without believing them *to have sprung from some common source, which, perhaps, no longer exists.* (Jones 1786, italics added)

The reverberations of these few lines cannot be overestimated. They prompted a feverish interest in Sanskrit, which, decades later, would lead to a European awareness of ancient grammatical treatises like that of Pāṇini, which we mentioned in chapter 2. The effects were not unlike those produced in the Renaissance with the rediscovery of classical Greek works, but augmented by the salutary realization that Europe and the Mediterranean world had no monopoly on great intellectual discoveries. More directly relevant to our story now is the radical effect of Jones' insight that *the common source* need *no longer exist.*

Historical linguists over the following century were to gradually work through the consequences of this idea, developing techniques for reconstructing what that common source was like, largely through the comparative study of languages of the Indo-European family to which Sanskrit and the other languages above belonged – with Hittite a later addition. It was in this heady period that two other major breakthroughs occurred. First was the realization that *regular sound correspondences* between languages need to be postulated and held to the strictest standards of scientific accountability, so that *exceptionless rules* need to be formulated. Second, it became clear that to meet these standards we often need to postulate *conditioning factors* in which sound changes are influenced by other sounds around them, so that a network of interlocking changes needs to be modeled.

These techniques have been adapted and integrated into a body of procedures called the *comparative method*, which allows us to deduce a great deal about the linguistic past by comparing descendant languages, as we shall see below. Given a computational sprucing up, these methods now underlie much work in molecular genetics on reconstructing original genome sequences in mitochondrial and Y-chromosomal DNA, and, more generally, the cladistic techniques used by evolutionary biologists to deduce the most likely phylogenetic relationships between organisms:

> There is a close connection between comparative linguistics and evolutionary biology. Both seek to account for the overall resemblance between entities that are now distinct; in both there are confounding cases of horizontal transfer of information; and both are bedevilled by spurious similarities that arise from convergence, parallelism or reversals in character states. Linguists require that comparisons of different lexicons should avoid circularity and emphasize exclusively shared innovations, and that such innovations should be appropriately weighted according to their importance. The same difficulties arise in interpreting molecules and morphologies. (Cann 2000:1009, with permission)

At the same time, in linguistics, these methods have gradually been transplanted from their original field of Indo-European linguistics. We now know they work just as well among the many other language families of the world, even those with no written tradition, such as with Leonard Bloomfield's masterful reconstruction of the Algonquian family in the 1930s.

The Careless Scribes

> Historical linguistics can then be thought of as the art of making the best use of bad data.
>   (Labov 1994:11)

As we have seen, it took scholars a long time to get the idea of a now-vanished common source that may no longer exist, but which contained all the information needed to derive large numbers of contemporary forms. Strangely, though, this general technique had already been used for centuries by scholars in a related field. Philologists like Erasmus were interested in clearing away the distortions wreaked by history on original Christian doctrine. They compared different versions of the Bible and other canonical texts with the goal of deducing the authentic original – something that, as we lack the "original New Testament," can only be arrived at by a series of deductive steps. To do this we must peel away the accumulated changes that scribes had introduced over the centuries. Just as a scribe would himself copy a manuscript by hand, introducing various "improvements," mistakes, omissions, and interpolations, so would his version in turn be copied by other scribes who took as their starting point a manuscript with its own accreted changes, and added others of their own. The "copies" these scribes made would then serve as "originals" for other scribes to copy from. As manuscripts were carried to new centers (perhaps new monasteries, or even newly evangelized countries) these would then found new "families" of copies, all inheriting certain characteristics acquired from these secondary founding documents. Children are just like these careless scribes. They replicate their parents' speech with less than perfect accuracy, then once they become parents themselves their speech serves as the blueprint for imperfect copying by the next generation.

Comparison of multiple texts allows scholars to deduce a family tree of manuscripts, whose nodes and branches make it clear at what point various changes are introduced, since shared changes are usually copied from a single *exemplar*.[3] By doing this we can generally deduce what the original exemplar must have contained, even if the actual original manuscript has been lost.

Jones' "common source which, perhaps, no longer exists" is like one of these reconstructed original exemplars. Nowadays we use the term "proto-language," and, in the particular case he was discussing, the common ancestor of Sanskrit, ancient Greek, and Latin (among others) is called proto-Indo-European, because the territory its descendants occupied extends from India to Europe – see figure 5.2.

Languages like Sanskrit and Latin, in their turn, have given rise to a number of descendants: Sanskrit to such languages as Hindi, Bengali, and many other languages of Northern India as well as Sinhala in Sri Lanka, and Latin to Italian, French, Romanian, and others. We

Figure 5.2   Proto-Indo-European and some of its ancient descendants

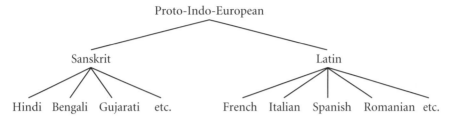

Figure 5.3   Three generations of Indo-European languages

can therefore extend figure 5.2 by adding another "generation." Focusing on just these two groups for simplicity, we then get a picture spanning a longer period.

The nodes of this tree have somewhat different statuses. All the modern languages are attested directly, and Sanskrit and Latin are attested through ancient texts, but proto-Indo-European is a hypothetical construct, gradually improved and elaborated through arguments based on comparisons between descendant languages – giving rise to the dig that no language changes faster than a proto-language.

But not all of the second-generation families of Indo-European have a classical language playing the part of Sanskrit or Latin. For the Celtic, Germanic, and Slavonic branches, the oldest substantial textual materials are post-Christian translations of the Bible – into Old Irish, Gothic, and Old Church Slavonic respectively. Particularly in the first two cases, these earliest written languages do not give a reliable guide to the proto-language of their family, because there had already been substantial further splits. For example Gothic represents just the eastern branch of Germanic – English, Dutch, and German are in a separate western branch, and Icelandic and the Scandinavian languages in a separate northern branch. So we need to reconstruct "proto-Germanic" by comparing all the modern Germanic languages, and then placing it between the youngest individual branches (e.g. Eastern Germanic) and our older "proto-Indo-European." One of the impulses driving the brothers Grimm to collect German dialect material along with their folktales was to have a good database of modern Germanic varieties to help them reconstruct proto-Germanic.

Let us get back to the logic of how the comparative method works. As I mentioned, we can think of each generation of speakers as producing very slight changes in the "manuscript" of the language that they copy as they learn it from their parents and others. These changes are very slight in any generation, but gradually add up, and every now and then a crunch comes. For example, my maternal grandmother pronounced the word "which" as *hwich* – a pronunciation still standard in many parts of the English-speaking world. But I pronounce it identically to "witch": I have "neutralized" the *w* vs. *hw* contrast, using *w* in both words. At least within the Australian branch of English, my generation has presided over the final death-throes of a distinct series descending from an Indo-European consonant reconstructed as *kʷ, as shown clearly by the Latin reflexes in *qu-* of the English *wh-* series: *quod* ("what," pronounced *kwod*), *qui* ("who," pronounced *kwee*), and so forth. (Note that historical linguists use the asterisk to warn that forms are hypothetical reconstructions.) An alien linguist, who would still have been able to transcribe distinct traces of this 8,000-year-old phoneme in my grandmother's speech, will no longer find it in mine.

We can use this sad casualty, incidentally, to illustrate the powerlessness of the individual to influence language change. Suppose that, having written the above lines, I decide I really should do something to conserve this vital part of my linguistic heritage, and start articulating *hw* every time I say "which" or "what." Even assuming I withstand the likely reaction of my peers, that I have become a foreigner or a pedant, my own rearguard action to conserve the proto-Indo-European labiovelars would have no influence on my kids' pronunciation. They are rightly more concerned with their own linguistic identities than with maintaining a private phonetic museum in their daily speech.

In vocabulary, too, there are always words that get lost, words that add meanings, and others that lose meanings, and new entries into the language. In general people are aware of the arrival of new words like "blog" or new meanings like "mouse," but less aware that old words or meanings are being lost. When my father was helping my children with their homework, he noticed that they had difficulty with the German word *Fell* ("fur, animal skin"), and was puzzled – didn't we all know the good English word "fell"? he asked. After all, his own father had worked as a "fell-monger" in New Zealand during the Depression, gathering the fleeces and skins of dead sheep. No one in our family had been aware of this unannounced little lexical loss until that moment – "fell" had quietly dropped out of use between my father's generation and my own.

Back to the Old Wording: How the Comparative Method Works

Trois frères unys. Trois licornes de conserve voguant au soleil de midi parleront. Car c'est de la lumière que viendra la lumière.

Three brothers joyned. Three Unicornes in company sailing in the noonday sunne will speak. For tis from the light that light will dawn.

(Hergé 1959:61)

The cumulative effect of small changes creates series like: "my heart," Dutch *mijn hart*, German *mein Herz*, Latin *cordis meus*, Italian *mio cuore*, Russian *moje serdtse*. If you hear Dutch, even for the first time, you would probably understand *mijn hart*, which sounds close to the Shakespearean-sounding "mine heart." You may not understand the German *mein Herz* first time around, but you will recognize it as related and remember it easily. The other versions are far less obvious, and may not strike you as cognate at all – apart from the *r* in "heart" and the *m* in "my," no sound runs across them all. But once we add more words a pattern starts to emerge. We will focus just on the initial sound in "heart."

In each of these examples, whenever you get *h* in Germanic languages like English, Dutch, and German you get *c* (pronounced *k-*) in Latin, and *s* in Russian. We can thus set up a "correspondence set" or

Table 5.1   Germanic *h* : Latin *k* : Russian *s*

English/Dutch/German	Latin	Russian
heart / hart/Herz	cordis	serdtse
head/hoofd/Haupt	caput	[–]
hundred/honderd/Hundert	centum	sot
OE *hæft/—/Haft*	captīvus	[–]
hound/hond/Hund	cane	[–]

proportion: Germanic *h* : Latin *k* : Russian *s*. The recurrence of the same correspondences led nineteenth-century historical linguists to speak of these as "sound laws," as dependable and regular as the laws of nature if only we can formulate them properly.

But sound laws are not simply regular, they are also locked into a larger *system*. If we now extend our search to other sounds, we find that the *h* : *k* : *s* correspondence is part of a broader set of changes in the Germanic languages (see table 5.2).

Table 5.2   The plot thickens: two more series of Germanic–Latin correspondences

f	*father, vader, Vater*	p	*pater*
	foot, voet, Fuß		*pedis*
θ/d	*three, drij, drei*	t	*tre:s*
	thunder, donder,		*tonāre*
	Donner thresh,		*terere* "rub"
	dorschen, dreschen		

Notice that *p, k,* and *t* all belong to the class of sounds known as *voiceless stops* – voiceless because they are made without any vibration in the voice box – and they turn into *voiceless fricatives* at roughly the same *point of articulation* (i.e. using the same part of the mouth). In other words, the *place they are made* in the mouth stays more or less the same, but the *way they are made* (the "manner of articulation") changes. Instead of making a complete closure, the articulating organs only close part way, creating the particular type of friction that defines the sound. (With the *th* sound we see that German and Dutch have *d* instead, but enough other Germanic languages have the *th* – such as Gothic *thriskan,* "thresh," or Old Norse *Thōrr,* the *Thunder* God – that English is shown to be more conservative here.)

This set of changes, discovered by Jacob Grimm, the older of the two brothers who collected and published the famous fairy tales, is part of the series of changes known as Grimm's law. These changes define all the languages of the Germanic family – making it an *innovation-defined subgroup*. It is the great systematicity of such changes that is the key in allowing us to reconstruct not just words, but the vast, intricate structures of whole lost languages.

Every Witness Has Part of the Story

Languages have a "story" to tell: it is our job to find these stories and figure them out. . . . It's harder for a group of dialects to hide their "stories". . . . Get related languages. They will tell related stories.

(Hyman 2001)

In general it is the case that every additional language increases our chance of catching some remnants of the past, and hence of having a more accurate reconstruction, since inherited elements are constantly bleeding out of some languages but surviving in others.

In the last few centuries, English has more or less lost its descendant of the original word for "man," while the original word for "woman" has seen some roller-coaster changes of fortune that have disguised its original meaning. The Indo-European root *wir* or *wīr* ("man"), as in Latin *vir* and its derivative *virīlis* ("virile"), is now barely hanging in there, preserved in aspic as the *were* in the compound "werewolf," which originally meant "man-wolf."

Meanwhile, its female counterpart *gwunā* ("woman"), related to Russian *zhena* ("wife"), Greek *gunē* ("woman," as in "gynecologist"), and Sanskrit *jani* ("woman"), and still present in Old English as *cwēn* ("woman"), had a riches-and-rags split. One line of development led to modern "queen," by the line "(lead) woman (of a country)." But another line, spelled *quean*, degenerated to the meaning "slut, harlot" and then dropped out of mainstream use altogether.

If we were approaching English with no record of the language's history – the situation we are in if we begin to document an undescribed language – and were wondering if there was any reflex of Russian *zhena*, "queen" would appear a rather forced candidate because of its meaning-shift. And if we were looking for a reflex of Welsh *gwr* ("man") the *were-* in "werewolf" would seem downright fantastical. But if we start casting our net further, into dialects of English, or other related languages, we turn up words that confirm the link. By adding words from some Scottish and northern English dialects we would get *quean* ("girl"), and by adding Swedish we would get *kvinna* ("woman"). If we went looking for languages preserving the "man" root we would have a harder time, since it has essentially disappeared from all the modern languages of the family. But if we include the Crimean Gothic word list that the enterprising Flemish envoy Count Busbecq recorded in Constantinople in 1562, not long before this language died out, we would finally get a hit: alongside the Latin translation *vir* he gives the Crimean Gothic form as *fers* (with a change from initial *v* to *f*).

Archaic words that would otherwise be lost can thus sometimes be fished back from related languages, from dialects, or from specialized uses like compounds or ritual languages. To illustrate the importance of individual dialects, consider this example from the Athabaskan languages of California and Oregon. These are cut off, geographically, from the main group of Athabaskan languages in Canada and Alaska, but also from the southern group that includes Navajo and Apache. This raises the question of how they got to California, and it would be consistent with what we know of Athabaskans further north – as arrow-shooting inland peoples getting around on snowshoes – for them to have come along the mountain ranges first, then gradually moved downstream. Support for this scenario would come from finding a reflex of the proto-Athabaskan "snowshoe" word, *ash* (< *ʔayh), which is reconstructed on the basis of languages in and around Alaska like Ahtna (ʔaas), Upper Tanaina (ʔoyh), and Central Carrier (ʔaih).

Once in California many groups became comfortably ensconced in warmer downstream areas and lost the need for snowshoes and their associated terminology. Others formed totally new words for snowshoe – again wiping out the linguistic trace we need. Luckily, however, we have one record, from one dialect, that is enough to clinch the argument. This comes from a vocabulary of the "Lassik" variety of Eel River Athabaskan collected from Lucy Young by Frank Essene.[4]

Essene transcribes the word as ŭss, a plausible transcription of ʔəʂ, which would be the regular Lassik reflex of proto Athabaskan *aʃ. Evidence from this one dialect is thus crucial in showing that this branch of Athabaskan speakers still had the old snowshoe word when they reached California, and more generally in evaluating a particular migration model. In fact it is likely that other Californian Athabaskan languages also had a comparable word. Most other linguists and anthropologists working in the area simply did not ask about a word for snowshoe, whereas Essene took great pains collecting terminology on material culture, filling hundreds of notebook pages. This illustrates the point that sometimes the most crucial words for hooking up linguistic to archaeological evidence are unlikely to be recorded by linguists as part of their regular documentation, making interdisciplinary work all the more important.[5]

This Lassik example illustrates how an individual language or dialect can end up being the only surviving witness that a word was present in the proto-language of a given subgroup. The importance of individual languages as witnesses is just as great whether we are dealing with particular sounds or with sound sequences that have changed or been lost in all other languages of the family. This is because each descendant changes the proto-language in a different way, leaving one daughter language with the information about vowel length, another as the guardian of consonant clusters, and a third as the vital witness for accent or a particular initial stop. Each modern language thus holds its own distinctive part of the ancient record.

Consider Eyak, an Alaskan language hemmed in by Chugach Eskimo to its north and Tlingit to its south. Eyak's already small population was devastated once salmon canneries were established in 1889, bringing environmental destruction, alcohol, opium, and disease. It dwindled further to around five speakers by the early 1960s, and it is largely thanks to the efforts of a single talented speaker, Anna Nelson Harry, that we understand its workings (see box 5.1).[6] Michael Krauss has described Eyak as the "missing link" offering definitive proof linking the Athabaskan languages to another Alaskan language, Tlingit, in the family now known as Na-Dene: "It is depressing to contemplate how frustrating the study of the Na-Dene relationship would have to remain without the independent and highly conservative evidence from Eyak. . . . Athapaskan-Tlingit comparison, without Eyak, would have to remain highly speculative and relatively infertile for insights from one side explaining the history of the other."[7]

In fact a series of more recent scientific developments that we will discuss in the next chapter have gone on to link Na-Dene, in its turn, to the Yeniseian languages of north Central Siberia. The most important contribution of Eyak to this demonstration is in its evidence about parts of the arcane system of verb prefixes, but this would take us along a longer path than I want to go down here,[8] so let us consider a simpler illustration.

One particularly tricky case for reconstruction comes when we are dealing with ancient clusters of sounds, which tend to get simplified giving different simple sounds that cannot, however, be derived from the same ancestral sound. If we try and relate the final sound of English "too<u>th</u>" to its German equivalent *Zah<u>n</u>* (pronounced *tsahn*) we would be making a mistake to think there was a single sound from which *th* and *n* both derive. But Dutch *tand* shows us there was an original *nt* or *nd* cluster; English and German then each kept one of these elements and lost the other. From outside Germanic, the presence of an original cluster is confirmed by Latin *dent-* (as in "dentist") and Greek *odont* ("orthodontist"). Languages that keep both elements, then, are the key in linking the two forms together.

Eyak plays a comparable role to Dutch, Latin, or Greek in allowing us to assemble cognates of this type between Athabaskan and the Yeniseian languages. The languages of these two families have been separated for long enough that there are not large numbers of cognate words, and the sound changes are sufficiently far-reaching that it is not always obvious that two words are related, so we need all the help we can get. Just like with the "tooth"/*Zahn* example, we have examples where the Yeniseian languages have shaved off

Box 5.1   Anna Nelson Harry, Eyak Shakespeare

Anna Nelson Harry was born at Copper River, Alaska, in 1906. At 12 she married an Eyak man, Galushia Nelson, but his own removal to boarding school had meant that his ancestral language was never completely secure, so that the dominant language of their household became English. Nonetheless, this couple managed to record a great deal about their culture, working first with anthropologists and then with a tag-team of linguists until 1961 when Michael Krauss began a long-term commitment to studying Eyak. By that time only five fluent speakers remained.

Anna Nelson Harry (third from left), working on language with Galushia Nelson, Johnny Nelson, Norman Reynolds, Kaj Birket-Smith, and Frederica de Laguna, Cordoba, 1933[9]

Anna Nelson Harry reveled in the intricacies of her mother tongue, and Krauss' introduction to a book of texts she recorded portrays her as a microcosmal Eyak Shakespeare in her blend of inventive language and richly humane characterization (Harry and Krauss 1982). Anna Nelson Harry passed away on February 1, 1982. Richard Dauenhauer had written, a little before her death:

> Eyak language
> three speakers left
> whose hearts have grown old,
> whose speech will die forever
> and the instance
> of human voice
> crystallize to text . . .[10]

the final stop, and the Athabaskan languages have skipped the nasal. An example is the root for "liver," which is *zid* in Navajo (final *d*), *se·ŋ* in Ket (final nasal), but in Eyak is *sahd*. The breathy vowel written *ah* in Eyak *sahd* presumably derives from a nasalized vowel that itself comes from a sequence *an*, and is the only surviving witness of the nasal in this word in proto-Na-Dene. This is crucial in allowing us to postulate a proto-Na-Dene form **sən't*',[11] which can be more readily linked to the Ket form *se·ŋ*. Eyak, like Dutch, is thus a language with the special characteristic of preserving at least a remnant of these clusters, so important as bridging evidence.

Synchrony's Poison Is Diachrony's Meat

A key insight of the great Swiss linguist Ferdinand de Saussure, who did so much to establish linguistics as a science early in the twentieth century, was that when we talk about languages we need to describe their *diachrony*, or history, separately from their *synchrony* – how they are at a given moment. He likened language to a chess game. A synchronic treatment of language is like a chess problem: all that matters is what is there on the board now, not what moves got them there. A diachronic treatment is like an account of the game listing each move in turn. More recently Noam Chomsky has given a powerful psychological reason for separating synchrony from diachrony: a child learning her language only gets access to what people are speaking now, and must deduce her grammar just from the words she hears. She has no direct access to how her now-silent ancestors spoke.[12]

The most challenging synchronic features of a language that learners have to cope with are "paradigms," which in linguistics refers to table-like lists, which largely have to be learned by heart rather than assembled by regular rules. While paradigms can be pesky for the language learner – and equally a headache for those trying to give an elegant synchronic description of how a language is now – they often turn out to be invaluable once we start to look for information about the language's past. And again, they illustrate the way the comparative method focuses not just on isolated words or sounds, but on the way they are organized into systematic crystalline structures, which can be reconstructed through careful comparison of related languages.

A particularly hairy part of paradigms are those cells in the table that are irregular or even *suppletive*, which is to say that the alternate forms have no logical basis at all (like "go"/"went"). It is a stumbling block for the language learner, whether adult or child, that while "bigger" and "biggest" are formed regularly from "big," you cannot extend this pattern to form "*gooder" and "*goodest" from "good" but need to learn the suppletive forms "better" and "best." Young children and second-language learners have been trying to straighten this out for thousands of years – each generation has a go – but time and again the community of adult speakers ends up pulling them into line and teaching them the "correct" but illogical forms. The verb "to be" is another nest of paradigmatic suppletions: while "to kiss, I kiss, you kiss, he kisses, they kiss, he kissed, they kissed" is completely regular, we have a whole string of one-off forms to learn with "to be, I am, you are, he is, they are, he was, they were." And then we have all the irregular verbs like "bring/brought," "think/thought," "run/ran," or "drink/drank/drunk."

Box 5.2   Mixed groups and language intertwining: the case of Michif

Occasionally contact between mutually unrelated groups engenders distinctive new tongues, mixing the features of two languages together in ways that were long considered impossible. Such a group is Michif in the prairie regions of Canada, which arose when the bilingual Méti (mixed) children of French-speaking trappers and their Cree-speaking wives gradually fashioned a distinctive style of code-mixing.

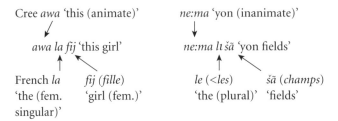

Cree and French elements in a Michif phrase

To say "this girl," for example, you say *awa la fij*, mixing the Cree-derived demonstrative *awa*, used for proximate (nearby) animates, with *la*, the French definite article used with feminine nouns like *fille* ("girl"). Michif noun phrases thus marry the Cree system, based on animacy and proximity, with the French system, based on gender and number, and Michif speakers have to keep both systems in their head when speaking.

This grammatical intertwining only happened once a particular set of social developments had cut Méti people off from both their French and their Indian relatives. This was intimately connected with the development of the fur trade, and with emerging ethnic categorizations in nineteenth-century Canada. At this point the Métis became a distinct social group, with their distinctive style of language-mixing a badge of their mixed identity. At some point this mixed code took on a life of its own, so that some speakers learned Michif without knowing either French or Cree.

Mixed languages like Michif defy many of our notions of possible language. They are a manifest challenge to the entrenched idea that "everything hangs together" in a single integrated whole, since they clearly merge two quite separate subgrammars, each with their own distinct sound systems and typological casts. They also show that, in suitable cases, languages can have more than one "parent," against the assumptions of the comparative method spelled out in this chapter. But the tenuous social status of mixed groups makes them even more fragile than traditional indigenous languages. Linguists only began to study them seriously in the 1970s, and already Michif is highly endangered, its last speakers being in their sixties and seventies.

Two of the caveats to drawing conclusions about relationships between languages from similar forms are overcome when we turn to paradigms, particularly when they contain irregularities like those just given.

The first caveat, that sometimes similar forms are due to chance like English and Mbabaram *dog*, is overcome once we discover whole paradigms whose cells match up systematically. This is because of the multiplicative effect that such multidimensional arrays have on probability. Although the chances of a single word being similar between two languages are not outrageous, the chances of both elements in a two-term paradigm matching up is the product of the individual probabilities of each similarity. The chances get correspondingly smaller each time we expand the paradigm: to three members, four, and so on.[13]

The second caveat, that the similarity may reflect borrowing, is largely put to rest by the observation that, while languages borrow words reasonably commonly, and borrow grammatical formatives sometimes, they only borrow complete paradigms in extremely unusual conditions of "language intertwining" (see box 5.2). As Ives Goddard[14] put it, when we want to establish evidence for language relatedness we look for examples that "are so tightly woven into the basic fabric of the language that they cannot be explained simply as borrowings." These tightly knotted lattices of paradigmatic information, which because of their arbitrariness create difficulties for language learners and grammarians alike, end up providing historical linguists with some of their best evidence for language relatedness.

This means that when we get cognate irregular paradigms or alternations, like German *gut : besser : beste* corresponding to English *good : better : best*, or *ist : war* to *is : was*, or *bringen : gebracht* to *bring : brought*, or *denken : gedacht* to *think : thought*, or *trinken : trank : getrunken* to *drink : drank : drunk*, an alien linguist examining these two languages would be quite safe in concluding that they are related. Let us turn now to two other language families and see how this sort of paradigmatic and irregular information can be useful.

First, a remarkable North American example. The Algonquian language family covers a huge area of the Great Plains, northeastern USA, and eastern Canada, and includes such well-known languages as Cree and Ojibwe. These languages and cultures have figured prominently in how Native Americans are represented to western eyes, from *Hiawatha* to *The Last of the Mohicans*: "Mohican" is an anglicization of *Mahican*, an Algonquian language traditionally spoken at the junction of Massachusetts, Vermont, and New York state. And as I mentioned above, Leonard Bloomfield's work on showing their relatedness was decisive in establishing that the comparative method could be applied to unwritten languages just as well as to the classical Indo-European languages.

Far to the west of the Algonquian languages, in adjacent tiny pockets in northern California, we find two languages, Wiyot around Humboldt Bay, and Yurok along the Klamath River (see figure 5.4). The last speaker of Wiyot died in 1962, but there are still a few very old speakers of Yurok, and tribal members are trying to revive the language. Thanks to recording efforts through the twentieth century, there are ample textual materials collected by various investigators – I already mentioned in chapter 2 how the anthropologist Kroeber transported hefty crates of aluminium disks upriver by canoe to record Yurok material early in the twentieth century.

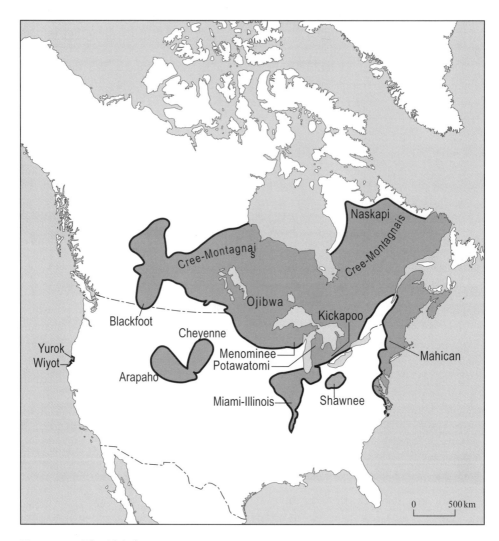

Figure 5.4　The Algic languages

The cultures of Wiyot and Yurok are typical of California rather than of the Great Plains, and the languages have many Californian features, such as ejective consonants. But they nonetheless display eerie similarities to Algonquian, which have led linguists to group them all in a larger family called Algic (see figure 5.5).

The recognition of this grouping poses interesting problems for understanding past movements of the Algic peoples. Was California a jumping-off point for Algonquian, or was it rather the case that Wiyot and Yurok headed west across the Sierra Nevada many years ago, or that all groups moved from somewhere like Washington state? And why are the similarities between these next-door neighbors barely greater than what each shares with geographically distant Algonquian, despite the fact that Wiyot and Yurok speakers were traditionally fluent in each other's languages as well as others of the region like Tolowa Athabaskan?[15] I will not go into these controversies here, however, since my

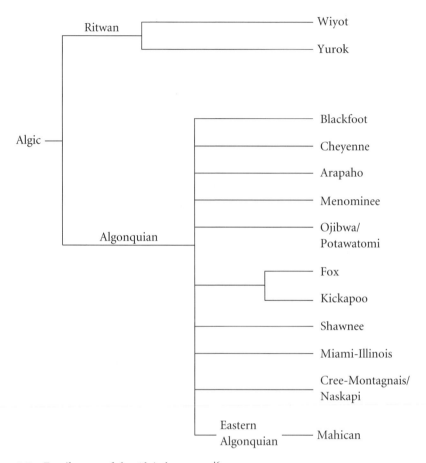

Figure 5.5 Family tree of the Algic languages[16]

goal is to illustrate the role of paradigms and irregular formations in relating them to Algonquian, and it is these nerdy details that enable us to pose the more stirring questions just mentioned.

A taste of these similarities (see table 5.3) can be obtained by comparing the possessive paradigm for "tooth," which is built on a cognate root. You can readily see the common proportion *n : k : w : m* for *my : your : his : a*, even though this is partly disguised in Wiyot by the fact that it has hardened the nasals *n* and *m* to the corresponding stops *d* and *b*.

Besides a shared paradigm, there is another grammatical pattern, derived from it, concerning verbs for certain types of kin. Let's start with another set of possessed nouns that have been reconstructed in proto-Algonquian: **ni:wa* ("my wife") and **wi:wali* ("his wife"), in which you will recognize the Cree prefixes *ni:-* ("my") and *wi:-* ("his"). Now in the Algonquian

Table 5.3 Possessive paradigm showing the similarities between Cree, Wiyot, and Yurok[17]

	Cree	Wiyot	Yurok
"my tooth"	ni:pit	dápt	ʔnerpel
"your tooth"	ki:pit	khápt	k'erpel
"his tooth"	wi:pit	waptáʔl	ʔwerpel
"a tooth"	mi:pit	bápt	merpel

languages it is possible to form verbs of possession like "to have a wife", and strangely, even if the possessed element belongs to the first person (e.g. "I have a wife") it is based on the "his" form given by the above paradigm. The verb stem "have a wife" is then *wi:w-i*, which with its two *w*s is based on the "his" form. Even if you say *newi:wi*, "I have a wife," it looks from its make-up like it should mean "I have his wife."

Now look at Yurok. First we build "my wife" as *ʔnahpew* and "his wife" as *ʔwahpew*, following the *ʔn : ʔw* pattern given above for "my tooth" and "his tooth." Then, just as in Algonquian, you build on the "his" form to get *-ʔwahpew* ("to marry (of a man)"), even if this is used with a first-person subject, as in *ʔneʔwahpewok* ("I am married," i.e. "I have a wife"). This seemingly illogical but deeply entrenched pattern, with its identical idiosyncrasies in Yurok and the Algonquian languages, is the sort of inexplicable irregularity that makes paradigms hard to learn, and that poses puzzles for description. But when shared across languages it becomes a veritable smoking gun in the detective work of historical linguistics.

By the Waters of Lake Chad

As a second example of how paradigms and irregularities can help establish family relationships, consider the vast and far-flung language family known as Afro-Asiatic. To those who associate language with race, the speakership of this huge family comes as a shock, for its speakers are found from Nigeria to Ethiopia to Morocco to Egypt to Israel (see figure 5.6),

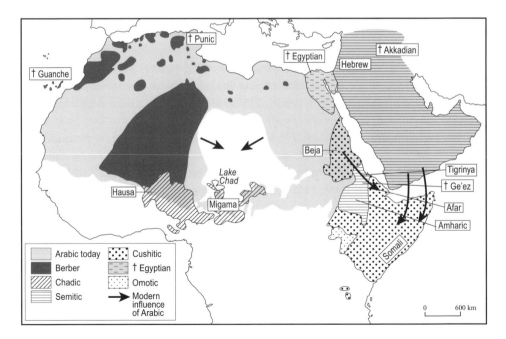

Figure 5.6   The Afro-Asiatic languages

embracing a huge range of physical types whose features range from Caucasian to West African. It includes 240 languages conventionally divided into six groups, and numbers over 250 million speakers, with Arabic, Amharic, and Hausa accounting for the lion's share.

We also know, from the long written histories of this part of the world, that the Berber family used to be much more widespread. It once included Guanche on the Canary Islands, which gave way to Spanish by the sixteenth or seventeenth century, and Libyan, which was submerged by the phenomenal spread of Arabic under Islam. Other Afro-Asiatic victims of Arabic's explosive spread were the Semitic language of the Carthaginians, and the single-language family Egyptian, whose most modern form, Coptic, may have been spoken in some remote villages as late as the nineteenth century, and still survives as a liturgical language of Coptic Christians. Many languages of the Omotic, Cushitic, and Chadic branches in particular are still little-studied and much new material of historical significance remains to be unearthed.

Five of the six component families of Afro-Asiatic are exclusively found in Africa, while the sixth (Semitic) has members in both Africa (Ethiopia and Eritrea) and western Asia – the Arabian Peninsula, the Levant, and the Fertile Crescent. Their geographical distribution suggests that the Semitic peoples, so pivotal in the development of Mediterranean civilization, had their earliest roots in Africa, but this argument has not always been accepted with open arms.[18] Indeed, the covert assumption that language and race will correlate held scholars back from recognizing the existence of this family for a long time, and it was not until Joseph Greenberg swept the cobwebs away in his foundational 1950s classification of African languages that the true dimensions of this family began to be accepted, as well as its squarely African center of gravity. It is likely that several of these families were once spread out across what is now the Sahara, at a time before the onset of desertification: about 7,000 years ago there were many large lakes (including an upsized Lake Chad) and fine grazing lands in a belt across the northern center of the continent.

Sometimes small clues are the picadors in establishing language relationships, before the matador of the comparative method enters the ring. Greenberg, trained early in Hebrew and Arabic, wrote his PhD on Hausa and was intrigued by the strange fact that, in Hausa and other Chadic languages, "water" is grammatically plural, just as in the Hebrew of the Old Testament. The familiar English translation "the waters of Babylon" is simply a literal translation of a Hebrew word that happens to require the plural for grammatical reasons.

However, it would be misleading to imply that the Afro-Asiatic construct hangs by this slender thread.

In addition to large numbers of reconstructed lexical items, the evidence includes grammatical formatives like the formation of plurals with a distinctive suffixed *w* (see table 5.4), and a distinctive way of marking the opposition of

Table 5.4 Examples of plural *-w* in four Afro-Asiatic families

Language (family)	Singular	Plural
proto-East Semitic[19]	*tšȝj* "neighbor"	*tšȝjw* "neighbors"
Berber	*im-i* "mouth"	*im-aw-ˀn* "mouths"
Afar (Cushitic)	*alil* "chest"	*alil**wa** "chests"
Hausa[20] (Chadic)	*itààc-èè* "tree"	*itaat-**uuwà** "trees"

Table 5.5 Incompletive formation in languages from four Afro-Asiatic families[22] by doubling a root consonant and inserting the vowel *a*. Beja has lost consonantal doubling but kept the distinctive vowel

Semitic		
Akkadian	ikbit	ikab<u>b</u>it
"get heavy"	preterite	imperfective
Tigrinya	säbärä	y-əsäb<u>b</u>ər
"break"	perfective	imperfective
Berber		
Tuareg	ifəɣ	if<u>f</u>aɣ
"go out"	past	habitual
Cushitic		
Beja	ʔiidbil	ʔiidabil
"collect"	past	present
Chadic		
Migama	náʔápìlé	náʔápàl<u>l</u>á
"wash"		

completed vs. uncompleted[21] actions by a combination of inserting an *a* inside the root (bolded in table 5.5) and geminating or reinforcing one of its consonants (I have underlined the doubled consonant).

The inexorable and essentially random nature of language change means that, the longer the time that passes, the more likely it will be that particular configurations of features will survive in only a single daughter language – although we can never predict which daughter will be the last custodian. In the case of Chadic, for example, most languages insert the inherited *a* in the imperfective, but do not employ gemination. Does this mean that proto-Chadic had already abandoned the gemination pattern? To answer this, we need to track our way up to the small group of Migama speakers in Chad, where at last we find evidence of gemination, along with the use of the *a* vowel. This one witness language is thus vital in proving that proto-Chadic, too, employed the same mixed pattern. Once again, this shows how important a single key witness language can be to the whole enterprise of linguistic reconstruction.

Examples like Afro-Asiatic and Algic show why discussions of language relatedness cannot simply be based on lists of vocabulary: the most convincing evidence often rests in complicated paradigms. Yurok, for its part, shows that even after putting together the basic paradigms there is still important descriptive work to do, since derived possessive verbs, built from the paradigm, are also decisive. To be sure of having all the basic synchronic evidence that we need to draw solid diachronic conclusions, we require nothing less than a complete and detailed grammar – plus as full a dictionary as it is possible to compile – for every language and dialect of a family. This is because we never know in advance which language or dialect is going to be a last inheritor of some piece of key evidence.

Loanwords as Complication and Resource

There is one further complication in applying the comparative method. Sound changes are historical events, and occur at a particular point in time, only hitting words that are in the language when the sound change happens. Words that have entered English in later centuries from Latin or Greek or French will miss out on particular changes, and instead will be stamped with the distinctive transmutations that occurred inside other languages. Grimm's change from *k* to *h*, for example, only affects "native" English words like "hundred" or "hound" or "heart," which have reached us through an unbroken line of development inside the English language. Cognate words that were borrowed from non-Germanic languages after Grimm's law had applied will thus show up in English with the initial k, p, or t unchanged. This is why we have "cardiac" and "cordial" alongside "heart," "canine" alongside "hound," "paternal" alongside "father," "pedal" and "podiatrist" alongside "foot," and "trinity" alongside "three."

The effect of loanwords like this on the comparative method starts off as a nuisance, because it makes it much harder to see the basic pattern, which is not properly discernible until all the loanwords have been filtered out. But it ends up as a boon, because you can turn the argument around and use it to work out when individual words came into the language, since they missed out on the "date-stamp" given by a particular sound change. Once a first-pass profile of the distinctive sound changes undergone by various families or branches is known, it becomes possible to identify "doublets" (or sometimes "triplets"), which are sets of words where one member has come through the main line of descent and undergone all relevant changes along the way, while other words in the set have undergone sound changes associated with some other family. An example is the English triplet *hemp* : *canvas* : *cannabis*, in which all words derive from the same word, widespread in early Indo-European, and all refer to different products of the same plant *cannabis sativa*. "Hemp" comes from Old English *henep*, changing $k > h$ in accordance with Grimm's law. "Canvas" is a loan from Norman French *canevas*. Since this version of the word was hiding out in the Romance languages at the time Grimm's law applied it was spared the change from $k > h$, although it underwent its own French-specific weakening of original $b > v$. Finally, "cannabis" is a recent loanword from Greek.

Loanwords often give us information about cultural contacts – since generally they are adopted because they denote new concepts or objects from another culture. We can use them to profile the cultural and sometimes also the geographical history of language families and subgroups, and to date some changes in the language through inferences from the appearance of new items in the archaeological record.

The Linguistic Lens on the Past

> Words [are the] tags that carry the imprints of the past: trace the origin of a word and one traces the historical development of whatever it refers to, be it object, activity, thought, or feeling. Trace the words that refer to everything related to an institution and one traces its existence.
>
> (Gewald 1994)

Humans have a deep need to understand their past, and the discipline of history – originating with chronicles commissioned by kings and rulers in literate societies over much of the world, from the Middle East to China to Sulawesi to Mesoamerica – has developed so much rigor and detail that it is easy to think this is our only way of knowing the past. But where does this leave those peoples where the written record only takes up with the coming of alien colonists? As Vansina puts it in his book on the precolonial history of the Congo region:

> Imagine that Caesar arrived in Gaul and landed in Britain in 1888, a mere century ago, and that your known history began then. You were not Roman, your language was not Latin, and most of your cherished customs had no historical justification. Your cultural history was amputated from its past. Would you not feel somewhat incomplete, somewhat mutilated? Would you not wonder what your cultural heritage was before Caesar? Unimaginable? Yet this is the situation of the So in Zaire, whose record seems to begin only with Stanley in 1877. (Vansina 1990:xi)

There may well be oral cultural traditions dealing with the doings of ancestors, but there is no knowing where the boundary within them lies between history and myth. Some Aboriginal mythological traditions have handed on eyewitness accounts of the floodings of river valleys, the marooning of islands by rising seas, and the eruptions of volcanoes, which geologists can date back 6,000 years or more, but mixed in with the confirmable geomorphological material are other elements that are esoteric, undatable, or simply inaccurate.

The language-based techniques that we have sketched in this chapter allow us to infer histories before history. Bringing in linguistic evidence can thus help eliminate the truncations of the past and the imbalances between regions of the world that arise if we confine our histories to the written record. But language reconstruction, as achieved by the comparative method, risks floating disconnected to the real world of places, times, and objects unless it is anchored to the models of the past given by other disciplines – particularly archaeology and genetics – and in the next chapter we see how this hooking-up can be achieved.

Further reading

There are many excellent textbooks in historical linguistics with good accounts of the comparative method. My personal favorites are Crowley (1997), which has a special emphasis on Oceania, and Campbell (1999), with particular foci on Mesoamerica and on the Finno-Ugric languages. *The American Heritage Dictionary of Indo-European Roots* is a good source for the Indo-European origins and far-flung cognates of English words. Haas (1958, 1966) and Goddard (1975) give the evidence relating Algonquian to Yurok and Wiyot. Hayward (2000) is a clear overview of Afro-Asiatic with many onward references; those wanting to get deeper into this family should see also Ehret (1995), Newman (1977), Ehret et al. (2003), as well as Jungraithmayr (1975) and Semur et al. (1982) for the Migama evidence. On Eyak culture see Birket-Smith and De Laguna (1976 [1938]). Richard Dauernhauer's poem, a short biography of Anna Henry Nelson, and a fine bilingual collection of Eyak texts appear in Harry and Krauss (1982); see Krauss (2006a) for a full history of research on Eyak. The most thorough study of Michif is Bakker (1997).

6

Travels in the Logosphere: Hooking Ancient Words onto Ancient Worlds

The historical "texts" of the *longue durée* are encoded not just in the ciphers of Western scribes; they exist equally as material traces dispersed over landscapes and sedimented in their depths, no less as patterns of cognate words in the linguists' comparative lexicons, or as indigenous traditions transmitted orally over long generations.

(Kirch and Green 2001:5)

My emphasis in the last chapter was on the techniques we can use to reconstruct languages from sound systems, words, and grammatical structures. These methods can take us back into past logospheres, enabling us to imagine smaller or larger fragments of proto-languages, and evincing "the great power of language evidence in displaying the history of the inner as well as the outer lives of those societies."[1] They can tell us how people divided their companions into kin or age-mate categories, and reveal unsuspected complex social algebras in societies that appear materially simple in the archaeological record.[2]

Or we can identify quite specific ancient cultural practices. In Kayardild, for example, there is a fundamental taboo against mixing land-food and seafoods on the same fire, e.g. fish and yams, for fear of potentially fatal stomach blockages and cramps. The sickness produced by violating this taboo is known as *markuriija* and is part of an interlocking set of beliefs about the need to keep land-based and sea-based creatures, foods, and smells separate from each other. Lardil people on Mornington Island, whose language and society has long been separated from Kayardild, have a comparable concept, known as *malkuri* (and now *mulgri* in local Aboriginal English). This is the expected form of a true cognate going back to their common proto-language, proto-Tangkic. We can thus reconstruct an ancient shared concept, part of the cosmological reality of their remote common ancestors. In a culture without written records, no other type of evidence – archaeological, ethnographic, rock-art, or genetic – can offer a comparable window on past thought-worlds.

The problem with the *mulgri* example, however, is that it is quarantined to the logosphere – it floats in a world of ancestral words without any necessary connection to place or time. To realize the full contribution that historical linguistics can make to our understanding of past worlds, the next step is to link it to other sciences of the deep human past, most importantly archaeology, genetics, and comparative ethnography. By carefully finding the points of contact between linguistic evidence and these other disciplines, we can begin to localize our reconstructed word-worlds to specific times, places, archaeological cultures, and flesh-and-gened peoples.

The logic of linking reconstructed languages to places, times, peoples, and archaeological records hinges on three points of contact: between language and language, between word and object, and between name and place. These three techniques will recombine in differing proportions in the stories we will look at this chapter, but first let us look one at a time at each of these word-hooks.

Tongue to Tongue: Localizing Languages One to Another

> If we possessed a perfect pedigree of mankind, a genealogical arrangement of the races of man would afford the best classification of the various languages now spoken throughout the world. And if all extinct languages, and all intermediate and slowly changing dialects, had to be included, such an arrangement would, I think, be the only possible one.
>
> (Darwin 1859:422)

Proto-languages at various stages can be placed in space and time, relative to other known languages and proto-languages, by three types of information: internal branching of family trees, evidence from loanwords, and structural convergence with neighboring (and possibly unrelated) languages. In family trees with several levels of nesting the evidence from branchings, incoming loanwords, and contact influences can be laminated to give a multistep scenario. And the scenarios suggested by the linguistic model can be checked against those given by two other disciplines of the human past: archaeology and historical genetics. Within genetics, moreover, we sometimes get the chance to track parallel family trees in humans and other animals, looking at the historical genetics of plant cultivars that humans took with them on their travels, and even of animal species that hitched a free ride, such as the rodents inadvertently carried in the holds of Austronesian argonauts out into the Pacific. This gives geneticists time-linked family trees in non-human species.

Before going on, let us look in a bit more detail at each of the three types of information outlined above.

(1) *The branchings of reconstructed language family trees.* What does the location of the full set of "sisters" at each level of the family tree suggest about where their mother language was spoken? A German proverb states that *Der Apfel fällt nicht weit vom Baum* – the apple does not fall far from the tree. Other things being equal, the area of greatest genealogical diversity is assumed to be the homeland, as each migrating population only takes with it a subset of the home-grown variants, and as diversification takes time wherever it is found. Just think of where the most variability is found with English dialects: Britain, the homeland of English, has far more than North America, which in turn has far more than recently anglophone Australasia.

The family-tree conception of language relatedness thus gives us a powerful tool in relating linguistic evidence to history. Related languages must derive from some common ancient community of speakers who each went their separate ways, carrying their languages off to differentiate independently of one another. The spread of most languages is propagated by "demic diffusion," the natural spreading out of their speakers, whose children learn the language, go forth, and multiply. Occasionally other factors produce a mismatch – the imposition of Spanish by colonial rule on indigenous people who formerly spoke Aztec, of Arabic by religious conversion on former Coptic speakers. But mostly we can take the tree of language relationships as a good measure of Darwin's "pedigree of mankind."

(2)   *The source and timing of loanwords.* Mostly loanwords (particularly big sets of them) are from next-door languages. This is likely to hold more reliably the further back in time we go, since the effects of writing and intercontinental trade are then removed. So while (1) locates related languages with respect to their shared inheritance, (2) locates them with respect to their contacts – possibly with quite unrelated languages. Later in this chapter we will play a star-witness role in tracing the route followed by the Gypsies (Roma) on their long trek from India to Europe.

(3)   *The patterning of linguistic features absorbed through contact with other languages.* The longer they are in contact – and the larger or more influential the number of bilingual speakers – the more languages tend to converge in sound, grammar, and semantic categories, as bilingual brains economize on storage and processing by maximizing the information that can be shared between languages. Evidence of structural convergence can thus point to sustained and intimate connections between speech communities at some earlier period.

Words to Things: Matching Vocabularies to Archaeological Finds

Forget grammar, think about potatoes.

(Stein 1973)

The most direct link between reconstructed phases of the logosphere and the real world of people and objects in time and place comes when we can hook reconstructed language states onto the localizable remains studied and dated by archaeologists. Sets of reconstructed words, which tell us about cultural inventories at particular stages of a language's history, can be linked to distinctive archaeological profiles. Unlike proto-languages, these can be directly and absolutely placed in space and time, thanks to the welter of mapping and dating techniques that archaeologists use. Traditionally this approach is known by the German term *Wörter und Sachen* – literally "words and objects."

A classic application of this technique is in dating the expansion of the Bantu peoples into southern Africa. The several hundred Bantu languages account for over 95 percent of the subequatorial population of Africa, with languages like Swahili touching the Indian Ocean coast, and Zulu and Xhosa reaching into South Africa. Yet the Bantu family is scarcely more internally divergent than the Germanic family, and is actually a sub-sub-sub-sub-sub-sub-sub-subbranch of a much more ancient and widespread family, Niger-Kordofanian, whose center of gravity is squarely in the Sahel of northern Africa. (This means, incidentally, that our best witnesses to the earliest phases of this vast family are those of the Kordofanian branch. These little-known languages, spoken in the Nuba Mountains, have been particularly devastated by recent wars in the Sudan, and their description is one of the most urgent tasks for understanding Africa's linguistic past.)

Moreover, it is clear that the Bantu languages are only recent arrivals in the southern half of Africa. It is true that much of the original pre-Bantu population of this vast region has been completely submerged, from a linguistic point of view. Pygmy peoples, for example, who are both ancient and genetically distinct from the Bantus, now all speak languages of the Bantu or the related Ubangian families, although Pygmy languages retain some individual "substrate" words from before the Bantu-Ubangian onslaught. But an indication of the pre-Bantu linguistic situation holds on in some areas, most importantly in the extremely diverse Khoisan families of Namibia, Botswana and South Africa, in two other click-language isolates in Tanzania (Hadza and Sandawe), and in the presence of click consonants in two Afro-Asiatic languages in Kenya, pointing to earlier contacts between them and click-language speakers who must once have lived far north of their current location.[3]

If Bantu speakers are relative newcomers to subequatorial Africa, where did they come from, when did they start arriving, and what technological and social mechanisms powered their spread? Here we have a classic case of the various linguistic techniques mentioned above converging with archaeological evidence (and more recently with genetic evidence as well). First of all, linguists have long known that the greatest diversity within the Bantu group, as well as the nearest cousins of the Bantu languages, are found in the Cameroon grasslands, suggesting their original homeland lay near there.

The set of proto-Bantu terms that we can reconstruct through the comparative method shows the proto-Bantus to have been a people with a characteristic West African crop package of legumes, yams, oil palms, and kola nuts (see table 6.1), who made new fences and traps round their fields each year, and who traded with specialized hunters and fishermen. This matches the technological profile found in archaeological sites in the Cameroon from around 5,000 years ago.

We can also peek forward to the next step through the equatorial jungles that had hemmed their southward expansion. Moving agriculture into these jungles required iron axes for felling, and new crops like the banana and Asian yam that would grow in forest clearings, and we can look at how far up the family tree common terms for these objects appear. It turns out that different subbranches of Bantu have different reconstructable terms for these crops and for metallurgical products, suggesting that distinct Bantu branches adopted and named them independently after heading south from Cameroon into the equatorial jungles.

Table 6.1   Some reconstructable proto-Bantu agricultural terms (material from Ehret 1998:105)

*-kúndè	"black-eyed peas"
*-jùgú	"Voandzeia groundnut"
*-bá	"oil palm"
*-bòndó	"raffia palm"
*-bónò	"castor bean"
*-kùá	"yam"

The triumphal package of wet-climate crops, iron tools, and military organization on age-grading principles, which was to carry eastern Bantu speakers as far as the southern tip of Africa, was not put together all at once. Rather, one branch had the chance to absorb these elements from Nilo-Saharan and Afro-Asiatic neighbors in the region of what is now Uganda around 1000 BC. The iron tools and wet-climate crops show up in the archaeo-logical record, and can be linked directly to reconstructed words like -*bàgò* ("adze"), and -*sòká* ("planting-ax"), each of which have relict distributions in rainforest Bantu languages spoken at the northern end of the family's distribution.[4] The presence of military age-grading, where age-mates go through initiation together and form a powerfully integrated cohort around which large armed forces transcending local family allegiances could be organized, is not directly visible archaeologically, but can be inferred by the reconstruc-tion of verbs like *-alik-* ("to enter circumcision rites"), *-aluk-* ("to finish circumcision rites and leave seclusion"), and *inkunka* ("circumcision observances").[5]

The greatest challenge to the words-and-things approach exemplified with our Bantu case study is that, in many parts of the world, the objects of most interest to archaeo-logists may not have seemed important enough to linguists for relevant vocabulary to be recorded. To an archaeologist, the crucial material signature of a particular cultural assemblage may be an arcane type of grindstone or tool, a distinctive pattern of pottery, or a wide spectrum of crop remains – and linguists often lack the expertise or interest to push their vocabulary-gathering out into these areas. In Australia, for example, with its sparse archaeological record sometimes summarized as "bones and stones," the vocabu-lary of grindstones is turning out to be a key to understanding adaptation to life in desert regions, which depended on crushing types of acacia seed into a type of wild flour.[6] Yet the limited word lists we have for many languages do not give us the vocabulary we need to work out when these items appear in the family tree.

Or consider the problem of recording plant names. Since the expansion of many language families was fed – literally – by their agricultural breakthroughs, there are many parts of the world where the most important match-up between language and archaeological profile involves the remains of crop plants. But to really nail whether a particular crop is indi-genous to a family, or a later adoption, we need more than just a single crop name (e.g. maize): we need the whole set of vocabulary items that spring up around it – phases of plant growth, parts of the plant, ways of preparing the soil, ways of cooking the food.

Consider the great Uto-Aztecan family, which extends from the southwestern USA down through Mexico to El Salvador. Their geographical range is strikingly similar to the early spread of maize cultivation, which had reached the Tucson basin between 1400 and 1100 BC from origins in Mesoamerica. This would suggest that maize cultivation was associ-ated with the earliest ancestral node of this family, proto-Uto-Aztecan, and that the rapid spread of this family northward from Central America could have been supported by "demic expansion" – maize-eating Uto-Aztecans displacing the more scattered hunter-gatherer pop-ulations as they expanded northward. But a problem with this scenario, until recently, was the apparent lack of cognates for maize-related items in the northern branch of Uto-Aztecan. This would suggest a rather different interpretation, in which proto-Uto-Aztecan lacked maize-based agriculture, and only the southern Uto-Aztecan branch, with its numerous reconstructable maize terms, was originally associated with maize-growing. This in turn would push back the inferred date for proto-Uto-Aztecan to a time before the arrival of maize cultivation.

But the recent production, by a team led by Kenneth Hill and late Hopi scholar Emory Sekaquaptewa, of the enormous Hopi dictionary – running to 900 pages – has turned the argument around. It shows that, after all, at least one northern Uto-Aztecan language, namely Hopi, possessed a good number of maize-cultivation terms cognate with terms in southern Uto-Aztecan, and the word-forms show them to be inherited vocabulary rather than loans. Sample Hopi words are *söŋö* ("corn cob," from proto-Uto-Aztecan **sono*), "corn products such as leaves, cane", *tɨma* ("griddle," identical with an ancestral pUA term meaning "tortilla, tamale"), and *qömi* ("oblong cake of baked sweet corn, flour," pUA *komal* "griddle"). Thanks to the detailed compilation of maize-related vocabulary in the Hopi dictionary, we now have a much firmer basis on which to correlate the branchings of the Uto-Aztecan family tree with archaeological dates given by particular crop items. The lesson of the Hopi dictionary for language documentation is that the vocabulary relevant to archaeologists may not emerge until very detailed terminological investigations have been carried out.

The vital role of plant vocabulary is not confined to terms for major food items. After all, the demographic crunch point for hunter-gatherers comes during famines, not feasts. It is the carrying capacity of the land during times of drought rather than plenty that determines the stable population of hunter-gatherer societies. Crop plants in incipient agricultural societies thus often emerge from marginal "drought foods." Yet it is these very drought foods – often rather unappealing – that are the first to be given up after contact with other groups. Native societies rapidly adopt outside elements (like traded flour or rice), making the terms for famine foods particularly vulnerable to a loss of intergenerational transmission. It is very rare for linguists to record these words properly.

Bob Rankin has done detailed historical work on the Siouan languages of the Mississippi corridor and the eastern USA, aimed at using reconstructed crop terms to link the linguistic chronology of the Siouan family to datable archaeological cultures of the Mississippi and Missouri valleys. These witnessed the slow emergence of more appealing domesticated gourd varieties: wild types appear from around 5,400 years ago but larger, fleshier domesticates do not start to appear before around 500 to 200 BC. Seeing how far back "gourd" words can be reconstructed would give us vital hooks to the archaeological records. But Rankin poignantly expresses his regret at how feeble linguists' efforts to record plant vocabulary were:

> Failure on the part of linguists (the author included) to collect pertinent ethnobotanical and agricultural vocabulary is a problem that will affect this and similar studies. We have almost no useful terms for parts of the corn plant including "cob", "tassel" and "leaf" (except the most general term), nor have we terms for different varieties of squash. To my knowledge no Siouanist has ever collected the terms for the known famine foods commonly gathered in food plains in preagricultural times. Chenopodium ("goosefoot, lamb's quarters"), amaranth ("pigweed") and iva annua ("marsh elder") are prominent among these. All might have turned out to be useful in comparisons between Proto-Siouan and the distantly related Catawban of the Carolinas. But these plants are no longer gathered and such comparisons are now probably beyond our reach. (Rankin 2000:13)

Getting this sort of information requires close cooperation between linguists and specialists in other fields. Jared Diamond,[7] in an article on interview techniques in ethnobiology, tells the story of anthropologist Ralph Bulmer, who had recorded around 1,400 species names from Kalam speakers in Papua New Guinea. Bulmer went on to quiz them about names for rocks, but was then told there was just one word for all types of rock. Returning the next year with a geologist friend whom he introduced to his Kalam teachers, he witnessed them giving his friend, within an hour, a long list of words for different kinds of rocks, classified according to texture, color, locality, hardness, and use.

When Bulmer reproached his Kalam teacher for not giving those words to him the year before, he was told:

> when you asked about birds and plants, we saw that you knew a lot about them, and that you could understand what we told you. When you began asking us about rocks, it was obvious you didn't know anything about them. Why should we waste our time telling you something you couldn't possibly understand? But your friend's questions showed that he does know about rocks. (Diamond 1991)

No linguist, however broad their ethnographic interests, has enough training to push out the documentation of vocabulary into all the avenues that future matchings of words to things may call for. This makes interdisciplinary teamwork essential, drawing in specialists who are more worthy conversation partners able to probe the encyclopedic depth we find so often in knowledgeable speakers.

The three key prerequisites for applying the words-and-things approach to link historical linguistics to archaeology are thus detailed dictionaries, joint fieldwork by linguists and disciplinary specialists, and the gathering of parallel data across as many languages and dialects as possible. Only in this way can the comparative method have the best possible set to draw on in its reconstructions. This is a tall order, but anything less risks sacrificing the huge potential that this method has to enlighten us about past worlds.

Name on Place: the Evidence of Toponyms

> [U]nlike DNA, which has wandered from country to country, place-names are fixed in space. The toponymy of the landscape can be compared to a palimpsest upon which successive linguistic groups have written their signatures, and continue to do so.
>
> (Sims-Williams 2006:1)

In chapter 3 I emphasized the fact that, before humans invented writing, extinct languages would leave no trace of their passing. In fact this formulation is slightly too negative: some relics of earlier languages may survive in the tongues that displace them. This may take the form of specific vocabulary items for which the newcomers had no name. I live in a land of kangaroos, wombats, mulga, and billabongs, all words taken from the various indigenous languages in which these objects were named long before Australia was claimed for the British Crown and the English language, to which such things were novel.

But the most important relics that earlier languages leave are generally in the realm of place-names or toponyms. Their special significance is threefold.

Quantitatively, they typically far exceed other loanwords in number. Australian English has at most a few hundred loanwords from Aboriginal languages, while the number of place-names of indigenous origin runs to the tens of thousands, from Canberra to Boggabilla. Indigenous groups throughout the world regularly had "a name for every riffle in the creek."[8]

Linguistically, the predictability of the formation of place-names – the preponderance of locative suffixes with meanings like "at," and the likelihood that a goodly number of names will refer to natural features like "lake" or "river" – makes informed guesswork about their meaning possible in many cases. There are even some ghostly phantasms of ancient languages, like Pelasgian and Lydian, whose elements are largely or entirely known from inferred roots in classical place-names.[9]

Geographically, toponyms are unique among the words of a language in being tied to particular locations, enabling us to map the spread of languages on the ground. We do need to beware of occasional whimsical outliers that can lead us astray – the pharaonic-ally named Memphis in Tennessee does not implicate an ancient Egyptian presence there. But, in general, the broad corpus of place-names, taken together, can give us a reliable map of earlier linguistic presences.

It is largely on the basis of toponymic evidence, for example, that we know that the Celtic languages once occupied a much larger part of continental Europe than any his-torical record of Celtic languages suggests (see figure 6.1). In this case, scholars can even work from much older forms of the names, as recorded by classical Roman and Greek authors, to detect Celtic elements like *brig* ("defended place"), *corn* ("horn"), and *dun*, which appear in many place-names. Although these have cognates in other languages (e.g. "bury" and "horn" in English for the first two), the specific form of the Celtic place-name can be used as long as the form it takes in the (currently) local language has changed. The plotting of place-names with Celtic etymologies by scholars like Sims-Williams (figure 6.1) reveals a widespread ancient Celtic presence out of all proportion to the marginal coastal areas that Welsh, Gaelic, and Breton now cling to.

Place-names, like words for obscure famine foods or highly specialized technical terms for pottery or spear types, can easily end up as the neglected wallflowers of linguistic documentation. Not all dictionaries include comprehensive lists of place-names. And even when toponyms are given, the source may omit information vital to interpreting their meaning – such as notes on the exact topography of the area, or what trees or rock types are present. It may also happen that place-names retain some trace of the sound system of an earlier language – an odd stress pattern, or an unusual sound – which phonological accounts obsessed with elegance may be tempted to tidy away. Just as with the words-and-things approach, the names-on-places line of evidence often turns on elements that, from the point of view of mainstream language documentation, can appear rather peripheral. So it is vital that the span of our recording interest not screen out these tale-telling blips.

Now that we have surveyed the various techniques for hooking up language to historical reality, we can turn to three stories of the deep human past and put them to work. Each story

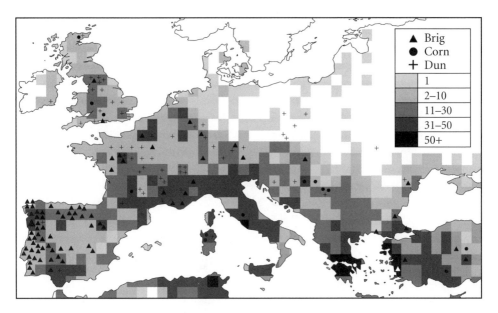

Figure 6.1 Distribution of place-names with Celtic etymologies in ancient Europe, as attested by classical authors (compiled from material in Sims-Williams 2006), showing number of attested Celtic place-names. Symbols in the white area refer to place-names whose exact locations are unknown, but there is enough reason for Sims-Williams to assume that they are/were in the locations indicated on the map

pushes outward in a different direction from the vast Asian continent: the Austronesian peoples and their migrations out of Taiwan across half the world's oceans, the Na-Dene peoples of North America branching off from their Yeniseian cousins in north Central Siberia, and the long uncharted trek of the Roma (Gypsies) from India to Europe.

Argonauts of Two Oceans

Perhaps no other language family demonstrates the value of the comparative method as clearly, or on such a vast scale, as the Austronesian family (figure 6.2), named from Latin *auster* ("south wind") plus Greek *nêso* ("island"). With over 1,200 tongues, it is the world's largest language family in terms of number of languages. A few have huge speaker populations, such as Javanese (76 million speakers) and Indonesian/Malay (40 million mother-tongue speakers, swelling beyond 200 million once you count second-language speakers). Others, like Naman in Vanuatu, are on the verge of dying out, and a few have already become extinct, such as Siraya in Taiwan, Waamwang in New Caledonia, and Moriori from the Chatham Islands east of New Zealand.[10]

The geographical reach of the Austronesian family goes halfway round the world and spans two oceans, the Pacific and the Indian Ocean, reaching from just off the African

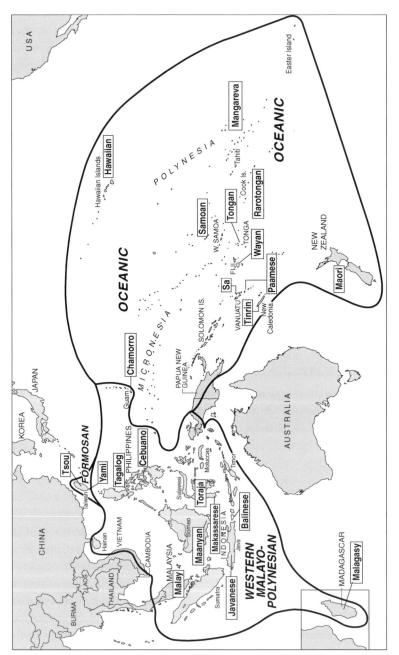

Figure 6.2 Distribution of the Austronesian languages

coast (Madagascar) almost to South America – spanning 240 degrees from west to east. From north to south it extends 75 degrees, from Taiwan to New Zealand. This made it the most extensive of any of the world's language families before European colonial expansion began in the fifteenth century. Its hemispheric span bespeaks a complex, adaptable navigator culture able to conceive and execute immense sea voyages, coupled with on-land agricultural adaptations that replenished the demographic and material base. Wherever they went the Austronesians intermarried with peoples they met, adding new crops and other local adaptations. All this was overseen by complex chiefly societies supporting specialized knowledge in astronomy, seafaring technologies unsurpassed at the time, and genealogical traditions reaching back many centuries.

Unlike most cultural traditions of comparable scale, the Austronesians were an oral culture, except for the recent adoption of literacy in parts of Southeast Asia from Indian and Arabic traditions. Thus linguistic evidence has had to bear most of the burden of working out their complex and dynamic history, although increasingly this has been integrated with material from archaeology, comparative ethnography, and genetics. This makes the Austronesian family a textbook case of how to combine the various disciplines of deep history. The fact that most steps in the Austronesian migrations were into virgin or thinly populated areas has been a great aid to this process, giving unambiguous archaeological datings of first occupations and clear genetic signals.

The stepwise nature of Austronesian migrations often involved leaps followed by centuries-long preparatory phases for the next move, such as those off eastern New Guinea and later in Fiji, during which clusters of diagnostic sound changes could accumulate. This stop–start pattern of expansion makes it much easier to detect successive branchings of a many-generational family tree (see figure 6.3).

Certain groups entered into sustained contact with other languages, taking on loanwords and converging with them structurally in interesting ways. Malagasy, which spent time on the East African coast before bouncing back out to Madagascar, was influenced by speakers of Bantu languages like Swahili. The Chamic languages along the coasts of Vietnam came into contact with a whole range of Southeast Asian languages, developing tone like in Vietnamese. And various groups who settled along the coasts of New Guinea became integrated with groups speaking Papuan languages.

Within Austronesian, then, we have a multigenerational family tree to which the comparative method applies beautifully. Some of its branchings correlate neatly with archaeological dates, while in other parts of the family we can study the messier effects of language contact, backgrounded by the controls that other parts of the family supply. Overall, cognates in most languages of the group are readily recognizable (see table 6.2) as long as we select conservative representatives of each subbranch, and a very large number of terms have now been reconstructed back to proto-Austronesian. Sometimes we have to beware of deceptively similar forms that are in fact loans, like the Malagasy words *hao* and *maso*: these look like they could be authentic Austronesian cognates, but are both loans from Swahili. At other times the meaning has changed a bit and I have put these in round brackets, as with Malagasy *sahiran*, which means "in difficulty" rather than "sick, in pain." The original Austronesian numbers in Chamorro are in square brackets, as they have now been replaced by Spanish ones and are only known from earlier records.

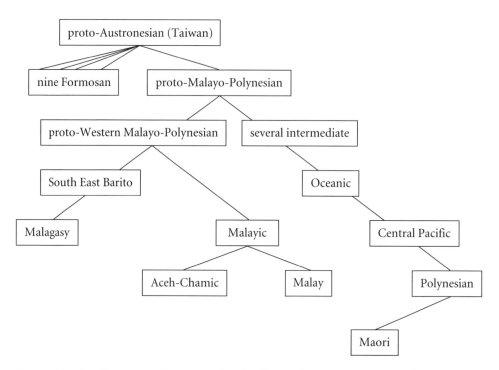

Figure 6.3 Family tree showing various levels of branching as they pertain to languages discussed in the text. To aid visualization, many branches and members have had to be omitted

Table 6.2 Sample vocabulary items across seven modern Austronesian languages, together with the reconstructed proto-Austronesian form. Non-cognate loanwords are in italics.[11]

Gloss	Tsou (Taiwan)	Yami (Taiwan)	Tagalog (Phili.)	Malay	Chamorro (Guam)	Maori (NZ)	Malagasy (Madag.)	proto-Austron.
child/ offspring	oko	anak	anak	anak	*patgon*	tamaiti	anaka	*aLak
louse	keū	kutuʔ	kutuʔ	kutu	hutu	kutu	*hao*	*kutu
breast	nunʔu	ṣuṣuʔ	susuʔ	susu	susu	ū	*nono*	*susu
new	farva	vajuʔ	bagu	baru	*nuebu*	hōu	(vao)	*baqeRuh
path	eroni̇	raraʔan	daʔan	jalan	calan	ara	lalana	*zalan
eye	meō	mata	mata	mata	mata	mata	*maso*	*mata
sick/pain	maʔeoŋo	miŋən	sakit	sakit	sageʔ	*māuiui*	(sahiran)	*sakit
three	turu	tiluʔ,atlo	tatlo	tiga	tulo	toru	telo	*telu
five	rimo	lima	lima	lima	lima	rima	dimi	*lima
ten	maski̇	sapuluʔ	sampuʔ	səpuluh	*manot*	ŋahuru	folo	*sapuLuʔ

The deepest-level branchings of the Austronesian family tree clearly identify Taiwan (Formosa) as the homeland, since nine out of ten primary branches of the tree are only found there,[12] and even the tenth branch (Malayo-Polynesian) is represented by Yami on islands off the Taiwanese coast that are presumed to be the jumping-off point for subsequent expansion. In other words, over 90 percent of the deep lineage diversity of a family that covers a huge part of the world's surface is concentrated on the small island of Taiwan. (Chinese varieties arrived much later.) Despite their key role for understanding Austronesian history, it is still the case that we know far less about the complex indigenous languages of Taiwan than we do about the languages of Polynesia, for example. Archaeological evidence linking early Taiwanese cultures to those of the adjoining mainland suggests that Austronesian languages were probably once spoken there as well, and indeed that the Chinese mainland may have been their ultimate point of origin. But no trace of languages from that period have survived on the mainland or left any clear attestation.

From Taiwan, just one adventurous group moved south into the northern Philippines, reaching the halfway Batanes islands more than 4,000 years ago, as revealed by carbon dates on distinctive occupation sites there.[13] All 1,200 Austronesian languages outside Taiwan descend from this single branch, generally called Malayo-Polynesian. Some of them stayed put, ultimately giving rise to large languages like Tagalog and Cebuano, each with tens of millions of speakers, as well as the 200 or so other languages of the Philippines.

One branch of Austronesian speakers then moved west across to Borneo. From Southeast Borneo a daughter group would set out, millennia later, to cross the Indian Ocean, ultimately reaching Madagascar off the African coast and engendering Malagasy. In Borneo, southeast Barito languages like Maanyan share a number of distinctive characteristics with Malagasy.[14] A distinctive sound change shared between Malagasy and the Barito languages is l > d: *kulit* ("skin") becomes *kudit* in Maanyan and *hoditra* in Malagasy, while *lima* ("five") becomes Maanyan *dime* and Malagasy *dimy*. Lexical innovations include the replacement of the original Austronesian word *miɲak* for "oil" with a new word reaching us today as *ilau* (Maanyan) or *ilo* (Malagasy). These linguistic arguments for placing Malagasy as a far-flung offshoot of the Southeast Barito languages have recently been confirmed by genetic work showing that y-chromosomal haplogroup markers in the Madagascan population match those in the Borneo populations of Banjarmasin and Kota Kinabalu.[15]

When did this migration across the Indian Ocean occur? An earliest possible date is set as the seventh century AD by the presence of Sanskrit loanwords filtered through Malay; this is when the Indian-influenced Malay state of Srivijaya was established in South Sumatra.[16] And archaeological excavations on Madagascar suggest there was no presence there before the eighth century AD. What seems most likely, given the almost equal mixture of Southeast Asian and African genetic lineages in the Madagascan population, and the presence of various Swahili and other Bantu-derived features in the grammar and vocabulary, is that the Austronesians did not go directly to Madagascar but first spent some time on the East African coast. There they would have intermarried with Bantu groups and developed a hybrid Austronesian-Bantu culture before heading back east to Madagascar.

Taking our main story back up in the Philippines, one group of languages fanned out through the Indonesian archipelago, while another branch made its way down through the Moluccas to the northern coast of New Guinea. Here it developed into the Oceanic branch, which is the common ancestor of all the languages of the Pacific Ocean as well as many along the New Guinea coasts.

During its New Guinea phase, between 1350 and 750 BC, groups living in the Bismarck Archipelago developed a distinctive new style of pottery known as Lapita Pottery.[17] Various scholars have suggested that this New Guinea pause was a necessary step in putting together the package of cultural attributes they would need for their move out into the near Pacific: domestic animals and wayfinding techniques, and durable tools, pots, and textiles. New names for many of these objects enter the lower reaches of the Oceanic branch at this point, and are readily correlated with datable objects in the archaeological record.

Proto-Oceanic speakers also intermarried with Papuan peoples, picking up a number of distinctive genes, which they took with them on their further travels – which together with genetic markers in rats and mice hitching rides in their boats provide a cross-species check on colonization genealogies. From there a branch hopped down through the Solomon Islands. From here one branch circled back up into Micronesia, a second struck south through Vanuatu to New Caledonia, and a third headed further out into the Pacific, to Fiji. Once they had left the Solomons they moved into what is generally believed to have been uninhabited territory. This makes it straightforward to track their arrivals, island by island, through the very distinctive patterns of occupation marked by shards of Lapita pottery.

The Austronesian express train, as dated by these means, is known to have reached Fiji by around 1000 BC. There it took another pause, with the striking consequence that the three languages of the small Fijian archipelago (Rotuman, West Fijian, and East Fijian) differ more among themselves than do all the languages of Polynesia. From the fact that East Fijian groups with the Polynesian languages, as against the other Fijian languages, we know that it was from East Fijian-speaking areas that the Polynesian explorers cast off out into the far Pacific. This Fijian interlude enabled the development of the double-outrigger canoe without which the daring long-distance voyages would have been impossible. In these legendary vessels the Polynesians were to discover virtually every inhabitable piece of land across that vast ocean – Samoa and Tonga, around 800 BC, Hawaii (AD 500), Easter Island (AD 800) and New Zealand (around AD 1000), and numerous other islands dotted through the Pacific.

This Oceanic phase has been reconstructed in minute detail, thanks to collaboration with scholars across many other disciplines – including boat-building, animal genetics, and astronomy, as well as the usual big four of linguistics, genetics, archaeology, and anthropology. The enterprise has been assisted by the high quality of linguistic and ethnographic documentation undertaken from the time of the nineteenth century missionaries on. We now have a detailed reconstruction of proto-Oceanic terminologies for every aspect of their known world, from canoe parts to fish traps, from stars to detailed plant names, including how proto-Oceanic speakers named each of the eight recognized growth phrases of the coconut tree.

This has been based on a pioneering new method of "lexical reconstruction," which integrates the reconstruction of word forms, by linguistic methods, with inferences about the items they stood for in the material world, obtained by comparative ethnography, e.g. by comparing the shapes of fishhooks or the design of boats. Here I will give you just a small taste of the level of detail that this approach makes possible.

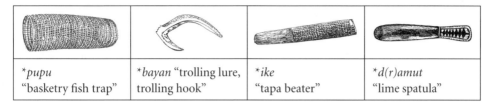

pupu "basketry fish trap"	*bayan* "trolling lure, trolling hook"	*ike* "tapa beater"	*d(r)amut* "lime spatula"

Figure 6.4   Four reconstructed named items of proto-Oceanic material culture[18]

Figure 6.4 illustrates four items of proto-Oceanic material culture along with their reconstructed names. The reconstruction of the items themselves is a job for comparative ethnography – by comparing detailed records of the relevant items in attested historical cultures – and archaeology, to the extent that they appear preserved in the archaeological record. Comparisons of material culture inventories are thus necessary to determine exactly how each item looked and was made.

The reconstruction of the names, however, is a job for historical linguistics. It draws on the comparative method to deduce the original form of the name, through comparison of descendant forms, and also to deduce how far up the tree the form goes by seeing which languages it appears in: in general it will be imputed to the highest node of the tree below which a regular reflex appears in two different branches.

Consider how this logic applies to the word *taba* ("bark cloth"), whose earliest appearance as a word with this meaning can be reconstructed for proto-Central Pacific. This implies that the use of this particular name for bark cloth was an innovation in the early Fijian speech community preceding their leap into the outer Pacific. However, bark cloth as an object is not just used for clothing across Oceania, but is also attested in Indonesia. And this widespread early use of the object by Austronesians is logically implied by the fact that *ike* ("tapa beater") goes back beyond proto-Oceanic to proto-Malayo-Polynesian: a cognate word *ike* ("tapa-beating mallet") is recorded for the Toraja language of Sulawesi in Indonesia. Comparative ethnographic studies indicate that the technology of making bark cloth, from a range of fig and paper mulberry-tree species (*Broussonetia*, *Artocarpus*, and *Ficus*), originates in Southeast Asia and was probably brought from the Philippines.

But, although the Austronesians may have made bark cloth well before they reached the Pacific, the name *taba* itself can only be reconstructed for it as far back as proto-Central Pacific, since reflexes with a sufficiently close meaning are confined to the languages of Fiji and Polynesia (see table 6.3). A couple of Solomon Islands reflexes have a possibly related meaning, suggesting that the word originally meant "limb, leaf, frond," later shifting to "skin, bark" in the Fijian languages, and then taking on the meaning "bark cloth" in the Polynesian languages.

The application of the comparative method to the Austronesian family has been so successful that in many ways we know far more about its prehistory than we do for Indo-European, despite the lack of substantial ancient sources. Our chronologies are far more certain and, unlike with Indo-European, there is complete agreement on where the original homeland was. Many specific factors have contributed to giving Austronesian

Table 6.3   Reflexes of proto-Central Pacific *taba* ("bark")[19]

Group	Language	Form	Meaning
Proto-Central Pacific	Wayan (West Fijian)	taba	skin, bark
Polynesian	Tongan	tapa	edge, rim, border (older meaning: bark cloth, not printed or stained)
	Samoan	tapa	white border of colored bark-cloth sheet
	Mangareva	tapa	bark cloth
	Rarotongan	tapa	cloth made from inner bark of certain trees
	Hawaiian	kapa	bark cloth

comparative linguistics a dream run: the huge number of witness languages, the stepwise nature of Austronesian expansion and the much clearer archaeological footprints that accompany virgin settlement, the conservation of millennially old customs and technologies in many speech communities, and the astute contributions of some brilliant scholars. Overall, the Austronesian languages show us just how much of the deep past can be recovered through the patient and principled comparison of modern languages, judiciously linked to the findings of other disciplines.

Long-Lost Subarctic Cousins

Imperfect as is our knowledge [of American languages] . . . it suffices to discover the following remarkable fact. Arranging them under the radical ones to which they may be palpably traced, and doing the same by those of the red men of Asia, there will be found probably twenty in America, for one in Asia, of these radical languages.

(Jefferson 1787, cited in Golla 2005:3)

[It] strikes me as intrinsically highly probable . . . that the linguistic differentiation of aboriginal America developed only in small part (in its latest stages) in the New World, [and] that the Asiatic (possibly also South Sea) immigrants who peopled the American continent were at the earliest period of occupation already differentiated into speakers of several genetically unrelated stocks. This would make it practically imperative to assume that the peopling of the Americas was not a single historical process but a series of movements of linguistically unrelated peoples, possibly from different directions and certainly at very different times.

(Sapir 1949b [1916]:454–5)

These quotes from Thomas Jefferson and Edward Sapir show how long people have been aware of a still-unsolved puzzle about the Americas. If the American continent has been settled for less time than any other, why does it contain so many language families – an estimate by Lyle Campbell suggests 150 genetic groupings for the Americas, compared to

37 for Eurasia and 20 for Africa. Only Sahul (New Guinea plus Australia) comes close with 85–90 groupings. But Sahul is known to have been settled 45,000–60,000 years ago, instead of the roughly 11,000–13,000 range for the generally accepted earliest dates for the Americas. And it had two distinct entry routes – one via Timor and a second via the Moluccas. Further, Sahul never had access blocked by massive barriers of ice such as the Bering Strait has held for much of its existence.

Have scholars in the Americas simply applied a more grudging yardstick that holds them back from grouping languages into larger families? That arch-lumper Joseph Greenberg, for example, fitted them all into just three groups – Eskimo-Aleut, Na-Dene, and "Amerind." This would flip the Americas into being the least diverse continent of all, but Greenberg's view has been almost universally rejected. Even if Campbell's figure of 150 lineages does err on the conservative side for language relatedness, and hence on the generous side for the number of distinct genetic groupings, a three-digit figure does not seem exaggerated when we confront the mind-blowing levels of diversity found among Amerindian languages. So most scholars maintain we are dealing with a real empirical problem, not just the artifact of a contingent of "splitters."

One explanation for the Jefferson–Sapir conundrum would be to claim that languages diversify faster in the Americas. But this position has no empirical support, and does not hold up when tested against specific language families like Mayan or Mixe-Zoquean, for which we have datable ancient written forms.

A second explanation would be that archaeologists have simply been too conservative about dating human occupation. Instead of believing the recent occupation dates they keep citing, should we instead listen to what language diversity is telling us, and open our minds to far earlier human migrations across the Bering Strait? After all, could there not be undiscovered evidence lying underwater along the Pacific coasts, from periods when the sea level was lower, or perhaps miraculously preserved somewhere under the Amazon forests? But this argument, too, is essentially an expression of faith and has yet to be bolstered by significant archaeological finds.

A third explanation would be along the lines ventured by Sapir: that a good part of the diversity had already been pre-evolved in Asia, where human occupation is much older. This explanation has the advantage of not forcing us to postulate outlandishly accelerated rates of diversification on one continent, or appeal to the Holy Grail of yet-to-be-found ancient datings. But it then runs against another problem. We would have to postulate a steady stream of immigrant groups – around one language family per hundred years on the maximally "exogenist"[20] view, where no Amerindian families differentiated in situ, but slowing down to almost plausible rates the more we are "endogenists" attributing a greater proportion of lineage diversity to post-arrival changes. Exogenist positions like Sapir's throw down the gauntlet to historical linguistics: can rigorous applications of the comparative method find evidence for language families that straddle the Americas and Asia? Note also that, since the immigration to the Americas is supposed to have involved such a rapid inpouring of different groups, we should then find connections "all the way down," not just in the northern regions.

Sapir himself spent much time on this problem, scouring the Sino-Tibetan languages for evidence connecting them to Athabaskan, although his evidence was unconvincing:

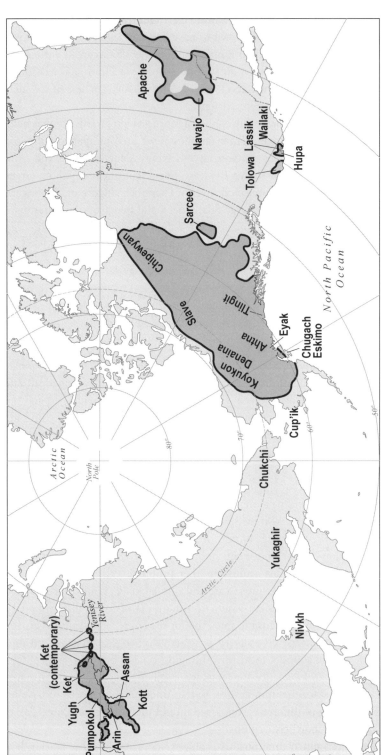

Figure 6.5 Distribution of the Yeniseian languages in Siberia, and the Na-Dene languages in North America

we now know how easily languages can develop tonal systems, making the common possession of tones between the two families an unconvincing argument. Although there have been many more proposals linking American and Asian language families, none bar the obvious and rather recent links of the Eskimo-Aleut languages across the Bering Strait have been convincing.

Recently, however, a much more plausible proposal has been put together by Edward Vajda, which goes a long way toward establishing a connection between the Na-Dene languages and the Yeniseian languages of Central Siberia (see figure 6.5). Na-Dene itself is a grouping that has taken much careful research to put together over the last century. We have already seen how evidence from the last speakers of the "missing link" language Eyak has helped chain the Athabaskan languages onto Tlingit. Although the Na-Dene family is primarily located in inland Alaska and Canada, groups like the Navajo and Apache have moved far down to the US southwest, while other groups moved to parts of northern California and Oregon as mentioned in chapter 5.

Let us move on to the Na-Dene family's remote Siberian cousins: all the Yeniseian languages except Ket have become extinct. As the only hunter-gatherers in north Asia they came under the strongest assimilatory pressures of all Siberian peoples. Even for Ket (see figure 6.6) there are only a few dozen fluent speakers, all middle-aged or older. For several languages of the group, we have to rely on eighteenth- and nineteenth-century records, such as those made in the Pallas expedition whose sponsorship by Catherine the Great was mentioned in chapter 2.

Ket itself is one of the most difficult languages on earth. Its structure is only now beginning to be adequately described after several generations of Ketological grapplings, and is right up there in the

Figure 6.6 A Ket shaman, photographed in 1967 by linguist Heinrich Werner[21]

complexity stakes with Navajo. Interestingly it shares many unusual typological features with Navajo and the other Athabaskan languages. Most distinctive is its shishkebab-like prefixing structure, interspersing grammatical and lexical information, with different positions for pronoun prefixes according to the verb. And, again like Navajo, it has alternate roots for animate and inanimate entities, such as Ket *tn* and Kott *te:n* ("animate lies down"), strikingly like proto-Athabaskan *ten*, with its Navajo reflex *tę* ("animate lies down").

Scores of lexical cognates between the Yeniseian languages and Na-Dene have now been assembled – I mentioned the role of Eyak in bridging some of these in the last chapter. There are even shape-classifying elements in Ket verbs, like *n-* ("round, around"), *d-* ("long, along"), and *hw-* ("area, flat surface"), which find echoes in some Athabaskan languages: Ahtna[22] has *n-* ("round, ropelike objects"), *d-* ("wooden object"), *ko-* ("space, time, large area"), and Navajo also has an "areal object" prefix *ho-*.

Although the evidence for a connection between the Yeniseian languages and Na-Dene has not yet reached the point of convincing all linguists, it is rapidly shaping up. By demonstrating a link across the Bering Strait, it supplies a second example (after Eskimo-Aleut) of an Amerindian language family with its roots in Asia.

The next step will be to link this to archaeological dates for assemblages matching the reconstructed vocabulary of proto-Dene-Yeniseic. We already have a good idea of what the proto-culture was like, in material terms. They used snow-sleds and canoes – shared vocabulary is reconstructable right down to the names of some sled and canoe parts – and they made widespread use of birch bark, conifer resin, and possibly snowshoes as well. Birch-bark technology, used by both Yeniseian and Athabaskan groups for teepees, boats, and dishes, is particularly important because this bark is virtually waterproof and is the only wood that can be lit while wet – just wipe it off and it's ready to burn. We also have some insights into ancient Dene-Yeniseic culture, in particular the importance of shamanic singing and shamanism, since cognate words for these are also found in both Siberian and American branches.

Archaeologists' estimates of when the ancestors of the Athabaskans arrived in Alaska range from a late-end 4,500 years ago (if correlated with the Taye Lake Phase of the so-called Northern Archaic Tradition)[23] to earlier estimates of 7,000–9,000 years ago for theories less correlated with archaeological phases. But, even taking the latest of these dates, 4,500 years ago gives us a significant foothold on the Jefferson–Sapir problem. The two northernmost American families (Eskimo-Aleut and Dene-Yeniseic), whose geographical position implies they are the most recent arrivals, between them take up at least the last 4,500 years of immigration into the Americas. If we cannot date the lower contents of the American bottle, at least we are moving toward a date for when the Na-Dene cork was put in.

Any further links that may be attempted between other Amerindian families and languages in Eurasia would have to be older than these, and correspondingly more difficult to demonstrate because of the steady decay of linguistic traces. This makes it unlikely that more than one or two other Amerindian families could ever be demonstrated to have Asian relatives within the time-band of what is reconstructable – leaving over 95 percent of the other Amerindian families without demonstrable Asian connections. The level of diversity throughout the rest of the American continent is left as a bigger mystery than ever – although my own inclination is to take seriously the linguistic evidence for a much greater time-depth of human occupation than archaeologists have yet been able to demonstrate.

But all of this will depend on fragile evidence equally at risk on both sides of the Bering Strait. As Ed Vajda[24] has put it: "Who would have thought that the ancient words Native American and Native Siberian boarding school children were punished for speaking aloud just a few decades ago would prove to wield a power vast enough to unite two continents?"

Lungo Drom: the Long Road

Syr te ryśół pałé pe dasavé droma,	*Jak powrócić na takie drogi,*	How to turn back to those roads
kaj dźidźónys chargá romá?	*gdzie żyli dawno Cyganie*	which the Gypsies once lived along?
Dźivno jamaró isýz dźiipén – paćén!	*Dziwne nasze było życie – wierzcie!*	Strange was our life – believe me!
. . .	. . .	. . .
Dakicý berśá ándre véš kałó dźidźónys romá,	*Tyle lat w lesie czarnym żyli Cyganie,*	So many years the Gypsies lived in the dark forests,
tradénys pe baré i tykné dromá.	*jeżdzili po wielkich i małych drogach.*	travelling along the roads and byways,
Vymarénys kałé, sýva grajá cherénca gilá apré bará.	*Wybijały czarne, siwe konie nogami pieśni po kamieniach.*	the hooves of their black, grey horses beating out songs on the roadstones.

(Papusza – Bronisława Wajs)[25]

Perhaps the most far-reaching use of loanwords to deduce the history and geographical provenance of a whole people comes from studies of Romani, the language of the people once called Gypsies, and now generally called Roma in English – I will return to the origins of this word below. Linguistic evidence from the words they have picked up in their travels has been crucial in mapping the long, slow road they followed from India to Europe (see figure 6.7).

The fate of the Roma has often seemed parallel to that of the Jews, both suffering as stigmatized outsiders of non-European origin. But the Roma differ from the Jews in not being a "people of the book" who zealously maintain a detailed written account of their earliest wanderings and banishments. As a result, their history has often been the subject of ill-informed speculation – such as that implied by the name "Gypsies," a corruption of the word "Egyptian," reflecting the erroneous old belief that they came from Egypt.[26] But evidence from several layers of loanwords in their language has allowed scholars to piece together the many way stations on their travels over two millennia – work that is now largely being corroborated by genetic studies – and to line these up against the often-conflicting shreds of historical evidence.

Before continuing I should emphasize that special problems of research are posed by the huge spectrum of Romani varieties, with its widely differing forms spoken in just about every European country. If we are talking about the pre-European phases of their migration we need to check that we are employing evidence from "common Romani" by ensuring that the terms are found right across these many varieties.

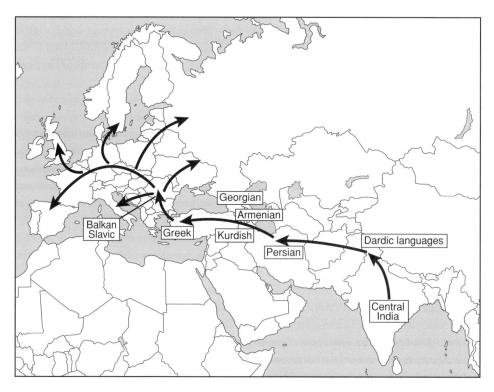

Figure 6.7   The Roma migrations from India to Europe

Wherever the Roma have gone, their language has been tugged in two opposing directions – pulled one way by convergence with the language of surrounding groups, resulting in many intimate grammatical borrowings, and pushed the other way by fostering divergent vocabulary so as to keep the language unintelligible to outsiders. Place-names, for example, regularly have special Romani versions: Rome is *u baro rašaj* ("the big priest"), and Switzerland is *kiralengro them* ("cheese country"). At the same time, there has been no equivalent of Hebrew and the Jewish scriptural tradition to serve as a point of convergence and common linguistic reference for the separated groups. Nonetheless, around one thousand lexical roots are shared across enough Romani varieties that we can assign them to a common ancestral lexicon.

Returning to the language's geographical origins in India, let us first consider the origins of their preferred name *Rom* for a member of their ethnic group. *Roma* is the plural form, and *Romani* or *Romani čhib* their name for their language. There are other related groups with similar names – *Dom* in the Middle East, who speak Domari,[27] and *Lom* in Armenia, who have a special vocabulary called *Lomavren*. All these terms are related to a caste-name in India: *Dom*, a caste of musicians, metalworkers, and sweepers who speak various Indo-Aryan languages according to where they live.

There is ample evidence that Romani is, in essence, an Indo-Aryan language of India, although it has been overlaid and reshaped again and again through contact with a host of other languages. Around 650 roots from the shared Romani lexicon have identifiable Indic origins. We can be even more precise about their geographical roots, since there is evidence that they originated in Central India, then moved north to live among speakers of Dardic languages in the northwest of the subcontinent, before moving westward out of India altogether. In support of their Central Indian origins are a number of changes specific to the Central Indian languages. One is the realization of the old cluster *kṣ* as *kkh* rather than the *cch* found elsewhere in India: consider Sanskrit *akṣi* ("eye"), which comes out as *jakh* in Romani (from middle Indo-Aryan *akkhi*). Another is the shape of the nominalizing suffix *-ipen*, as in *sastipen* ("health"). This is descended from the ancient Indic suffix *-itvana*: this became *-ittan* to the north and south of the Central Indian area, but in the Central region became *-ippan*, a form from which *-ipen* derives by regular changes.

Other features of Romani, however, can best be explained by appealing to developments that took place in the Dardic subgroup of Indo-Aryan, spoken in Kashmir and northern Pakistan. One such development concerns the past inflections of verbs: the Dardic languages developed a new way of marking the past tense by adding reduced pronouns to the past participle, e.g. *kerdo-jo-me* ("done by me") for "I did," and *kerdo-jo-se* ("done by him/her") for "he/she did." Modern Romani forms like *kerdjom* ("I did") and *kerdjas* ("(s)he did") derive from these innovative Dardic structures.

From Northern India, the Roma's next move was to an Iranian-speaking region, as indicated by the seventy or so Persian and Kurdish loanwords. Significantly, there are no Arabic loans,[28] suggesting that the ancestors of the Roma had already left Persia before the

Table 6.4 Vocabulary strata in the common Romani lexicon[29]

Stratum	Romani word(s)	Source
Indic	*trin* "three"	Skt *trīni*
	pandž "five"	Skt *pañča*
	štar "four"	Skt *čatvāras*
Persia (70 Persian or Kurdish)	*ámbrol* "pear"	Persian *amrūd*
	avgin "honey"	Persian *angubīn*
	xulaj "lord"	Persian, Kurdish *xuda/xula*
	xer "donkey"	Persian *xar*
	bi- "without"	Persian *bī*
	káko "uncle"	Kurdish *kak-*
Southern Caucasus (40 Armenian)	*bov* "oven"	Armenian *bov*
	grast "horse"	Armenian *grast*
	khilav "plum"	Georgian *khliavi*
	orde "here"	Ossetian *orde*
Anatolia (200 Greek)	*foro* "town"	Greek *fóros* "market"
	drom "road"	Greek *drómos* "road"
	kurko "week"	Greek *kyriakí* "Sunday"
	papus "grandfather"	Greek *pappús* "grandfather"
	efta "seven"	Greek *epta* "seven"
Balkans	*dosta* "enough"	Macedonian, Serbian, Croatian *dost* "enough"

Muslim conquest. Following this was a lengthy period in Anatolia, which must have been at a time when it was still a Greek-speaking part of the Byzantine Empire, and hence before it was conquered by the Seljuk Turks. We conclude this because only the Turkish varieties of Romani have Turkish loanwords, these being totally absent from all European varieties. Extensive loans in the domains of metalworking and horse-and-wagon-based nomadism entered the language from Greek and Kurdish during this Anatolian period. There are also some loanwords from languages of the southern Caucasus, which has led some scholars to argue for a southern Caucasian stopover. It is more likely, however, that these entered Romani during its Anatolian period, since the multilingual nature of Byzantine Anatolia would have given ample opportunity for Roma to have contact with Armenian, Georgian, and Ossetian speakers.

There may have been one final staging post in the shared history of the Roma, in the Balkans, before their breakup into many local European groups each picking up loanwords not shared with other Romani dialects. A few words with Balkan Slavic etymologies are found throughout all European Romani varieties, and bespeak a shared Balkan period: examples are the words for "enough" (*dosta*), and "bed" (*vodros*).

From the Balkans on there is no further European donor language whose loanwords show up in all modern varieties, in the way that each earlier sojourn picked up a linguistic inheritance that would be passed on to all subsequent descendants. Each regional variant has its own portfolio of local loanwords – *vreme* ("weather") from Bulgarian among the Bulgarian Roma, *ježo* ("hedgehog") from Polish among Polish Roma, *thalasa* ("sea") from Greek among Greek Roma. These words – which can be inferred as recent and localized by their absence from other Roma varieties – tell of a scattering of Roma tribes across Europe in many different directions, following the disruptive medieval wars in the Balkans. At that point begin the individual stories of particular Romani varieties, each a final but localized chapter in the narrative of the Roma people's long travels through time and space that the linguistic evidence has allowed us to piece together.

Further reading

Good discussions of the linguistic and other evidence for Bantu prehistory can be found in Ehret (1998), Vansina (1990). Much of the material on the Na-Dene connection to Yeniseian is still unpublished but Vajda (2008) gives a good summary. An interdisciplinary collection on the prehistory of maize in the Americas is Staller et al. (2006). Linguistic evidence for the Roma migrations is in an unpublished paper by Kaufmann (1973), but the most authoritative reference is Matras (2002), along with the online resource "The Romani language – an interactive journey," available at www.llc.manchester.ac.uk/Research/Projects/romani. On genetic links of the Roma to southern India see Kivisild et al. (2003); Fonseca (1996) is an excellent ethnography-cum-travelogue. There is an abundance of books on Austronesian prehistory – Bellwood et al. (1995) is particularly good. Two excellent volumes, edited by Adelaar and Himmelmann (2005) and Lynch et al. (2002), give detailed information about the western and eastern sides of the Austronesian world respectively, while Kirch and Green (2001) contains a detailed synthesis of Polynesian cultural history. The multi-volume collection edited by Ross et al. (1998, 2003) contains detailed reconstructions of proto-Oceanic vocabulary.

7

Keys to Decipherment: How Living Languages Can Unlock Forgotten Scripts

Un funud fach cyn'r elo'r haul l'w orwel,	A moment before the sun sets
Un funud fwyn cyn delo'r hwyr l'w hynt	A moment before night takes over from day
I gofio am y pethau anghofiedig	To remember the unforgettable things,
Ar goll yn awr yn llwch yr amser gynt.	Now lost in the dust of past times.
Camp a chelfyddyd y cenhedloedd cynnar,	The wonder and culture of early nations,
Anheddau bychain a neuaddau mawr,	Small habitations and large arenas,
Y chwedlau cain a chwalwyd ers canrifoedd,	The elegant fables destroyed centuries ago,
Y Duwiau na wyr neb amdanynt 'nawr.	And Gods long bereft of their followers.
Mynych ym mrig yr hwyr, a mi yn unig,	These come to me alone at the end of days,
Daw hiraeth am eich 'nabod chwi bob un.	And loss and longing from knowing you all.
A oes a'ch deil o hyd mewn cof a chalon,	Will you always have covenant in memory and heart
Hen bethau angofiedig teulu dyn?	Old things unforgettable to the family of man?

(Waldo Williams)[1]

So far we have been focusing on evidence from spoken languages and the reconstructions made from them. But another resource for understanding the past comes from the many writings, often still undeciphered, that have come down to us from ancient times. Once a culture adopts writing, the disappearance of speech no longer needs to mean the death of a language, and the loss of an oral tradition does not delete this knowledge for all time.

Unlike the reconstructions I talked about in the last couple of chapters, these texts directly represent the reality of their time, with all its detailed naming of kings, gods, and laws. They are datable thanks to the archaeological context they occur in, or even more precisely if they give actual dates themselves. By preserving long passages, they can give us more idea of how the language's syntax works than we get from comparative reconstruction. And they are often also a great read in their own right.

Ancient written languages sometimes provide a check on what the comparative method reconstructs. A celebrated example is the use of deciphered Hittite inscriptions to confirm Ferdinand de Saussure's hypothesis about Indo-European laryngeals. De Saussure had postulated these – under the obscure term "sonant coefficients" – to account for certain abstract congruities of patterning in ancient Indo-European vowel systems, even though no language then known had sounds corresponding to them. Boldly, he wrote them into his reconstructions of proto-Indo-European, despite the lack of direct attestation. Later, when Bedřich Hrozný deciphered the Hittite inscriptions during World War I (see p. 81), he discovered a symbol directly representing one of these laryngeals, confirming Saussure's proposal. A previously unknown language thus gave direct evidence for the sounds that De Saussure had reconstructed on the rather abstract grounds of symmetrical patterning.

Outwitting the Conquering Barbarians

Although conquerors have usually been intent on wiping out every trace of the cultures they destroy, they sometimes overlook concealed written records, which succeed in preserving the history the conquerors want to erase. Take the extinct Tangut language of the once-prosperous Buddhist empire in Central Asia known to the Chinese as Xīxià, and to the Tangut themselves as *phiow-bjij-lhjij-lhjij* ("The Great State of White and Lofty," see figures 7.1 and 7.2). This is a case where what we now know is due to bilingual inscriptions (e.g. Buddhist texts with parallel translations) rather than the evidence of a surviving descendant language.

Close to the mountains of Tibet, the Xīxià empire adopted Buddhism from its Tibetan and Chinese neighbors. But to its north lay the marauding Mongolian hordes of Genghis Khan. During his lifetime, we know that Tangut was one of the six tongues in which the Mongols' decrees were issued. But it ceased to be spoken in the years after the Tangut empire was destroyed by Genghis Khan.

Figures 7.1 and 7.2　Tangut stupa at the northwest corner of the Khara-Koto site[2] (left), and the Tangut title of the ancient Xīxià phonology book Ge_ ləu (*"The Homophones,"* right), called 同音 *Tóngyīn* (*"Homophones"*) in Chinese[3]

The rich literary tradition of Tangut, we now know, included Buddhist scriptures and original secular works. It even included treatises on phonology like *The Homophones*, whose title is shown in figure 7.2. First published in 1125 with a definitive revised reprint in 1187, it would prove to be a godsend to subsequent decipherers because of the direct information it gives about Tangut phonology.

This Central Asian literary patrimony was believed lost to all time until, in 1908, the Imperial Russian Geographic Society sent Colonel Pyotr Kuzmich Kozlov on a botanical expedition to Sichuan. On his travels he discovered a large collection of Tangut manuscripts hidden inside a stupa in the old city of Khara-Koto, on the bank of a dry riverbed. In the century since, most of these works have been transcribed and translated successfully, giving historians an inside picture of the empire, and linguists a rich set of texts to understand how this ancient Tibeto-Burmese language functioned grammatically. Interestingly, although Tangut writing looks rather like Chinese script, later work was to show that, unlike Chinese characters, Tangut characters are componential assemblages of sound-symbolizing strokes, which entirely lack a pictographic basis.

The prudence and foresight of the Buddhist monks who concealed these documents – aided by the crisp desert air of Central Asia – have ensured that we have a vivid and detailed record of their kingdom, culture, and language, which we would be almost completely ignorant about today were it not for these old records. But such cases are unusual, and many obstacles stand in the way of deciphering written texts from the past.

Dying a Second Death

> Our work together began with his somewhat paradoxical caution that to read a Makassarese
> sentence in *lontaraq beru* or *jangang-jangang* script, one first had to know what it said.
> (William Cummings, commenting on his language teacher,
> Djohan Daeng Salengke, in Cummings 2002:xii)

Although writing is in principle capable of preserving language material after the passing of its last speakers, the written records themselves are always vulnerable to a second death through physical destruction, misplacement, or decay. Stone inscriptions are eroded, oracle bone engravings are ground up for Chinese medicine, manuscripts are burned, eaten through by mice, or decomposed, and materials are displaced or recycled. The clay tablets that brought to our attention the previously unknown Ugaritic language, vital for our understanding of Semitic and of some aspects of Biblical interpretation, were only unearthed in 1928 when an Alawite peasant in Syria accidentally opened an old tomb while ploughing his field. It is certain that many written records – probably including dozens of completely unknown ancient languages[4] – have been irretrievably lost.

We now take cheap paper for granted. But in early Christian times a single folio of parchment – a sheet folded into four pages – required the skin of an entire sheep. This would have necessitated the slaughter of around 90 sheep for a single copy of the book you are holding in your hands. Even at its wealthiest, the Church could not always afford enough parchment for all the scribes busily copying manuscripts. We know this from complaints about lack of parchment that some scribes grouchily wrote into the margins of their manuscripts. So we can understand why cash-strapped monastic copyists often erased uninterpretable old materials and rewrote over the top of them. This gave rise to palimpsests, where the original writing (perhaps in another language) is just discernible under a more recent layer. Sometimes these faint overwritten marks are the only ghostly record of an ancient written language, as in the case of Caucasian Albanian, a story we will take up later in this chapter.

In the last couple of paragraphs I have been focusing on the physical integrity of ancient written materials. But we should also not forget the importance of culture in transmitting the knowledge of how to read and interpret them. Given the imperfections of many writing systems, reading traditions are even more fragile than spoken ones, since they involve a sustained interplay of oral transmission with the curation and study of written texts.

In a minority of cases, the supporting culture has maintained an unbroken millennial thread of reading and exegesis, as with the Hebrew, Coptic, Sanskrit, and Chinese traditions of reading, studying, and writing comments upon holy scriptures or other types of classical writing.

But it is all too easy for such traditions to be disrupted. Take the Makassarese script of Sulawesi, written on leaves of the Lontar palm and thus known as Lontara.[5] In this script only the first CV (Consonant + Vowel) of each syllable is represented, and there are no spaces between words. The writing system simply leaves out any consonant "coda" closing the syllable. This is not as bad as it sounds, since syllables only have three possible codas: zero (as in *ma*), an unspecified stop whose articulation varies with what follows but comes out as a glottal stop at the end of the word, and an unspecified nasal whose articulation also depends on what follows, but comes out as *ng* at the end of a word. This means that ⟨⟩ (KA) can be read *ka*, *kang*, and *ka?*, and that a sequence spelled KA KA (⟨⟩ ⟨⟩) can be read variously as *kaka*, *kakang*, *kaka?*, *kakka*, *kakkang*, *kakka?*, *kangka*, *kangkang*, and *kangka?*. To give a more realistic example, a sequence like ⟨⟩, transliteratable as BA LA DA TO KA, can be read either as *balla? datoka* ("the Chinese temple") or as *balanda tokka?* ("the bald Dutchman"). This is in addition to 241 other readings (i.e. 3^5 minus 2), which are mostly nonsensical but phonologically possible.

An important factor in maintaining correct readings of Lontar manuscripts was thus oral transmission from one generation of readers to the next, supplementing the written representation with remembered pronunciations. This made accurate reading a hybrid of memorization and reading off the page: "only by knowing the subject of the sentence can it be read. According to some Makassarese, the written script only 'becomes' Makassarese when it is spoken aloud."[6] But younger Makassarese now mainly read and write in Indonesian, and when Makassarese is written, it is now done with the Roman script. With the passing of this reading tradition, our ability to give definitive readings to the considerable body of Lontara manuscripts – which chronicles six centuries of the history of one of Southeast Asia's preeminent maritime powers – has been severely curtailed. So "last readers" are a category not much less important than "last speakers."

Once a tradition of reading disappears – especially if it does so before there has been any bilingual commentary or other documentation – we need to painfully reconstitute this knowledge from the most meager of surviving clues, cracking these abandoned codes through decipherment, one of the most difficult pieces of detective work humans ever undertake.

Living languages can help us in that process. These languages themselves are often obscure or endangered. Many peoples who were once in command of powerful nation states, possessing their own tradition of monumental or commercial inscriptions, have seen their fortunes decline to the point where their script is no longer used, and their descendants live as marginalized groups among the ruined monuments built by their ancestors. Just think of the Mon, now reduced to a minority ethnic group in southern Burma. They were once the most powerful kingdom in Southeast Asia, whose monumental inscriptions bequeathed us the first written records of the region and the first written form of any language of the Austro-Asiatic family.

The Keys to Decipherment

> The main problem with unknown ancient languages is to find related languages, ancient or modern, which are known. If an unknown language cannot be linked with any known language, and if there are no extensive bilingual texts, translation is probably impossible.
>
> (Rilly 2005:2)

The inspired coterie of geniuses who have accomplished the great decipherments have had to bring together many personal qualities, and many realms of knowledge. In most cases the baton has passed through the hands of several scholars from the first discovery of the written material to something like a definitive decipherment.

To begin with, they have often needed bravery and physical stamina. Sir Henry Creswicke Rawlinson, who copied down the Behistun cuneiform from a cliff-top site containing three parallel inscriptions in Elamite, Babylonian, and what turned out to be Old Persian, had to hang from suspended ropes 500 feet above the ground just to copy down the scripts. Zaza Alexidze, who needed ultraviolet light to see the underlayer of Caucasian Albanian in the Sinai palimpsest, could only get sufficient darkness by locking himself in the monastery lavatory for hours, balancing the manuscript on his lap and a lamp in his left hand while copying the shape of each letter onto a pad with his right.[7]

When parallel texts are available, a first point of anchorage across the languages is usually proper names. Champollion, in his decipherment of Egyptian hieroglyphics, began by cross-tabulating the proper names written in cartouches – cartoon-bubble-like motifs surrounding key words like "Rameses." Making the reasonable assumption that proper names tend to be pronounced similarly even in unrelated languages, he could get some purchase on the phonetic values of some glyphs.

General knowledge of the target culture is also indispensable. For the Mayan decipherments, the intricate calendrical cycles of the Long Count and vigesimal (base 20) number systems opened entry points in the texts. Knowing about classical Mediterranean practices like writing "owner inscriptions" on valuable gifted objects, as with the Etruscan inscriptions *mi titasi cver menache* ("I was offered to Tita as a gift") or *ecn turce selvansl* ("this (she) gave to Selvans"), can unlock guesses about the words for "I" (*mi!*) or "this" (*ecn*). Still in the ancient Italic world, the knowledge that on ancient dice the numbers on opposite faces always added up to seven tells us that the first six Etruscan numbers, found spelled out on dice in archaeological digs, could be paired as *mach* + *zal* = seven, *thu* + *huth* = seven, and *ci* + *ša* = seven.[8]

In languages from the Christian tradition, it helps to know about the practice of abbreviating frequently occurring words (like "God" and "Jesus Christ") to the first and last letters of the word, and writing them with a line or "titlo" above those specific words to mark them as abbreviations: like cartouches, these can give a first toehold in the decipherment since it is likely the forms for such words will be phonetically related to those in other languages.

Because so much decipherment relies on mathematical inferences from recurring symbol combinations, an intimate knowledge of canonical texts of a cultural region is also indispensable. Sometimes this can suggest where to look for a parallel text in other languages of the culture area. One of the breakthroughs in Zaza Alexidze's Caucasian Albanian decipherment came when he noticed that a certain passage in the Mount Sinai palimpsest repeated the same word nine times in close succession (see if you can recapitulate his discovery by finding the nine repeated sequences in figure 7.3!). He spotted this as the passage from St Paul's letter to the Corinthians (2 Corinthians 11:26–7), which then identified a lengthy parallel text he could use for further decipherment.

The sharp reader will notice that, in the English King James translation, the word "peril" only occurs eight times, not nine. The same figure of eight is found in many other translations into modern European languages, such as Luther's German translation, and

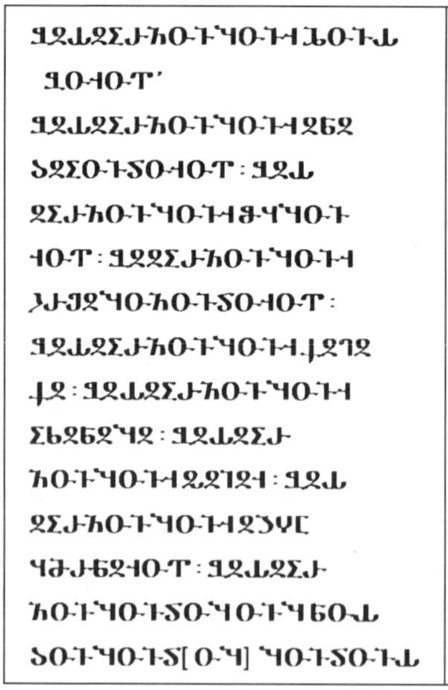

| | [26] In journeyings often, *in perils* of waters, *in perils* of robbers, *in perils* by mine own countrymen, *in perils* by the heathen, *in perils* in the city, *in perils* in the wilderness, *in perils* in the sea, *in perils* among false brethren; [27] In weariness and painfulness, in watchings often, in hunger and thirst, in fastings often, in cold and nakedness. |

Figure 7.3 Nine times in perils: the crucial passage from the Caucasian Albanian manuscript[9]

modern French and Dutch translations. The rather bland remake in the *Good News for Modern Man* translation removes us further from the figure of nine, with only six:

> In my many travels I have been in danger from floods and from robbers, in danger from fellow Jews and from Gentiles; there have been dangers in the cities, dangers in the wilds, dangers on the high seas, and dangers from false friends. There has been work and toil; often I have gone without sleep; I have been hungry and thirsty; I have often been without enough food, shelter, or clothing.

In Caucasian Christian traditions, though, the phrase we are interested in comes up nine times, since "in weariness and painfulness" is rendered as "with perils and with troubles." A central step in the decipherment thus depended on Alexidze's familiarity with the Georgian and Armenian bibles, which suggested a numerical parallel not found in English or other western European versions.

A final, crucial type of information that has been indispensable in many decipherments comes from known varieties of the target language (or of a closely related language) in a more recent form. The prodigious Egyptologist Champollion grasped this early in his life. Having conceived the ambition while still a boy to decipher the Egyptian hieroglyphs, he moved from France to Geneva with the express purpose of studying Coptic, which is the final stage in the long lineage from ancient Egyptian, only extinguished when it gave way to Arabic throughout Egypt. Although no longer spoken in everyday life, Coptic is still used as a liturgical language by Egyptian Coptic Christians. Champollion guessed that knowing Coptic would give him a useful leg up in his decipherment of hieroglyphs, and by his teenage years had learned it well enough to write his diary entries in it.

One step in Champollion's decipherment, for example, followed the hunch that some words would be written by the *rebus* principle: recycling an easily drawn symbol to represent something more abstract but with the same phonetic value, e.g. drawing a bee to represent the English verb "be." Having guessed that the cartouche ⊙𝕄𝕝 represented the word Rameses, and knowing that the Coptic word for "sun" was *re:*,[10] he hypothesized that the symbol for sun could also be used with the value rV (using V to abstract away from the exact vowel quality). He then needed to establish the next symbols, which he guessed might be $m + s + s$ (spelling Rameses without vowels as *rmss*). Looking at other words, he came across another group, (𝕝𝕝), again in a cartouche, showing a drawing of an ibis plus the same symbols that he thought might represent *m* and *s*.

Knowing that "thoth" was the name of the Ibis-god, he guessed this cartouche would contain the name of Thoth-mes: that is Tuthmosis of Manetho's Eighteenth Dynasty. To confirm this reading, he went back to the Rosetta stone, where the $m + s$ sign occurs in a group corresponding to Greek *genethlia* ("birth day"), suggesting the Coptic word for "give birth," ***mise***, and confirming the reading. His earlier studies of Coptic thus furnished Champollion with crucial inferential steps in his decipherment.

Champollion used one ancient variety of a language to decipher an even more ancient one – the liturgical language Coptic, extinct in everyday life for a thousand years, helped decipher Ancient Egyptian, extinct for more than two millennia. In the rest of this chapter we show how modern languages can play a similar role.

Reading the Clear Dawn: Mayan Then and Now

Varal xchicatzibah-vi, xhicatiquiba-vi	Here we shall inscribe, we shall implant
oher tzih v ticaribal, v xenabal	the Ancient Word, the potential and source
puch ronohel xban pa tinamit quiche,	for everything done in the citadel of Quiché,
ramac quiche vinac.	in the nation of Quiché people.

  (*Popol Vuh*, Quiché version from Jena 1944:2, English translation from Tedlock 1996:63)

As a first example of how contemporary languages of indigenous groups have helped unlock an ancient writing system we consider the decipherment of the ancient Mayan script, drawing here on the account in Michael Coe's wonderful book *Breaking the Maya Code*. Attempts at decipherment had limped along for centuries, and got badly bogged down during the mid-twentieth century when the British archaeologist Eric Thompson managed to convince most other researchers that Mayan glyphs "represent, not Maya words or constructions, but universal ideas."[11] If they didn't directly represent a language at all, then it was a waste of time seeking clues to decipherment in the 20 or so modern Mayan languages spoken by over four million people in central America. Dogmatic, opinionated, and forceful, Thompson made his views dominant for decades, turning scholars away from the idea that contemporary Mayan languages could help them in any way.

One piece of evidence that swung the field back on track, to seeing ancient Mayan as a true writing system representing an actual language, was work by linguist Benjamin Lee Whorf. Although not a specialist in Mayan, Whorf had studied enough about Mayan languages to know that many, such as Yucatec Maya, have the distinctive VOS (Verb + Object + Subject) word order illustrated by the Mayanized pseudo-English sentence "wrote the story the scribe." We now know that this rare order is found in only 3 percent of the world's languages, so Whorf was right to take it as distinctive evidence. Through a study of the glyph blocks over each picture in the Dresden codex, he was able to show that the glyphs, too, appeared to have a VOS order, usually with a god last, in the position you'd expect of the subject in a Mayan language. This suggested that they did, after all, represent words from a language directly, rather than just non-linguistic ideas as Thompson had maintained.

Decades later Floyd Lounsbury, who had prepared himself for grappling with the Mayan script by teaching linguistic field methods courses in New Haven with speakers of Yucatec and Chortí Maya, was able to put this more detailed knowledge of Mayan ordering principles to good use, working with epigraphers Linda Schele and Peter Mathews. Modern Mayan languages typically follow the order:

Time/Date :: Verb :: Subject

By assuming this order in Ancient Mayan as well, it was possible to spring off from date expressions in texts, and plug in the limited set of verbs or "event glyphs" for the three major kingly life-events of being born, acceding to the throne, and dying. Suddenly "[t]hey had laid out the life stories of six successive Palenque kings, from birth to accession to death . . . the most complete king list for any Maya site."[12]

Perhaps the most philologically challenging part of any decipherment is in deciding which rival readings of given passages make the most sense. I gave a couple of examples above of how specific cultural knowledge can play a crucial part in unraveling the riddles of old texts. The course of Mayan decipherment supplies many cases where classical cultural schemata have survived right through to contemporary Mayan-speaking cultures, and there has been an increasing involvement of speakers of modern Mayan languages in the decipherment process. Despite five centuries of Christianization their cultures have maintained many key beliefs and terms that can resolve puzzling glyphs.

Let us illustrate this with the example of a glyph appearing on an old Mayan vase. As with many Mayan inscriptions, there is a large pictorial glyph combined with a textual representation alongside it. The vase inscription shows the Waterlily Jaguar floating in the sea (see figure 7.4), with an accompanying text reading *WATERLILY JAGUAR u way(a) SEIBAL ahau.* Note that we write the meaning of phonetic syllable signs in lower case, and that of ideographic characters like the place-name SEIBAL directly in capitals, indicating we are not sure of their pronunciation. The bracketed *(a)* in the word *way(a)* may or may not be pronounced, so the word we are interested in could either sound like English "wire" or more like "why." *Ahau* was known to mean "lord." But what did *u way(a)* mean, was it pronounced *u way* or *u waya*, and what did the whole passage signify?

Information from speakers of modern Mayan languages resolved these questions. Throughout the traditional cultures of Mesoamerica, from a time going back to the

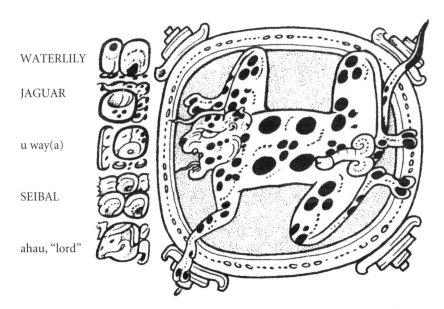

WATERLILY

JAGUAR

u way(a)

SEIBAL

ahau, "lord"

Figure 7.4 Water-pool jaguar and the *way* glyph, from an ancient Mayan vase[13]

ancient Olmec civilization, a key notion is that of "animal alter ego" or "animal counter-part," known in Spanish as *nagual*, a word it took from Aztec. Every individual has their own *nagual*, whose fate is linked to their own. The kind of *nagual* you have reflects your social status: if you are a high-ranking noble you may have a jaguar, if you are humble, a mere mouse.

Now it turns out that words relatable to *way* occur in a number of modern Mayan languages. In Yucatec *way* means "transform by enchantment," and a number of Mayan speakers around Quintana Roo in southern Mexico told Mayanist Nikolai Grube of a sorcerer able to transform himself into a cat or spider monkey. The animal he changes himself into would be called *u way* ("his nagual"). This exactly matches the puzzling phrase from the inscription, secures a particular phonetic reading, and enables a reading of the whole vase text, which can now be translated clearly as "the king of Seibal's nagual (animal counterpart) is water-pool jaguar" or, following the Mayan word order more closely, "water-pool jaguar is the nagual of the Seibal lord."

In this case, then, key phonetic, semantic, and cultural information came from speakers of modern Mayan languages living near the monuments of their ancestors. Despite the collapse of the great Mayan city-states and the sustained assault on their traditions through five hundred years of Spanish colonialism, their culture and language have kept alive many of the ancient words, ideas, and practices depicted and written about so vividly in these monuments. Input from Mayan speakers continues to help epigraphers read their way ever more closely into the fascinating texts of ancient Mayan.

Released by Flames: The Case of Caucasian Albanian

The Caucasus – labeled *Jebel Al-Alsan* or *Jabalu l-'alsân* ("the mountain of tongues"), by a tenth-century Arab geographer – has long been famed for its incredible Babel of languages, with around 40 languages (see figure 7.5). Its linguistic diversity is not simply a matter of brute numbers, but also of deep lineage diversity: in an area smaller than France, it includes more deep-level linguistic lineages than the rest of Europe put together. The rest of modern Europe contains representatives of just three language families: Indo-European, Basque, and Finno-Ugric (particularly Hungarian and Finnish). But the Caucasus contains representatives of five: Indo-European (e.g. Armenian), Turkic (e.g. Azerbaijani), South Caucasian or Kartvelian (e.g. Georgian), Northwest Caucasian (e.g. Abkhaz, Kabardian, and Ubykh), and Northeast Caucasian (e.g. Archi, Avar, Chechen, Ingush, and Lezgian). Except for émigré groups, the last three families are only found in the Caucasus.

It is a miracle that so many small groups, often confined to just one village, have managed to cling to these languages in their mountain fastnesses, as one wave of warlike hordes after another surged past out of Central Asia. These invaders laid level the lowland civilizations in their path, but left the Caucasus mountains as what Johanna Nichols has called a "residual zone," preserving an ancient linguistic mosaic at the crossroads of Europe and Asia that is likely to be much more representative of what the linguistic picture looked like in Neolithic Eurasia.

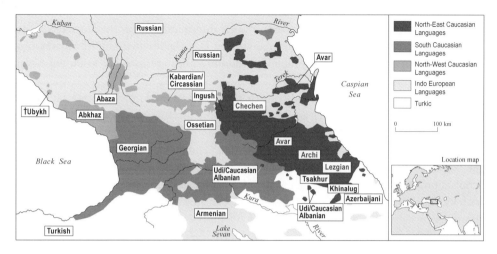

Figure 7.5   Languages of the Caucasus

As we saw in chapter 2, two Christian kingdoms of the Caucasus – Georgia and Armenia – were among the earliest states to convert to Christianity. By the fifth century AD the Armenian scribe, monk, and missionary Mesrop had developed a distinct writing system for Armenian, and some scholars have attributed to him the development of the Georgian alphabet as well. As a result, both these languages boast a long literary tradition. However, most other Caucasian languages remained unwritten until the nineteenth century or later. The lack of old texts for the entire Northwest and Northeast Caucasian families has limited what we can find out about the history and development of these dauntingly complex languages.

The talented Mesrop is also credited with the invention of a third alphabet: the long-lost script of a people generally known as "Caucasian Albanians." (Note that these people have nothing to do with the Albanians of the Balkans, with whom they confusingly share a name.)[14] In an ancient Armenian manuscript, the "History of the Albanians,"[15] it is said that Mesrop "created with the help [of the bishop Ananian and the translator Benjamin] an alphabet for the guttural, harsh, barbarous and rough language of the Gargarac'ik." The Gargarac'ik (the *c'* is pronounced as an ejective or popped *ch*) were one of the peoples of the kingdom of Albania, a region south of the central Kura river in present-day Azerbaijan. This alphabet is known to have been used at least until the twelfth century. However, a sequence of events including crackdowns on varieties of Christianity espousing the Monophysite[16] heresy (which they followed), and then an Arab conquest, led to their eventual conversion to Armenian (Gregorian) Orthodox Christianity. Reduced to a fragmented minority, and with their original version of Christianity castigated as heresy, they saw their alphabet fall into disuse.

Until recently only the merest traces of the Caucasian Albanian alphabet were thought to have survived: a few short inscriptions on candleholders, roofing tiles, and a pedestal unearthed by archaeologists in 1947, and a fifteenth-century Armenian manuscript listing Albanian letters in a comparison of a number of scripts, although subsequent work has shown that many of the "Albanian" letters there are wrong or have a misleading phonetic value. We also have some shreds of early information about the language of the Caucasian Albanians: a second-century papyrus by Heracleides gives the Albanian word for "beard" as *mile:kh*, and some Albanian month names are listed in a few medieval Armenian manuscripts.

Although the "beard" word is difficult to relate to any modern Caucasian language, some of the month names are clearly relatable to words in a language called Udi, spoken now by around 4,000 people in the villages of Nizh and Oguz in northern Azerbaijan and another 200 in the village of Okt'omberi in eastern Georgia (see figure 7.5). For example, the Caucasian name for August[17] is given as *Toulen* or *Towlēn* in the manuscripts, and scholars proposed it could be related to the Udi word *t'ul* ("wine grape"), citing parallels with its Georgian counterpart *stulisay*, which means "(month) of the vintage." And in fact the modern Udi name for August is based on the same root: *t'ulaferek'alxaš*, literally "month of the consecration of the wine grape." Udi belongs to the Lezgian group of the Northeast Caucasian family, and is completely unrelated either to Armenian or Georgian. Interestingly, while speakers of most other East Caucasian languages are Muslims, Udi speakers are Christians even today.

Figure 7.6 St Catherine's Orthodox monastery on Mount Sinai in Egypt.[18] The library is on the side backing Mount Sinai.

The linguistic similarities mentioned above gave rise, already in the nineteenth century, to the hypothesis that the Albanians spoke an early form of Udi. But without extensive textual materials in the script this idea was untestable. Then, in 1975, a fire broke out in the ancient orthodox monastery of St Catherine's, far away on Mount Sinai in Egypt (see figure 7.6). As the brethren were assessing the damage from the fire, they discovered a concealed cellar room underneath the chapel floor with over a thousand ancient manuscripts, and one of these was to unlock the Caucasian Albanian mystery.

In the next two decades these manuscripts were gradually cataloged by scholars. The majority were in Greek, but over one hundred were in a Caucasian language – Georgian. Georgian monks had a connection to the monastery that went back to the sixth century, and in 1990 two Georgian scholars – Zaza Alexidze

Albanian	Georgian	
(letter)	(letter)	[j]
(letter)	(letter)	[tç]
(letter)	(letter)	[i]
(letter)	(letter)	[s]
(letter)	(letter)	[w]
(letter)	(letter)	[p]
(letter)	(letter)	[b]
(letter)	(letter)	[r]
(letter)	(letter)	[o]
(letter)	(letter)	[d]
(letter)	(letter)	[v]
(letter)	(letter)	[ʒ]
(letter)	(letter)	[q']
(letter)	(letter)	[tsʰ]
(letter)	(letter)	[m]
(letter)	(letter)	[tʃ']
(letter)	(letter)	[tʃ]
(letter)	(letter)	[u]
(letter)	(letter)	[e]

Albanian	Ethiopian	
(letter)	(letter)	[ṣa:],[ṣo:]
(letter)	(letter)	[na:]
(letter)	(letter)	[ro:]
(letter)	(letter)	[næ]
(letter)	(letter)	[gæ]
(letter)	(letter)	[u:]
(letter)	(letter)	[hi:]
(letter)	(letter)	[ju:]
(letter)	(letter)	[pæ]
(letter)	(letter)	[tæ]
(letter)	(letter)	[hæ]
(letter)	(letter)	[hu:]
(letter)	(letter)	[da:]
(letter)	(letter)	[ni:]

Albanian	Armenian	
(letter)	(letter)	[ɛ]
(letter)	(letter)	[ɛ:]
(letter)	(letter)	[i]
(letter)	(letter)	[k]
(letter)	(letter)	[z]
(letter)	(letter)	[t]
(letter)	(letter)	[f]
(letter)	(letter)	[s]
(letter)	(letter)	[q]
(letter)	(letter)	[h]

Figure 7.7 Letters from the Caucasian Albanian manuscript, compared with their Georgian, Ethiopian, and Armenian counterparts (adapted from Alexidze and Blair 2003, with permission)

and Mikhail Kavtaria – finally visited the monastery to catalog and assess the collection. Part of their job was to define the languages and scripts on the underlayers of those parchments that were palimpsests – old Greek and Ethiopian manuscripts were a particularly common source for recycled parchment. On his last day Alexidze noticed one palimpsest, with a barely legible original layer under an upper layer written in Old Georgian. He wondered if the rather unusual lettering it contained might be Ethiopian.[19] But it was not possible to complete the analysis on their short first visit, and in any case many of the parchment manuscripts had solidified in the intense heat of the fire. So a second expedition was organized, in 1994, this time including conservators expert in gently parting the clumped old pages. The more extensive readable materials these conservators opened up revealed that other letters in the palimpsest resembled Georgian or Armenian letters. Counting Ethiopic, the mysterious text now appeared to comprise letters drawn from at least three languages (see figure 7.7).

On his third expedition to Mount Sinai, in 1996, Alexidze took along photos of the Albanian alphabet from the fifteenth-century Armenian manuscript mentioned above, and from the other inscriptions unearthed by archaeologists. Comparison with these materials convinced him that the lower text on the palimpsest was in fact Caucasian Albanian. The apparent mixture of three scripts – Ethiopic, Armenian, and Old Georgian – simply reflected the fact that letters from each of these scripts were drawn on in devising the Albanian script. With around 52 phonemes to represent, the inventor of the Albanian script had to seize on as many symbols as he could get his hands on. There were ancient connections in early Christian times between the mountain kingdoms of the Caucasus and Ethiopia, and scholars from all these lands had mingled in the cosmopolitan monasteries of Constantinople.

Once it became clear that the language of the palimpsest was Caucasian Albanian, the task of decipherment was clearer. As mentioned above, previous scholars had hypothesized that Udi, with its tiny and marginalized population of under 6,000 speakers, was the language of the descendants of the ancient Caucasian Albanian kingdom. But to put this knowledge to advantage four things were needed: an educated guess at what texts the Mount Sinai palimpsests represented, reliable grammars and dictionaries of the Udi language, enough information on other Daghestanian languages to show that it was Udi rather than another language of the area, and historical reconstructions of how the candidate language had changed in the last two millennia.

Earlier in this chapter we have already seen how Alexidze used the ninefold recurrence of the key phrase "in perils of" to pinpoint the text. Like Champollion, he also drew on distinctive proper names, such as Korintha (Corinth), Ebra (Hebrews, Jews), Epesa (Ephesus), and Paulos (Paul), and used these to identify particular passages. His ingenious detective work in the months that followed led to the conclusion that the manuscript represented an early "lectionary" – a Church service book containing liturgical lectures read at given points in the Church calendar, and mainly made up of readings from the New Testament and psalms from the Old Testament.[20]

Equally indispensable to the decipherment process was information about modern Udi. In Tsarist Russia, and then during the Soviet era (both in Moscow and in Tbilisi), there was a fine tradition of studying the languages of the Caucasus. Indeed, the great Russian general Baron Petr Karlovich Uslar made a practice, after taking his Caucasian counterparts prisoner, of using them as captive language teachers. This enabled him to write an excellent nineteenth-century description of Lezgian, as well as descriptions of six other Caucasian languages – a feat that Martin Haspelmath, in his own more recent grammar of the same language, has labeled tongue-in-cheek as "perhaps the greatest military achievement in history."[21]

Further north, in the isolated villages of the Caucasus mountain range, the fabled two-man team of Alexandr Kibrik and phonetician Sandro Kodzasov, accompanied by a dozen or so postgraduate students, made "linguistic expeditions" every summer, driving up into the mountains in an army lorry, living in the village school, and dividing up the task of description among the team members, each given a particular topic to pursue. Days were for working with informants, nights for collective discussion and analysis.[22] Magnificent grammars of Archi, Khinalug, Tsakhur, and other Caucasian languages have appeared from this team.

Taken together, we now have a reasonable picture of most languages of the Caucasus, an understanding of their formidable phonology and morphology, and of the historical relations between them. In the case of Udi, a grammar was published in 1863 by the linguist Schiefner, and in the century and a half since then extensive descriptive materials, including Udi–Russian and Udi–Georgian dictionaries, have been developed by Russian,

Georgian, and Udi linguists (Voroshil Gukasyan and Evgeni Jeiranishili), as well as scholars from Germany (Jost Gippert and Wolfgang Schulze) and the USA (Alice Harris). Thanks to this work, evidence from these dictionaries and grammars was available for the decipherment process.

Consider the little excerpt from Corinthians that we mentioned above (which I now cite in a version closer to the Caucasian original): "In journeyings often, *in peril* by rivers, *in peril* by thieves, *in peril* by (my) tribesmen, *in peril* by the Gentiles, *in peril* in the city, *in peril* in the wilderness, *in peril* in the sea, *in peril* by false brethren." We can infer from this that in these repeated phrases there should be a recurrence of the word "peril," and some sort of locational indicator – which in Udi and other languages of the Lezghian group is shown by a case suffix.

As we saw earlier, though, we have to beware of naïvely seeking a direct equivalence to the English structure. In Georgian, "in peril(s) of" is often translated as "seeing trouble[s] of," e.g. "seeing trouble[s] of robbers," and it is this latter structure that is represented here. Let's zoom in on a transliterated and analyzed version of the second of those phrases, "seeing trouble(s) of robbers," drawing on an analysis made by German Caucasologist Wolfgang Schulze.[23] The top line gives Zaza Alexidze's transliteration made from the Mount Sinai palimpsest, the second gives glosses breaking it down into meaningful parts, and the third gives the modern Udi equivalents for the same morphemes.[24]

(1)　Script　　　　　ᲧᲛᲚᲛᲘᲯᲐ�-Ი-ᲧᲦᲚ-Ი-Ი　　ᲛᲑᲛᲘᲛᲘᲝᲦᲑᲝ-Ი-ᲥᲝ-Ი0-Ი
　　　Transliteration　mar-ak'esown-owx　　　　abazak'-owg^-oxoc
　　　Gloss　　　　　trouble-seeing-dative2　　thief-plural-ablative
　　　Udi equivalent　ak'sun-ux　　　　　　　　abazak'-ug^-oxo
　　　Translation　　　"in danger of thieves"

The modern Udi structure gives us a remarkably clear insight, not just into the structure of the original text – rather different from English – but also into many of the specific forms. The ablative *-oxoc* comes out as *-oxo* in modern Udi, and the dative2 and plural suffixes are recognizable as well. What was written *ow* in Caucasian Albanian is pronounced *u* in Udi, but in fact *ow* may just have been a Greek-influenced convention for writing the sound *u* in Caucasian Albanian anyway. With similarities like this between Caucasian Albanian and modern Udi, it was possible to identify morphemes in the original text quite easily, and go on from there to deduce what forms they represent by cross-tabulating with alphabetic values given elsewhere.

By such means Alexidze, Gippert, Schulze, and other scholars have now achieved an almost complete decipherment of the Mount Sinai manuscripts. To historians of religion these are interesting because they are one of the earliest lectionaries found in the Christian tradition. To linguists they make it possible to know, directly, the grammar of a variety of Udi close to one and a half millennia older than what we would otherwise have. This in turn will help scholars understand the historical development of other languages of Caucasian Daghestan.

But it is not just a matter of science and scholarship. The Udi's links to their indigenous orthodox tradition were severed more than 1,000 years ago when they were forced to convert to Armenian Gregorian Christianity or to Islam. Now they have begun efforts to reclaim their ecclesiastical vocabulary – and perhaps their script as well – and incorporate these into contemporary religious practice. In a couple of decades, thanks to this decipherment, they have gone from a forgotten and anomalous minority to being the direct heirs to one of the major historical cultures of the Caucasus.

Zoquean Languages and the Epi-Olmec Script

ʔineʔwe   The stones that he set in order
jeʔtzʉ   were thus symbols.
kiʔpsi

(La Mojarra Stela, Epi-Olmec transcription and translation by Kaufman and Justeson (2001).[25]

Among the many archaeological cultures packed cheek-by-jowl into Mesoamerica, that of the Olmecs has a good claim to be the earliest. Excavations in the steamy lowlands of Veracruz state on the Gulf Coast of Mexico have unearthed a complex urban culture going back to 1500 BC, sustained by systematic agricultural exploitation of the fertile lands around. Although stone is rare in the area it was transported great distances, probably by boat, and fluidly chunky figures (see figure 7.8) were hewn out of these great blocks of stone. A common Olmec sculptural theme shows a parent emerging from an underworld cave with a child in their arms and it is tempting to see this as representing how the newly emerging urban civilization saw itself as coming out of the inchoate mode of life that preceded it.

Figure 7.8   An Olmec Figure, La Venta Park, Villahermosa, Tabasco, Mexico (photo: Nick Evans)

The Olmecs did not just carve figures. They also carved inscriptions, and developed what many consider to be the mother of all Mesoamerican writing systems, known in the literature as Epi-Olmec. Only four substantial inscriptions are known so far. The longest of these, the so-called Stela 1 of La Mojarra (see figure 7.9), was fished out of the muddy sludge of the Acula River in 1986, near the village of La Mojarra. It contains 465 glyphs, neatly arranged in two columns, and the image of a ruler. Although the glyphs do not resemble other known writing systems of Mesoamerica, its use of the Long Count dating system, also found with the better-understood Mayan systems, allows the identification of dates in the texts[26] and, amazingly, the monuments themselves. The dates span a five-century range, from 300 BC for an early inscribed potsherd, to AD 162 for the well-preserved Tuxtla Statuette with its long text.

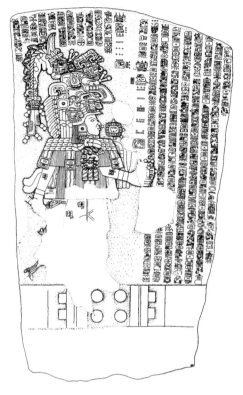

Figure 7.9   The La Mojarra Stela[27]

There were no Rosetta stones, no bilingual inscriptions counterposing other known Mesoamerican writing systems. But the Mayan decipherment process I discussed above had left Mesoamericanists with a clear game plan. A concerted campaign to tackle Olmec epigraphy, by systematically drawing on the evidence from indigenous languages still spoken in the region, has enabled rapid progress to be made. In fact, the Olmec decipherment is arguably the most successful example of using living modern tongues to decipher ancient monoglot texts.

The cracking of the Epi-Olmec code, by a long-running project led by linguist Terry Kaufman and epigrapher John Justeson, drew on the following six steps:

(1)   *Geographical localization.* An initial guess was that the most likely candidate language for decipherment was an ancestral form of indigenous languages still spoken in the region, namely the dozen or so languages of the Mixe-Zoquean (also spelled Mije-Sokean) family around the Mexican isthmus (see figure 7.10). Their populations range from 188,000 for Mixe to extinct or virtually so for Tapachulteco. An example of the fragility of some Mixe-Zoquean languages is Olutec (also called Oluta Popoluca), a particularly revealing witness in reconstructions because of its conservatism, but which we only know about in detail thanks to recent fieldwork by Roberto Zavala with Antonio Asistente and others (see box 7.1).

(2)   *Linguistic reconstruction.* As much as possible of the lexicon, grammar, and sound system was reconstructed for each language and family of the region – not just Mixe-Zoquean,

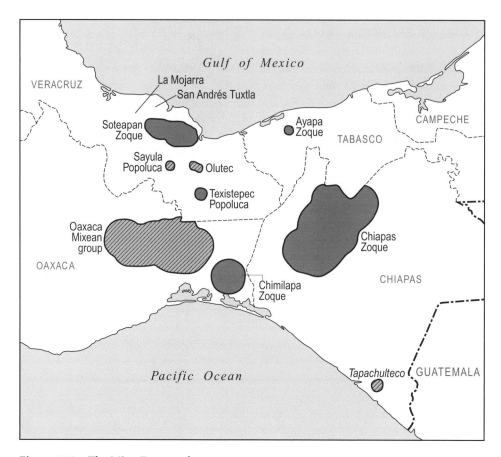

Figure 7.10   The Mixe-Zoquean languages

but also Mayan, Otomanguean, Uto-Aztecan, Totonacan, and other small isolates like Xinca and Lenca. Obviously such reconstructions depend, first of all, on having good descriptions of all the languages because, as we saw in the preceding chapters, each new language nets further reconstructable words: the more languages, the greater the accuracy and scope of the reconstruction. Mixe-Zoquean languages are mostly not very well described, particularly the smaller and endangered ones. So, although tentative results of this stage have been posted since work by Kaufman in the 1960s, this process still has a long way to go, and depends on careful fieldwork with each candidate language.

(3) *Determining the direction of borrowing.* Step 1 suggested that the Olmecs spoke an ancestral form of Mixe-Zoquean. As a check, the etymologies of words denoting cultivars and items of material culture associated with the Olmec archaeological culture were assembled, drawing on all languages of Mesoamerica. This is an example of the "words and objects" approach I outlined in chapter 6.

Box 7.1 Oluteco, Olmec echo

Antonio Asistente (photo: Nick Evans)

In the small town of Oluta, in Mexico's Veracruz state, Antonio Asistente (see photo), a tiny mischievous man in his eighties, lives with his younger sister Alfredina. Neither ever had children of their own and the younger people in their community have gone over to speaking Spanish. The Asistente siblings are among the handful of people who still speak Oluteco (Oluta Popoluca), a particularly important witness in reconstructions of proto-Mixe-Zoquean thanks to its generally conservative features.

Already in the 1960s, Oluteco was being described as moribund. In the early 1990s a brilliant young Mexican linguist, Roberto Zavala, was asked by Terry Kaufman to visit the town of Oluta and check out if anyone alive still remembered the language. In fact he found several speakers, and through his work with Antonio Asistente and others has been able to produce a detailed grammatical description of Oluteco and a full collection of vocabulary items, feeding into the Olmec decipherment project. Had this work been delayed by just a few years, we would have known next to nothing about Oluteco.

The idea is to see in which languages there are reconstructable words for the suite of archaeologically attested objects, and in which other languages they were likely to be more recent borrowings from a more innovative prestige culture. This gives a material profile of different proto-languages to see which best matches the archaeological signature of excavated objects from Olmec sites. The word *kakawa* for "cocoa," for example, can be reconstructed to proto-Mixe-Zoquean, and cacao appears in Olmec sites, suggesting they were the first or among the first to domesticate this plant.

Loanwords can be identified by a variety of techniques.

Segmentability is one criterion. Words like *ʔason* appear with the meaning "cloud" in many Mayan languages, but cannot be further segmented within the grammar of those languages. But in proto-Zoquean the word **nas-oʔnaʔ* ("fog"), from which these are likely to have been borrowed, can be segmented as "earth-cloud," marking it as a Zoquean loanword into Mayan.

Phonological fit to the language is another criterion. Inherited English words can start with *sl*, *sm*, or *st* ("slow," "small," "stick") but not with *shl*, *shm*, or *sht*. This would allow a Martian linguist to readily identify words like *shlemiel*, *shmuck*, or *shtick* as loanwords, and it wouldn't take them long to identify Yiddish – or German in the case of *schmaltz* – as the donors. (Actually the English spelling system helps us keep track of where loans come from – German-derived words are written *schm* and Yiddish ones as *shm*,[28] even though they're both pronounced the same. But we don't have this luxury with unwritten languages.) Identifying the direction of borrowing between Mixe-Zoquean and Mayan languages is helped by the fact that real proto-Mayan roots were usually monosyllabic, while proto-Mixe-Zoquean abounded in disyllables. Words like *(š)koːyaːʔ* for "tomato" in many Mayan languages thus stand out as likely Mixe-Zoquean loans, and in fact **koːyaːʔ* is clearly reconstructable as the word for "tomato" in proto-Mixe-Zoquean.

By integrating arguments of this type, Lyle Campbell and Terry Kaufman made a persuasive case for proto-Mixe-Zoquean as the carrier language of original cultural developments in Mesoamerica, liberally strewing loanwords out into the surrounding languages thanks to the technological innovation and prestige of its associated culture. At the same time, their reconstructed inventory of archaeologically detectable items linked proto-Mixe-Zoquean to the material profile of the Olmec sites: cocoa, tomatoes, squash, beans, sweet potato, guavas, papayas, zapotes (sapodilla plums), manioc (cassava), turkey, maguey (agave cactus), stages of maize preparation including corn grinding and mixtamal (leached corn), ritual items like incense (copal), woven mats and axes for human sacrifice, and central calendrical concepts.

(4) *Identifying the type of writing system.* Independently of steps (1) to (3), the basic typology of the writing system needed to be established, primarily by counting the number of recurring elements and their contexts. The most plausible hunch was that Epi-Olmec mixed syllabic elements employing CV-syllable signs representing the sound, and direct (logographic) representations of the meaning of some items.

This is very similar to the Mayan system, but also to some well-known modern systems. In Japanese, for example, a word like *yama* ("mountain") can either be written with two syllable symbols, や (*ya*) and ま (*ma*) giving やま (*yama*) – or with a single *kanji* or pictographic symbol 山. The symbol 山, in turn, can be used for the same meaning but with other pronunciations. For example, it is pronounced as *san* in 山水 *sansui* ("landscape"), literally ("mountains and water"), where 水 represents *sui* ("water").[29] There is even a third possibility, used in school primers or when writing obscure characters, of putting the syllable symbols in tiny print above the character (then known as *furigana*) to show how it should be pronounced. Mayan, Epi-Olmec, and many other mixed syllabic-logographic scripts sometimes employ similar double representations, and where this happens it is an obvious boon in decipherment since it tells us how logographic characters can be pronounced.

(2) 　　山^{やま}　　　　　　　　　　　　山水^{さん すい}

| "mountain" written with the syllabic phonetic symbols (*furigana*) for *yama* above the pictographic symbol | "landscape" written with the syllabic phonetic symbols (*furigana*) for *sansui* above the pictographic symbols |

Finally, in the same way that the meaning of a few Sino-Japanese symbols can readily be guessed from their form, like 門 for "gate" or 森 for "forest," some Epi-Olmec symbols are realistic enough to allow plausible guesses about their meaning. With the symbol , for example, it is not too outrageous to assume it means "turtle." By reconstructing from known words for "turtle" in modern Mixe-Zoquean languages, we can guess that its pronunciation should be *tuki*.

(5) *Statistics and combinatory properties of syllables.* Armed with the above assumptions, the next step was to look at how the existing modern languages work, and make some smart guesses about what the most common syllables were, based on how often certain elements turn up in running texts, and on what sort of words they are likely to combine with. By comparing these elements across all languages of the family, the comparative method can show what forms they would have taken in earlier phases of the language. Meanwhile, statistics on morpheme frequency in texts can be gained from corpora in the modern languages.

We can get a feel for the logic of this by reasoning that, if we knew spoken English and were trying to decipher a writing system representing it, a good place to start would be from the overwhelmingly high frequency of the syllable representing "the," and also from its combinatory profile: it combines happily with nouns ("the dog") but not adjectives (?"the small"), verbs (?"the eat"), or proper names (?"the Henry"), so it can be used to sort the words it combines with into classes. By matching the statistical distribution of candidate syllable signs in Epi-Olmec script with the distribution of syllables, it was possible to make a first guess at sound values of some signs, then ratchet up from there.

A providential feature of the Mixe-Zoquean languages that helped this step is that many grammatical affixes are exactly one syllable, giving them a one-to-one correspondence with syllable symbols. We can illustrate with two of these syllabic morphemes, which happen to have survived unchanged into Antonio Asistente's language, Olutec. These are the third-person possessive prefix ("his, her, its, their"), which takes the form *ʔi-*, as in *ʔiʔawok* ("his son"),[30] and the "independent incompletive verbal suffix" *-pa*, used for ongoing (uncompleted) actions in main clauses, as in *tani:motowüpak* ("they obey me"). (As this example shows, verbs in Olutec are complex and have accreted a lot of other affixes in the course of their evolution from proto-Mixe-Zoquean, but the key suffix *-pa* is still alive and well.)

Without trying to recapitulate all the intricate steps that led Kaufman and Justeson to figure out which syllables went with which signs in the texts, we can skip forward and see these affixes busy at work back in the Epi-Olmec texts in (3a) and (3b), paired with reconstructed proto-Mixe-Zoquean words that match them in (4a) and (4b); both have a , pronounced *Ɂi*, as their first (top) element.

(3) a.

(3) b.

(4) a. *Ɂisaj*
         "his shoulder"

(4) b. *Ɂikuwna Ɂki Ɂpsi*
         "his set-aside symbol"

Likewise, we can compare the three Epi-Olmec representations of the three words in (5a) to (5c) with the reconstructed proto-Mixe-Zoquean words that match them (6a) to (6c). You can readily observe that all have a or , pronounced *pa*, as their last (bottom) element, representing the incompletive (here translated by the English suffix *-s*.)

(5) a.

(5) b.

(5) c.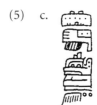

(6) a. *kajpa* "he faints (incompletive)"

(6) b. *wejpa* "he shouts (incompletive)"

(6) c. *wanetzɨkpa* "he sings (incompletive)"

Reasoning in this way, Kaufman and Justeson were able to propose the following table of syllabic signs for the Epi-Olmec script (see figure 7.11).

Note that a couple of theoretically possible syllables seem to be missing. In any language some syllables are rarer than others, so these gaps would probably need more textual material before they can be filled. But at the same time the members of the project are doing all they can to collect relevant words with the right phonological structure by making up all possible words whose pronunciation would include these syllables (appropriately changed through the operation of language-particular sound-laws) and asking Mixe-Zoquean speakers if they correspond to real words in their languages.

(6) *Testing by reading.* The last step, and the keystone to the whole hanging arch of the preceding ones, is to try reading a complete new text with the proposed phonetic and semantic values of the preceding analysis, and to see how far it makes sense. Justeson and Kaufman, who had initially developed their decipherment on the basis of the Tuxtla statuette, then went on to cut their teeth on the La Mojarra Stela after the director of the Anthropology Museum in Xalapa made it publicly available for research. A summary of their decipherment was published in the journal *Science*, and their full reading of the La Mojarra Stela

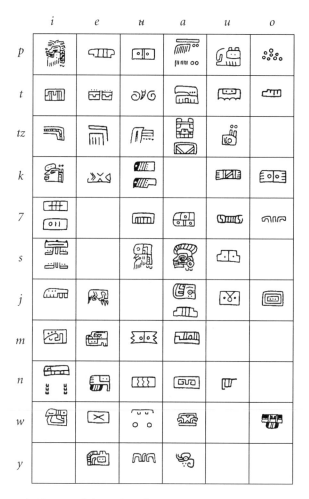

Figure 7.11   The Epi-Olmec syllabary (Kaufman and Justeson 2001)

is available online. A flavor of the La Mojarra text – regal history in the grand style – can be gained from the first few lines: "It was the third day of the seventeenth month, the long count was 8.5.3.3.5, and the day was 13 Snake. A sun-eating moon (solar eclipse) takes place. Piercingly the bludgeon star (Venus) had shone earlier, as a late-in-the-day one (i.e. as evening star). Coronated ones hallowed by sprinkling fought against noble(s) and war-leader-type succession-supporters (would-be successors/usurpers)."[31]

Once we become able to read texts like this, there is a sudden increase in the precision with which we can know the past: the voices of kings – or at least of their scribes – start speaking to us directly. Of course, given the meager textual material at our disposal and the still early stage of our understanding of Mixe-Zoquean languages, there remain many gaps in the interpretations. This is particularly true for the interpretation of logographic signs, as unlike the syllabic ones they cannot be directly related to reconstructed Mixe-Zoquean forms, unless by good fortune they are accompanied by partial or complete syllabic representations. Not surprisingly, unanimity has yet to be reached, and since the ability to extend the readings obtained with one text to a newly discovered text is one of the main hurdles that a confirmed decipherment must clear, the search for new textual materials is paramount.

A potentially crucial new text has in fact been found, but it is currently in the private possession of a collector, holding up open scrutiny of the decipherments to be outlined below. Despite the problems with points of detail, however, the back of the decipherment has been broken, and the stones that the Epi-Olmec sculptor-scribes set in place have become interpretable symbols once again after nearly two millennia, training a clear new lens onto a pivotal moment in the history of the Americas. Without the evidence of the modern Mixe-Zoquean languages that today's speakers have been able to provide, none of this would have been possible.

Darkening Pages

In this chapter we have focused on three case studies where languages still spoken by dis-possessed modern groups hold the keys to unlocking the accounts of the past, which their more powerful predecessors engraved on stone or wrote on parchment. Much of the know-ledge of how their ancestors spoke, from sounds to grammatical suffixes to metaphors and semantic compressions, has somehow been passed through their ears and mouths over untold generations, across the millennia of perils that followed the collapse, dismember-ment, defeat, or cultural conversion of their forebears' societies by other peoples.

Dozens of other ancient scripts around the world remain partially or wholly undeciphered, from the Indus script in south Asia to other still-mysterious Mesoamerican scripts such as Zapotecan. Many will undoubtedly keep their secrets forever, as the languages whose earlier stages they recorded have disappeared as oral traditions as well. In other cases we stand a chance of cracking their codes through a resourceful use of material from surviv-ing modern languages. But again and again our attempts at decipherment are held back by our ignorance of the languages of the area. Take the Meroitic script of the Kingdom of Kush in northern Sudan, now on the brink of decipherment. Claude Rilly, who has begun this decipherment, argues that it represents an early language of the Northeastern Sudanic branch of Nilo-Saharan. But key daughter languages needed to reconstruct Northeastern Sudanic – little-known tongues like Afitti, Tama, Nara, and Nyima – are threat-ened by war, displacement, and cultural assimilation to Arabic. The chance to carry out the sort of decipherments we saw for Caucasian Albanian and Epi-Olmec will not be with us for much longer.

Further reading

On Tangut see Gong (2003) for an accessible introduction and Dunnell (1996) for a history of the Tangut empire. On Lontara script and its ambiguities see Cummings (2002) and Jukes (2006), the sources for the examples discussed here. Davies (1990) and Bonfante (1990), respectively, give clear accounts of the decipherments of Egyptian hieroglyphics and attempts at deciphering Etruscan, while Coe (1999) is a gripping account of Mayan decipherment by someone who played a key role in it himself; the *nagual* story is in Coe (1999:240–2). On Caucasian Albanian see Alexidze and Mahé (1997), Alexidze and Blair (2003), Schulze (2003, 2005), Gippert (1987), and Gippert and Schulze (2007). Good linguistic descriptions of Udi are Schulze (1982), Harris (2002), and Schulze's online grammar at www.lrz-muenchen.de/~wschulze/Uog.html; also interesting is Schulze's (2001) annotated version of the Udi gospels.

The best materials on the Olmec decipherment are downloadable from the website of the Project for the Documentation of the Languages of Mesoamerica (www.albany.edu/anthro/maldp), but see also Campbell and Kaufman (1976) on the original linguistic arguments for linking Mixe-Zoquean languages to the Olmecs, Justeson and Kaufman (1993, 1997) for published accounts of the decipherment, Wichmann (1995) on the historical linguistics of the Mixe-Zoquean languages, and Zavala (2000) for a detailed treatment of Olutec. Not all scholars accept the Justeson / Kaufman decipherments – see the Wikipedia entry for "Epi-Olmec script" for pointers to alternative views. On Meroitic see Rilly (2005), who claims a decipherment linking it to Nilo-Saharan languages; for a dissenting view linking Meroitic to the Cushitic languages and containing a detailed history of attempted Meroitic decipherments see Rowan (2006).

Part IV

Ratchetting Each Other Up: The Coevolution of Language, Culture, and Thought

die Sprachen [sind] nicht eigentlich Mittel [...], die schon erkannte Wahrheit darzustellen, sondern weit mehr, die vorher unerkannte zu entdecken.

Languages are not actually means of representing a truth already known, but rather of discovering the previously unknown.

(Humboldt [1903–36]:L.IV:27)

Grammar is restless and earned.

(Stein 1973:60)

Language diversity, as should be clear by now, is intimately tied up with the great plasticity of human experience. The critic Harold Bloom once wrote that "we read ... because we cannot know enough people."[1] Equally, one could add, we study other languages because we cannot live enough lives.

The value of this insight is not just to remind ourselves of how differently we might have experienced this world. It is becoming increasingly clear, in the field of human evolutionary biology, that the crucial defining feature of our species is precisely this openness to *enculturation* – by whichever intricate tapestry the culture and language of our group weaves onto the weft of our baby mind-loom. But to discard the ancient blueprints of instinctual control is a rash evolutionary gamble. For it to work, we need minds able to learn from whatever culture we grow up in. And that culture, in its turn, has to have a rich and finely adapted set of patterns ready to teach us.

The evolution of our species, then, has been an intimately coordinated dance. One partner is physical evolution, its steps danced out as changes in our genes. The other is cultural and linguistic evolution, choreographed by complex, structured, and everchanging social institutions, which we learn from our caregivers, and then pass on with enrichments, losses, and restructurings, to the next generation. Human evolution, in other words, has involved an intense interplay between our hardware, in the form of our genes and physiology, and our software, in the form of our language and culture.

We can understand this *coevolution* easily by thinking of recent advances in computer technology. Advances in hardware and software constantly spur each other on. New software drives the need for, but at the same time is enabled by, hardware breakthroughs like the mouse, optical fiber, and satellite networks linking computers together through the Internet. It would be sterile and artificial to try and study the evolution of just hardware in isolation, or just software, and the same is true when we look at human evolution. Unfortunately the unrecorded disappearance of most of our ancestors' languages leaves a huge gap on the software side. But in compensation the wild linguistic diversity we still have enables us to draw on a stock of natural experiments in evolving complex language systems.[2]

As our early human-like ancestors were increasingly freed from instinctual control of behavior, a second line of information transmission was produced across the generations. Besides the primordial track of genetic transmission that we share with all other species, there appeared a new track – culture – and this in turn was increasingly mediated through language. New techniques and observations about the world could now quickly be added to the shared repertoire of a human group, without having to wait for the slow process of genetic selection. This rapidly widened the bandwidth at which information could be passed from one generation to the next, by summing the genetic and cultural transmission pathways.

Just consider how our ancestors would have dealt with the problem of whether a particular berry was edible. The epithet "eat, die, and learn"[3] can work two ways. If you rely on genetic transmission, many individuals must eat and die before a species can be said to have "learned" to avoid a given food source, through an inherited instinct to avoid it. But once you have culture – preferably including language – a single death is enough to bring about the change. The information that "eating *kirriwuk-kirriwuk* berries[4] causes death" can now be transmitted culturally to other members of the group, without needing to wait for the slow work of genetic selection.

Because human cultures and languages can rapidly integrate many thousands of such observations, about all aspects of the world, they act as a vast memory bank. Each refinement, added from one generation to the next, ratchets up the sophistication of human culture, to use the image proposed by Mike Tomasello:

> These new forms of cultural learning created the possibility of a kind of ratchet effect in which human beings not only pooled their cognitive resources contemporaneously, they also built on one another's cognitive inventions over time. This new form of cultural evolution thus created artifacts and social practices with a history, so that each new generation of children grew up in something like the accumulated wisdom of their entire social group, past and present. (Tomasello 1999a:527, with permission)

At the same time, human groups began to live across a range of ever more distinct ecological niches, as the power of culture extended their adaptive reach, and drove the differentiation of local cultures. This trend would have been accelerated further in many cases by a conscious quest for diversification to mark local group membership and keep out untrusted, freeloading alien busybodies. But since we have kept intermarrying (and inter-adopting) throughout our time on earth as humans, our children have always needed the genetic flexibility to learn whatever culture(s) and language(s) they happen to grow up in.

This work-space for culturally modulating behavior can only be opened up by releasing a proportion of behavior from genetic, instinctual control – in other words, by increasing the *developmental plasticity* of the organism, so that decisive information can be transmitted culturally rather than genetically. One well-known consequence of this is the long period of dependency that we humans need while being enculturated by our parents and other group members. Another is that as a species we need exceptional learning skills to cope with widely variant cultures – in particular, those skills needed to solve the "triple mapping problem" I mentioned in chapter 3 in connection with learning radically different linguistic systems. And it is increasingly clear that these learning skills are dependent on the exceptional *mind-reading* or *intention-attribution* skills that are needed to function in complex human societies. These are harnessed by the child trying to figure out what her caregivers' words are referring to, which in turn depends on tracking what the caregivers are *attending to*. Crucially, then, in order to cash in on the information bonanza that the cultural transmission track offers, the evolutionary pathway to being human had to include – now as a *genetic endowment* – remarkable learning and mind-modeling abilities.

The best-known coevolutionary approaches focus on the interactions between genetic and cultural pathways of development: for example, the mutual feedback between a cultural change like adopting cattle-herding, and a genetic change like evolving lactose tolerance to benefit from the availability of cows' milk. In the history of language, the gradual development of phonological and grammatical devices – each one perhaps inadvertently stumbled upon by some unsung and genetically favored wordsmith who could invent what his or her contemporaries could only imitate – would have kept the pressure on for the selection in the next generation of brains and vocal tracts best able to learn and benefit from the ever more elaborate language systems available for use.

But coevolution is not limited to the interplay of culture and genes. Within the broad cultural track, there are also coevolutionary relationships between language and the rest of culture, and this is the focus of the next two chapters. In particular, we will look at the relationship between language and habitual thought patterns (chapter 8), and between ordinary "unconscious" language and the curated "poetic" use of language that leads to the most valued and powerful creations of individual cultures (chapter 9). In each case, it is language diversity that provides us with the variety of case studies we need to check our causal and evolutionary models, just as species diversity enabled the development of evolutionary theory in biology.

Unlike with the questions investigated earlier in parts II and III of this book, which could be studied just through documenting the languages themselves, we now need to expand our focus to the other coevolving elements. Purely linguistic studies remain fundamental, of course, enabling us to find language systems that bring together unusual elements, or that have just the right combination of structural features to help us test particular hypotheses. But beyond this, we are witnessing a radical expansion in what questions we ask of the cultures we are studying. We must now bring in psychological evidence of how people think and how babies learn and attend, and evidence from poetics and musicological

methods to understand how outstanding creative individuals compose, and how their creations are then fed back into the everyday language system.

Even at the linguistic level, there is a broadening clutch of data-gathering techniques:
semi-controlled elicitation games, the recording of concomitant gestures, eye-tracking
to monitor attention, fine-grained phonetic analysis across large corpora to detect the
subtle incipient growth of new grammatical categories. As has happened so often in the
history of our engagement with the world's myriad tongues, new questions are demanding an ever greater range of interests on the part of the field linguist.

8

Trellises of the Mind:
How Language Trains Thought

*Prise en elle-même, la pensée est comme une
nébuleuse où rien n'est nécessairement délimité.*

Without language, thought is a vague,
uncharted nebula.

(Saussure 1979:155)

Мысль не выражается в слове, но
совершается в слове.

Thought is not merely expressed in words;
it comes into existence through them.

(Vygotsky 1962 [1934]:307)

We have seen, again and again, how different are the categories into which languages
carve up the world. Disparate languages are not just collections of different names for the
same concepts in a hypothetical universal "mentalese" that is the same for speakers of all
languages. Rather, many of the concepts we use to apprehend the world are built up in
the very process of learning to speak – with the result that our conceptual stock differs
markedly with our language background.

It follows that different languages induce different patterns of thought at the most obvious level that, in order to speak or understand a language, you need to have the right concepts ready in your mind. Until you have the concept of "matrilineal parallel relative two
generations up or down" in place, you cannot use the Kunwinjku word *kakkak*, covering
as it does the concepts of mother's mother (English "maternal grandmother"), mother's
mother's brother (English "maternal great-uncle"), and their corresponding reciprocals:
daughter's child from a woman's perspective, and sister's daughter's child, from a man's
perspective. Until you have the concept of "harmonic" vs. "disharmonic" generations you
cannot make the even more basic and unavoidable move of using Dalabon subject pronouns correctly (see chapter 4).

Passing from kinship to numerals, to speak a language like Arammba with a base 6 number system (see chapter 3), you need a well-oiled mastery of powers of 6, instantly seeing
217 as $216 + 1 = 6 \times 36 + 1 = 6^3 + 1$. A natural and commonly named numerical unit in
south New Guinea languages is 1,296, the fourth power of 6. Among the nearby Keraki

people, for example, a family's seasonal yam harvest should fill its yam storehouse with at least a *dameno* – namely 1,296 stored tubers.[1]

Likewise, to speak Japanese you have to be at ease making mental calculations that bundle numbers into units of 10,000 (remember *man* 万 "10,000") rather than the units of 1,000 we are used to from English. Reflecting this, a number like 10 million is expressed by taking 万 (10,000) as the multiple in Japanese – 1000,0000 ("a thousand *man*") – rather than 10,000,000 as in English.

None of these concepts are so complex that you can't work them out in a few seconds with a pencil and paper. But this is not something you can do each time you want to say or comprehend a word. You need to have it ready to use, at the top of your mental stack. Children's games often pep up this conceptual fluency. In one Kunwinjku children's game, someone calls out the kin group name of another, who must respond instantly by calling out the name of the kin group that is in their *kakkak* (matrilineal grandparent) relation. I suffered a series of humiliating defeats at the hands of children playing this game one night at Yikarrakkal outstation in the heart of Arnhem Land. Although I understood both the term *kakkak* and the kin group system in theory, I needed to think through the calculations, whereas they could give immediate answers, drawing on the same overlearned and rapid-fire fluency that oils their language use.

The centrality of language-specific concepts in speakers' minds – and in particular the role they play in ensuring that fellow members of the same language and culture are thinking in the same groove – is shown in other ways. There is a type of experiment known as a "convergence task," devised by the psychologist Thomas Schelling to demonstrate our abilities to "mind-read" – more accurately to second-guess – what other people are thinking. The tests go like this: you and I are separately told something like "imagine you have to meet your partner in an unknown city, but didn't make arrangements where" (this was in the days before mobile phones). Our joint goal is for each to guess what the other person will guess – to *converge* or *coordinate our thoughts* without communication. Schelling's experimental subjects achieved this with extraordinary success, nominating stereotyped locations like "under the main clock at the central railway station" (he did his original experiments with Europeans, with a shared orientation to the role of the railway station).

Another of his tasks involved asking people to "think of the same large number as your partner." Again, (European) people converged remarkably, nominating 1,000, 1 million, or 1 billion. But if you do this test in Japan, people will nominate a different number, namely one of the powers of 万 – 10,000 (1,0000) or 100 million (1,0000,0000). These numbers would not normally occur to speakers of English or other European languages.

Tok Pisin, the national language of Papua New Guinea, distils this idea that we are on the same wavelength as speakers of our language, and can therefore trust and call upon them, into the word *wantok* ("one talk"). The Arammba, Japanese, and Kunwinjku examples above show that culture- and language-specific concepts do not just select what is salient for you, the speaker. They also shape what you assume is salient for your *wantoks*. Cultures and the languages they coevolve, in other words, are a powerful channeler of convergence between their members.

The Linguistic Relativity Hypothesis and Its Precursors

No two languages are ever sufficiently similar to be considered as representing the same social reality.

(Sapir 1949 [1929]:162)

But how far do the consequences of linguistic differences for thought really extend? Do speakers of different languages actually think differently – even when they are not talking or using inner speech? And are we talking about the outer reaches of what it is possible for them to think about, or simply what is habitual for them? After all, geniuses throughout history have regularly thought outside the grooves that guided the thoughts of those who spoke their language before them. Does learning a new language later in life entail learning new modes of thought, as we adjust to the new lens it gives us to perceive the world through? And do bilinguals switch between thought-modes as they switch between languages?

An interest in these questions runs back to Romantic thinkers like Vico, Herder, and Humboldt, all intoxicated with the individual creative destinies of different nations (see chapter 2). But it was the American linguists Edward Sapir and Benjamin Lee Whorf who gave the idea of linguistic relativity its real bite in the first half of the twentieth century. They leavened their cosmovisionary musings with examples drawn from the dramatically different conceptual worlds offered by North American languages like Nootka, Shawnee, and Hopi.

Whorf formulated these ideas as the "principle of linguistic relativity": "users of markedly different grammars are pointed by their grammars toward different types of observations and different evaluations of externally similar acts of observation, and hence are not equivalent as observers but must arrive at somewhat different views of the world."[2] His interests in this problem took a more specific turn in the 1930s when he met Hopi speaker Ernest Naquayouma, then living in New York City, and began studying the language with him. He followed this up with fieldwork on the Hopi reservation in Arizona in 1938. Based on this work, Whorf declared that

the Hopi language is seen to contain no words, grammatical forms, constructions or expressions that refer directly to what we call "time," or to past, present, or future, or to enduring or lasting ... Hence, the Hopi language contains no reference to "time," either explicit or implicit. At the same time, the Hopi language is capable of accounting for and describing correctly, in a pragmatic or operational sense, all observable phenomena of the universe. (Whorf 1956:57–8)

In place of our linear notion of time, Whorf imputed to the Hopi language a concept of "eventuating" – a process transforming successive states of the universe – augmented by various subjectively based notions roughly comparable to "hoping" used for mental projections of the future.

It is well worth reading Whorf's evocative essay to get more of the flavor of his discussion than I can convey here. By the standards of modern linguistics it is lamentably short on actual example sentences, leaving you sensing that there is some tantalizing alternative cosmology out there just beyond your grasp until you have more Hopi under your belt than Whorf can currently provide you with. But it conveys a powerful, almost hallucinatory feeling that there may well exist a completely different but internally coherent model of the physical universe, right down to the base ontologies of space and time.

How Closely Coupled

Como lingüista conoce sólo las lenguas de los pueblos, pero no sus pensamientos, y su dogma supone haber medido éstos con aquéllas y haber hallado que coinciden.

As a linguist he only knows the languages of peoples, not their thoughts, and his dogma supposes the measurement of the latter to coincide with the former.

Ortega y Gasset (1983 [1937])[3]

As intoxicating as Whorf's cosmological adventure into Hopi time was, it failed on two counts, one empirical, one procedural.

Its empirical failures were shown up decades later, when Ekkehart Malotki published a detailed account of the manifold ways of talking about time in Hopi. Malotki cheekily begins the fly-page quote with this Hopi gobbet: *pu' antsa pay qavongvaqw pay su'its talavay kuyvansat pàasatham pu' paw piw maanat taatayna* ("then indeed, the following day, quite early in the morning at the hour when people pray to the sun, around that time then he woke up the girl again").[4] His work de-exoticizes Hopi, presenting a completely familiar array of grammatical structures – distinguishing future from non-future by grammatical tense, and supplemented by more precise time-denoting adverbs. For Malotki, then, Whorf's Hopi cosmology was a figment of inadequate, exoticizing fieldwork.

But there was a deeper, procedural failure in Whorf's method, which has plagued the field for longer. To talk about language influencing thought, we need an independent yardstick for each. Otherwise we end up overstretching exotic language examples to double duty: linguistically, they show how the language works, and psychologically they are also taken to be a direct indicator of thought itself. This circular procedure makes the claimed correlation between language and thought a simple artifact of measuring the same thing twice.

In the last few decades the Sapir–Whorf hypothesis has suffered a peculiarly schizophrenic fate. It is seen by some heavy punchers in the fields of philosophy and psychology as a sort of glandular fever that briefly infects romantic college students exposed in their dorms to factoids about the number of Eskimo words for snow,[5] before emerging cured into a more sober and orderly world in which facts are facts, and where they can join philosopher Jerry Fodor in hating relativism "more than anything else, excepting maybe fibreglass powerboats."[6] Some recent popular scientific books – such as Pinker's *The Language Instinct* – summarily trash the significance of the Sapir–Whorf hypothesis, saying it is "wrong – all wrong" and that "There is no scientific evidence that languages dramatically shape their speakers' way of thinking."[7]

At the other extreme, many postmodern scholars and anthropologists have outwhorfed Whorf by digging into extreme relativist foxholes. These scholars assert the ultimate incompatibility of different discourses, with scant regard for the recurrent similarities in ontological categories like time, space, and causality exhibited across the world's languages. But a belief in the shaping power of words over thought is also alive and well outside the charmed salon of postmodernist scholars, in the inexorable flow of relabelings undertaken in the service of political spin (from "fetus" to "unborn child") or inclusive social policy (from "chairman" to "chair," or "blind" to "visually impaired").

Clearly the Sapir–Whorf hypothesis has unfinished business. But to answer and refine the questions it poses, we need to go beyond the methods of linguistics proper – which can only ever get directly at what people say, not at how they think – and turn to the experimental methods developed by psychology. These allow us to catch thought alone, away from language's jealous embrace, and thus to measure the two independently. In fact, psychologists usually go further, and break "thought" down further into various categories, such as representing, categorizing, remembering, and reasoning: "The linguistic relativity question, interpreted nonvacuously, is whether by having learned these languages speakers differ in the very basis of their inductions, whether they are representing, categorizing, remembering, and reasoning in terms of a (partially) different set of experiential categories."[8] Factorizing the problem in this way makes it easier to tackle more specific and experimentally tractable psychological processes, through methods we will explore in this chapter.

Move This Book a Bit to the South

Bujuku kurrij, jirrkaanmaruth,
ngudija riinki miburi.

Crane looked from the north,
from the east he cast his eye.
(Dugal Goongarra, in Evans 1995a:612–3)

A time-honored tradition in western philosophy and psychology treats the way we think about space as universal, pre-wired and essentially egocentric, its anthropomorphic coordinates established through the planes of our body: left vs. right, front vs. back, up vs. down. This point of view lies behind the instructions I might give you to look for the frozen fish *on your right* when you go in through the supermarket door: I am projecting myself onto you in an imaginary bodily orientation to the supermarket's entrance. But recent research has shown that some languages have radically different linguistic strategies for encoding spatial information. Associated psychological experiments have demonstrated how far different languages can influence the way we conceive of, and work with, space.

Let me first illustrate the point with an anecdotal example. When I began learning Kayardild from Pat Gabori, Darwin Moodoonuthi, and others, I suddenly had to add a whole new channel of ongoing attention to how I thought about space. I needed to use "absolute reckoning," orienting to the points of the compass for every waking moment, if I was to follow what was being said, and talk in a way that people would understand. In Kayardild, this starts from the first greeting. There is no word for "hello." Rather, you ask *jinaa nyingka warraju?* ("where are you going?"), to which a typical reply might be *ngada warraju jirrkurungku* ("I'm going northward").

The obsession with compass orientation continues through conversations, through little instructions to move a smoldering stick a little southward on the fire (perhaps an inch!), and the way you call out to an approaching unidentified person in the dark: *riinmali!* ("hey you approaching from the east!"). It frames people's recollections, their dreams, even their visualizations of hypothetical scenarios. The late Dugal Goongarra, another of my Kayardild teachers, was once boasting to me about a spear he had just made, which sported a fearsome row of barbs. It would penetrate a big queenfish, he said, as far as the second barb; a turtle's fin, as far as the fourth. And speared into a dugong, *burrija bathinyinda thawurri,* ("the western end (of the spear) would come out of its throat"). The spear was newly made and had not seen any action yet, so he must have been describing an imaginary scenario. But, in his mind, the dugong's throat was still clearly oriented to the compass. On the basis of this and similar interactions with Kayardild people I believe they virtually never think, imagine, or even dream without orienting their mental scenes to the compass.

Words for "right hand" (*junku*) and "left hand" (*thaku*) do exist. They are mainly used to locate things like a pain in the left side of your body where compass-based coding would keep shifting around. But they are never employed to locate objects or places, as we do in English with expressions like "the righthand book," or "the path to your left." One aspect of speaking Kayardild, then, is learning that the landscape is more important and objective than you are. Kayardild grammar quite literally puts everyone in their place. Some Kayardild compass expressions are shown in table 8.1, which gives a set of derivatives based on *ri-* ("east"). Equivalent sets exist for the other three compass points.

It is not that I never thought by compass before learning Kayardild. Sometimes I had needed to do it, in occasional boy-scout mode, when orienteering, or navigating a city with a grid layout. And if someone had sprung the command to "point north" upon me, I could eventually have answered

Table 8.1 Some Kayardild compass-point derivatives, based on the root *ri-* ("east")

riya	"east"
rilungka	"to the east, eastward"
riyananganda	"to the east of"
rilumbanda	"easterner"
riinda	"moving from the east"
riliida	"heading ever eastward"
riliji	"far to the east"
rinyinda	"at the eastern extremity of"
ringurrnga	"east across a geographical discontinuity"
riinkirida	"at the boundary you meet moving from the east toward the point of speech"
rimali	"hey you in the east!"
riinmali	"hey you coming from the east!"
rilumali	"hey you going eastward!"
rilumirdamirda	"in the dugong grounds to the east"
rilunganda	"easterly wind"
rilurayaanda	"previous night's camp in the east"
rilijatha	"turn (self) round to the east"
rilijulutha	"move something to the east; sleep with one's head to the east"
rimarutha	"look to the east"
riinmarutha	"look from the east"

after checking for the sun or shadows out the window. But the experience of speaking Kayardild was something quite different – an incessant need always to know the compass directions, and always to attend to them, or face an embarrassment equivalent to not knowing my wife's name, or not noticing whether you are male or female.

These mental reprogramming effects result from what psycholinguist Dan Slobin has called "thinking for speaking." However we think – and we can certainly do a lot of it word-free – we end up having to mold it into words if we want to pass our thoughts on to others. At that point, the free-wheeling non-verbal part of our minds that Pim Levelt has christened our "conceptualizer" has to pass on a preverbal message to the "formulator" whose task is to put into words. And since we do this so often, it is likely that "messages must, to some degree, be *tuned* to the target language."[9] In other words, the need to talk and listen in particular ways, over and over, trains our minds to pay constant attention to certain aspects of reality.

But introspective reports based on incomplete language learning by an outside linguist are at best suggestive. To really see how language structure can affect thought, a barrage of psychological methods needs to be brought into play. It would have been fascinating to try these out with Kayardild. But, unfortunately, it was too late by the 1980s to carry out carefully designed experiments. The surviving speakers were too few and too old, reflecting a general principle that psycholinguistic experiments need to draw on a larger community of speakers, across a greater age range, than are required for descriptive linguistic work, which at that point was still possible. Luckily, though, such "absolute" systems are not confined to Kayardild. Other investigators have been able to look at these questions in more tightly controlled conditions with different Aboriginal languages, such as Arrernte in Central Australia and Guugu Yimithirr from Cape York. These languages have similar systems, but unlike Kayardild they are still in regular daily use by a substantial speech community.

Guugu Yimithirr, from the Cooktown region, was the first Aboriginal language to be written down, and gave the English language the word *kangaroo* in 1770 when Captain Cook's crew transcribed the word *gangurru*, which properly denotes a species of large black or grey kangaroo (notwithstanding the resilient urban myth, which I have heard in many parts of the world, that it means "I don't know"). Thanks in part to the positive attitudes of Lutheran missionaries to the language, Guugu Yimithirr has managed to survive into its third century of contact with English against the generally dismal trend of indigenous language loss in Australia.

When linguistic anthropologists John Haviland and Steve Levinson went bush with Guugu Yimithirr speakers in the 1970s and 1980s, they were struck by the way absolute reckoning of space pervaded conversation and storytelling – very much like what I mentioned above for Kayardild. In the 1970s and 1980s, both Haviland and Levinson had independently filmed tellings of the same story by Jack Bambi, of an escape from an overturned boat in shark-infested waters, and by good fortune he had happened to be facing different ways on the two tellings. They went on to discover, in their transcriptions, that even though Jack Bambi was facing in quite different directions when telling the story, he oriented his gestures to exactly the same compass points (see figure 8.1). And the Guugu Yimithirr style of conversation was continuously puzzling to those thinking from a

European perspective. Levinson recalls being completely stumped when another Guugu Yimithirr speaker told him he was wrong about the location of frozen fish in a store 45 km away, gesturing "on this side" with two flicks of his right hand. Levinson thought he meant "on your right, coming into the store," but when he finally got to the store he discovered they were on his left. The man had, in fact, been gesturing to the *northeast*, taking it for granted that any reasonable interlocutor would note the absolute direction of his gesture and save the memory for when he went back to the store.

Dagugulnguynhayun, miidaarrinyarrbagurray.
"Well, the boat was lifted up; it went like this."

Miidarrinyarrbath . . . thambarrin.
"It lifted it up like that – and threw it."

Figures 8.1 and 8.2   Jack Bambi telling the same story of a boat turning over in shark-infested waters, on two occasions. He gestures in the same absolute direction in both tellings, even though his body is oriented differently. In the first frame (in 1980) he is facing west and, to describe the boat turning over westward, he makes a forward-rotating gesture. In the second frame (in 1982) he is facing north, and shows the boat turning westward with a sideways-oriented gesture clear from his raised right hand. Photos courtesy of Steve Levinson; transcriptions and translations from Haviland (1993).

Various checks on Guugu Yimithirr speakers' dead-reckoning abilities suggested they were oriented at all times, even while traveling through dense bush. Haviland and Levinson checked this by stopping vehicles halfway along bush roads, asking Guugu Yimithirr speakers to point to various known locations and recording their gestures with a compass. On average, over 120 trials, the error rate deviated by less than 4 percent from the true direction. On another occasion, a dozen Hopevale men who had attended a land-rights meeting in Cairns, 250 km to the south, were asked more than a month later about the layout of their hotel room and of the meeting room – which had lacked windows. They gave immediate, accurate answers, with complete agreement between them, to questions about the orientation of the speaker and the blackboard, and the location of the breakfast room in the hotel.

To get a more experimental perspective that makes it possible to compare speakers of different languages systematically, Levinson's Language and Cognition group at the Max Planck Institute for Psycholinguistics in Nijmegen devised a series of tasks that could get at how people perceive, categorize, memorize, and talk about spatial layouts. Here is one, the rotation experiment. Subjects are shown a row of plastic animals laid out in a row on a table in a room – say a pig, a sheep and a cow– and asked to memorize the layout. Then they are led to another identically furnished room with a table, given a set of the plastic

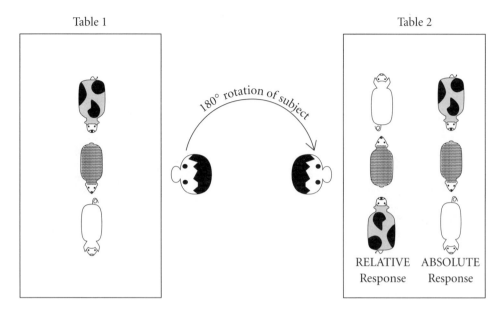

Figure 8.3 The rotation test for distinguishing absolute from relative systems of spatial orientation (from Levinson 2003:156)

animals, and asked to lay them out the same way. Unobtrusively, the new room's layout has been rotated through 180 degrees (figure 8.3).

There are two ways of responding to this situation, corresponding to "relative" and "absolute" frames of reference in how the situation is perceived and stored in memory. A typical English speaker might remember something like "the pig is on the left ahead of the sheep, which is ahead of the cow, which is on the right." Coding the layout relative to your own body's orientation, you lay the animals out this way on the new table. But what Guugu Yimithirr speakers do is remember the absolute layout – something like "the pig is south of the sheep, and the sheep is north of it." They reproduce this in the new room, even if it means the pig is now on their right instead of their left; this is labeled the "absolute" response in figure 8.3. A number of other experiments were also carried out, such as getting people to memorize domino-like card layouts, or asking them to supply the missing part of a maze that could be filled out in two ways according to relative and absolute orientations.[10]

These and other similar experiments have been run on a range of languages from around the world, selected to represent absolute vs. relative strategies. (There was also another "intrinsic" strategy, based on orienting to the projected layout of objects themselves, such as the front vs. back of a car, which I won't go into here.) In languages where one linguistic strategy was predominant, performance on the tasks consistently aligned with the languages' preferred coding method. Speakers of absolute-predominant languages like Arrernte in Australia, Hai//om[11] in Namibia, Tzeltal in Mexico, and Longgu in the Solomon Islands, all consistently gave absolute responses. Relative responses, however, were preferred by speakers of relative-coding languages like Dutch, Japanese, and English.

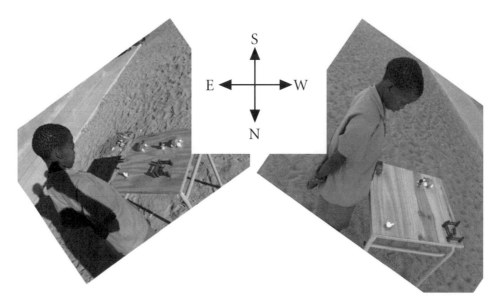

Figure 8.4   Nine-year-old Hai//om speaker Licias Goboseb from Namibia shown carrying out a spatial memory task. He was asked to memorize the layout of a farm scene (left), then led to another table 25 m away, so that he had been rotated through 90 degrees (right). In the presentation scene (left) he was facing south; in the translation scene (right) he was facing west. Hai//om uses an absolute compass-based orientation system like Kayardild or GuuguYimithirr, and he has reproduced the exact compass orientations of the farm scene (e.g. with the animal pen on the western side) even though this means arranging them differently with respect to his own orientation (e.g. the small hen, which in the presentation was to his left, is now to his right, but is in the northwest corner under both conditions) and also with respect to the long and short sides of the table (photos by kind permission of Daniel Haun)

These experiments, then, show a strong correlation between a language's coding style and the cognitive performance of their speakers on experiments of this type. But is there necessarily a causal relation between language and thought? Could not both, for example, result from predominant cultural practices? Perhaps, in cultures where people are instilled with the importance of looking and orienting in absolute fashion, they simply learn to think non-verbally in an absolute-oriented way, and meanwhile the frequency of talk about orientation ends up affecting the structure of the language? This would then be a case of parallel causality (with culture impacting in parallel on thought and language) rather than a true Whorfian effect.

The relevant sets of conditions are difficult to tease apart, but one method is to look for odd gaps in the linguistic system. In one variety of Tzeltal, for example, spoken around Tenejapa in Mexico, there is an absolute system based on projecting the predominant topography onto all spatial layouts. North is downhill, south is uphill, but east and west are both simply "across." The "uphill" vs. "downhill" contrast is projected so thoroughly onto the overall landscape that a Tzeltal woman, staying with her husband in a distant hotel away from their home environment, might ask "is the hot water in the uphill tap?" She would be referring to the tap that would lie in the uphill (southerly) direction if they were back at home.

Now this system gives us a crucial experimental chink in the less specified "across" dimension. This quirk of the Tzeltal system opens up a weak point for confusion, not found in a true compass system like Kayardild or Guugu Yimithirr. "X is across from Y," in other words, does not specify the direction accurately, since what is "across" could be either east or west. When Tzeltal speakers were tested in a rotation-based reasoning test[12] where object locations could be specified using their "strong" axis (uphill/downhill, i.e. south/north) they were significantly more likely to use an absolute strategy than they were when the rotation set was aligned to use their "weak" axis. Just in this latter case they were more likely to use a relative strategy. Effects like this are difficult to account for simply by appealing to a single path of culturally based causation on language and thought, since they show that different cognitive preferences snugly follow idiosyncratic asymmetries in the linguistic system.

The Flow of Action in Language and Thought

And from the first declension of the flesh
I learnt man's tongue, to twist the shapes of thoughts
Into the stony idiom of the brain,
To shade and knit anew the patch of words
Left by the dead who, in their moonless acre,
Need no word's warmth.

(Dylan Thomas 1988)

To round out our survey of areas where the impact of language on thought has been investigated, I will consider three other domains concerning the fleeting world of events. By their very intangibility, events are more liable than much of what we talk about to have their boundaries chalked out in different ways by different tongues.

Recently a window on a strikingly unusual system of time metaphors has come from work with speakers of Aymara, from the stretch of the Andes where Bolivia meets Peru and Chile. Most languages of the world draw on space–time metaphors that see the future as in front of them, just as in English, and the past as behind them. Kayardild *buthanji yari* ("last year"), for example, is based on the root *buda* ("behind"). This crosslinguistic effect holds whether speakers are using a metaphor where the observer is moving through space, as in "we're coming to the end of spring," or one where it is time itself that is flowing toward the observer, like "the end of spring is approaching."

In Aymara, however, the metaphorical flow of time runs the other way. *Nayra* ("eye, sight, front") gives rise to expressions like *nayra mara* ("last year, literally front year"), *ancha nayra pachana* ("a long time ago, literally at time far front"), and *nayra pacha* ("past time, literally front time"). Conversely, *qhipa* ("back, behind") yields *qhipüru* ("a future day," literally "behind day"), *akata qhiparu* ("from now on," literally "day back from this"), and *qhipa pacha* ("future time," literally "behind time").

It is likely that this particular way of thinking about time is connected with another interesting feature of Aymara: its use of "data-source marking" or "evidentials." Evidentials (see chapter 4) are like a grammatical footnoting device that makes speakers give the source of their information for each statement they make. Linguistic anthropologists Andrew Miracle and Juan de Dios Yapita Moya got incredulous responses when they exposed Aymara speakers to written texts stating "Columbus discovered America." Was the author really there with Christopher Columbus, they would ask scornfully? In Aymara such a plain statement could only be made if its author was a direct witness of the other event. Otherwise – if you are working it out from other evidence, or passing on what you have heard from others – you need to add special evidential marking suffixes to the word "discovered."

Evidentials interact with time, as we can only be certain about the past, not the future. And in general we are most sure of things that we have seen ourselves. So the space in front of our eyes is where events known for certain – those of the past – are played out. In other words, since we can only see events in the past – the future is speculation or inference – this sets up a clear connection between the seeing eye, the space before you, and the past, especially since *nayra* means both "eye" and "front."

But how psychologically real are these etymological connections? Couldn't they just be dead metaphors that speakers use unconsciously? For example, most speakers of English do not think of the relation between time and the fore-and-*aft* of a boat when they use the word "after." So could the Aymara usages not just be historical baggage with no consequences for how speakers really think about time?

To resolve this question, Rafael Núñez and a team of Chilean researchers spent 18 months collecting ethnographic interviews with Aymaras from northern Chile, videotaping them so that their gestures could be analyzed. The first part of the interviews asked participants about upcoming events and past customs in their communities, while the second got them talking about expressions for time. The gestures that speakers made, reasoned Núñez, would directly reveal speakers' cognitive models, giving a check on whether these lined up with their actual words.

Among Chilean Aymaras language shift is in full swing, owing to obligatory Spanish education and a widespread notion that economic progress depends on shifting to Spanish. By varying the age and language dominance of their interviewees, it was possible to examine the whole spectrum from Aymara monolinguals, through bilinguals with differing balances between the languages, to Spanish monolinguals of Aymara descent.

The researchers found that, at least at the two extremes of the language transition, gestures directly mirrored the metaphorical system of the dominant language for talking about time.

Older speakers, for whom Aymara was the dominant language, consistently pointed forward when talking about the past (see figure 8.5), and back over their shoulder when talking about the future, in line with the Aymara metaphorical system. For younger, Spanish-dominant speakers, however, pointing forward designated the *future*, as it would

01:13:11   01:13:14   01:13:17
(a)   (b)   (c)

Figure 8.5   An old Aymara speaker gesturing forward during a bilingual interview as he refers to his ancestors in pre-Spanish times (Núñez and Sweetser 2006:430, with permission)

for standard Spanish (or English) speakers, and pointing backward denoted the past (see figure 8.6).

Interestingly, the past-is-in-front gestural system held for older speakers even when they were speaking Spanish – which admittedly was "Andean Spanish," essentially Spanish poured into an Aymara mold. This suggests that their metaphorical placement of the past is sufficiently ingrained that it persists even when they speak another language.

The work by Núñez and his colleagues raises a host of new questions. How do more balanced bilinguals perform? Are there individuals who move back and forth between the two gestural systems? And how do these gestural systems impact on strictly non-verbal reasoning tasks, when there is no speech at all? It is already clear, however, that the distinctive Aymara notion of time goes beyond mere word-metaphors and is built on a much more pervasive, non-verbal cognitive system that we can glimpse by looking at gestures.

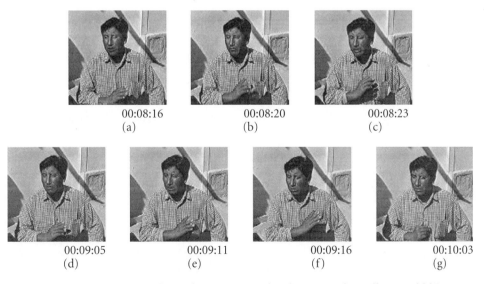

00:08:16   00:08:20   00:08:23
(a)   (b)   (c)

00:09:05   00:09:11   00:09:16   00:10:03
(d)   (e)   (f)   (g)

Figure 8.6   A younger Spanish-speaking Aymara, also discussing the millennia-old history of his culture, points backward (Núñez and Sweetser 2006:436, with permission)

In a sense that mirrors Aymara attitudes to evidence, we become surer of how they think about time once we go beyond the hearsay of their words and actually see their gestures.

As our parting example, we return to a distinction discussed in chapter 3: how languages divide up motion events. The original work by Talmy discussed in chapter 3 was concerned just with *language structure*, but thanks to more recent work by Dan Slobin[13] and his collaborators we can now see how far these structural differences impact on thought.

Recall that "satellite framing" languages, like English, put *manner* characterizations like "rolling," "skipping," "staggering," and "gamboling" at the clausal core. They then delegate the job of showing path to a "satellite" like the preposition "down," as in "he rolled down the roof" or "the bottle floated into the cave"; for this reason languages like English are termed "satellite-framed." Other languages put the *path* at the core, in the verb, and are hence termed "verb-framed." They then optionally specify the manner information with an extra gerundial expression, as in the Spanish-style "he descended the roof (rolling)" or "the bottle entered the cave (floating)."

Slobin's psycholinguistic work has shown that a suite of cognitive differences follows from this basic architectural decision. This reflects the syntactic separation of manner and path-coding, in languages like Spanish or Turkish, as well as the optionality of manner-coding (like "rolling"), typically in a separate clause. Speakers of path-framed languages learn manner expressions later and more sparsely, notice and remember manner less, and have less rich mental imagery when they read. Even their gestures can be different, as has been shown in experimental work by Sotaro Kita and Aslı Özyürek. An English speaker depicting someone "rolling down the street" will typically make a conflated descending-and-rolling gesture (see figure 8.7). But speakers of languages like Turkish and Japanese, which separate manner and path into distinct clauses, also tend to divide their gestures up into two phases (see figures 8.8 to 8.11), a rolling phase and a moving phase, just as they do in speech.[14]

Blicking the *Dax*: How Different Tongues Grow Different Minds

> ontology recapitulates philology
>
> (James Grier, in Quine 1960)[15]

> We began the study with an expectation that there was a basic set of semantic notions that all children would try to express by some means. . . . We were repeatedly surprised to discover how closely learners stuck to the set of distinctions that they have been given by their language. . . . [W]e are left, then, with a new respect for the powerful role of each individual language in shaping its own world of expression.
>
> (Berman and Slobin 1994:61)

If adults speaking different languages think differently, using distinct categories, how do they get to this point, and how soon? To answer this question we need to find languages whose semantic structures carve the world at different joints from ours, look at children

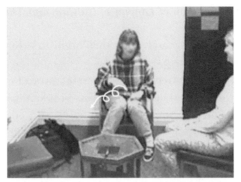

(a)   English: "He rolls down the street into
a bowling alley"

(b)   Turkish: *Yuvarlana yuvarlana gidiyor*
rolling   rolling   goes
"(the cat) goes while rolling"

(c)   Japanese: *koo nanka   kaiten-shi-nagara booru-mitai-ni   korogari-ochi-te-t-te*
like somehow rotation-do-as   ball-like-DATive roll-fall-CONNective-go-
CONNective
"Like somehow, as (s/he) rotates like a ball, (s/he) descends rolling"

Figures 8.7 to 8.11   Gestures accompanying descriptions of rolling motion events in
English (a), Turkish (b), and Japanese (c)[16]

learning them, and work out how and when they begin to diverge in the categories by which they apprehend reality.

Recall the logical problem that faces anyone hearing a word in a language they do not know, and needing to work out what it means. This problem has come to be known as "Quine's problem" after the philosopher Willard Quine who posed the following problem in his book *Word and Object*: suppose you see a white rabbit appear and hear the word *Gavagai* in an unknown language. How do you know if it means "(Lo, a) rabbit!," "rabbit," "animal," or "white" – or even "stages or temporal segments of rabbits"?

To use an example more like what a language-learning child encounters, suppose they hear the word *blick*[17] being used when their mother is carrying them. How can they tell whether it refers to carrying events in general (like "carry" in English), or carrying in a special device for carrying children, or carrying in both arms, which is what the verb *pet* denotes in Tzeltal (see table 8.2). Clearly the child needs to sum their memory of the word over a number of rather different contexts, seeing which elements of the situation are always present.

The "carry" example pertains to a rather specific, lexical category – solving it will only help with the use of one word. But the child also needs to work out some more general problems. For example, is there a basic ontological division between *substances* and *objects*? Will the child, in other words, need to divide words into countables (like "two apples" in English) and non-countables or mass nouns, which cannot be counted directly but need to combine with special words that dollop them out as "two sheets of paper" or "two slices of bread"? And if there is a boundary between objects and substances, where is it? Why can I put "two chickpeas" on my spoon, but if I move to gravel, stuff that is made up of things about the same size and degree of differentiation, I cannot put "two gravels" on my spade?

English, as it turns out, makes a pretty clear grammatical distinction between objects, which are denoted by *count nouns* that take the plural and combine directly with numbers ("two candles"), and substances, which are denoted by mass nouns like "water," "mush," and "gravel." Grammatically, we are unable to count any of the last types of entity directly. Rather, we first need to measure them out, as in "two buckets of water," "three spoonfuls of mush," or "four spadefuls of gravel." Quine thought, in fact, that it is the

Table 8.2 The many ways of carrying in Tzeltal (Brown 2001:529)

	Ways of carrying things	Verbs for carrying
carry/hold (no generic term)	in both arms	pet
	weight on head/back	kuch
	weight cross shoulders	k'ech
	in hand, supported from top	lik
	vertically extended from hand	tuch'
	in mouth	lut
	etc.	etc.

count/mass grammatical distinction in a child's grammar that leads them to understand the ontological distinction between objects and substances.

But not all languages work like English. Yucatec and Japanese, to take two quite unrelated languages, do not normally inflect nouns for the plural, and generally use the equivalent of the "two slices of bread" construction for all nouns regardless of whether they denote objects or stuff. In Japanese, for example, all nouns, even those for humans, can combine with the number + classifier construction, and there are a huge number of specific classifiers, like *hiki* for animals, *wa* for birds, *soku* for pairs, *tsuu* for letters, *satsu* for books, and *hon* for long cylindrical objects.

You might think that the choice of classifier itself would give a clue to the difference between objects and substances. *Hon*, for example, duly prefixed with a number form like *ni-* ("two"), typically combines with long thin objects like a pencil, as in a sentence like:

(1) *enpitsu ga*   *ni-hon*   *arimasu*
  pencil Subject.marker two-long.thin.cylindrical be
  "There are two pencils."

But it can also combine with substances formed into that shape (e.g. a stick of butter), or in a container of that shape (e.g. two long thin tubes of water). Yucatec and Japanese grammar,[18] then, do not give the learning child the kinds of systematic linguistic clues that they should need, on Quine's view, if they are to learn the ontological distinction between substances and objects. Does this have consequences for how children growing up in these languages develop the substance/mass distinction?

Psychologists Mutsumu Imai, Dedre Gentner,[19] and their colleagues have probed the way Japanese and English map new words onto the substance vs. object distinction, to see whether they are affected by the very different grammatical patterns of these two languages. Working with speakers from the age of 2 up, they exposed them to novel items, using the made-up name *dax* in a grammatically non-committal frame like "Look at this *dax*!" or its Japanese equivalent *Kore wa dakusu [dax] desu*. The new stimuli were presented in one of three ways:

- as *complex objects*, favoring an *object construal* owing to their manifest internal structure;
- as (unformed) *substances* like hair gel or sand, favoring a *substance construal*;
- as *simple objects* made of a single material formed into a simple shape, e.g. clay formed into a kidney shape.

It is this last category, the simple objects, that was crucial to the experimental design, since the objects are ambiguous as cues – they could plausibly be classed as substances or as objects, depending where the ontological boundary is drawn.

Children were presented with stimuli of the various types and asked to find another exemplar, along the lines of "Can you point to the tray that also has the *dax* on it?" Contending trays would contain either other objects of the same material (favored if *dax* is taken to be a substance name), or instances of the same object made from different material (favored if *dax* is construed as an object name). If our ontology is independent of language, speakers of English and Japanese should not differ in their categorization. But if language structures ontology, then differences should emerge.

The results from the *dax* experiment were equivocal. Overall – counting all three sorts of stimuli – neither group showed significant difference in categorization. Both groups treated complex objects as objects, suggesting that the basic categorization between substances and objects is language-independent. However, the groups parted company on how they treated the simple objects and substances. English children pointed to other *daxes* of the same shape as the simple object stimuli, but gave random responses to the substance stimuli. And Japanese children pointed to other same-substance *daxes* when the stimulus was a substance, but gave random responses to simple-object stimuli. These results were consistent with a more Whorfian view, that English count-noun-oriented grammar favors object construals in word-learning, while the grammar of Japanese, oblivious as it is to the count- vs. mass-noun distinction, favors substance construals – at least at the hair-gel end of the continuum.

The original *dax* experiment is limited to showing whether there are any language-related effects on how children learn the meaning of new words. But does it show they actually construe the world differently when they're not using language? A way of finding this out would be simply to ask them to point to "the same" object, without the interposition of any made-up name. Imai and another colleague, Reiko Mazuka,[20] therefore tried a different, "no-word," experiment, which got subjects to simply find another stimulus that was "the same as" the one presented, without using any names like *dax*.

Their results were fascinating, showing that English-speaking 4-year-olds on the no-word trial were closer to their Japanese-speaking peers than either group were to English-speaking adults. Learning English, it appears, gradually induces an attentional bias toward shape and construal as objects, away from the start-up attention to material that is found in both Japanese and English 4-year-olds, and maintained in Japanese but not English adults. This raises the question of whether there is a "wild type" of attentional channeling, which children start out with, but which can be reshaped to some extent by the language they learn.[21]

These studies show that language learning does indeed influence categorization, although it cannot give the whole universe a makeover. Speakers of both English and Japanese distinguish objects from substances, and agree in their categorizations of the clear cases. What is different is where they draw the boundaries in the unclear or ambiguous cases, and it is in these soft areas that languages mark out different joints to carve the world at: "When the perceptual affordance of a given entity strongly suggests the entity's status of individuation, then there is little room for language to affect people's default construal . . . [W]hen the entity's perceptual affordance is weak and ambiguous . . . language exerts its maximum influence. Human cognition is neither absolutely universal nor absolutely diverse."[22]

The youngest children in the above studies were already in their third year of life. But a series of studies by Melissa Bowerman and Soonja Choi have uncovered even earlier influences of language on thought, this time in the semantic field of words for the placement and removal of objects.

The English word "put" is highly generic, and is generally accompanied by a preposition like "in" or "on" that specifies the spatial location of one object with regard to another, paying attention to categories like containment ("in") or support ("on"). I can *put* a pen

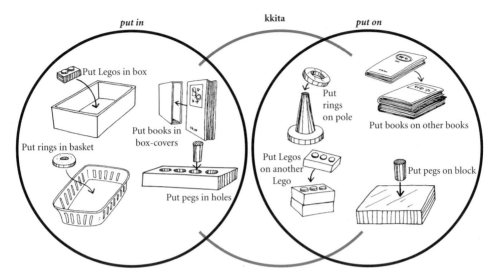

Figure 8.12 Contrasting placement-event categorization in English and Korean (Bowerman 2007, with permission)

in a box, or *put* a peg *in* a hole (both examples of containment), and I can *put* a book *on* another book or *put* one Lego piece *on* another (both examples of support).

In Korean, by contrast, verbs focus on rather different relationships. Take the verb *kkita* (끼다 in the Korean script, Hangul),[23] for example, which focuses on the tightness or snugness of fit – it means something like "move into a tight-fitting configuration with something else," without regard to the "containment" vs. "support" contrast expressed by "in" vs. "on" in English. Another verb *ppayta* denotes the opposite situation of removing from a tight-fitting situation. The different ways English "put on" and "put in" and Korean *kkita* carve up the space of events is shown diagrammatically in figure 8.12.

The meanings of verbs like *kkita* and *ppayta* suggest that Korean speakers need to attend more closely to tightness of fit than English speakers do. But can this be shown experimentally? And if it can, how soon do children start to tune in to the difference?

New experimental techniques allow us to track the attention of young infants even before they can speak, by presenting stimuli on adjoining video monitors in a specially outfitted baby lab, then monitoring their gaze direction with eye-tracking devices. Since young children look longer at scenes that repeat a category they have just seen, this gives us a window on their category structure.

Say we want to check when children begin to build categories like English "put in" or Korean *kkita* ("put into a tight-fitting situation"). We first present them with a "conflated pair" of stimuli (see figure 8.13), contrasting a situation that fits both categories (English and Korean) with one that fits neither, and asking them "where's she PUTTING IT IN?" or the Korean equivalent meaning "where's she KKITAing it?" Then we pass to a second, "split pair" of stimuli: one continues the "put in" theme but is not describable by *kkita* (e.g. putting a small object in a large bowl), while the other one continues the tight-fitting *kkita* theme but is not describable by "put in" (e.g. putting a tight-fitting ring on a peg). Again we ask:

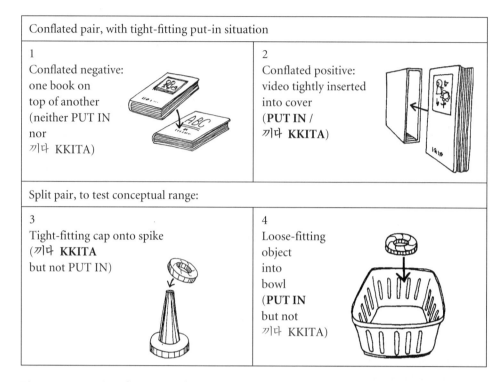

Conflated pair, with tight-fitting put-in situation	
1 Conflated negative: one book on top of another (neither PUT IN nor 끼다 KKITA)	2 Conflated positive: video tightly inserted into cover (PUT IN / 끼다 KKITA)
Split pair, to test conceptual range:	
3 Tight-fitting cap onto spike (끼다 KKITA but not PUT IN)	4 Loose-fitting object into bowl (PUT IN but not 끼다 KKITA)

Figure 8.13 Pairs of scenes used to test infants' comprehension of the "put in" and *kkita* concepts in the preferential looking task[24]

"where's she PUTTING IT IN?" or "where's she KKITAing it?" As good psychological experimenters we control for all relevant variables, randomizing the order of presentation, which scene appears on which screen, and using a sufficient number of experimental subjects.

If children are already learning the concepts appropriate to their mother tongue, they should differ in which follow-ons they prefer to look at. The Korean children should prefer to track the scene sequence that continues the *kkita* category (2, then 3 in figure 8.13), while the English-speaking children should prefer to track the scene sequence that continues the "put in" category (2, then 4). And this is in fact what Bowerman and Choi found. Astoundingly, they discovered that 18- to 23-month-old children were already tuning in to the respective categories of their language before they could even produce the words. The children's concept-formation was being driven by linguistic categories they could already comprehend but not yet produce.

Follow-up experiments by Soonja Choi and colleagues[25] pushed the age even further back, checking whether babies from English- and Korean-language backgrounds, aged 9, 11, and 14 months old, were still open-minded enough to pay attention to either dimension.

This time the test stimuli were presented without any language labels – simply to see what events the infants were considering similar. The children were first exposed to successive instances of one category (tight fit vs. loose containment) and then exposed to new variants. And the experiment found, in fact, that children this young, from both language backgrounds, easily learned both sets of contrasts. Infants aged between 9 and 14 months are still open to either possibility, reserving judgment on which dimension of contrast they will end up needing in their own language. Grown-ups, in contrast, turned out to lack this open-mindedness: English-speaking adults simply could not get the tight vs. loose-fitting distinction, even after repeated trials. Fascinatingly, sensitivity to the tight vs. loose contrast in English speakers was almost gone by 36 months old, closely tracking their acquisition of the English vocabulary ("put in, put on") for the cross-cutting semantic dimension.

Just as bits of our genetic code get switched off in our development to adults of a particular species, forsaking one path to take another, possible avenues of attention still present in our infancy appear to atrophy as we settle into the grooves of one language, leaving those dimensions of reality for speakers of other languages to worry about. And this process of zeroing in on language-specific meaning categories, the Bowerman and Choi research shows us, is already well launched by halfway through our second year of life. We are built to tune in to variant meanings almost as early, and certainly with as much attentional focus, as we are to tune in to variation in sound.

Language and Thought: A Burgeoning Field

> It is peculiarly important that linguists, who are often accused, and accused justly, of failure to look beyond the pretty patterns of their subject matter, should become aware of what their science may mean for the interpretation of human conduct in general.
>
> (Sapir in Mandelbaum 1949:166)

Despite the pillorying they took in the early 1990s, Sapir, Whorf, and the linguistic relativity hypothesis have been making a comeback. The construals of the world that our languages make, whether with their grammars or their lexicons, do after all turn out to have a powerful influence on how we attend to and represent what is going on around us. What starts out as "thinking for speaking" – making sure we have the categories and information we will need to express ourselves in a given language – ends up creating habits of thought that shape what we remember and guide what we pay attention to, whether we are speaking or not. In the end, "we must mentally encode experiences in such a way that we can describe them later, in the terms required by our language"[26] – to our *wantok* who, we presume, have encoded their own experiences similarly to how we have.

Language differences, then, impact on thought in many ways. They act as the cookie-cutter shaping the categories we use from the dough of experience, like Korean *kkita*. They guide our attention to different facets of reality – like the boundary between substance and shape. They nudge our reasoning in different directions by suggesting different metaphors and analogies, as with the strikingly different way of conceptualizing time in Aymara. These effects have been shown in a growing number of experiential domains – space, time, number, color, causality, event structure, the substance vs. thing distinction – although other areas of cognition, like the representation of the social world that we looked at in chapter 4, still remain unexplored.

To explore these fundamental questions properly, psychologists and linguists need to be paired up. But they usually make uncomfortable bedfellows. Psychologists, in general, are rarely interested in strange languages, and like nice tidy experimental designs with plenty of experimental subjects and in carefully controlled experimental settings – none of which sits well with fieldwork in small chaotic communities. Linguists, particularly of the field variety, are usually naïve about statistics, happy to sail with their intuitions from key texts and speakers, and buck at the straitjacket of picky experimental designs. Getting linguists and psychologists to talk to each other and plan crucial experiments, let alone work together in remote field settings, is thus a matchmaker's nightmare, so it is no surprise that meaningful collaborations have been limited.

For many questions that require real collaboration between them, we have not yet reached the point where sufficiently portable technology is available for use in the field. And no amount of technological progress will ever make it possible to carry out statistically kosher experiments with languages that just have a few old speakers left, who may be happy to teach their language in their own way, but not to bend to the instructions of an experimenter. Some of the key results we have discussed in this chapter have thus used large languages like Turkish, Japanese, or Korean as accessible proxies for the outermost reaches of language diversity. This is particularly so when it comes to really early language learning, where highly specialized equipment, like eye-tracking devices, is needed.

For these reasons, the real gamut of language diversity has yet to make its full potential impact felt on the field. If we have already been able to show such major effects using such relatively well-documented languages, how much further will they be seen to reach when we really get to know how you think as a speaker of the thousands of other languages like Guugu Yimithirr and Tzeltal and Aymara?

Already, though, the research we have surveyed in this chapter shows up the naïvety of "simple nativism" – the view that there is a predetermined set of categories in our minds, independent of language, to which we simply attach language-particular labels when we learn the language(s) of our community. Rather, the process of learning a language goes hand in hand with constructing a particular thought-world, and the pervasive web of integrated cultural practices that go with it. These distinct thought-worlds are neither ultimately incompatible nor hermetically sealed from each other. The contrasting ingredients of reality from which a given language makes its selection are already available to open-minded infants. But our attention to many dimensions of the world then withers if these ingredients turn out not to be needed in our mother tongue – unless they are maintained in a bilingual or multilingual environment.

Further reading

Whorf's *Language, Thought and Reality* (1956) is worth reading in the original for its hypnotic posing of the problem; you can then hose down your excitement with sober Hopi linguistic fact by reading Malotki (1983). A thorough discussion of the various logical strands to the relativity hypothesis is Lucy (1992a) and its companion volume (Lucy 1992b), which contains an exemplary comparison of how English and Yucatec grammar affects number cognition, a topic I could not fit into this chapter. Levinson's (2003) fascinating *Space in Language and Cognition* contains the results of a decade of research on spatial cognition in a range of languages, including the Guugu Yimithirr and Tzeltal examples discussed in this chapter; a more detailed discussion of Jack Bambi's gesturing in his storytelling can be found in Haviland (1993). Bowerman and Levinson (2001) achieves a comparable synthesis in the field of how language acquisition shapes cognition. Gentner and Goldin-Meadow (2003) assembles contributions to the Whorfian debate from advocates on both sides, including work by Dan Slobin on thinking-for-speaking and Imai and Mazuka on English vs. Japanese ontological development. The Aymara gesture work is reported in Núñez and Sweetser (2006); for more on Aymara language see Hardman (1981).

9

What Verse and Verbal Art Can Weave

chwilio am air a chael mwy   to search for a word and find more

(Islwyn, as cited in Williams 1992:80)

The epigraph of this chapter comes from a poem by the Welsh poet Islwyn, entitled "Gwel uwchlaw cymylaw amser" ("See above the clouds of time"). In it he describes how the challenge of working within a chosen set of complex formal templates – in his case the intricate rhymes and alliterative patterns of the bardic tradition – can lead poets to compressed mnemonic densities which they may not have found in the slack comfort zone of free form.

The bardic tradition has, in fact, played an important role right up to today in holding the Welsh language steady against the English tide. The graded ranks of bardic status are hotly coveted, and the bardic competitions or *eisteddfodau* confer heroic status on those who can maneuver their creations along the narrow path of its intricate alliteration schemes, known as *cynghanedd* (pronounced *kung-han-eth*).

Let us look briefly at two to examine their workings. *Cynghanedd draws*, literally "traversing *cynghanedd*," divides each poetic line into three sections. A neutral middle section is removed, then within each alliterative rump all consonants except the last must match up, as in (1a) or (1b). I have capitalized the alliterated consonants to show it works.[1]

(1) a. DaGRau GWaéd | ar | DeG eiRy GWyn
         "tears of blood on fair white snow"[2]
     b. DRúd | yr adwaenwn dy | DRó
         "I recognized your vain deceit"

A second scheme, *cynghanedd sain* or "sonorous *cynghanedd*," combines alliteration with another device, internal rhyme. This chain-like structure links the first part of a line to the second by internal rhyme, and the middle part to the last by alliteration (as in 2a and 2b):

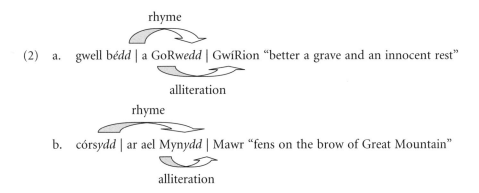

(2) a. gwell b*édd* | a GoRw*edd* | Gwí Rion "better a grave and an innocent rest"

b. córs*ydd* | ar ael Myn*ydd* | Mawr "fens on the brow of Great Mountain"

Across the logosphere, each language has developed its own special repertoire of curated styles – ranging from language-games, riddles, and rhyming duels to poetic or song forms and vast epics, not to mention the special registers of a language that may be acquired at initiation or used in ritual settings. The Welsh bardic tradition illustrates a universal valuation that takes creative mastery of special styles as the hallmark of an expert speaker, whose productions are savored and imitated, and whose intense and beautiful performances are regarded as the ultimate distillation of the culture's achievements. Meanwhile, the tightly organized formal structures they deploy greatly assist memorization and transmission.

Extraordinary Language

Aweten' "Sū!" atsoi'a.	"Now then, enough!" said Earthmaker.
"Solim' ūmā'kan," atsoi'am.	"There will be songs –
Wīī'men-makan," atsoi'am.	there will always be songs,
"Kömā'ankano minsöm'," atsoi'am.	and all of you will have them."

(Maidu myth from Dixon 1974:24, English translation from Shipley 1991)

In some areas, such as western Arnhem Land, every small clan group has at least one distinctive song style of its own (see figure 9.1). Each has its own characteristic didgeridoo accompaniment – and remember from chapter 1 that in Warramurrungunji's heartland we are often talking about populations of fewer than a hundred people per language. There is even a special song cycle that systematically switches between three languages – Mawng, Kunwinjku, and Kunbarlang – as it describes the amorous night-time goings-on observed by a voyeuristic trilingual owl, who is said to have dictated the cycle to the Mawng song-man Balilbalil.[3]

For members of each group, having their own distinctive style provides a public showcase of linguistic identity when performed at ceremonial gatherings such as funerals. It also ensures that each clan group is indispensable to the overall musical fabric, and will thus be guaranteed an invitation to perform at region-wide events. Against the modern backdrop of language endangerment, these songs also provide a powerful motivation for

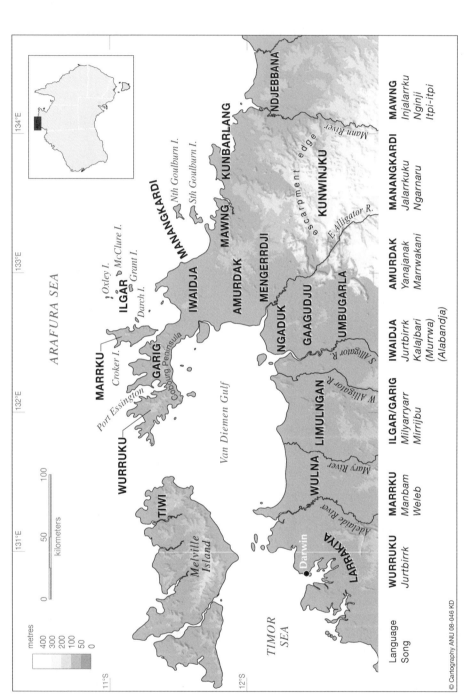

Figure 9.1 Languages and song types in western Arnhem Land

younger people to learn their own linguistic traditions. During the Iwaidja documentation project, many young men on Croker Island, who had sometimes been diffident about using the spoken language, showed themselves to be passionately interested in learning their clan songs.

Given all this, members of small speech communities naturally assume that linguists, in their quest for the essence of their language, will place special value on these higher forms. And in fact those two great universal linguists Edward Sapir and Roman Jakobson explicitly argued for the inseparability of "poetics" – the study of what makes verbal messages works of art – from the rest of linguistics. As Jakobson put it: "the linguist whose field is any kind of language may and must include poetry in his study."[4]

Yet all too often contemporary linguists turn back from the bardic threshold, as if these higher forms of speech – through their leap into art, away from the realm of regular abilities like normal speech, which all children simply learn without effort – are no longer a core concern of linguistic inquiry.[5]

In this chapter I shall follow Jakobson's affirmation that linguistics and poetics are inextricably intertwined, while continuing the theme of how language and cultural systems coevolve. The concerns of the verbal artist with form, semantic subtlety, and the power of intricate literary architecture may be conscious, unconscious, or semi-conscious, but they always strive to convey more than normal words allow. Paul Friedrich, an anthropological linguist who moved back and forth between the canons of Russian literature and the improvisations of Tarascan village poets in Mexico, puts it well in his book *The Language Parallax*:

> the medium of poetry can enable one to simultaneously constellate personal and general, subjective and objective statements in order to handle situations or realities that are simply too subtle or complicated or multidimensional to be dealt with succinctly in any other way; in brief, one job that a poem often can do better than a discursive statement is to distill gist. (Friedrich 1986:5)

In non-literate traditions, multiple performances of the same work offer the chance to gradually improve "oral drafts." We have already encountered some impressive specimens of how speakers of polysynthetic languages build up whole sentences' worth of material into a single complex verbal word. But, as Marianne Mithun has remarked for Mohawk,[6] the most elaborated examples do not just come out cold – they are found in texts that master-speakers have successively polished and elaborated through numerous retellings.

Let's think back to our earlier take on Borges' Library of Babel. So far in this book we have been exploring those library wings that hold grammars and dictionaries of obscure languages, or the variant manuscripts of the careless scribes from which a language's genealogy and history can be deduced. Now it is time to reward ourselves for these sometimes arid pursuits, and look at some of the masterpieces composed across the neglected languages of our horizon, by the oral equivalents of Cervantes, Du Fu, and Basho, transcribed from their spoken traditions in appropriate notations to take their place on the Library's shelves.

Carving with the Grain

> Some forms of verbal art – verse, song or chant – depend crucially on morphological and phonological, even syntactic properties of the language in which it is formed. In such cases, the art could not exist without the language, quite literally.
>
> (Hale 1998:204)

Like the great works of written literature, the poetic architecture of oral masterpieces is intimately tied up with the form of the languages they are composed in, following the lines of cleavage given by their phonology. The raw material that different languages supply affects how poetry is organized. Do we match word-finals (rhyme) or word-initials (alliteration)? Do we measure out lines by stress, by quantity (e.g. syllables), or by tone? And of course it is possible to combine these elements in different ways.

Classical Chinese poetry, for example, had roughly eight hundred patterns known as *cí* (詞). Each was a structural template of tones and rhymes, associated with its own theme or mood, into which the poet would set words by *tian cí* (填詞) ("filling out a (*cí*) pattern"). It is the manuals or "rhyme tables" compiled to help poets write *cí*, incidentally, that give us our best insights into early Chinese phonology. And you will remember that the adaptation of this tradition by Tangut speakers left us with the keys, nearly a thousand years later, to decipher their mysterious script, thanks to their adaptation of the Chinese rhyme-table tradition to describe the sounds of their own language.

But while the patterns for weaving verse vary – in such multifarious ways that we have yet to achieve anything like a cross-linguistic synthesis of poetic styles – what remains constant is their intricacy and the valuing of verbal artistry.

For many unsung tribal geniuses, only a tiny audience can appreciate their verbal art, tied up as it is with the tissues and ligaments of a language spoken by just a few people. Consider Anna Nelson Harry, whom Mike Krauss has ranked as an "Eyak Shakespeare," telling her vividly worded stories for the last few remaining Eyak speakers, or an Iwaidja Basho like David Minjumak, composing brief, achingly evocative *Jurtbirrk* lyrics[7] whose subtlety can be savored only with the knowledge of Iwaidja found among at most a hundred people. Nonetheless, the glimpses we can snatch from outside show how much richer our world's literary universe is than even the most inclusive and erudite compilation of comparative literatures would indicate – filled with fresh figures of speech, intricate metrical devices, genres as small as haiku and as large as a Homeric epic. Much of this creation is forged in the heat of improvisation and performance, embroidering inspired riffs on a noble old garment, bringing together feats of memory and creativity in equal measure.

A terminological problem I have been dodging so far is what to call the special forms of language we are looking at in this chapter. "Oral literature" is the name sometimes used to cover those productions of oral societies that most resemble our notion of literature, like songs, chanted epics, and traditional stories. But it is not a perfect term. Although some of the language material we are dealing with here is in fact literature, in the literal sense of being written, its traditions of commentary and translation are confined to the much more fragile route of oral tradition, and these aspects are often little known, with documentary work urgently needed: the epics and historical chronicles of the Bugis and Makassarese peoples of Sulawesi in Indonesia, which I mentioned in chapter 7, are an example of such a literary/oral hybrid.

The term *oral literature* also risks downplaying the interesting question of what difference it makes, in aesthetics and formal organization, when an oral tradition becomes written. This set of questions is often investigated under the banner of *ethnopoetics*, which Richard Bauman has defined as "the aesthetic patterning of oral literary forms and the problems of translating and rendering them in print in such a way that the artfulness of their performance is not lost."[8] Many investigators employ the term *verbal art* for what is being studied here. Others use the term *comparative literature*, which has the advantage of promoting the value of oral traditions alongside more familiar canons. But the preconceptions we have about what is included in "literature" may make us neglect other sorts of extra-ordinary language use, which, although cleverly curated and out of the ordinary, are not exactly literary or artistic. An example is the special initiation language Damin, which I will discuss at the end of the chapter. This, too, is clearly a conscious creation, although its interest is not so much literary or artistic as philosophical.

Improbable Bards and Epic Debates: the Singers of Montenegro

πολλῶν δ'ἀνθρώπων ἴδεν ἄστεα καὶ νόον ἔγνω,	Many were the men whose cities he saw and whose mind he learned, aye,
πολλὰ δ'ὅ γ'ἐν πόντῳ πάθεν ἄλγεα ὅν κατὰ θυμόν	and many the woes he suffered in his heart upon the sea,
ἀρνύμενος ἥν τε ψυχὴν καὶ νόστον ἑταίρων.	seeking to win his own life and the return of his comrades.

(Homer, *The Odyssey*, I:iii–v, translated by A. T. Murray)

The founding masterpiece of western literature is Homer's pair of epics, *The Iliad* and *The Odyssey*. One impetus driving the early development of linguistic study among the Greeks was a concern to understand Homeric language, the better to preserve it, as it was already archaic by the time they had developed an alphabet able to stabilize and preserve the double masterpiece.[9] This raises a central question, which has arisen again and again since ancient times, and which perches on the conventional line between literature and lore: could such a complex and densely wrought epic have been composed through any means but writing? Could its creator really have made it up as he went along?

A related question concerns its authorship, given that it so far antedated the beginning of reliable written records: was it really composed by a single person, traditionally the blind old bard whom Homer writes into the fabric of the epic itself as Demodocus? Or is the identity "Homer" simply a conventional label for the accumulated labors of a tag team of oral composers over centuries, each adding new episodes and figures? This latter view would explain the existence of various inconsistencies, and the presence of different dialect forms and archaisms from different periods. It is also more consistent with our knowledge that Greek writing did not exist at the time the Homeric poems were composed around the ninth century BC.

But if the Homeric epics were composed orally, their incredible length poses an explanatory challenge to the known bounds of human memory. Even the longest versions of oral traditions known up to the early twentieth century, such as the Finnish *Kalevala*, came nowhere near the Homeric epics in length, making experts skeptical that they could have been composed and transmitted by oral tradition alone.

In the 1920s the American scholar Milman Parry began his studies in Paris, following the hypothesis that the Homeric epics preserved an oral tradition that predated any written literature in Greek.[10] His first move was to study the *formulaic epithets* – "a group of words which is regularly employed under the same metrical conditions to express a given essential idea."[11] These formulae, it had been suggested, win time for the bard while he composes the next couple of lines, and are hence a hallmark of oral performance. In support of the bardic-tradition view, Parry found that more than a third of the lines in Homer occur more than once[12] – like the formula in the epigraph above, ἐν πόντῳ πάθεν ἄλγεα ὅν κατὰ θυμόν ("the woes he suffered in his heart upon the sea").

Parry's doctoral supervisor was the great Caucasologist George Dumézil, whom we met in Turkey in chapter 3 working on Ubykh with Tevfik Esenç. One of Dumézil's interests was to understand the cosmology of the early Indo-Europeans through fieldwork on the languages and oral traditions of peoples, like those of the Caucasus, whom he believed to have conserved practices paralleling those of the ancient Indo-Europeans. Parry realized that the Homeric authorship question could only be resolved by a fieldwork-based existence proof, and set out to find a contemporary Homer in some part of the world that still maintained the ancient bardic traditions:

> the aim of the study was to fix with exactness the form of oral story poetry, to see wherein it differs from the form of written story poetry. Its method was to observe singers working in a thriving tradition of unlettered song and see how the form of their songs hangs upon their having to learn and practice their art without reading and writing. (Milman Parry, quoted in Lord 2000:3)

Parry had originally wanted to work in Central Asia, but Soviet permission to go there was out of the question for an American fieldworker during the Stalinist 1930s. In the end he set off on a recording expedition to Montenegro in Yugoslavia from 1933 to 1935, accompanied by his student assistant Albert Lord. Suitable technology for capturing real performances in the field was just being developed, although it was still cumbersome. Parry needed to transport over half a ton of aluminium discs through the mountains of Montenegro, and since each one only ran for a couple of minutes, he had to commission a special recording device that allowed him to toggle between two turntables so as to capture long unbroken runs. Parry recorded performances from a number of singers – and sometimes the same song several times from the same singer – singing in what was then called Serbo-Croatian.[13] He also interviewed tale-singers about their lifetime careers, and how they learned, memorized, and composed. Parry and Lord gradually became acquainted with the league of Montenegrin bards, often by sponsoring performances in the coffee shops of small dusty towns still redolent of centuries of Turkish rule. One day they discovered Avdo Međedović (see figure 9.2), an illiterate peasant farmer, around 65 years of age:

Figure 9.2   Avdo Međedović

> Finally Avdo came and he sang for us old Salih's favorite of the taking of Bagdad in the days of Sultan Selim. We listened with increasing interest to this short homely farmer, whose throat was disfigured by a large goiter. He sat cross-legged on the bench, sawing the *gusle*, swaying in rhythm with the music. He sang very fast, sometimes deserting the melody, and while the bow went lightly back and forth over the string, he recited the verses at the top speed. A crowd gathered. A card game, played by some of the modern young men of the town noisily kept on, but was finally broken up.
>
> The next few days were a revelation. Avdo's songs were longer and finer than any we had heard before. He could prolong one for days, and some of them reached fifteen or sixteen thousand lines. Other singers came, but none could equal Avdo, our Yugoslav Homer. (Lord 2000:xii)

Avdo Međedović's performances, comparable in length to the Homeric epics, finally established without doubt that talented bards were capable of astonishing feats of memory. Scholarly skepticism about these capacities, it now appears, stemmed from a fundamental reconfiguration of human ability when we cross the threshold of literacy: even as books are opening up other minds and worlds to us, the stability of preservation and access they now afford lets us demand less of our memories.

In a preliterate society human memory is the only archive – what we forget is gone forever. Just as the human invention of culture released genes from a heavy burden of information transmission, so the invention of writing released us from the duty of memory – whether "us" refers to our individual minds or to the cultures whose practices vivify, order, turn over, and reinforce what is held in them. Our ability to remember then rapidly withers. My Aboriginal language teachers are repeatedly astonished when I fail to remember, for example, the pairing of a bush and a name they have given me for it a month or a few years ago. "I already bin show you this one before" they say, with an expression suggesting I should be struck from the list of recognized linguistic practitioners. And I once heard of an Aboriginal mother who was reluctant to let her daughter learn to read and write because of her fear that this would atrophy her memory.

Besides demonstrating the feasibility of staging such epic performances from memory, Parry and Lord found striking similarities to Homer in the use of formulae by Avdo and other singers. "The formula is the offspring of the marriage of thought and sung verse,"[14] they found, since these repetitions facilitate sung composition. Sometimes these formulae marked stages in the action, sometimes with slight variations (3a, 3b); at other times they would frame the time of the action (4a to 4c). The toolbox of formulaic variants assists the bard because, according to need, they can plug the first half of a line (4a), its second half (4b), or all of it (4):

(3) a. *Jalah reče, posede đogina*
         "By Allah," he said, he mounted the white horse.
     b. *Jalah reče, posede hajvana*
         "By Allah," he said, he mounted the animal.

(4) a. *a na kuli* "in the tower"
     b. *na bijeloj kuli* "in the white tower"
     c. *na bijeloj od kamena kuli* "in the white tower of stone"

Parry and Lord's fieldwork with these living bards gives a direct insight into how Homer would have worked: learning massive stretches from previous singers, adding material of his own, drawing on a rich personal stock of formulae to play for on-line creative time, and lengthening, shortening, or updating the tale according to the occasion – "the singer of tales is at once the tradition and an individual creator."[15] The virtuosity of Avdo Međedović invites us to rethink our notions of literary creativity:

> A culture based upon the printed book, which has prevailed from the Renaissance until lately, has bequeathed to us – along with its immeasurable riches – snobberies which ought to be cast aside. We ought to take a fresh look at tradition, considered not as the inert acceptance of a fossilized corpus of themes and conventions, but as an organic habit of re-creating what has been received and is handed on. It may be that we ought to re-examine the concept of originality, which is relatively modern as a shibboleth of criticism; there may be other and better ways of being original than that concern for the writer's own individuality which characterizes so much of our self-conscious fiction. (Lord 2000:xxxi)

Parry and Lord's study came at just the right historical moment. Even ten years earlier the technology to record such long performances did not exist. And by the later part of the twentieth century bards of this caliber were no longer to be found, at least in Montenegro. The inexorable forward march of literacy has hobbled people's capacity for such feats of memory, and the globalization of entertainment has rapidly eroded the patronage given to such local performers.

But other researchers would pursue these epic wanderings along pathways worthy of Odysseus' travels. Despite Parry and Lord's demonstration that the bard himself could be illiterate, there remained scholars who adopted a fallback position: that even though individual performers could not read or write, the actual literary form of the epic was tied to at least a regional awareness of literacy, which would allow the filtering of elaborated written models for the Homers and Međedovićes to adapt. Epics, on the view espoused by scholars like Ruth Finnegan and Dennis Tedlock, would never be found beyond the outer reaches of the literate world:

> When we look at cultures known to have been free of alphabetic or syllabic writing, not only African and Amerindian but also Chinese, we find no epic. Wherever we find epic today, in Islamic Africa, in Central and Southeast Asia, in the Balkans, it always exists within a literate tradition that uses alphabetic or syllabic writing, and the oral versions, *though sometimes performed by individuals who are themselves illiterate*, always exist in close proximity to written versions. (Tedlock 1983:250, italics added)

Dennis Tedlock, the author of this passage, could hardly be labeled a narrowly Eurocentric scholar. A student of Mayan ethnopoetics, he has written thoughtfully about the problems involved in catching the magic of oral performances in written form, and has produced a masterly translation of the Mayan cosmological epic known as the *Popol Vuh* or *Book of the Mat*,[16] whose momentous feel you can gauge from the excerpt below.

V cah tzucuxic, v cah xucutaxic,	the fourfold siding, fourfold cornering,
retaxic, v cah cheexic,	measuring, fourfold staking,
v mehcamaxic, v yuccamaxic.	halving the cord, stretching the cord
"V pa cah, v pa vleu	in the sky, on the earth,
cah tzuc, cah xucut",	the four sides, the four corners,
chughaxic rumal ri tzacol, bitol,	as it is said, by the Maker, Modeler,
v chuch, v cahau gazlem, vinaquirem:	mother-father of life, of humankind,
abanel, guxlanel,	giver of breath, giver of heart,
alay rech, guxlaay rech zaquil amaquil,	bearer, upbringer in the light that lasts
zaquil al, zaquil gahol;	of those born in the light, begotten in the light;
ahbiz, ahnaoh chirech ronohel	worrier, knower of everything,
ato, gol-vi cah,	whatever there is:
vleu, cho, palo.	sky-earth, lake-sea

(*Popol Vuh*,[17] Tedlock 1996:63–4)

The *Popol Vuh* comes from the northwestern end of the Mayan world, in what is now Guatemala, and was composed in Quiché (K'ichee'). It was originally written in giant illustrated Mayan books employing the writing system we met in chapter 7. When the Spaniards encountered these marvels of New-World literature in the sixteenth century they made every effort to destroy them. Only four volumes in this genre have survived – three that were removed to Europe by Cortes and others (the so-called Dresden, Madrid, and Paris codices), and a fourth found in 1966 by looters in a dry cave in the Chiapas.

While they were destroying the originals, however, the Spanish taught Mayan nobles to write their languages in an adapted form of the Latin alphabet, so as to produce Mayan translations of Christian prayers and sermons. But very soon these students adapted the new tool to write down their own founding religious texts – thereby leaving us "a literary legacy that is both more extensive than the surviving hieroglyphic corpus and more open to understanding"[18] – although its existence was carefully kept secret from the Spaniards. However, between 1701 and 1703, in Chichicastenango, friar Francisco Ximénez happened to get a look at one of these manuscripts while he was serving as parish priest, and he made the only surviving copy of the Quiché text of the *Popol Vuh*, adding to it a Spanish translation. Thanks to this politically complex series of events we now have various versions – hieroglyphic Mayan, Latin-transcribed Quiché, and Spanish, plus the English translation cited above – which indubitably establish the existence of a great epic tradition in the Americas as well as in the Old World.[19] But, importantly for our debate, it is again a product of a literate world, that of pre-Columbian hieroglyphic writing. Tedlock, long immersed in both the oral and written traditions of the Quiché, explains why he sees literacy as a prerequisite for the emergence of epics:

> The measuring out of long runs of lines with equal numbers of syllables, moras, or feet does not occur in audible texts from cultures whose verbal arts are not under the direct influence of literary traditions. In most languages, such fine-grained metrical schemes require an atomization of speech sounds that is precisely the forte of alphabetic and syllabic writing systems. (Tedlock 1983:250, note 12)

This formulation expresses a widely held viewpoint about how much conscious "metalinguistic" awareness people have of the structure of their language: that without exposure to literacy, and the dissociation that this brings between integral words and individual speech sounds, humans are incapable of working with the complex phonological concepts needed to construct meters and fit lines to them. But is this actually true, or is it one more unfounded prejudice of modern literate cultures?

There are two grounds for being skeptical about the above formulation. First, we know that language-games in preliterate cultures regularly play on metalinguistic awareness of various units, such as syllables in the case of Arrernte Rabbit Talk, or tonal patterns in the case of Ibibio erotic riddles. So the claim that one needs writing to develop a metalinguistic awareness of these units is ill founded.

Second, just because literates are capable of being analytically aware of phonological units when they are thinking like linguists does not mean they do this when engaged in artistic creation. To be sure, sometimes they are quite explicit about the reasoning behind their architecture. Dante, in planning his *Divine Comedy*, consciously reflected the centrality of the number three in Christian imagery – the Trinity of the Godhead, and the three realms of Hell, Purgatory, and Paradise. He allegorically organized its hundred cantos into three books of thirty-three (plus an introduction), and even invented a new rhyme scheme, his famous *terza rima* (triple rhyme), to bring the rule of three down to the verse level. But this does not mean poets in literate cultures are always so conscious of what they do – as we will now see.

The Case of Khlebnikov's Grasshopper

Language is rough drafts for poetry,
just as poetry is "the blazoned book of language"

(Friedrich 1986:35)

Verbal art can also help us understand one of the great mysteries of language evolution – the incessant emergence of complex patterning, often with no conscious planning. Roman Jakobson, whom I mentioned earlier, once wrote a fascinating essay[20] examining how far poets are conscious of the phonological structures they create. It focuses on the Russian poet Velimir Khlebnikov's poem "The grasshopper," composed in 1908, and in particular on its first, crucial sentence:

Крылышкуя золотописьмом тончайших жил   **K**rylyšk**ú**ja zolotopis'm**ó**m tončaj**š**ix *ž*íl
Кузнечик в кузов пуза уложил   **K**uznéčik v k**ú**zov p**ú**za uložíl
Прибрежных много трав и вер.   Pribréžnyx mnógo tráv i vér.

Winging with its gold script of veins most fine,
The grasshopper packed his hollow gut
With many foreign weeds and faiths.[21]

In Russian this poem has a hypnotic, dreamlike perfection, due in part to the almost unbelievable mathematical symmetry of its phonetic makeup. Although he had been unaware of it at the time of writing, Khlebnikov realized years later that

each of the sounds *k*, *r*, *l*, and *u* occurs five times "without any wish of the one who wrote this nonsense" (*pomimo želanija napisavšego ètot vzdor*) and thus joined all those poets who acknowledged that a complex verbal design may be inherent in their work irrespective of their apprehension and volition . . . – to use William Blake's testimony "without Premeditation and even against my Will." (Jakobson 1987b:251)

I have bolded the *k*, double-underlined the *u*, and italicized the *r* in the transliteration above to make them easier to find. But the formal symmetries do not stop here, since Jakobson discovered even more fivefold recurrences – which the poet himself did not notice at the time of writing the above! The initial word *krylyškúja* is a neologism, derived from the word *krylyško* ("little wing"), thus meaning "small-winged." Stripping away its feminine suffix *-ja* to leave the neologistic three-syllabled stem *krylyškú-*, Jakobson noticed that this word contains each of the sounds participating in the "five-fold structuration" of the first sentence: five *k*, five *r*, five *l*, five *u*, as well as five "hushing" sibilants (*ž*, *š*)[22] that Khlebniko had failed to notice even the second time around. In the transliteration I've also underlined the occurrences of *ž* (pronounced like *zh* in Zhivago) and *š* (pronounced *sh*).

The opening word thus projects a set of fivefold phonological proportions that vault out the poem's whole first sentence. Moreover, the ten stressed vowels group themselves into balanced sets of five, whichever of two alternate criteria they are grouped by:

five rounded vs. five unrounded (i.e. [3 ú + 2 ó] vs. [3 é + 2 í]), and
five high vs. five mid ([3 ú + 2 í] vs. [3 é + 2 ó]).

On the basis of this example – where even a literate and metalinguistically tuned-in poet like Khlebnikov could construct an interlocked set of alliterative constraints without any awareness of having done so – Jakobson concludes that

> phonology and grammar of oral poetry offer a system of complex and elaborate correspondences which come into being, take effect, and are handed down through generations without anyone's cognizance of the rules governing this intricate network . . . Intuition may act as the main or, not seldom, even sole designer of the complicated phonological and grammatical structures in the writings of individual poets. (Jakobson 1987b:261)

Is it possible that the lofty bard's-eye view for patternings latent in a language, crystallized into poetic form, can end up influencing not just the literature composed in it, but even the language itself? We still have virtually no idea, in fact, how far there is feedback from the more curated forms of language into everyday speech.

It is striking how often linguists invoke criteria from out-of-the-ordinary language as evidence for a particular analysis – from syllables, to rhymes, to semantic groupings. Personally I believe that linguists' arguments are mostly just reproducing, consciously, what native speakers work out for themselves unconsciously, and linguists' "tests" for identifying particular units or relations are merely formalizations of grouping principles that speakers are unconsciously aware of anyway. If this is true, then the emergence of a particular special device in oral literature – a new language-game cutting syllables a particular way, or a new type of alliteration, or a new metrical template in poetry – can actually nudge the whole language system in a particular direction by adding another cookie-cutter for speakers to use on the dough of the speech around them. It is for this reason that a coevolutionary framework is helpful in studying verbal art: it reminds us that the impact of artistic creativity does not stop at the work itself, but flows on to the rest of the language system.

Unsung Bards of the New Guinea Highlands

Kanab taka nyiba mudupa e   As I see, it quietly reports itself,
Kanab take taka nyiba e   as I see, quietly, quietly it speaks
                                     (*Tom Yaya Kange* narrative, in Rumsey 2001:208)[23]

The metalinguistic facility attested by language-games on the one hand, and the importance of unconscious creative patterning even in highly literate poets like Khlebnikov on the other, suggest that it is an overstatement to see literacy as a prerequisite for the development of metrically structured forms. But what would really decide the issue would be to find a culture that clearly lacked either literacy itself or any contact with an outside literate tradition, yet nonetheless possesses its own tradition of large-scale metrical narratives.

The linguistic anthropologist Alan Rumsey has recently done just that, working with peoples of New Guinea who possess a tradition of sung tales known as *Tom Yaya Kange* in the Ku Waru language of the Western Highlands Province. These contain the same structural elements found in epics like the *Odyssey*, the *Popol Vuh*, or the Montenegrin tradition, but in an area that irrefutably lacked any contact with literate traditions until very recently.

The New Guinea Highlands were the last densely populated region on earth to become known to Europeans. When Australian explorers finally "discovered" this region in the 1930s they were amazed to find hundreds of thousands of highland farmers. Although the people were exotic in their armed, feathered near-nakedness, villages and hamlets stretched across a landscape that was almost Bavarian in its picturesque rural orderliness, with fenced, irrigated mountainside fields. It would be wrong to suggest this population had remained completely isolated from the rest of the world – over the millennia they had adopted pigs and new root crops from the Austronesians along the coasts, through the mediation of intermediate groups. But they certainly represent an almost completely independent cultural tradition, and one that has remained entirely separate from the nearby world of Asian maritime empires and their literate cultures. The oldest practitioners of

Tom Yaya Kange were already adults, and well launched in their poetic craft, when they first encountered people writing.

Tom Yaya Kange are metrical narratives, themed on the romance of exogamy, with a young hero who must roam far and overcome many obstacles before finding a wife. A well-defined line structure is established by regular stepwise alternation between pitch levels plus added overlong vowels at the end of each line. There is also extensive use of parallelism, a standard set of literary tropes known as *ung eke* ("bent speech"), and recurrent formulae of the type we have seen in Homer and the Yugoslavian epics.

Neat correlative formulations adorn the performances. The perfect proportion of female beauty in this culture – big eyes and big nose – is expressed in the Ku Waru language by the doublet formula *kubin topa mong wali jirim e, mongn topa kubi kelin jirim e* ("the nose makes the eye

Figure 9.3 Paulus Konts performing *Tom Yaya Kange*, 2004[24] (photo: courtesy of Don Niles)

(appear) small, the eye makes the nose (appear) small"). And just as Homer makes overt reference to an inspiring muse beyond his conscious creative power – "sing in me, Muse, and through me tell the story," goes one English translation – *Tom Yaya Kange* singers employ parallel formulations to capture the feeling of the story "telling itself" as they mentally watch the action they are depicting: "as I see, it quietly reports itself; as I see, quietly, quietly it speaks."

A rough idea of the flavor of *Tom Yaya Kange* verse can be gained from the following excerpt, performed by a tale-chanter called Koma:[25]

(5)	a.	*kang mel we mel kaniyl e*	Though the tiniest slip of a lad
	b.	*kang mai pup yaka nyirim e*	That boy strode from perch to perch
	c.	*kang komunga mong yaka nyirim e*	That boy strode from mountain to mountain
	d.	*ukuni yabu tobu midi nyirim e*	He wanted to slay the Ukumi
	e.	*kobulka yabu tobu midi nyirim,*	He wanted to slay the Kobulka
	f.	*kang mel we mel kaniyl e*	Though the tiniest slip of a lad
	g.	*kang pidi-tap mel kaniyl e*	Who'd been ignored since he was born
	h.	*pilyini kub nai-ko, nyirim e*	And who's ever heard such a tale?
	i.	*kanuni kub nai-ko nyirim e*	And who's ever seen such a thing?

But to appreciate their poetic structure, we need to understand a bit more about the meter and the larger-scale interaction of verse lines with melody. In the version just given each line is organized into six feet, whose length are held constant no matter how many syllables need to be squashed into them. The monosyllabic *mel* of *kang mel* in line (a), the disyllabic *pidi* of *kang pidi* in line (g), and the trisyllabic *komunga* of *kang komunga* in line (c) are all timed to the same length, rather like the "vanishing foot" in English poetry. Each line has an overall pitch contour starting low, rising to high in the middle of the line, and dropping back by its end. Other performers cast their verse into somewhat different molds: another singer, Koj (Paulus Konts), uses lines of five feet rather than six, with a higher-level melodic cycle of eight-line verses split into pairs of four-line groups.

Field investigations of a tradition like this need to proceed on two fronts. First they need to record, transcribe, translate, and metrically analyze actual performances, or the fragile tradition is lost forever – itself no mean task, in a language still lacking a full dictionary or grammar, and for long tales chanted at high speed and sometimes exceeding a thousand lines. But to understand how the tradition is maintained and elaborated, through con-stantly repeated fusions of memorization and re-creativity, it is also necessary to record a number of well-known performers, compare their individual styles, and interview them about their performing histories and their methods of composition and performance. To achieve this, Rumsey and his colleagues organized special "Chanted Tales" workshops, which have winkled out performers from across a broad region of the Highlands and done much to assure the continued prestige and liveliness of this tradition. Although the surface of this independent epic tradition has so far just been scratched, it has already established beyond doubt that there are Papuan as well as Yugoslav Homers. We must now definitively accord, to talented individuals in preliterate cultures, the ability to compose massive and metrically structured epics without the benefit of writing or editing.

No Spice, No Savor

> Poetry is of so subtle a spirit, that, in pouring out of one language into another, it will all evaporate
>
> (John Denham 1656, in the preface to his translation of the second Aeneid)

I mentioned earlier that each language elaborates a set of compact devices that give the stories and poems told in it a particular flavor and cast. Within the western tradition, for example, many of the special characteristics of Russian literature have been linked to specific linguistic features. An example is the use of the grammatical device known as *verbal aspect* to plant the reader directly in the unfolding narrative – giving that characteristic feeling of being tossed on the wave of the moment that we get reading Dostoyevsky – and the use of a whole range of grammatical devices that economically express the characters' powerlessness in the face of an unstoppable fate.[26]

Masterful speakers use these compact grammatical techniques to color their audience's reactions to characters and events in vivid ways that are impossible to translate without sounding cumbersomely explicit – and also to give savor to ordinary conversation. Consider a set of verbal modifications from the Nootka language of Vancouver Island, now more usually known as Nuu-Chah-Nulth. These were described in a classic article by Edward Sapir in 1915, at a time when the Nootka oratorical tradition was still thriving. Each of these affixes, when added to a word like *qwís-ma'* ("he does so") or *hín-t'-ciL-we'in*[i] ("he comes, it is said"), emphasizes some abnormal features of the hearer or referent, as shown in table 9.1.

Various affixes and other types of modification – shown in bold in table 9.1 – are used to denote abnormal features of the hearer or referent. In addition to those shown in the

Table 9.1 Some Nootka "abnormality" markers

Affix	Meaning	Example	Translation
-'*is*	diminutive – "dear little"	*qwís-is'-ma'*	"he does so, the little one"
-*aq'*	augmentative	*hín-t'-ciL-aq'-we'in*[i]	"he comes, the fatty, it is said"
-'*is* plus palatalization of sibilants	abnormal diminutive	*hín-t'-śiL-iś'-we'in*[i]	"he, little man, comes, they say"
-'*is* plus replacement of sibilants by lateral fricatives[27]	eye defect	*qwíł -ił'-ma'*	"he does so, the squinty / cross-eyed / sore-eyed one"

Box 9.1   Animal language in Ceq Wong (Malaysia)[28]

Kapiyat Patong of Kula Gandah in Malaysia (photo: Nicole Kruspe)

Ceq Wong speakers believe that all creatures are really human and speak Ceq Wong, but that we hear them through our human ears with different "dialects." These are manifested by making distinctive changes to the speech of each species. When long-tailed macaque monkeys talk, for example, the prefix *ruŋ* is added to the beginning of each word (displacing all but the last syllable), and the vowel of the remaining syllable is nasalized (shown by the tilde above the vowel). The following speech is from a narrative by Kapiyat Patong about a lazy long-tailed Macaque son-in-law, who was making excuses for his misbehavior; it is told by Kapiyat Patong of Kula Gandah in Malaysia. The top line gives the Macaque version; the second line its rendition in ordinary human speech.

Ɂu-ruŋyãh	ruŋjãɁ	ruŋcɨ̃h	ruŋhũɁ	ruŋmõɁ
Ɂu-liyah	jaɁ	cɨh	jhũɁ	tramoɁ
it-fell.off	we	fell	tree	tree.type

"It fell off (when) I was felling the teramoɁ tree."

table, there are distinct modifications for referring to hunchbacks, lame people, left-handed people, circumcised males, and greedy people.

Many of these have special additional uses in myth, based on particular stereotyped features of particular animal characters. The "eye defect" form is used to refer to the Deer (said to have weeping eyes) and to the Mink. The "left-handed" form is used to refer to the Bear, considered to be left-handed, and the "greedy" form for the Raven, noted for his gluttony. These forms can then be used to track the actions of these mythical characters through the narrative, without naming them explicitly. (See box 9.1 for another, Malaysian, example of special animal talk in storytelling.)

At the other end of the twentieth century, Tony Woodbury decided to investigate empirically how far a culture's central expressive vehicles get narrowed when they shift away from their traditional language. He decided to focus on how far the availability of such shorthand coloration devices influences the inclusion of information of this type, but based on a language far north of Nootka, namely Central Alaskan Cup'ik Eskimo (here I'll just call it Cup'ik for short, pronounced *CHOOP-pick*). Cup'ik, like Nootka, has a battery of compact "affective" devices, though compared to the Nootka ones they are tender rather than mean: -*rurlur*- ("poor dear one"), -*ksaga(r)*- ("darned"), -*rrlugar*- ("funky"), -*llerar*- ("shabby old"). They can go either on nouns (e.g. *cavilqu**ksaga**at*, "darned strips of metal") or on verbs, in which case they apply to the subject of the action: *maqicurlagcite**ksagar**ciqaakut-ll'-am* ("the darned (one) might ruin our bath").

Woodbury hypothesized that, because these suffixes stand out less than independent words do, they could be used more often without diminishing the aesthetic effect by sounding overdone. In English we do not like to reuse whole words too frequently – "the *poor dear* girl went outside and then *poor dear* she started shivering" sounds repetitive. But repeated grammatical affixes do not bother us: we do not even notice if we repeat the verb inflection -*s* in "she come*s* outside and then start*s* shivering." Thanks to this effect, repeated uses of a suffix like -*lurlur*- should be able to slip under the radar, building up a resonant coloring effect without sounding clunky.

To see if there would in fact be differences between Cup'ik and English storytelling, Woodbury carried out an experiment to "test the fate of given features of the Cup'ik under different conditions of interlinguistic performance." In 1978 he recorded a traditional myth or *quliraq* from Leo Moses in his home in Chevak, Alaska, first in Cup'ik then in English (see figure 9.4).

Some years later, Woodbury played the Cup'ik original back to Moses, section by section, and got him to give a running translation/interpretation for a second tape recorder. Leo Moses, 45 years old at the time of the first telling, was not just a master storyteller himself, but was widely recognized for his skills as an interpreter. So "his renderings must be seen . . . as instances of performed interlinguistic mediation by a skilled, methodical practitioner making creative choices that draw on mature narrative abilities in both languages."[29]

The myth concerns a champion young hunter who is blinded by his grandmother so as to cut down his catch. When loons on a nearby lake restore his sight he thanks them by painting them in the colors they now have, goes off to win as his wife the daughter of another famous hunter, and eventually returns home with her to find his grandmother

Figure 9.4   Leo Moses and Tony Woodbury working on Cup'ik, 2002 (photo: Mary Moses)

dead from neglect. In the Cup'ik version there are a number of affective suffixes, referring in turn to the poor dear grandmother (*anuuruluruluagguq*), the poor dear young man (*cikmi'urlurlun'*) as he was blinded, the shabby old great hunter (*nukalpialleraam*) about to test the younger hunter's worthiness to marry his daughter, and the shabby old grandson (*tutgararululleraq*) getting up early at dawn. But hardly any of these made it through to the English rendition. Rather, we just get "the grandmother," "a great hunter" and "he went . . . when the day was about to come," except for a single description of "that poor young man" being blinded.

The overall effect produced on the narrative by removing this suffixal coloration is to weaken the emotional engagement with the characters, the sympathetic portrayal of characters dwarfed by the greater forces of fate. Leo Moses, of course, is still in full command of his native linguistic traditions, which he inhabits and savors when he chooses to speak his ancestral tongue, Cup'ik. But for younger people Cup'ik is becoming moribund, and language loss means cultural loss. These generations will not be able to appreciate the full richness of their forebears' stories once their emotional bandwidth has been narrowed as they are recast in an alien tongue: "[A]estheticized and emotionalized traditions of language use are dependent for their stability – if not their very definition – on particular features of a traditional lexicogrammatical code and are therefore not transplanted (or readily transplantable) into a new language."[30]

The Great Semanticist Yellow Trevally Fish

Some days after the subincision,[31] all the *warama* [second-degree initiates] taught the new *warama* the second initiation language, Demiin . . . They whistled as if whistling to a dog, and they laughed derisively as if to say, "Ah you think you know something. But like a dog you know nothing."

(McKnight 1999)

So far we have been concentrating on the use of language for poetic or narrative purposes, but a more conscious forging of linguistic codes is also found in special *registers* – distinct ways of talking learned by adults for specific purposes. We can illustrate this with a ritual register called Damin (classically pronounced *Demiin*), which was taught to Lardil men on Mornington Island as part of their initiation as *warama*.[32] Damin is said to have been created by an ancestor known as Kaltharr (Yellow Trevally Fish), and has a rich inventory of sounds, some echoing what "fish talk" would sound like.

The legendary Ken Hale, who was able to bring his brilliant language-learning skills to bear on transcribing Damin from its last fluent practitioners in the 1970s, noted that it bore all the hallmarks of a "brilliant invention." One feature that points to this is the fact that all sounds with unusual airstream mechanisms occur in only one word each (except for those with clicks).[33] Moreover, historical reconstruction of archaic word forms since Hale's work has shown that some of them clearly involve disguising normal words by substituting a similar but more exotic sound: the *m* of the proto-Tangkic word **miyi* for vegetable food is converted to a nasalized bilabial click in the Damin correspondent, *m!ii* – phonetically [ŋ͡ɓiː], which you can make by directly following a smooching smack of your lips with the sound *ee*. Likewise, the *k* of a proto-Tangkic word for "eye," *kuwa*, is converted to an ejective in the Damin word *k'u*.

Because grammatical affixes are simply taken over from everyday Lardil, it is only the word roots that display these special phonemes, as can be illustrated by the following sentence equivalents from everyday Lardil (6a) and Damin (6b): Damin substitutes *n!aa* for *ngada*, *didi* for *ji-*, and *l*i* for *yak-*, but leaves the grammatical suffixes intact (other than slight differences in the form of the object-marking suffix).[34]

(6) a. *Ngada ji-thur   yak-ur*
         ŋada   ciṯuɻ   yakuɻ
         I   eat-FUT   fish-OBJ
         "I will eat fish." (ordinary Lardil)

     b. *N!aa didi-thur   l*i-ngkur*
         ŋ͡!aa tiṯiṯuɻ   ɬ↓iŋkuɻ
         I   eat-FUT   fish-OBJ
         "I will eat fish." (Damin)

However striking its phonetic exoticism, it is the semantic structure of Damin that represents a true tour-de-force in language analysis. As I mentioned in chapter 3, since the time of Leibniz philosophers and semanticists in the western intellectual tradition have been seeking an "alphabet of human thought," which would allow all meanings to be decomposed into a small stock of elements. Damin comes close to achieving this goal – out of nowhere in terms of prior philosophical traditions, and without drawing on any tools of written logical notation. It maps the many thousand lexical items of everyday Lardil onto around 200 words by a combination of highly abstract semantics, extended chains stringing together meaning extensions,[35] paraphrase, and supplementation by hand signs.

In the above example, *n!aa* does not simply equal *ngada* ("I") but can denote any group including the speaker. This corresponds to nine different pronouns in everyday Lardil, representing the three-dimensional matrix formed by *ngada* ("I") plus the eight possible ways of saying "we."[36] Thus ordinary Lardil *nyarri* ("we two, not you, in even-numbered generations"), *nyaan* ("we two, not you, in odd-numbered generations"), *ngakuli* ("we more than two, including you, in odd-numbered generations"), five other "we" pronouns, and *ngada* ("I") all come out as *n!aa*. English, with "I" and "we," sits somewhere between the terminological exuberance of Lardil and the abstractness of Damin.

To give another example, *didi* does not simply correspond to *jitha* ("eat") but also includes all actions producing a change to the affected object, such as *barrki* ("chop"), *betha* ("bite"), and *kele* ("cut"). Another word, *diidi*, which sounds similar but has a long vowel, includes all actions of motion and caused motion, such as *waa* ("go"), *jatha* ("enter"), *murrwa* ("follow"), and *kirrkala* ("put"). Sometimes the motion is to be understood metaphorically, involving a change in possession (*wutha* "give," *wungi* "steal"), or a transfer of information (*kangka* "speak").

By these means Damin achieves a total semantic analysis of the entire vocabulary into a small number of elements, and Hale is not exaggerating when he refers to it as a "monument to the human intellect." Elsewhere he has drawn attention to the fact that its association with rituals outlawed by the missionaries in power on Mornington Island meant that its transmission was interrupted well before the transmission of everyday Lardil: "The destruction of this intellectual treasure was carried out, for the most part, by people who were not aware of its existence, coming as they did from a culture in which wealth is physical and visible. Damin was not visible for them, and as far as they were concerned, the Lardil people had no wealth, apart from their land."[37] Tucked away in the oral traditions of a people regarded as primitives by mainstream Australian society, this singular logical breakthrough had been completely invisible to the outside world – and was casually eliminated by missionary policy that had no inkling of what it was destroying.

Unfortunately my use of the words "total semantic analysis" in the preceding paragraph needs to be tempered by the observation that the last *Demiinkurlda* or "Damin-possessors" died before it could be comprehensively recorded and charted. The fragmentary recordings that we have from the 1960s and 1970s leave many questions unanswered about how ambiguities would be resolved, or whether some words allow different paraphrases using alternative criteria.

Consider the verb "eat." Since it produces both a physical displacement and a physical change to its object, we might expect it to allow paraphrase with *didi* ("produce physical change to") as well as *diidi* ("move"). My teacher Bob Dixon, working in the 1960s and 1970s with the Dyirbal people a few hundred kilometers to the east, recorded and analyzed Jalnguy, their "mother-in-law language." Although it was learned as part of polite adult etiquette rather than ritual observance, it is similar to Damin in its many-to-one semantic compression, although it does not drive its vocabulary compression so far. Dixon's patient work, which involved carefully quizzing different old speakers like George Watson and Chloe Grant, showed that for many words speakers disagreed on the best mother-in-law rendition. We can't tell whether there were cases like this in Damin, or what speakers would do with proper names like place names or personal names, whose semantics is not always analyzable but which in principle form an unbounded set.

An Oral Culture Always Stands One Generation Away from Extinction

> The . . . culmination occurs when the ceremonial life of a traditional people is threatened by language erosion. That is, when the most deep- and far-reaching forms of expression the people possess . . . grow pale, lose significance and coherence, and begin to die.
>
> (Jocks 1998:231)[38]

Must a culture be lost when its ancestral language ceases to be spoken?[39] This question is of burning interest to speakers of small languages around the world as they try to preserve their fragile traditions, but there is no simple answer to it. People may well manage to maintain hunting practices, food preparation, distinctive costumes – or even ways of using language such as avoiding direct questioning or the use of personal names, which many indigenous peoples in southern Australia have carried over as they switched to speaking English.

What is certainly clear, though, is that among the many perceptive and moving insights tied up in that intangible flow we call language, those held most dear by the cultures themselves are the ones sculpted through and into their verbal art. Their conspicuous maintenance – whether through Welsh eisteddfods, Ku Waru chanted tales, Cup'ik storytelling, or Jurtbirrk song performances – acts as a point of attraction for younger community members drawn to the prestige and wisdom of their master storytellers, singers, and bards. As R. McKenna Brown puts it: "[L]iterature, both in spoken and written forms, is a key crossover point between the life of a language and the lives of its speakers. Literature gives a language prestige; and knowledge of its literature enriches a language's utility for its speakers. Both act to build the loyalty of the speakers to their own language."[40] Luise Hercus, one of the great veterans of linguistic fieldwork in Australia, recalls that at the end of her first day of recording from Wemba-Wemba speaker Stan Day in Echuca in 1962, he insisted on singing her a song he had learned from his grandfather:[41] "To him and to other 'last speakers' language and song were inseparable, and a song was something very special. People wanted the songs and traditions to be recorded for the future: they somehow felt that this was the voice of their culture."[42] The unsuspected creative masterpieces we have considered in this chapter should make it clear why linguists should heed their valuation and make the recording of verbal art, in its full richness, one of their highest goals.

Further reading

On Welsh poetic traditions see Parry (1955). Good discussions of ethnopoetics, verbal art, and oral literature include Bauman (1989), Sherzer and Woodbury (1987), Fox (1988), Finnegan (1992), Hymes (1981), and Fabb (1997). Jakobson (1987a), although more oriented to poetics in written literatures, is a stimulating collection by someone who believed in the inescapable unity of all linguistic questions. Albert Lord's *The Singer of Tales* (2000) is the best source on Parry and Lord's Montenegrin studies, and two works by Tedlock (1983, 1996) pair an initial study of the problems of representing oral performance with a sensitive translation of the *Popol Vuh* and a discussion of its history and cultural background. Rumsey (2001) was the first report of the *Tom Yaya Kange* chanted tales, with further refinements in Rumsey (2006). Sapir's classic study of Nootka "abnormal speech" is still fascinating reading and can be found in Mandelbaum (1949); the Cup'ik study is from Woodbury (1998). The best discussion of Dyirbal mother-in-law language is Dixon (1971).

Part V

Listening While We Can

Marrija kangka ngakuluwanjina jungarrana dangkana,
karrngijuruya bilwanjuruya ngungukuruya bana birrjilkuruy.

Listen to the words of our old people,

so that we can hold on to their stories and their ways.

(Darwin Moodoonuthi, Kayardild speaker, recorded 1982, deceased 1983)

Hablar la lengua de su madre, de su padre
y de los abuelos es manifestar el amor
de su pueblo.

To speak the language of your mother, your father and your grandparents is to manifest the love of your people.

(Luís E. Campos Baca, in García Vega and Gasché 2007:3)

Throughout this book I have emphasized how tenuous language knowledge is when it is held in just a few frail minds. But an ever-growing range of techniques, from alphabetic writing to phonetic notation, from wax cylinders to born-digital sound and video recordings, have successively broadened the scope and accuracy of the physical records we can make to assure its survival outside mortal brains. At the same time, technologies have telescoped its portability down from the canoe-loads of wax cylinders and truckloads of aluminium disks, which Kroeber in California and Parry in Yugoslavia had to transport back from the field, to wallet-sized recording devices and laptops the size of a leather-bound notebook. And by offering the potential to place languages out there on the Internet, with interactive sites and chat networks and video shots in their rich cultural context, these technologies can give small languages a whole new type of appeal to younger generations of speakers.

As these technical advances extend the quality and quantity of language data that linguists can record, although arguably not the rate at which linguists can learn the language in the field,[1] there has been increasing debate about how language documentation should proceed. In this final part of the book we first take stock of just how huge and extensive the problem of language endangerment is – of how many peoples are on the threshold of losing the languages that are so precious to them, and of the symptomatic stages that communities go through as they shift away from their ancestral tongues. We then proceed to the question of how we can best go about using the assembled insights and technologies of modern linguistics to help the world record as much of this heritage as possible, while it is still there to be heard.

10

Renewing the Word

Ngurrahyawoyhkarrudjerrnguhmiyan,
ba wurdurd bulahduluwoniyan
bulahlngbengkiyan.

We're going to make our ways new again, so
that the children can understand our words
and then they'll know.

(Maggie Tukumba)

One by one, at a quickening tempo, many of the world's six thousand languages are falling mute and withdrawing from the parliament of tongues. The silence may come decades before the actual death of the last speaker. An old lady, who for decades has stubbornly kept addressing her children in her mother tongue though they only ever answer back in another language, suffers a stroke and loses the power of speech. Or two old sisters become separated when one moves into an old people's home, and without anyone noticing the last conversation in their language has slipped past.

It is not always outside forces that halt the talk. Aaron Lansky, whose battles to save the forgotten patrimony of Yiddish literature took him right across the American Jewish diaspora, "marveled that Yiddish still existed at all, since it seemed everyone I met who spoke the language refused to speak with everyone else."[1] Or the poet Gary Snyder tells the following story from his travels in northern California in the mid 1970s:

> We spoke for some time of people and places along the western slope of the northern Sierra Nevada, the territories of Concow and Nisenan[2] people. Finally my friend broke his good news: "Louie, I have found another person who speaks Nisenan." There was perhaps no more than three people alive speaking Nisenan at that time, and Louie was one of them. "Who?" Louie asked. He told her name. "She lives back of Oroville. I can bring her here, and you two can speak." "I know her from way back," Louie said. "She wouldn't want to come over here. I don't think I should see her. Besides, her family and mine never did get along." (Snyder 1990:3–4)

To a young community member wanting to hear and learn their ancestral tongue, or to a linguist wanting to make last-ditch recordings, these biographical vagaries can be decisive in cutting short the afterglow of a language's final years.

Box 10.1   **Rumors of our death have been greatly exaggerated**

The Kusunda[3] are a little-known group of hunter-gatherers who may help us understand the pre-Hindu civilization in India. This tiny people somehow managed to hold onto their distinctiveness in the remote jungles of Nepal: their language is unrelated to any other. First mentioned in 1848, when a British envoy wrote that "amid the dense forests . . . dwell, in scanty numbers . . . two broken tribes having no apparent affinity with the civilized races . . . and seeming like fragments of an earlier population," by the late twentieth century the language was being declared extinct, disappearing almost without record.

But Nepalese officials recently intensified efforts to locate speakers. In 2000 they discovered a man who could remember some of his parents' speech, and in 2004 they found a couple more Kusunda and brought them to Kathmandu to give them citizenship papers. One, Kamala (center) is only 30, and still speaks

Kusunda speakers Gyani Maiya Sen, Kamala Singh Khatri, and Prem Bahadur Shai Thakuri in 2004, Kirtipur (left to right) (photo: Dave Watters)

the language with her monolingual mother, who was too old to make the journey to Kathmandu. Her 60-something cousin Gyani Maiya (left) is also fluent, although she had not used the language for 20 years; the two knew of one another but had not met until both came out to Kathmandu. And these speakers know of a couple more, six days' walk into the jungles. Yogendra Prasad Yadav, David Watters, and Madhav Prasad Pokhrei have now been able to record and analyze a good part of the language.

Amazingly for hunter-gatherers, this language has native words for domestic animals (horse, cow, sheep, goat, chicken), for 15 different castes of tribal groups, for king, police, gold, and money. All these words are completely unrelated to those found in other languages of the region. This suggests that the Kusunda, against first expectations, have not always been hunter-gatherers, but were once the bearers of a much more sophisticated civilization, predating the Indo-Aryans of Vedic times, from which they had to retreat into a marginalized hunter-gathering existence once more powerful groups encroached.

Sometimes the final silence can be staved off for a little while, as when linguists Luise Hercus and Mary Laughren located two Wanyi-speaking cousins, Archie Dick and Roy Seccin, at the turn of the millennium, in quite separate parts of northern Australia. Each cousin was only vaguely aware the other was still alive, and the two lived far apart, leaving each with nobody to talk to. Wanyi had only been poorly documented during the 1960s and 1970s, and was believed in some quarters to be extinct.

Roy Seccin, in his seventies, was living near Borroloola in the Northern Territory. Archie Dick, after escaping a boarding school in Doomadgee run by the "bashing brethren,"[4] embarked on a life of factory work in southern cities and droving on pastoral properties. He ended up at Narylco Station in southwest Queensland, a thousand kilometers away from his cousin. Hercus and Laughren, in a bold pincer movement, were able to bring the two together for a week in September 2000 in a Cunnamulla caravan park, and continued working with the two whenever they could for a few more years until Roy Seccin's death in February 2006. This brief reflorescence of the language enabled the recording of naturalistic conversational material impossible to collect from a single isolated speaker, enough to form the basis of a grammar and dictionary that Hercus and Laughren are completing.[5]

In fact it is not all that rare for people to turn up who speak languages that have been declared extinct – see box 10.1 for the dramatic case of Kusunda in Nepal, a language completely unrelated to any other.

Or, in a speech community in which the few remaining elderly speakers are less than fully fluent, a younger speaker may be discovered whose life circumstances enabled them to learn the language to a level that effectively turns back the clock of language obsolescence by a generation. This recently happened with the Pacific Coast Athabaskan language Hupa. Mrs Verdena Parker, now in her sixties, had lived until recently with her mother, born in the nineteenth century in a remote town in Oregon. When she made contact with Athabaskanist Victor Golla she turned out to be a highly fluent speaker of this language, speaking a pure classical form of Hupa at least as fluently as the first speakers he had worked with in the 1960s.

Another example was reported by the late Terry Crowley, who visited the village of Vinmavis on the island of Malekula with a ni-Vanuatu friend in December 1999, to see in the new millennium. He happened to take with him a vintage 1934 ethnography by Bernard Deacon, which contained some old textual material in the Neve'ei language that he wanted to check with contemporary speakers. While Crowley was doing this Temo Saiti, a man in his forties, spotted a heading saying "texts in the dialect of Lagalag" and volunteered that it was "his language." Crowley was skeptical, as the language was believed extinct or nearly so, with virtually no records other than the texts in Deacon. But Saiti insisted, and Crowley read out the transcription, doing the best he could for a language he had never heard. Once Saiti heard it, he declared "yes, that's my language. I can understand all of it." Crowley went on to work with Temo Saiti and others he knew, and on the basis of this work was able to publish a grammatical and lexical description of the language.[6] Examples like this show how premature it can be to declare a language "extinct."

Although stories like those above focus on "last speakers," the final faint echo of a language's existence is that held in the minds its "last hearers." These are people a generation below the last speakers, who grew up hearing and understanding the language, typically from their own parents, without ever getting the confidence or opportunity to speak it.

Sometimes such last hearers can make a huge difference to the value of existing documentation. In the prologue I described the distressing funeral of Charlie Wardaga on Croker Island, the last speaker not only of Ilgar but of several other languages of the Cobourg region. When we buried him, in 2003, it looked like that was the final nail in the coffin of our hopes of recording the Marrku language.

There were, however, a few hours of taped material from the 1960s, made on the hop by two different investigators – Bernhard Schebeck and Heather Hinch – in the course of their fieldwork on other languages. Unfortunately, these lacked any transcriptions or translations, and basically consisted of a few old people mumbling on unchecked, just in Marrku. Marrku is so different from all other languages around that without assistance from someone who could at least understand it, this material was almost useless. I had played these recordings back in the 1990s to Charlie and another old Marrku speaker, Mick Yarmirr, in the hope they could help me transcribe and translate it, but both were too impatient and hard of hearing by that time in their lives. "I can't hear what they're talking there – turn it off!" Mick had said in his peremptory way. As Charlie and Mick were the only two people around who spoke any Marrku beyond a few fixed phrases, I had decided it was a lost cause and simply gave up on the recordings.

But the wet season after Charlie's funeral, while up on Croker Island to work on Iwaidja, I was rain-bound for a few days and spent some time listening back through the tapes. I decided to make a simple ranking of the taped Marrku material from easiest to hardest in terms of how understandable they were. Among the slurred ramblings of the old men was a 20-minute passage in a woman's voice, clear as a bell. A couple of days later, sitting on the beach with our main Iwaidja teacher, Joy Williams, I tried playing her that passage. She sat rapt, laughing and crying as she listened. "That's my mum!" she said. "She used to talk to me in that language all the time. I can understand that right through."

Over the next couple of years we gradually worked through the taped material, getting a transcription and translation of almost all her mother's speech – which turned out to be stories that Joy had heard many times. At first the work was agonizingly slow – Joy was reluctant to say anything out loud, preferring to correct my own guessed repetitions of the taped material. Later she had an ear operation that considerably improved her hearing, and after that she would sometimes say words herself. But under no circumstances would she ever repeat a word she did not know. It later turned out that another old Iwaidja man, Khaki Marrala, could understand some of what these other speakers were saying, and could help in a comparable way with one of the male speakers on the tape, who had brought him up. Thanks to the knowledge of these two "last hearers" it has been possible to get a certain amount of information on this language – although still falling far short of what we would need to write a full grammar or dictionary.[7]

The Process of Language Shift

Roger had learned his tribal language before he was removed from his family around the age of six. I first heard him speak the language without hesitation, however, sixty years later. After a long trek back overland, he and I stumbled out onto the beach where he had been born. The country he had not seen for sixty years, its trees, rocks, and animals, seemed to speak to him in his childhood tongue, and he was only there able to respond fluently.

(Haviland 2006:137)

So far these vignettes have focused just on the final phases of language death. But leaving aside natural disasters or genocide, the passing of a language takes at least a lifetime to occur, from the birth to the death of whoever turns out to be its last speaker, often as an octogenarian or older. More often the process takes longer, and this gives a way of diagnosing how far the language has moved between health and death.

Table 10.1 reproduces one method for doing this, developed by Michael Krauss. First, to count as "safe" (A⁺ rating), a language needs either to have over a million speakers, or be the official language of a sovereign nation state, such as Icelandic. Once below this threshold the best rating a language can get is "stable" (A), on the assumption that even if things seem fine for a small traditional speech community, its very smallness renders it at risk from all sorts of disasters, ranging from volcanic eruptions or tsunamis to the establishment of large mines on its territory with their devastating impact on the local population. From then on, the indicators essentially pick up the relentless demographic shifts outlined in the next paragraph.

First, some communities begin switching to another language, but the language is maintained in more isolated locations (A⁻). Then a day will come when there is no household left where children still learn their language, although at first this is barely noticeable – teenagers may be heard speaking the language to their elders, but not to their younger siblings. Decade by decade the speaker profile ages, until the youngest are in the parental generation (B), then the grandparental (C), then just a few old speakers survive from the great-grandparent generation (D). Finally the language becomes extinct with the death of its last speaker (E). (Krauss' scheme does not include a category for a situation where there are still some "last hearers" alive, which I would add as an additional phase before definitive extinction.)

One difficulty in applying this scheme is that at any point along the trajectory, people will typically mix words from the dominant language into their own. This may give the impression of incipient language shift. But it is not always clear whether speakers are doing this out of choice, and could have said everything in

Table 10.1 Krauss' schema for assessing language endangerment (Krauss 2006b:1, with permission)

"Safe"	A⁺	> 1 million speakers, or official language of monolingual nation
stable	A	all speak, children and up
unstable; eroded	A⁻	some locales where children speak
definitively endangered	B	spoken only by parental generation and up
severely endangered	C	spoken only by grandparental generation and up
critically endangered	D	spoken only by very few, of great-grandparent generation
Extinct	E	no speakers

their own language if necessary, or out of necessity, because they no longer command the full grammar and vocabulary needed for a language to survive as a viable medium of complete communication.

These problems aside, classifications like Krauss' give us reasonable accuracy in diagnosing how far language shift has progressed in a particular community. But it is not always easy to make these assessments, and it is often impossible to assign an accurate figure until you have worked with the speech community for a number of years.

Estimates of how much of the world's linguistic heritage is endangered attempt to compile scores like this for every part of the globe. They range from pessimistic estimates that 90 percent of the languages spoken today will have become extinct by the end of the century[8] to more "optimistic" estimates that put the figure closer to 50 percent[9] – a statistic that still works out at one language dying every two weeks.

There are three main difficulties in coming up with accurate predictions at the global level. First, like all predictive enterprises, they cannot foresee the impact of unknown future

---

Box 10.2   Small languages in the big city

Dam yoqta e'esa qomi qom wetai' dam qartaGayaGak enawak qom yawelaGa nawa doqshe laqtaqa qalaGaze sapaguenaq nam qozalaqpi daetek dam qadataGaq, dam qadtaGayaGak cha'aze qom sanalda himétawoguet. Ena'an na alwa da wetaguet na lacheogue da la'añaGak na etaGat hiche'kta qaq qome na alwa rqatawek da lañaGak . . . nawa qom laqtaqa eko' alwa, na etaGat doqshe l'aqtaqa. qalaGaze dam wo'o na lacheoguepi waña dam na alwa nalemaqchiguiñi, qaika da qaiche'k. Enawak qomi qom, qalaGaze heGatae shenakta'at. na lañaGak na etaGat nache wa'a nache qayayaten qayatakta e'esa alwa.

The real meaning of what we are is in our language, Toba (*qom laqtaqa*). We all like to learn Spanish, but we must teach our children our customs, our language, because otherwise everything gets eaten away. It is like the earth next to a river, and the force of the water is wearing it away and then the earth loses its strength. *Qom laqtaqa* is the earth, and the water is the language of the whites. But there are rivers where the earth holds its ground and doesn't get eaten away. We are all Indians, but we are not all the same. By the force of the water one can know what is the real earth.

El verdadero sentido de lo que somos está en nuestra lengua, qom laqtaqa. A todos nos gusta aprender el castellano, pero debemos enseñarles a nuestros hijos nuestras costumbres, nuestro idioma, porque si no todo va carcomiéndose . . . Es como la tierra que está al lado de un río y la fuerza del agua la va gastando y entonces la tierra va perdiendo su fuerza . . . qom laqtaqa es la tierra, el agua es el idioma de los blancos. Sin embargo, hay ríos en donda la tierra se mantiene, no se carcome. Todos somos indios, pero no todos somos iguales. Por la fuerza del agua, así se conoce cuál es la verdadera tierra.

(Valentín Moreno, Toba Elder, Ciudadela, Buenos Aires, July 1992)[10]

factors. It is likely that technological changes that are now taking global media and global languages into the remotest villages in the world will hasten language shift even further, as will the accelerating destruction of traditional environments for many small peoples.

Besides technological factors, much will also depend on who comes out on top in major ideological battles. Traditional languages are seen as the enemy of economic development by monolingualist advocates, from economists through nationalist governments to disenfranchised minority parents who want their children to get ahead in the national language and therefore talk to them in whatever scraps of it they can manage. But other speech communities, from Catalan industrialists in Barcelona to Miskito traders in Nicaragua, have demonstrated that retaining their traditional language is not incompatible with economic development and self-determination.

It is the belief that humans are basically monolingual, rather than the presence of world languages per se, that is the crucial factor in determining whether communities maintain their own language.[11] Ever more psycholinguistic studies illustrate the cognitive benefits

Not all members of small speech communities have the luxury of holding onto their traditions in their ancestral lands. For many, the only hope of escape from poverty and exploitation is to move to a city, where the social fabric of tradition comes under threat. And for most groups wanting to retain an ancestral tongue, realism dictates that it will form part of a bilingual or multilingual ecology alongside English, Spanish, Hindi, Indonesian, or some other world language. For these groups the challenge is to maintain their own language and traditions as part of this mix, in a distinct communicative space where it goes on being transmitted and valued alongside the national language. Many ingredients go into making this work, including Maori-style "Language Nests" where children get minority-language exposure at the critical pre-school age, but also ethnically centered religious organizations and festivals. Equally important is a shared locale where the language can be heard on the streets and doorsteps – like the Derqi community recently set aside near Buenos Aires so that Toba people from the Chaco, a thousand kilometers to the north, can live as a community while pursuing work in the Argentine capital.

Valentín Moreno with two younger Toba community members in the community of Derqi, on the outskirts of Buenos Aires (photo: courtesy of Cristina Messineo)

of multilingualism. But in large predominantly monoglot countries they tend to be ignored in public policy and discussion, and the majority's monolingual mind-set can easily get foisted on minorities who traditionally regarded multilingualism as the norm. So, while some communities may see isolation as the key to maintaining their culture, it is plural-ism and a positive valuation of multilingualism that holds the real ideological key to supporting language maintenance around the world (see box 10.2): "Except in cases of great geographical or social isolation, the long-term maintenance of a small language implies not just the persistence of one language but the enduring coexistence of two or more."[12]

The second cause of uncertainty in our projections is that there are some regions – par-ticularly Africa – where the effective collapse of nation states and research infrastructure makes it almost impossible to gather data. Meaningful statistics are thus hard to obtain for this part of the world. Yet the huge number of languages in Africa – at an estimated two thousand, it contains around a third of the world's languages – magnifies the impact of uncertainties there on any global projection.[13]

Third, there are huge differences at continental and national levels. Figures of 90 per-cent extinction rates or worse seem likely for the English-speaking settler lands (Australia, USA, Canada) and in the islands of the Caribbean and Uruguay all indigenous languages are already extinct. However, in much of South America, indigenous languages are on a better footing – going from the listings of languages and their vitality levels in Adelaar (2006) and Moore (2006), it appears that 71 percent of indigenous South American lan-guages (except for the southern cone of Chile, Argentina, and Uruguay) are still being learned by children, giving the much less pessimistic projected extinction rate of 29 percent for this part of the world by the end of this century.

However crude the figures, this comparison should be enough to demonstrate that the situation around the world is rather variable. Even between what would commonly be regarded as two rather similar Melanesian countries, each preserving high levels of linguistic diversity – Papua New Guinea and Vanuatu – there are big differences.

In Vanuatu, the world's most lin-guistically diverse nation on a *per capita* basis, almost all languages are still being transmitted to children,[14] against a com-plex national language policy giving triple recognition to English, French, and the national creole, Bislama, as well as a general ethos of encouraging tradi-tional culture (see box 10.3).

In Papua New Guinea, on the other hand, many regions are witnessing rampant language shift to Tok Pisin, another Melanesian creole. There have now been several detailed studies of

Table 10.2 Summed number of languages in each category for South America (excluding Chile, Argentina, and Uruguay), based on figures in Adelaar (2006) and Moore (2006). Summed figures for the A and A⁻ show languages still being transmitted to children, summed figures for B and below are those unlikely to survive the century

Krauss category	Summed number	Adelaar (2006) (%)	Moore (2006) (%)
A⁺	261	66.4	70.7
A⁻	17	4.3	
B	2	0.5	29.1
C	14	3.5	
D	79	20.1	
E	20	5.0	

Box 10.3 *Duan apay*: living in Sa custom at Bunlap

Sali, Olul, and Bong, three young Sa speakers (photo: Nick Evans)

Speakers of Sa from Pentecost Island, Vanuatu, represent one successful if radically traditionalist approach to language maintenance. Their "custom" villages rejected Christian missions and the schooling that went with them, and live a self-sufficient, traditional lifestyle.

Bu Mangrikaan, grandfather of one of the boys shown above, worked with American soldiers on Santo Island during World War II and was offered the chance to go to America after the war. But he was so disenchanted by what he saw of the outside world that, instead, he returned to his native village. After dismantling the church, he advocated a return to *duan apay* – traditional *kastom* (custom, culture). The objection to outside schooling was based on its association with mission-era Christianity, rather than a rejection of literacy per se, and many villagers are open to bringing in non-denominational schooling in the future, provided it is on their terms. Bunlap residents continue to lead traditional lives, with a subsistence economy based on yams, horticulture, and a wide range of products from the surrounding forest, supplemented by exports of kava and occasional earnings from staging traditional land-dives (the forerunner to bungee jumping) for tourists.

Sa is the first language of all, and the only language of most, although some men learn Bislama, Vanuatu's national language. In January 2003, when I visited Bunlap, only one woman spoke a language other than Sa – French, learned at a Catholic school in a nearby village.

A positive traditional identity is maintained through ceremony and music, advancement through a complex graded system of ranks, and integration of young men into lineage-based men's houses. Virtually all Bunlap marriages are contracted with *kastom* Sa speakers. Of the roughly 2,500 Sa speakers, around 800 live in *kastom* villages like Bunlap. Inhabitants of non-*kastom* villages also overwhelmingly maintain Sa, but with some Bislama influence.

Sa is a radical example of a small speech community maintaining its language as an incidental outcome of isolation and cultural traditionalism, with core values revolving around traditional religion, and social structures backed up by secure land tenure and economic self-sufficiency. Many factors play a role in the high retention rate of Vanuatu's traditional languages: tolerant multilingualism, limited urban drift, demographic breathing space as the country recovers from catastrophic population declines a hundred years ago, and government recognition of traditional land rights, thus giving village groups full ownership of their means of subsistence.

language shift in Papua New Guinea – Don Kulick's study of Gapun being the most detailed[15] – and, while many factors are at work, the widespread belief that a complete shift to Tok Pisin (and English) will bring economic gain appears to be crucial in driving the abandonment of local languages. In many parts of Papua New Guinea the unparalleled levels of linguistic diversity will soon be a thing of the past, despite the lack of any true engagement of villages with economic and educational development. The younger generations have traded away their heritage without receiving the hoped-for integration into the world economy.

To summarize, there is considerable uncertainty in our estimates of how many of the world's languages face extinction by the end of this century, even if we can confidently place the percentage between an upper limit of 90 percent and a lower limit of 50 percent. An obvious factor is the degree to which small speech communities are able to retain control of their destiny on their traditional lands, but the reality of economic migration means that attempts to maintain indigenous languages in urban settings will play an increasingly important role.

In general, the more desperate the case, the more uncertain are our figures. The most urgent scenarios are equally prone to wild overestimates and premature obituaries that leave unknown last speakers out of account. This means that it is often more helpful to just get out and start careful documentation, which often turns up further speakers, rather than over-investing in broad-brush surveys that can deliver untrustworthy results.

Whether the 50 percent or the 90 percent figure ends up being more accurate, the magnitude of the task facing us in documenting so many languages is enormous. And for every language where the chance to do something will disappear within months, there are many more where we still have decades to respond. Compared to the rapid extinction reported for some natural species with shorter life spans, such as the Golden Toad of the Costa Rican cloud forests, which became extinct in a few short years due to climate change,[16] language death potentially gives humankind a generation or two to respond, provided we are prepared to commit adequate resources to the task.[17] In this section I discuss the key questions that face us as we respond to these mass extinctions of the mind. These can be grouped into three main issues – people, approach, and archiving technology.

Let Us, Ciphers to This Great Account . . .[18]

Bulngahmarneyangyurruniyan,
winjkûnngan, winjkindjanngan,
wurdurdngan, ngahdjayidjnjaninj,
bûlahmarneyunginj kahnûnda bulunganyih.

I want to put down my language forever,
for all the grandchildren
and children that I have had,
as my fathers laid it down for me.

(Alice Boehm, Dalabon speaker, 1994)

In most cases, speech communities are eager to have their languages put on record for posterity. Individual speakers most often focus on their own descendants – their grand-children and great-grandchildren. But, out of pride in their own culture – so often despised or undervalued by outsiders – they typically also want to share this with the rest of the world. Maggie Tukumba (see figure 10.1), put her reasons as follows, in the preface to the dictionary of Dalabon that she worked on with Francesca Merlan and myself: *Nunh kahlng-barrhkarrminj, warlahmikun bulah-bengkan nunda yang, bah yibungkanh kaye-djayu nunh kanh karruno, ba kinikun mahkih mak bulu-dulu-bengkan* (So that it can spread everywhere and people everywhere can know about the different stories and meanings that are in it).[19]

Sometimes an older generation are actually proud that their modern children speak a prestige outside language, and they see language shift as an inevitable ticket out of the ghetto. Some cases of this are cited by the phonetician Peter Ladefoged[20] in a much-quoted article defending the rights of minority-language speakers to make their own choices for modernity and away from poverty and marginalization. Nonetheless, even such people may be committed to making an abiding record.

This is not to deny that there are situations where, for a range of reasons, the speakers themselves, or the community as a group, may be opposed to language documentation. Some individuals simply decide to take their spurned language to the grave, being so distressed at what has happened to their world that they deem nobody worth of receiving such a treasure. At other times, such as with some Pueblo groups in Arizona and New Mexico, the indigenous religious culture associated with the language is something that should not be shared with outsiders. A third and more ethically problematic case

Figure 10.1 Maggie Tukumba (photo: courtesy of Sarah Cutfield)

is when knowledge (or purported knowledge) of the language has become a political commodity that some community members wish to ration, sometimes against the stated wishes of their elders.

In situations like this, linguists may simply need to bow to speaker or community wishes – after all, no speaker produces good language material against their will. But persistence and goodwill, or simply a change in community leadership, often produces turnarounds in people's attitudes. In general, my own experience and that of most field linguists I have talked to around the world is that small speech communities generally see language documentation as a vital, interesting, and desirable task, and that they are keen to make it happen as long as they are satisfied that a long-term, mutually supportive relationship can develop with the linguist(s), with appropriate return of language materials back to the community.

Successful language documentation draws on and cross-fertilizes the work of a wide range of people, and achieves the best results when it capitalizes on the different talents and motives that each brings to the task. One of the satisfactions of linguistic fieldwork, for both sides, is that it establishes a sophisticated, evolving and life-long conduit between people of quite different worlds brought together by their shared interest in a language that one speaks and the other wishes to learn and understand. In what follows, to avoid covert assumptions about the ethnicity, educational level, or role of the various parties, I will simply refer to them as the "insider" – the person who by their upbringing has been socialized inside the language at issue – and the "outsider" – the person who is seeking to record information on a language they do not themselves speak with fluency.

Literate and linguistically trained insiders with an interest in recording their own language played a key role in Fray Sahagún's early work on Aztec, as we saw in chapter 2, and in the gathering of textual and grammatical materials for many North American languages. Examples are William Jones, a native speaker of Fox who produced major text collections in Fox and Ojibwa, or Ella Deloria, coauthor with Franz Boas of a classic 1940s grammar of Dakota.

Often insiders, although commanding great respect within their own small community for their traditional knowledge, may lack formal education altogether and be unable to read or write, yet rapidly reveal themselves to be formidable natural linguists. Indeed, I personally believe that it is a natural interest in and flair for language that enables a subset of individuals from the last generation of speakers to acquire their ancestral tongue in the adverse circumstance of language obsolescence.

Figure 10.2   Saem Majnep at work (photo: courtesy of John Dumbacher)

Perhaps the most compelling example of how a brilliant insider with limited formal schooling can contribute directly to documenting indigenous knowledge, this time at the boundary between linguistics and ethnobiology, is the case of Saem Majnep (see figure 10.2), a speaker of Kalam in the Upper Kaironk valley of Madang Province, Papua New Guinea. Majnep started out as a field assistant to anthropologist Ralph Bulmer, who noted his outstanding bush knowledge. Bulmer was committed to

> the need in ethnographic reporting for two-sided partnerships in which the informant is given equal status with the anthropologist. He meant not only joint authorship, but, above all, a form of ethographic reporting in which the insider is allowed to speak for himself, instead of having his words filtered through the prism of the anthropologist's interpretation and reformulated in Western forms of discourse. (Pawley 2007:xxi, in preface to Majnep and Bulmer 2007)

To make this happen he needed an orthography for Kalam, and enlisted linguists Bruce Biggs and Andy Pawley in this task. Majnep, although he had only got as far as the second year at primary school, learned to write Kalam in this orthography and began putting together a vast compendium of ethnobiological essays, working by talking onto a cassette recorder in Kalam and Tok Pisin, and then transcribing these in a series of notebooks. Bulmer then helped arrange these thematically, and worked up an English translation aided by a Kalam dictionary that Pawley, Majnep, and others developed over the decades. This material eventually grew into two immense published treatises on traditional Kalam biological knowledge, one on birds and one on mammals,[21] with a third on plants soon to appear. An example of the depth of Majnep's knowledge is his discussion, in *Birds of my Kalam Country*, of a bird with poisonous feathers – something that western science at that time believed impossible. The Kalam name for this bird is *wobob* (pronounced *wompwomp*) and Majnep wrote about it that "some men say the skin is bitter and puckers the mouth." Some years later western biologist Jack Dumbacher picked up this lead, and reported on its toxic properties in the pages of *Science*.[22]

Saem Majnep, too, has recently departed this world. As Andy Pawley wrote in his obituary: "What made Majnep unique in the world of natural history is that he had almost no education and was able to write about the biology of his region, not as a western-trained scientist, but as a member of a traditional community."[23]

On a more mundane level, it is normal within speech communities that insiders vary widely in what they are good at. With Kayardild, for example, I discovered that Pluto Bentinck, although his grammar was oversimplified and irrevocably shot through with pidgin, was far and away the most knowledgeable source of plant names – somehow the mangling of his grammatical knowledge had not touched his ethnobotanical competence. And it often happens that the most inspired storytellers are not temperamentally suited either to the slow work of transcription or the grinding systematicity of working through complex paradigms. Working with a wide range of speakers, then, gives a richer and more varied profile of the language, and creates a sense of shared enterprise in the community. It is also vital to draw in younger speakers who might otherwise be left out of the process, in ways that can range from transcription and translation to taking a major part in the documentary process (see box 10.4).

But this is only the beginning. How best to tap and develop the full talents and knowledge of the "natural linguists" so commonly encountered during fieldwork is one of the greatest challenges facing linguistics today.

The benefits to linguistic science are clear – native speaker insights can have a depth and precision that outsiders can still be struggling to reach after decades of work. As Ken Hale wrote in 1972: "I question whether significant advances beyond the present state of knowledge of the world's languages can be made if important sectors of linguistics continue to be dominated by scholars who are not native speakers of the languages they study."[24]

The benefits to the speech community itself are equally great. Advanced training of community members creates new possibilities for the whole community to understand and

---

Box 10.4   For our words to beach safely . . .

Kuikuró speakers engaged in documenting their own languages as part of the Kuikuró language project in the Mato Grosso of Brazil: Takamā and Munai documenting a traditional ceremony (left; photo by Mara Santos) and Kuikuró speakers Mutua and Jamatua entering transcriptions/translations (right; photo by Vincent Carelli)

The Kuikuró documentation program in the Upper Xingu region of Brazil, led by Bruna Franchetto with support from the Volkswagen Foundation's DoBeS program, shows how far it is possible for members of speech communities to participate in the documentation of their own language. Although their remote setting may seem geographically distant from institutions of formal education, the Kuikuró have a deeply

shape the impingement of the outside world. At the level of social and economic justice, formal education of native-speaker linguists gives them the skills and recognition their talents deserve, and creates a more interesting and interactive research dynamic.

Obvious and desirable as the goal is, however, we are still a long way from meeting the challenge of properly training native-speaker linguists. There are many obstacles. Universities in many parts of the world are conservative in their admission requirements, and generally unaware of the advantage that pre-existing language knowledge can bring for native speakers interested in language analysis. Most institutions are (rightly) willing to admit PhD candidates with a training in linguistics but no knowledge yet of the language they will study. But they do not extend the converse recognition to those with a deep knowledge of their language but no formal training yet in linguistics.

ingrained interest in the workings of their language. This is epitomized by the metaphor they use for grammatical particles and deictic words anchoring meanings to context: *tisakisü enkgutoho*, roughly "made for our words to beach safely."

After gaining the endorsement of tribal chiefs to carry out their own documentation, and overcoming the reluctance of some community members to have insiders carrying out the role of language documenter, several young Kuikuró have embarked on a comprehensive program of recording their own language in a wide range of contexts. One of them, Mutua, recently submitted his undergraduate thesis on the intricacies of plural semantics in Kuikuró through an innovative program at the Indigenous University of Mato Grosso (UNEMAT) – testimony to the ability of some insiders to harness their traditional knowledge in formal western education despite their non-standard educational backgrounds.

Native-speaker linguists, apart from an initial lack of formal academic training, may face special demands that traditional community life places on them, such as the obligation to attend ceremonies and funerals whose timing may be unpredictable and may clash with crucial academic dates. If they come from small communities and end up as the best-educated person, they may face so many demands – educational, legal, and administrative – that they lack the time to concentrate solely on linguistic matters. It may also happen, paradoxically, that communities can be less receptive to linguistic work by insiders than by outsiders, as the O'odham linguist and poet Ofelia Zepeda has pointed out.[25]

Despite these problems, some notable programs for training native-speaker linguists have begun to emerge in recent years. One of the most instructive is OKMA (*Oxlajuuj Keej Maya' Ajtz'iib'*) in Guatemala, established as a linguistic research and training group dedicated to Mayan linguistics. This was set up in the late 1980s to help reestablish a Mayan identity after the ravages of the Guatemalan civil war, along with other Mayan-language institutions like the Academy of Mayan languages. Mayan speakers asked US linguist Nora England to give them the training they needed to carry out their own linguistic research. She was able to use the five years granted to her through a Macarthur Fellowship to train an initial "generation" of linguists, with further support from the Norwegian government.

The structure of the OKMA program is interesting. From an initial recruitment of a larger number of young would-be linguists, two trainees per language were selected for two years of training. From this starting point, subsequent "generations" were brought in to be trained each couple of years by a combination of previous generations, England herself on a less intense basis, and other linguist visitors. Many graduates of this program have now gone on to more conventional linguistic studies.

Do the roles of insider and outsider linguist differ, from a scientific point of view? Felix Ameka[26] has written a thoughtful assessment of the history of grammatical descriptions of his mother tongue, the Ghanaian language Ewe. In it he weighs up the varying contributions of both native-speaker and outsider linguists in the century since the first Ewe grammar appeared in 1907, by the German missionary linguist Diedrich Westermann. Ameka is well placed to evaluate this question, having worked as an insider on his mother tongue and as an outsider on another language of the Ghana-Togo mountains, Likpe, and in addition has trained both insiders and outsiders to work on Ewe. He concludes that each perspective is both vital and inadequate by itself, citing the late Mary Haas, who worked on so many Native American languages: "We gain insight from the outside looking in as well as from the inside looking out."[27]

This brings us to the other challenge – that of training "outsiders" as field linguists. In a way this is a problem that linguistics has been facing for a long time, since the golden days of Boas and Sapir. Strangely, though, there have also been recent periods where powerful figures in the most academically influential countries have denigrated or ignored the role of descriptive work, compared to the supposedly nobler and more scientifically challenging task of "theoretical" work in formal paradigms like generative grammar. Since the ascent to dominance of Chomskyan generative linguistics in the 1960s, the focus in North America and in many countries that followed its academic trends has been on theoretical modeling of fragments of well-known languages, rather than on new empirical work. Indeed, it is currently the case that in most US universities a reference grammar of a little-described language is not a permissible doctoral topic, despite the fact that it is about the most demanding intellectual task a linguist can engage in.[28] This has led to an explosion of work on English and a dozen or so other well-known languages, and a corresponding neglect of the other 6,000 languages of the world.[29]

Doctoral work is perhaps the ideal moment in a young scholar's life for undertaking fieldwork – with the freedom to spend long periods in a remote location, and the opportunity to concentrate exclusively over several years on the task of figuring the language out. Yet the talented and committed human resource offered by doctoral students is being squandered by the very field that we would expect to have the greatest interest in charting the world's linguistic diversity.

This is not to say that every linguistics PhD student has the personality, interests, or life circumstances to make a go of fieldwork, but the proportion is certainly much higher than the depressingly low percentage that Newman found. Luckily world academia is not a monoculture, and some countries (e.g. Australia and the Netherlands) have held to the value of descriptive work in doctoral degrees in defiance of the dominant North American trend. And more recently there has been a revived receptiveness to the value of doctoral fieldwork in a few US universities. But the field of linguistics still needs a massive turnaround of professional priorities, an expansion of field training, and a proper recognition of the value and the time demands of descriptive work. Only then can we marshal the number of trained linguistic scholars that is needed to document our fragile linguistic heritage over the coming decades. As the British colonial administrator Colonel Lorimer put it, in the preface to his 1935 grammar of the enigmatic Burushaski isolate language of northern Pakistan: "How much can now be done will again be governed by the time factor – the harvest is ripe, but the labourers are few."[30]

Bringing It Out and Laying It Down

> Descendants of speakers will not be learning the language so that they can order a meal in a restaurant or ask directions to the railway station. They will want to know what is special about their heritage.
>
> (Mithun 2007)

In chapter 2 we mentioned a tried and true approach to illustrating the many facets of a language in an approachable form: the so-called Boasian trilogy, named after Franz Boas, which can present a rich portrait of a language in three mutually illuminating volumes: grammar, texts, and dictionary. But, however useful it is, this trilogy will not supply answers to all the questions that future linguists and community members will want to ask.

To begin with, no matter how hard the linguist has tried to be comprehensive in their grammatical description, and to represent the functionings of the language in a way that does justice to its own unique genius, there will always be phenomena they have overlooked or failed to understand. As Andy Pawley once wrote, "a language should not be assumed to have just the characteristics of its linguistic description."[31] Text collections, and a rich set of sample sentences distilled into dictionary entries, are a useful reservoir of material whose significance the grammarian may have overlooked, and in which later researchers may find undetected patterns.

As we saw in chapter 2, the idea of making substantial, ethnographically informed text collections goes back a long way. This was the basis of Sahagún's epocal Aztec/Spanish compendium, *General History of the Things of New Spain*, and it has kept resurfacing in text collections by linguists ever since. But, however rich and extensive they may be, such collections do not capture every aspect of language use. They typically favor the formal and literary at the expense of the casual and slangy. They filter out the hesitations and mistakes of actual speech that may play a crucial part in pointing the way to future changes in the language. And they can be uninformative about exactly how people speak to each other in intimate situations.

Since the mid 1990s a number of scholars, Nikolaus Himmelmann[32] foremost among them, have argued that we need a new subfield of linguistics in its own right, *documentary linguistics*, independently of the traditional concerns of descriptive linguistics. This subfield would be concerned with the compilation and preservation of linguistic primary data, and with securing a lasting, multipurpose record of a language:

> The net should be cast as widely as possible. That is, a language documentation should strive to include as many and as varied records as practically feasible . . . Ideally . . . a language documentation would cover all registers and varieties, social or local; it would contain evidence for language as a social practice as well as a cognitive faculty; it would include specimens of spoken and written language; and so on. (Himmelmann 2006:2, with permission)

Essentially, this approach is concerned with elaborating a set of procedures that have two goals. First, to make sure that linguists are scrupulous in making their primary data available to other investigators. Second (and this is more difficult) to ensure that all phenomena of a language are well-sampled in the recordings they make. Only in this way can we ensure that documentary linguists do what Wittgenstein exhorted philosophers to do: "plough over the whole of language."

The paradox that documentary linguistics must confront is how to provide for future questions that the original documenter does not ask. Throughout this book we have seen how widely linguistic research must roam. Grammar is important for all sorts of reasons – it is central to our task of understanding possible human languages, lays down the most insistent grooves of habitual thought, and conceals the evidence of distant historical relationships inside the pesky irregularities of its paradigms. But the lexicon is equally important: crucial information linking languages or families to the archaeological record may depend on obscure place-names or plant terms, and every one of a language's thousands of vocabulary items needs its own sensitive investigation. It is only with multiple attestations that we can really understand what a word or prefix means, as we saw with our *molkkûn-* ("unbeknown to someone") example in chapter 3.

Each language possesses certain structural densities of its own that require targeted investigation and whose logic may not become apparent in a naturalistic corpus, because even a large corpus contains all sorts of gaps. Consider English for a moment. A breakthrough in Chomsky's theory of syntax in the 1950s came with the recognition that syntax can be recursive, feeding the output of a rule back into that very same rule to create multiply embedded structures. An example is the following line from a Rolf Harris song, deeply etched into my memory from singing it on long childhood car journeys:

> Now the fascinating witches
> [who put the scintillating stitches in the britches
> [of the boys [who put the powder on the noses
> [of the faces [of the ladies [of the harem
> [of the court [of King Caractacus]]]]]]]]
> are just passing by.

This builds up its lung-challenging structure by two recursive "looping" tactics that generate "center-embedding": possessive *of*-phrases ("the noses of the faces of the ladies of the court"), and relative clauses ("witches who put . . . boys who put"). In writing this example out, I have indicated each level of embedding with square brackets.

In principle, the computational power needed to generate such sentences allows infinitely many embeddings, although limited in practice by lung and memory capacity. This property of *unbounded recursiveness* was a linchpin in Chomsky's demonstration that human grammars could not be modeled by certain types of device that were at that time believed sufficient to represent natural language – the so-called finite state grammars. Yet a recent study by Fred Karlsson has shown that naturally occurring spontaneous English speech essentially lacks structures with more than two degrees of embedding. A grammar constructed just from sentences collected by a Martian linguist recording what people say would not need the computational power Chomsky argued for.

Yet this would be wrong. Any English speaker, if asked, will judge King Caractacus-style examples perfectly acceptable. In other words, speakers tend to have an inner grammar of what their language permits that is much richer than what they actually say. The trick for the linguist is to sense where these shadowy nodes of complexity are, and to probe them by targeted questioning that enriches the documentary record beyond what natural speech would yield. (Of course, if the Martian linguist was interested in the sort of verbal art discussed in chapter 9, they would certainly be recording Rolf Harris songs and would end up getting these intricate sentences. This is because elaborately rehearsed performances enable speakers to push the boundaries of complexity much higher than that found in normal unrehearsed speech.)

Just where the linguist will need to apply these techniques of systematic probing depends on the genius of the language. In one language, it will be important to vary all the dimensions of a verb or noun paradigm to make sure all logical cells are recorded, since paradigms tend to be nests of irregularity where each combination needs separate checking.

In a second, we will need to vary all tonal combinations in a given sequence of words to see how the tones interact or reveal hidden "floating tones." As Larry Hyman has shown,[33] if you want to check out all combinations of floating tones in a language like Kuki-Chin from Nagaland near the Indian–Burmese border, you will have to construct unnatural-sounding sequences like "chief's beetle's kidney basket" or "monkey's enemy's snake's ear" in order to get the right tonal line-ups to test particular hypotheses.

It is unlikely that even an infinitely large corpus would contain all the combinations needed to work out the answers to questions like this. If linguists merely point the microphone, without shaping what is to be gathered through their own evolving analysis, future scholars will be deprived of key data. On top of that, to be really useful a corpus must contain discussions of the various ways that each sentence in it can be interpreted in different contexts – a semantically annotated metacorpus. Again, this can only be produced by embroidering structured probing onto the original text.[34]

The best guarantee for the future usability of a documented corpus is thus a complex hybrid of natural and elicited data. In practice linguists proceed best in an everlasting spiral of texts, grammar, and dictionary, with advances in each informing how the others are understood.[35] For those parts of a language where the linguist glimpses the outlines of a well-organized structure, rigorous description and analysis makes sure that all relevant combinations are asked about and recorded. As a report on what makes documentation adequate put it, "analysis is itself critical to assessing the sufficiency of a documentation corpus."[36]

One of the key qualities of a good field linguist is their ability to sense where these nodal zones lie and zero in on them for more structured intensive questioning. But for other parts of the language, a more free-flowing approach that emphasizes balanced sampling is the best hedge against unasked questions.

Two final key ingredients go into making a robust and broad documentation. First, the more rangingly curious the linguist is – and we have seen in this book just how widely the phenomenon of language engages with questions touching on many areas of knowledge – the more they will sense where to probe deeper. The great lexicographer James Murray, founding architect of the Oxford English Dictionary, credited much of his success to his omnivorous interest in every conceivable topic that humans talk about.[37]

This leads on naturally to the second crucial ingredient. The more investigators work on a given language – insiders and outsiders, linguists with different foci of interest, other investigators ranging from ethnobiologists to musicologists to specialists in material culture – the greater the range of issues that, in Maggie Tukumba's words, will be "brought out" from the minds of speakers into dialogue, and "put down" in some more durable form for the sake of future generations:

Nunh kenbo, kardu marruh-kûno nga-yawoh-dulu-burlhkeyhwoyan nga-yawoh-yungiyan bebakah . . . Nunh kenbo ngahlng-burlhkeywoyan rerrikah, duludjerrnguno, kanhkuno ngah-yungiyan kanunh bebakah. Kenbo yilah-dulu-burlhkeyhwoyan, mak kaduluwanjingh, bah kadjahlng-ngongno kanh duluno, kanh drebuy njelng yilaye-yenjdjung.	From now on, whenever, I bring out a story or word, I'll put it in the book. And other things, that I'll bring out later, new words, I'll put them on paper. Then we'll bring out the meaning of things, not just one idea, but all sorts of meanings, including the subtleties of what we say.[38]

From Clay Tablets to Hard Drives

Today's linguists can access printed and handwritten documentation that is hundreds (sometimes thousands) of years old. However, much digital language documentation and description becomes inaccessible within a decade of its creation ... In the very generation when the rate of language death is at its peak, we have chosen to use moribund technologies, and to create endangered data.

(Bird and Simons 2003:557, with permission)

It is no use recording detailed language and cultural material if the recordings themselves are not properly conserved and archived – or our fragile recordings may follow the speakers they contain into oblivion.

The enthusiastic uptake of each new technological advance can leave orphaned recordings in abandoned and inaccessible media. A central challenge for language archives is to ensure that endangered materials do not go the way of the languages they record. This often requires complex technical conversion procedures to ingest the materials into a digital format, including a small museum of playing devices such as wax cylinder players, wire recorders, and old-fashioned reel-to-reel recorders.

The media themselves, too, are often perishable. Cassette tapes become demagnetized, hard drives crash, books and manuscripts burn or go moldy. To get around this problem, a number of new digital archives have been set up, such as PARADISEC[39] in Australia, LACITO in France, AILLA in the United States, and the DoBeS archive in Germany and the Netherlands.

A mundane but typical example is a set of 11 tapes that reached PARADISEC from New Caledonia a couple of years ago. They had been recorded by Leonard Drilë Sam in his own language, Drehu, from the Loyalty Islands, then kept for about 20 years in his home. But he could no longer play them, both because of the lack of a reel-to-reel player, and because the tapes themselves had grown a visible white mould. Before they could be read into a more abiding digital format, they needed to be cleaned and demolded by being placed in a vacuum oven at low temperature for a few weeks.

Even when converted into a digital format, archives are not yet safe. Electronic records can become gobbledygook as proprietary fonts[40] and data formats change – they only remain accessible if contained in an archive that assures their automatic and ongoing format migration with correct preservation of all fonts.

In this regard, Sumerian clay tablets still remain unsurpassed for archival stability and long-term interpretability. Initiatives like the Rosetta Project[41] are now seeking to make permanent physical records available in the form of micro-engraved materials that could, with ingenuity, be accessed by our remote descendants or by extraterrestrial visitors, even if some physical disaster on our earth were to wipe out the complex infrastructure that maintains our digital records.[42]

At least as problematic as physical degeneration or format marooning is the likelihood that recordings or field notes will be forgotten in a dead scholar's trunk, or thrown out as worthless junk by people who do not realize their worth. There is a great temptation to hold onto your own field material until you have analyzed it definitively — and spare yourself the embarrassment of being shown up for your poor transcriptions or overlooking grammatical analyses obvious to other scholars. But death or Alzheimer's often arrive before analytic perfection is attained. Even where the material is salvaged by an executor or other relative, the crucial metadata – about who is speaking, when, where, and about what – may be lacking from the record, sometimes rendering it all but useless.

So it is not just languages that can be fragile – their recordings can be too. The last decade has seen raised awareness of these issues, and the beginnings of a consensus about how long-term archiving of material can be secured. This involves a large number of issues. From the depositors, it entails the use of open-source software to avoid locking up data in proprietary formats, a commitment to archiving their materials with full metadata, so as to make them available to the speech community and other scholars. From the archives, it requires appropriate systems to ensure that some material can remain restricted following community requests, a commitment to massive data storage, permanent format migration, and the mirroring of data across several "cybraries" to get around the potential vulnerability of any one location.[43]

Among scholars and institutions, there still needs to be a shift of responsibility, from researchers and universities who typically measure time in decades to the institutions most knowledgeable about long-term conservation: museums and libraries. These have the know-how and the right time perspective, but in many cases do not yet value digital data from oral cultures in the way they value books and objects – I hope that the examples I have used in this book have shown how wrong this attitude is.

Further reading

On the difficulties of identifying and locating "last speakers" see Evans (2001) and references therein. Brenzinger (2006a), a survey of the worldwide language situation, organized by region, is an invaluable resource. Newman and Ratliff (2001) treats linguistic fieldwork, with many chapters discussing ethical or logistic quandaries, and Crowley (2007) is a delightfully frank personal account of work in Vanuatu, Papua New Guinea, and Australia. Good discussions of the issues surrounding long-term storage of linguistic data are in Bird and Simons (2003) and Barwick and Thieberger (2006), while Gippert et al. (2006) is the most up-to-date and practical compendium of articles on the documentationist paradigm. For an example of a North American group maintaining its language through traditionalist means, see Kroskrity (1998) on Arizona Tewa. For a fuller description of Kusunda see Watters (2006) and the website at www.linguistics.ucsb.edu./HimalayanLinguistics/grammars/HLA03.html.

Epilogue:
Sitting in the Dust,
Standing in the Sky

ถ้าศึกษาภาษา ก็ศึกษามรดกของความคิด

When we study language, we study the heritage of human thought.

_ พระเปร่ง ปกสุสโร

(The Venerable Phra Preng Pathassaro, as cited in Morey 2005:1)

I interrupted the writing of this final part of the book to make a field trip to Croker Island in Arnhem Land. Although Charlie Wardaga's death in 2003 took away the last speaker of Ilgar, there are still a couple of dozen knowledgeable Iwaidja speakers, and for the past few years I have been working with the community there on a multidisciplinary documentation of that language, along with a number of colleagues, particularly Bruce Birch. It was an exciting trip, throwing up information across a wide spectrum from instrumental phonetics to terminology for the growth stages of turtles.

The presence of a couple of guest fieldworkers enabled us to get into areas that Bruce and I couldn't have figured out on our own. Phonetician Andy Butcher toted up some electronic palates to measure tongue movements on some of the more elusive sounds. Turtle biologist Scott Whiting fronted up with a whole series of questions about nesting sites and turtle behavior. He rigged up an accompanying PowerPoint show in the guesthouse, which got a lively biological discussion tumbling along among the Iwaidja men – Khaki Marrala, †Tim Mamitba,[1] and Archie Brown. One of Scott's slides showed the Australian snubfin dolphin (*Orcaella heinsohni*), newly recognized as a distinct species by western science. Old Khaki was having difficulty peering at the computer slides, but as he caught the gist of what the younger men were saying he casually mentioned that Iwaidja had a name for that species, *manimuldakbung*. Picking up on our reaction, he made the laconic observation that *Iwaidja kalmu*. Literally this means "Iwaidja is many" but a better translation would be "Iwaidja – there's a whole lot of it!"

While we were working with Khaki, Tim, and Archie, another linguist colleague, Murray Garde, was camped on the Arnhem Land escarpment, a couple of hundred kilometers southward down the Warramurrungunji track. There he was working with another elder, Lofty Bardayal Nadjemerrek, on the vocabulary of traditional fire management in Bininj Gun-wok. This is an intricate topic, as traditional fire drives are so finely tuned to the landscape and seasons, and Murray and Lofty have steadily been unearthing a host of specific terms denoting particular micro-eco-zones and burning strategies. At two thousand speakers or so, Bininj Gun-wok is a relatively big language by Australian standards, and it is still being passed on to children. But even in this language a lot of the more fine-grained traditional knowledge is being lost and a mini-research community has been established at Kabulwarnamyo to bring together western researchers and knowledgeable Aboriginal elders.

The Kabulwarnamyo project illustrates how suddenly a domain of traditional knowledge can be transformed from purely theoretical interest into a resource of great economic value.[2] With global warming and the advent of carbon credits has come the realization that a huge fraction of Australia's CO_2 emissions arise from hot-burning forest fires in its northern savannahs, and that these can be significantly reduced by following traditional Aboriginal burning regimes. A number of resource extraction companies have become interested in gaining future carbon offsets by supporting the maintenance and reinstatement of these indigenous burning practices. Research with elders like Lofty is closely tied in with the training of young fire rangers interested in working on their traditional country and finding out as much as they can of their ancestors' time-tried burning practice. This information is intimately interwoven into their traditional language.[3]

In the midst of all this I received a terrible piece of news. Pat Gabori, the Kayardild man who led us into this story, had passed away. Mingled with my grief were bitter doubts and self-recriminations. Should I have spent more time sitting and talking with him in his last months instead of working on this book, or instead of making the Croker field trip? To settle my mind I walked along the beach in the late afternoon, soothed by the similarity between its casuarina trees and sandbanks and those on the beaches of Bentinck Island. A Croker tradition says that when someone dies, so does a casuarina along the beaches of their country – and this is mirrored by what people say across on Bentinck Island, calling out to a dying casuarina with the names of dead people who were born in their shade. I found a dead casuarina and sat on the soft carpet of needleleaves at its foot, grateful for the reminder that everyone must die sometime, the focus of my pain shifting to regret that I would not be able to get across to old Pat's funeral.

You may be wondering about the second part of this epilogue's title. In the Jiliwirri initiation language of the Warlpiri people of Central Australia, which systematically replaces sentences by their antonyms, "I sit on the ground" is expressed as "you stand in the sky."[4] Perhaps no words can do better justice to the reversed perspective we can gain on the innumerable possibilities of language, mind, culture, and history by squatting in the dust, doing fieldwork.

My task in this book has been to show why we should care about the silent epidemic of language loss that is occurring throughout the world, how diverse and profound are the lessons that these obscure and neglected tongues have to offer to the sum of our human heritage, and how we can go about listening to and learning from them before it is too late.

We have seen how languages can carry forward otherwise forgotten information about each group's history, allowing us to reconstruct the travels of the Gypsies, the unsuspected links between Siberian Kets and North American Athabaskans, and the venturesome fanning out of the Austronesians from Taiwan across half the world's oceans. They can provide the key that unlocks mysterious ancient scripts, like Caucasian Albanian or Epi-Olmec, whose chronicles would otherwise remain forever undecipherable. They shape and sharpen the ways of thought that give each culture a different set of insights into the nature of time, space, events, social reality.

The different patternings of their sounds and grammars provide a wealth of distinct raw materials from which unsung Shakespeares can construct poetic and literary forms that transcend what ordinary language can say. And at the same time, the way that intricately organized grammars with their datives and evidentials emerge from the every-day activities of ordinary speakers, from their explaining and gossiping, hosting and intriguing, wooing and fibbing, declaiming and mumbling, is perhaps the best example we have of how self-organizing human systems of great complexity emerge without centralized planning.

The crucial evidence for any of these questions, and for others we have yet to think of asking about, may lie in Eyak, Migama, Kayardild, Kusunda, or any of the world's 6,000 languages. And as a language dwindles it can end up in the frail heads of just a few and finally just a single person. In this light, Alice Boehm's Dalabon statement *kardû ngah-molkkûndoniyan* ("I might die unbeknownst," see chapter 3) has a deeper resonance, for what is "unbeknownst" can be the whole vast world that a language holds. I also mentioned in that chapter that the prefix *molkkûn-* does not specify *who* is affected by the lack of knowledge. This is especially appropriate here, as the loss from her death may be felt not only by her own dispossessed descendants as they are left aching to speak how their ancestors did, but also by wondering and curious souls right across the world.

Never before in history have languages and the knowledge they hold been disappearing at a faster rate. But, equally, never before have we been aware of the dimensions of what is being lost, or had the curiosity, appreciation and technology to document what is still hanging on. Bringing this knowledge out on the scale it deserves, before the Khaki Marralas and Lofty Bardayal Nadjemereks who are still alive join the Pat Gaboris and Charlie Wardagas in their graves, is a quest that must call scholars of many types – both insiders and outsiders – from right around the world. I hope this book has shown something of how deep, fascinating, and pressing is the task we face.

Notes

Prologue

1 The English translation of this poem is by Alistair Reid.
2 The Aboriginal people I refer to typically have a "whitefeller name" and a traditional name, e.g. Pat Gabori and *Kabararrjingathi bulthuku*. Traditional names often have a strong element of privacy, sometimes even comparable to a pin number on a bank account, and are used sparingly if at all, so in general I will use their whitefeller names in this text.
3 Pinker and Bloom (1990:715).
4 And if we take more complicated sentences as examples, we see that other nouns (basically all nouns except the subject) also get the tense-marking. "He speared the turtle with big brother's spear" is *niya raaja͟rra banga͟na thabujukarrangunina wumburungunina: thabujukarra* means "big brother's," *wumburung-* "spear," *-karra* "belonging to," and *-nguni* "with, using." As you can see, "turtle," "big brother's," and "spear" all get the past tense suffix *-na*. The instrumental suffix *-nguni* also ends up on all words in the noun phrase "big brother's spear." This penchant for agreement is another highly unusual characteristic of Kayardild, which I do not go into here: it can lead to nouns stacking up four case suffixes at a stretch, to a level of complexity not found in any other human language – see Evans (1995a, 1995b, 2003b, 2006).
5 It turns out, in fact, that quite a number of languages mark tense on nouns – see Nordlinger and Sadler (2004) for a comprehensive survey and discussion.
6 For the moment I simply assert this figure, but we return to the grounds it is based on in chapter 10.

Part I   The Library of Babel

1 See e.g. Mauro (1995) and Alesina et al. (1999).
2 Steiner (1975).

Chapter 1   Warramurrungunji's children

1   Laycock (1982:33).
2   Gossen (1984:46–7).
3   Based primarily on the author's own field notes, with additional input from Murray Garde (personal correspondence), Mark Harvey (personal correspondence), and Birch (2006).
4   Green (2004).
5   When he told me this story in the late 1990s, Pluto was an amiable and gentle old man, around 80 years old. Violent as it is, his story promised to provide crucial evidence in an upcoming Native Title claim. Against similar claims elsewhere in Australia government lawyers had advanced the argument that, if traditional laws were only described as ideals without case studies of sanctions taken against violators (including white people), their evidentiary status was weakened. Although his evidence was potentially important, it could also have led to charges being mounted against him for a murder that until now had not appeared on the radar of the Australian justice system. Asked whether he was willing to submit his statement and take the risk of perhaps being sent to prison, Pluto looked around the room of the old people's home and laughed – "ah, so they might send me to prison, eh?" Undeterred, he signed off on his affidavit with a thicket of spidery marks, grasping the pen like a hand-axe. In the end he passed away just days before the official hearing commenced, and he was buried in his own country on Bentinck Island. Parts of his affidavit, including the statement recounted here, were read out at his funeral.
6   Lynch and Crowley (2001:6).
7   Campbell (1997:122).
8   Laycock (1982).
9   Nettle and Romaine (2000:88).
10 Lee and DeVore (1968); a similar figure is given in Hassan (1981), although some scholars, such as biological anthropologist Rob Foley (personal correspondence), think a figure of 6–7 million is more likely.
11 Daniel Nettle (1999:102), who goes through more careful estimating procedures than I have given here, nonetheless comes to a very similar estimate, giving "the late Palaeolithic language diversity as between 1,667 and 9,000 languages."
12 I base this date on the assumption that the ability to use language only evolved once, and must thus not postdate the archaeologically attested dispersal of modern humans, coupled with extrapolations from the degree of typological divergence of modern languages paired with known dates like the settlement of Australia some 50,000 years ago. However, a date this early is not uncontroversial. A study by Lieberman and McCarthy (1999) of the evolution of the modern human vocal tract, which can be inferred from skulls, suggests that neither Neanderthals nor a 100,000-year-old "modern" human skull excavated in Israel could have had modern vocal tracts, which is taken to suggest a more recent date for the evolution of fluent human speech (though this raises the question of whether a hybrid of signs and sounds could have been in earlier use). At present different lines of evidence point to different time-depths, and scientific consensus on the date when human speech emerged remains some way off.
13 See e.g. Bellwood and Renfrew (2002).
14 Pulgram (1958:268).
15 The Etruscan language of the Romans' original mentors is unusual in that we know exactly when it was last spoken. In AD 408 Rome was threatened with destruction by Alaric, king of the Goths. "[S]ome Etruscan priests went to the emperor, offering to perform certain magic

rites and recite Etruscan prayers and incantations to ward off the enemy. But they were unsuccessful, for Rome was sacked, and it was the last time the Etruscan language was spoken" (Bonfante 1990:328–9).

16   Nettle and Romaine (2000).

17   This estimate is from Nettle and Romaine (2000). Their ranking of language-diverse countries differs somewhat from that given in the first column of table 1.2; they include Ghana (72), Benin (51), Vietnam (86), and Laos (92), and omit a number of others.

18   My source for data in the first and third columns is Harmon (1996), whose own sources for endemic language numbers are derived from Grimes (1992), and for species from WCMC (1992:139–41). I calculated the figures for the second column myself, using data from the genealogical language listings in the World Atlas of Linguistic Structures (Dryer 2005), descending to the second-level clades, e.g. 7.6 (Semitic) or 9.10 (Slavic), and counting how many such families were represented in each country on their (admittedly incomplete) list. "Higher vertebrates" is just one possible measure of biodiversity; these numbers include mammals, bird, reptile, and amphibian species. Species figures for the following countries do not include reptiles, because the number of endemic species is not reported in the source table: USA, China, Papua New Guinea. Column 1 and column 3 figures for Ethiopia include Eritrea.

19   Harmon and Maffi (2002).

20   Moore et al. (2002).

21   Manne (2003).

22   Stepp et al. (2004).

23   Note: "endemic diversity" counts only languages whose original historical association is with where they are spoken: Hokkien speakers in Malaysia, Hindi speakers in Fiji and English, Spanish, Portuguese, and French speakers anywhere in the New World will be discounted. Clearly if we count immigrant languages in cosmopolitan first-world cities the picture would be changed.

24   And, to be fair to the scientists of the Green Revolution, many were involved in establishing this process of archiving land-races.

25   Fishman (1982:6).

26   Bernard (1992:82).

27   Felger and Moser (1973).

28   Torr (2000:4).

29   Evans (1997).

30   See Gerrand (2007) for some examples of problems with Ethnologue's speaker-population estimates.

Chapter 2   Four Millennia to Tune In

1   See Chaloupka (1993).

2   This is not to deny the value of other writing systems for representing the languages they were developed for. Many scholars have stressed the unique advantages of the Chinese writing system in holding together a vast empire of peoples speaking mutually incomprehensible varieties, like Cantonese and Mandarin, which although they are often called dialects are at least as different as two Romance languages. And syllabic scripts like Japanese hiragana and katakana are a highly effective way of writing Japanese. But these are all so finely tuned to the structure of the particular language they have been developed for that it is effectively impossible to extend them to cover all the possible sounds of the world's languages.

Hangul, the remarkable Korean alphabet, was commissioned by King Sejong in the fifteenth century to facilitate literacy among his subjects and is sometimes said to be a second independent invention of alphabetic writing. However, we also know that the Koreans were aware of other writing systems used for Buddhist scriptures, such as the Tibetan Phagspa script and other Indian scripts, so I do not consider it a completely independent invention.

3 Material adapted from Rogers (2005:119, 156).

4 See Allen (1956).

5 Though see Wright (1999) for a skeptical take on this widely cited story.

6 Rau (1977).

7 Though there was one aspect of Sanskrit that they did not manage to commit to writing – the system of musical accent. Interestingly, this has also been transmitted to us today by another route: the hymns of the Rigveda were "strictly preserved by exact repetition through rote learning, until today. It must be underlined that the Vedic texts are 'tape recordings' of this archaic period. Not one word, not a syllable, not even a tonal accent were allowed to be changed" (Witzel 2005:90).

8 Pedersen (1962 [1931]:2), from whose discussion this story is taken.

9 Dionysius of Halicarnassus (1914:30).

10 In fact, one bilingual inscription was discovered in the 1960s on a gold tablet near a Roman temple, but the other language is Punic – which we do not know too much more about than Etruscan! There are also the Pyrgi tables, from around 500 BC, which are bilingual in Etruscan and Phoenician.

11 Robins (1979:23).

12 *Anabasis* 2.15, 16.

13 Dibble (1982:11).

14 See Karttunen (1995) for an evocative portrait of the life of one such collegian, Antonio Valeriano.

15 See Lockhart (1993) for an interesting account of the discrepancies between the Aztec and Spanish perspectives, drawing substantially on this source.

16 Karttunen (1995:116).

17 Cited in Jankowsky (1995:179).

18 One language of this family, Ket, is still spoken by older people today, while for another, Arin, materials were gathered in the 1730s by G. F. Miller (Mueller). Although Arin had already died out by the middle of the eighteenth century, it is a star witness in current research on the more distant affiliations of the Yeniseian languages, as it preserves certain word-initial consonants, lost in all other languages of the family.

19 As cited in Ergang (1931:265).

20 Herder (1877:212–13).

21 Jankowsky (1972:44), summarizing Humboldt.

22 Sapir (1924:149).

23 Sapir (1929:166).

24 Tate (1993), Maud (2000); I thank Marie-Lucie Tarpent for tracking down these references.

25 Boas (1911:1).

26 Hinton (1994:194).

27 Perhaps the most amazing such story is that of Nicaraguan Sign Language, where linguists have been able to track the birth and growth of a completely new language system in just three generations since Nicaraguan deaf children were first brought together in new sign communities in the 1970s. See Senghas, Kita, and Ösyürek (2004).

28 Roe (1917:237–9).

29 Zeshan (2002:243).

Part II   A Great Feast of Languages

1   It is likely that by dividing off the object of their research (physics, chemistry) from their descriptive system (mathematics) it became easier for scientists to play around with and recombine elements of their representational system and thereby deduce the possibility of hitherto unknown configurations. In linguistics, by contrast, we suffer from the problem that the object (language) is also the descriptive system (metalanguage). Studying languages of great structural difference is one of our best methods for inducing the required distance between object and descriptive system.
2   Ribenboim (1988).
3   Becker (1995:2).

Chapter 3   A Galapagos of Tongues

1   Kawano (1990:1).
2   Bowerman and Levinson (2001).
3   Photo courtesy US National Archives, originally from US Marine Corps, No. 69889-B.
4   Henderson (1995); Maddieson and Levinson (in prep.).
5   I am grateful to Ghil'ad Zuckermann for supplying this version of the Hebrew text, with quotation and punctuation marks added to the original.
6   Such as a pharyngealized voiced labiodental fricative, which you can make by pumping up your pharynx Arabic-style while making a *b* sound.
7   Photo courtesy of Christfried Naumann.
8   The widely differing figures depend on whether certain complex sounds are treated as unit phonemes, or as clusters of simpler sounds – should the !X at the beginning of the language name !Xóõ, for example, be treated as a single coarticulated sound (with a tsk-tsk style dental click performed at the same time as a guttural fricative) or as two distinct sounds clustered together? Miller (2003) advocates the first type of analysis, while Traill (1985) and Nakagawa (2006) have gone for the second. A team led by Tom Güldemann is currently studying Taa in the hope of resolving this debate.
9   This is an oversimplification, as it is increasingly seen that the different gestures making up many consonants and vowels – like nasalization or retroflexion – are also independent "tiers" in some languages.
10   Breen and Pensalfini (1999).
11   Of course there are always weaker versions of these formulations – e.g. that the Maximal Onset Principle is an initial heuristic that children try out first, but are able to abandon if the evidence against it is too strong. That would predict that it would then take them longer to learn an Arrernte-type phonological system. Testing hypotheses like this requires us to know more about the language than is needed just to write a grammatical description: we can't just work with a few knowledgeable adults, but have to then go on and see how children acquire the language. Hypotheses about language acquisition thus take decades longer to evaluate than hypotheses about structure, and at the moment we simply do not know whether this prediction is true.
12   Japanese does use tone, but in a different way: it has a pitch-accent system where one place in the word is marked by the pitch dropping from high to low, but there can be at most one drop per word. The Japanese system thus works by varying the change-point, rather than allowing each syllable to contrast as in Navajo or Chinese.
13   Quine (1969:27).

14   Kotorova (2003).

15   Pawley (1993).

16   Evans (1994).

17   Etymologically, *bengdi* means "mind-stand" and *bengkan* means "mind-carry," with *kan* ("carry") suggesting continued holding, but *di* ("stand") suggesting momentary awareness – see Evans (2007) for more detailed discussion.

18   In his masterpiece *Ethnobiological Classification*, Brent Berlin suggests that the languages of cultivator groups make more classificatory distinctions than those of hunter-gatherers, partly reflecting the detailed observation of minor differences necessary to breed plant varieties, but it is noteworthy that his information on cultivator groups is generally better than that for hunter-gatherers, in terms of the number and depth of studies he reports. Berlin (1992:274) claims that, with the exception of the Seri, "the recognition of folk species in the ethnobiological systems of traditional nonagricultural peoples is essentially non-existent." But further cases have emerged (such as many Australian Aboriginal groups) where folk species are recognized, and there are even examples of names for sub-species varieties, such as the terms *an-bardbard* ("grevillea heliosperma: lowland variety") and *an-djen.gererr* ("grevillea heliosperma: upland variety"). Baker (2007) even claims that, for many plant genera in Australia, species terms rather than generic terms are the basic ones (or even that generic terms are lacking altogether, at least for such populous genera as *Eucalyptus* and *Acacia*), perhaps recognizing the botanical dominance of these two plant genera over the continent, making them inappropriately general to serve as basic-level categories. Detailed work on the ethnobiological knowledge contained in hunter-gatherer languages remains an urgent priority.

19   From Munn (1973:104) with permission. The motif derives from women's *Yawalyu* designs; it also has a number of other meanings including headbands, paths, and teeth.

20   Sapir (1964:128).

21   Boevé (2003).

22   Talmy (1985).

23   "I caused runny icky material to move into the fire by acting on it with a linear object moving axially," e.g. in a situation where I prod some guts into a fire with a cooking stick.

24   In Aboriginal culture it is very important that everyone concerned be notified of a death, so they can come to the funeral, and in retrospect it seems most likely to me that this is what Alice Boehm was wanting to convey by her use of the prefix *molkkûnh-* here: that her death would not be known to me, and that hence I would be unable to attend her funeral. Sadly for me, this fear proved justified.

25   Although you do not need to know the sound system to work out what is going on, the other parts of the Navajo orthography that are used here, besides the lateral fricative ł that we discussed earlier in the chapter, are the use of acute symbols (e.g. é) to mark high tone (unmarked vowels are low), and of Polish-style hooks under the vowels to indicate nasalisation, so that ą, for example, is the nasalised ã sound close to what is spelled *an* in French (e.g. in *blanc* "white"). The data is based on a problem presented in Stockwell, Elliott, and Bean (1977:48).

Chapter 4   Your Mind in Mine: Social Cognition in Grammar

1   A wide range of English translations are given for this famous proverb, of which the most common is probably "new language, new soul." Its literal meaning is "as many languages as you know, so many people you are."

2   Ortega y Gasset (1983 [1937]:444).

3   The first two sentences of this translation are from Trask's 1957 translation of *Man and People*; the rest is my own. (This is because Ortega y Gasset repeated the first part of the original 1937 text from "Miseria y esplendor de la traducción" in his subsequent work *El hombre y la gente*, which is the source of the Trask translation.)

4   Compare Roman Jakobson's famous formulation: "Languages differ essentially in what they must convey and not in what they may convey" (Jakobson 1992 [1959]:149).

5   Crowley (1996).

6   Crowley (1982:211).

7   Osumi (1996).

8   Hargreaves (2005).

9   McLendon (2003).

10 Hardman (1986).

11 McLendon (2003).

12 Fleck (2007).

13 Photo courtesy of David Fleck. The village is Nuevo San Juan on the Gálvez River, in north-eastern Peru.

14 Evans (2003b), Garde (2003).

15 And indeed the root *bon* ("go") is part of the language name: *Dala*, a form of *dalû*, means "mouth," i.e. "language," and Dalabon is thus the "mouth [language] where the word for 'go' is *bon*"). Next-door peoples form their own names for this language by substituting their word for "mouth" and combining it with *bon* in the same way: Kune speakers take their root *dang* ("mouth") and name it Dangbon, while Jawoyn speakers use *ngalk* ("mouth") in a parallel way and call it Ngalkbon.

16 De Lancey (2001).

17 Landaburu (2007).

Part III   Faint Tracks in an Ancient Wordscape: Languages and Deep World History

1   Boas (1911:70–1).

Chapter 5   Sprung From Some Common Source

1   For many other fascinating insights into Dixon's fieldwork in North Queensland, see Dixon (1984).

2   An engraving of Sir Joshua Reynolds' portrait of William Jones by J. Hall, 1782. The original portrait was painted c. 1768 or 1769 and depicts William Jones aged 22 or 23. Photo source: Murray 1998:Ill.3b.

3   Dunning (2000).

4   Published as an appendix ("A comparative list of Lassik and Kato nouns") to Essene (1945). I thank Victor Golla for supplying this reference.

5   I am grateful to Victor Golla for this example and the associated data.

6   Anna Nelson Harry was survived by one younger Eyak speaker, Marie Smith Jones, but she too recently passed away, while I was finalizing this manuscript.

7   Krauss (1969).

8   See Vajda (2008) for details.
9   Photo courtesy of Michael Krauss.
10 "Epiphany," reprinted courtesy of R. Dauenhauer.
11 It is likely both the nasal and the stop were glottalized, shown here by the apostrophes, as final velar nasals in Ket regularly correspond to glottalized nasals in Na-Dene (Ed Vajda, personal communication).
12 In some cultures, formal education may then overlay some knowledge of the history of the language, as in the inculcation of Greek schoolchildren and students with a detailed knowledge of their language's history, which can end up bringing the past back into their use of the language – see Joseph (2006).
13 See Nichols (1996) for some examples – e.g. she calculates that the probability of finding an "Indo-European gender paradigm" is roughly one in 2 million.
14 Goddard (1975:249).
15 Some scholars have argued that Wiyot arrived in California around AD 900, and Yurok in around 1100, based on the likeness of their archaeological assemblages to those found along the Columbia river. On this view, the Wiyot and Yurok were the importers into California of woodworking technology, river fishing, and wealth consciousness – see Moratto (1984).
16 Simplified from a more detailed classification in Campbell (1997:153).
17 See Goddard (1975) for the examples in Table 5.3. Reprinted with permission of the author.
18 Such a major scholar as Militarev (2002) has proposed a Levantine origin. This view invites a close shave by Occam's razor, as it requires us to assume six separate migrations to Africa (half of Semitic, Cushitic, Omotic, Egyptian, Berber, and Chadic).
19 Since most Semitic roots consist of a consonantal skeleton (see chapter 2), only the consonants are reconstructed for these proto-East Semitic forms.
20 The grave signs in Hausa mark low tone: it has developed tone contrasts through contact with tonal languages of other African families.
21 The languages sometimes rejig the nature of this contrast to past vs. habitual, past vs. present, and so forth but it is always the value associated with present, habitual, or uncompleted action that has the special marking.
22 Following my source (Hayward 2000), I give third-person singular forms for all languages except Migama, which is first-person singular.

Chapter 6   Travels in the Logosphere: Hooking Ancient Words onto Ancient Worlds

1   Ehret (2000:295).
2   See McConvell (1985), Evans (2003c).
3   Our understanding of the Khoisan languages is still rudimentary. Many early classifications (including Greenberg's) treated them as a single family – partly because their common possession of welters of click phonemes carried all perceptions of other differences before it – and Hadza and Sandawe have also been stapled onto the same construct, again often on the basis of clicks, though some scholars have proposed shared etymologies with Hadza. More recently it has become clearer through work by Tom Güldemann (2006) that there are in fact three quite unrelated families. Two families, Tuu and Ju-ǂHõa, represent an original hunter-gatherer population, while a third (Khoe-Kwadi) represents a more recent pastoralist intrusion from South Eastern Africa, and is possibly related to Sandawe in Tanzania. Although all three families possess click

inventories, the grammar of Khoe-Kwadi is organized on radically different principles from those of the other two families, and is in general much more similar to other languages of East Africa. Whether or not the details of Güldeman's proposal gain acceptance, it is clear that there is far more deep-level linguistic diversity in southern Africa than the misleading umbrella term Khoisan suggests, in keeping with the 70–140,000 years that a lineage continuous with some modern Khoisan speakers has been in southern Africa (Traill and Nakagawa 2000).

4   Ehret (1998:113).

5   Ehret (1998:157).

6   McConvell and Smith (2003).

7   Diamond (1991).

8   Collins (1998:262).

9   See e.g. Dolgopolsky (1988).

10 On Siraya see Adelaar (1997); on Waamwang see Haudricourt et al. (1979:17).

11 Most data from Tryon (1995), supplemented by Williams (1971) for Maori and Topping et al. (1975) for Chamorro.

12 Some scholars have tried to reduce the number of Formosan lineages, but I regard Blust (1999), who posits nine indigenous Formosan lineages, as the most convincing analysis.

13 Bellwood and Dizon (2005).

14 Adelaar (1989).

15 Hurles et al. (2005).

16 Adelaar in press a, b.

17 The archaeologist's type name is doubly misleading, being based on a chronologically late site in New Caledonia that happened to be discovered first, and, to boot, on the mistranscription of a word beginning with a voiced velar fricative rather than an *l*. *Xaapeta* [ɣa:peta] simply means "the place where they are digging" (i.e. where the archaeologists are excavating) in the Haveke language – see Rivierre et al. (2006). I am grateful to Claire Moyse-Faurie for this detail.

18 Reprinted with permission from Ross et al. (1998:77, 96, 218, 220); original lime spatula drawing from Nevermann (1934:226).

19 Adapted from Ross et al. (1998:96–7), with permission.

20 I take the terms "exogenist" and "endogenist" from the interesting discussion in Golla (2005).

21 Reproduced with kind permission of H. Werner.

22 Kari (1990:33).

23 See www.nps.gov/akso/akarc/interior.htm for more information.

24 Vajda (2008).

25 My translation from the version cited in Ficowski (1956:108–9), which gives the Romani in a polonizing orthography and a Polish translation; I thank Yaron Matras for getting hold of the Wajs text for me and Robert Debski for assistance with the Polish.

26 Another widespread name for the Roma, in many European languages, is a variant of *tsigane* (this is the French version) as in the Polish *Cyganie* given here. This most likely derives from the Turkic word *chighan* ("homeless").

27 Only a handful of elderly people in Jerusalem still know Domari, which is giving way to Palestinian Arabic. Ongoing linguistic work by Yaron Matras with these old speakers, however, suggests Domari results from a separate migration out of India, rather than a branch of the Gypsy migration.

28 At least, no primary loans. There are occasional words of ultimate Arabic origin, such as *dzet* ("oil," cf. Arabic zēt "olive oil"), whose form suggests they were borrowed through Persian or Armenian.

29 Largely compiled from material in Matras (2002).

Chapter 7   Keys to Decipherment: How Living Languages Can Unlock Forgotten Scripts

1   This poem, "Cofio" (in English "Remembering"), was read out at the funeral of my sadly missed archaeologist friend Rhys Jones, and translated from the Welsh by his nephew Dylan Evans. The translation is reprinted here with his permission and some slight alterations by myself. The Welsh version is from Parry (1962:503).

2   British Library Photo 392/29(95). © British Library Board. All rights reserved 392/29(95). Reproduced with permission.

3   Cook (2007:6).

4   In a few cases, such as Tangut and the Caucasian Albanian case we discuss later in this chapter, the existence of the language and its writing system was already known about before the discovery and decipherment of substantial written materials. But in many other cases, such as Tokharian (an ancient Indo-European language of Central Asia), even the existence of the relevant languages, let alone the writing systems, was unknown before the discovery of the writings.

5   Sometimes this is spelled Lontaraq, with the *q* indicating a final glottal stop (i.e. *lontaraʔ*). Words borrowed into Makassarese that end in anything except a vowel, glottal stop, or *ng* add an echo vowel plus the glottal stop; thus *dollar* ends up as *dolaraʔ*. This is a useful marker for identifying loanwords – in this case showing that *lontaraʔ* is a loanword from Malay *lontar* – and equally useful for identifying which Indonesian loanwords into Aboriginal languages of the Australian north coast come from Makassarese and which from Malay (see Evans 1992b).

6   Cummings (2002:xii).

7   In a second session in 2005, the palimpsest pages were photographed using MuSIS spectroscopy, which refined the reading of some rather corrupt lines beyond what was possible from the ultraviolet photos (Wolfgang Schulze, personal communication).

8   We then need other clues to narrow down the exact meaning of each number.

9   Here I give a slightly cleaned-up transliteration of the original, courtesy of a version by Wolfgang Schulze; to see what the original looked like (and with the nine passages marked up) see the account by Zaza Alexidze and Betty Blair on www.azer.com/aiweb/categories/magazine/ai113_folder/113_articles/113_zaza_secrets_revealed.html. I give the King James Version alongside, which is more likely to be familiar to readers. A more accurate rendition of the Caucasian Albanian text is: "in peril by rivers, in peril by thieves, in peril by (my) tribesmen; in peril by the Gentiles, in peril in the city, in peril in the wilderness, in peril in the sea, in peril by false brethren, with perils and with troubles."

10 Davies (1990:127–8).

11 This characterization of Thompson's position is taken from linguist Archibald Hill's 1952 review of Eric Thompson's influential book *Maya Hieroglyphic Writing*.

12 Coe (1999:205).

13 From Houston and Stuart (1989), figure 3, with permission. Also published in Coe (1999), illustration 65.

14 We do not have a definitive etymology for the term Albania as used in the Caucasus (Albania or Albanis in Greek, and Alowank' in Armenian), although some suggest it derives either from Alpan, a village in the Shah-Dagh mountains, or Alpan, the name of a pre-Islamic deity in Lezgistan.

15 Parts of this manuscript date from the seventh century AD, although the crucial part quoted here appears to be more recent, from the ninth or tenth centuries (Wolfgang Schulze, personal communication).

16 Monophysites believed that Christ had only a single, divine, nature, rather than mingling divine and human natures as asserted by the Nestorian doctrine.

17 For full discussion of the month-name data see Gippert (1987).

18 Forsyth and Weitzmann (1973: frontispiece).

19 In other words Ethiopic or Ge'ez, the South Semitic language of ancient Ethiopia, which had been written for liturgical purposes since the fifth century.

20 Another manuscript, in a different hand and style, contains the Gospel of St John.

21 Haspelmath (1993:23).

22 A vivid picture of one such expedition is given in Borshchev (2001); for a shorter but more accessible English version see Kibrik (2006).

23 Schulze (2003), available online at www.lrz-muenchen.de/~wschulze/Cauc_alb.htm

24 This "modern Udi" puts together several different sources, for expository purposes. The "thief" word *abazak'*, for example, originally an Armenian loanword into Caucasian Albanian, was still present in nineteenth-century Udi (appearing in Schiefner's texts) but has now been replaced, at least in the Vartashen dialect, by another word of unknown provenance. I am grateful to Alice Harris for discussion of a number of points concerning the modern Udi, and to Wolfgang Schulze for supplying the line from the Caucasian Albanian original.

25 Their transcription uses "7" instead of "ʔ" for the glottal stop but otherwise I follow their exposition.

26 Long Count dates follow a day-to-day count that begins, intriguingly, in 3114 BC, so the cycle was well and truly launched by the time the Olmec monuments checked in. Archaeologists have yet to unravel the riddle of who and what event kicked off the start of the count.

27 Drawing by George E. Stuart reproduced from Kaufman and Justeson (2001).

28 Of course, Yiddish is written in the Hebrew script, not with Roman letters, but the normal transliteration conventions transcribe the Yiddish/Hebrew letter שׁ as *sh*.

29 *Yama* is the original Japanese word, while *san* derives from a Chinese word and is used in compounds.

30 This can also combine with verbs, then meaning "he, him, she, her, they, them," under conditions too complicated to go into here. But in case you have been wondering whether the *ʔi* at the beginning of *ʔineʔwe* in the chapter citation has something to do with this prefix, you are right on track: it is the so-called ergative use of the same prefix, here signifying "he (acting upon something or someone else)."

31 Justeson and Kaufman (1997).

Part IV   Ratchetting Each Other Up: The Coevolution of Language, Culture, and Thought

1 Bloom (2001).

2 See McWhorter (2001) on the evidence pidgins and creoles provide for the evolution of language – a topic that I lack the space to tackle in this book.

3 Webb (1969).

4 *Kirriwuk-kirriwuk* is the name, in the Bininj Gun-wok language of western Arnhem Land, for a beautiful red berry known by the Linnean name *Abrus precatorius* (and now sometimes as "jungle beads" in local English). They are threaded together on necklaces but are deadly poisonous.

Chapter 8 Trellises of the Mind: How Language Trains Thought

1 Williams (1936:227).

2 Whorf (1956:221).

3 English translation by Elizabeth Miller Gamble in Ortega y Gasset (1992). Ortega y Gasset was commenting on a paper by Meillet – ironically, Meillet's paper was asserting that anything can be expressed by any grammar, so that Ortega y Gasset was attacking an anti-relativist position, but his methodological caution is equally applicable from either angle. See Ortega y Gasset (1983 [1937]:442) for an anthologized version.

4 Malotki (1983).

5 And this particular delusional virus has proven particularly resistant to contrary evidence. The widespread misconception that Eskimo has – according to the version – dozens or even scores of words for snow has been summarily deflated by anthropologist Laura Martin (1986), and more recently in a satirical critique by Geoff Pullum (1991), who show the gradual inflation of the figure through uncritical and undersourced quoting and adornment of the original sources. But the myth dies so hard that the first response of a well-read person to whom I mentioned that I was writing this chapter was – "ah, you mean like the Eskimo words for snow?"

6 Fodor (1985).

7 Pinker (1994:58).

8 Papafragou et al. (2002:216).

9 Levelt (1989:71).

10 See Levinson (2003) and Majid et al. (2004) for further details of how the experiments were carried out.

11 The symbol // in the language name stands for a lateral click, like the giddy-up sound made to get horses to go faster.

12 In this "transitive reasoning" test subjects saw the relative location of A and B on the first table, then saw B and C on the second (rotated table) before being led back to the first table and asked where C would be placed relative to A. See Levinson (2003:163–8) for details.

13 See particularly Slobin (1996, 2000, 2003).

14 Kita and Özyürek (2003); see also McNeill and Duncan (2000) for similar findings regarding English vs. Spanish.

15 This playful twist on the old endocrinologist's saw that ontogeny recapitulates phylogeny appears in the epigraph to Quine's *Word and Object*, in which the philosopher anticipates the thrust of the developmental work outlined here, four decades earlier. I have been unable to locate its source more precisely.

16 I am grateful to Aslı Özyürek and Sotaro Kita for kindly extracting these frames from their video files of the experiments reported in Kita and Özyürek (2003), and for permission to reproduce them here.

17 I draw this appetizing word from the many child-language experiments, reported on below, in which children are exposed to stimuli of various sorts and then asked to get one puppet to *blick* another, revealing what they understand the word to mean.

18 There is an important difference between Yucatec and Japanese, which I gloss over here (but see Imai and Mazuka 2003 for a good discussion). Yucatec does not in general make lexical distinctions between different shapings of the same stuff. *Che* ("wood"), for example, refers not just to the same material but to various objects composed of wood, such as trees, sticks, and boards, with the sense disambiguated by the choice of classifier, for example "one 1-dimensional.unit *che*" for "one stick." Japanese, however, resembles English in generally having distinct words

for different objects composed of the same material. The beauty of this is that it supplies us with languages that vary the dimensions we are interested in – by comparing Yucatec, Japanese, and English we now have three different linguo-experimental conditions (Yucatec: classifiers without lexical differences, Japanese: classifiers with lexical differences, English: no classifiers but lexical differences). This means we can in principle examine the relative contribution of grammar (classifiers) and lexicon to helping the child learn the form / substance distinction.

19   Imai and Gentner (1997).

20   Imai and Mazuka (2003).

21   Although exactly what this is remains unclear. For example when Lucy and Gaskins (2001:274) compared English with Yucatec (which is grammatically like Japanese in this regard), they found that Yucatec children start out attending to shape but then attend increasingly to material. At 7 years old, their Yucatec subjects attended to material only 10 percent of the time, but this rose steadily to between 60 and 70 percent at the age of 15, compared to levels of around 20 percent among their English-speaking contemporaries. We do not yet understand why Lucy and Gaskins' results seem to go the other way to those of Imai and Mazuka.

22   Imai and Mazuka (2003:461).

23   Pronounced like *kee-da* with a "fortis" first sound, which is unaspirated and very tensely articulated.

24   Compiled from material in Bowerman and Choi (2001).

25   McDonough et al. (2003), Choi (2006).

26   Gumperz and Levinson (1996:27).

Chapter 9   What Verse and Verbal Art Can Weave

1   Parry (1955:123).

2   I am grateful to Helen Ouham, via Russell Jones, for translations of these four *cynghanedd*, which in Parry (1955) are simply given in Welsh.

3   Berndt and Berndt (1951).

4   Jakobson (1987a:93–4).

5   In the same article Jakobson suggested the following reason for the disengagement of linguistics from poetics: "If there are some critics who still doubt the competence of linguistics to embrace the field of poetics, I believe the poetic incompetence of some bigoted linguists has been mistaken for an inadequacy of the linguistic science itself." I believe the main reason is a more democratic one, and follows from Chomsky's emphasis on the ability of all normal individuals to gain complete grammatical mastery of their language, which thereby downplays the linguistic characteristics of specially gifted speakers.

6   Mithun (1984).

7   On this song style, a sort of didgeridoo-accompanied cross between haiku and the blues, see Barwick et al. (2005) and Barwick et al. (2007).

8   Bauman (1989:181).

9   The earlier development of Linear B to write Mycenaean Greek was a cultural dead end and does not appear to have intersected with Homer's epics.

10   Parry (1928).

11   Parry (1930:80).

12   Finnegan (1992 [1977]:59).

13　In a Warramurrungunji-comes-to-the-Balkans scenario, the breakup of the former Yugoslavia has now created at least three named official languages (Serbian, Croatian, and Bosnian) from what was in Parry and Lord's time known as Serbo-Croatia – essentially a dialect chain with two orthographies, Cyrillic for Serbian and Latin for Croatian. It remains to be seen whether Montenegro, Međedović's homeland, which became independent while this book was being written, will add a fourth language (Montenegro) to this list.

14　Lord (2000:31).

15　Lord (2000:4).

16　Based on a widespread Mayan metaphor of mats as symbols of regal power, upon which conferring nobles sit – hence another translation of "Popol Vuh" as "Council Book."

17　This version of the Quiché text is from Jena (1944:2). Visit the Museo Popol Vuh website for links to the Quiché original and a range of Spanish, English, and German translations: www.popolvuh.ufm.edu.gt/eng/popolvuh.htm.

18　Tedlock (1983:27).

19　Although not all the books are structurally identical, and some are more like an almanac than an epic.

20　Jakobson (1987b).

21　I have given what I believe is a more accurate translation than Jakobson's.

22　Slavic linguistics, faced with the wealth of sibilants in Slavic languages, traditionally groups them into "hissing" and "shushing" consonants, categories Jakobson draws on here.

23　Rumsey points out how closely the emphasis on the self-manifesting nature of the poetic narrative parallels that found in the opening muse invocation from Homer.

24　Photo courtesy of Don Niles, Institute of Papua New Guinea Studies.

25　Rumsey (2001:228).

26　Wierzbicka (1992:395).

27　This is Sapir's transcriptional system; in IPA ł = ɬ and L = tɬ.

28　I am grateful to Nicole Kruspe for this example, taken from her ongoing analysis of the Aslian language Ceq Wong.

29　Woodbury (1998:250).

30　Woodbury (1998:257).

31　On Mornington Island, as over much of Australia, first-degree initiates are circumcised, while second-degree initiates are subincised by making a cut along and through the underside of the penis as far as the urethra, a bit like preparing a Kransky sausage for pan-frying. There are many anthropological theories about the significance of this ritual, but the Lardil themselves explain it simply by saying that Kaltharr the Yellow Trevally ancestor was himself subincised. The current author managed to talk his way out of undergoing this ritual by promising to obtain a second-degree initiation within his own culture (i.e. submitting his PhD) within a time frame agreed upon with senior Mornington men.

32　For more details on Damin, see Hale (1973a), Hale and Nash (1997), McKnight (1999).

33　In fact, its phoneme inventory is unique among the world's languages in employing five distinct ways of launching the sound-making airstream. At a stroke it adds two previously unknown airstream mechanisms for speech sounds (c and d below) to what we need to teach in phonetic classes: (a) Breathing out from your lungs ("pulmonic egressive"), which is the normal type in most languages and the only type in all other Australian languages. (b) Breathing back into your lungs while making the sound, as on the inward phase of a mouth organ ("pulmonic ingressive"). This airstream mechanism, unreported for any other language, occurs in the ingressive lateral fricative *l** in the word *l*i* ("fish," phonetically written ɬ↓i), made like a

Welsh *ll* (roughly *thl*) but breathing in. (c) Velaric ingressive, where a click is made by suck-
ing air back under the velum. This is the mechanism for making Khoisan-style clicks, and in
fact Damin's clicks are the only known use of click phonemes outside Africa. (d) A unique labiove-
lar lingual egressive (*p'*), where air is farted out through the lips by velaric pressure. (e) Glottalic
egressive (*k'*), like the ejective sounds found in languages of the Caucasus, Ethiopia, and many
parts of the Americas.

34 This is slightly oversimplified, since the allomorph *-ngkur* is restricted to Damin and may
    represent an archaic postvocalic form – see Hale (1973a).
35 Evans (1992a).
36 The eight "we" forms are given by working through all combinations of the oppositions dual
    vs. plural, inclusive vs. exclusive, and harmonic vs. disharmonic. Remember that Lardil is one
    of the Australian languages, like Dalabon, with a special "disharmonic" category for designat-
    ing groups whose members do not belong to even-numbered generations.
37 Hale (1998:211).
38 The title header is from the same source.
39 See Woodbury (1993) for an astute discussion of this question.
40 McKenna Brown (2002:1), with permission of the author and publisher.
41 Hercus (2008:176).
42 In the same article, Hercus recalls that some influential academics at the time felt that mixing
    disciplines was amateurish and that "songs were to be left strictly to the musicologists" – to
    the point where she received a letter from her funding body, the Australian Institute of
    Aboriginal Studies, saying her fieldwork grant would not be renewed unless she stopped
    recording songs! (Hercus 2008:176).

Part V   Listening While We Can

1   Indeed, the vast amount of material that new technologies spawn can beget a great deal of busy
    work which actually slows down the initial phases of analysis and language learning, although
    it pays dividends later.

Chapter 10   Renewing the Word

1   Lansky (2004:131–2).
2   Nisenan and Konkow (= Concow) are two languages of the Maiduan family.
3   This is the term most widely used in the literature, although it is actually a deprecatory term
    based on the Nepalese word Kusuṇḍā ("savage; uncultivated person"), so that members of
    the group understandably prefer the term Ban Rājā ("kings of the forest") or their own term
    giloŋ-dei mihaq ("people of the forest").
4   His term for the Plymouth Brethren, who ran the mission, and were one of the most repress-
    ive religious groups to operate in Australia.
5   See Laughren (2001) for the full story. At the time of writing it appears that there remains one
    very old full speaker, Eric King, in the Queensland community of Doomadgee.
6   More generally known as Naman – see Crowley (2006:xv), from where this anecdote is
    drawn.

7   The three of us recently published a collection of transcribed stories with Iwaidja and English translations for use in the community, with an accompanying CD (Evans, Williams Malwagag and Marrala 2006).

8   Krauss (1992).

9   Crystal (2000).

10   Quoted in its Spanish version in Messineo (2003:i). Cristina Messineo originally recorded this passage in Spanish from Valentín Moreno, who then worked with her on a Toba version, which he wanted to appear in this book.

11   Nettle and Romaine (2000), chapter 8.

12   Dorian (1998:17).

13   See Blench (2006), Connell (2006), and Brenzinger (2006b) for informed discussion of the African situation.

14   Crowley (2000). As an exception he mentions inland parts of Malekula island and other areas heavily affected by epidemics last century.

15   Kulick (1992); see also Dobrin (forthcoming).

16   Flannery (2005).

17   Attempts to estimate the cost of documenting a language depend on how much you set out to cover. Dixon (1997:138) estimated US$ 200,000. Language documentation projects supported by the Volkswagen Foundation's ambitious and successful DoBeS program (www.mpi.nl/DOBES/dobesprogramme/) often run at around EUR 350,000 at the time of writing, leading to impressive collections of linguistic material but, even with these resources and excellent personnel and archiving facilities, most teams have yet to produce complete descriptions that contain a full grammar and dictionary in addition to the textual material that formed the main target of this project.

18   Shakespeare, *Henry V*.

19   Evans et al. (2004).

20   Ladefoged (1992)

21   Majnep and Bulmer (1977, 2007).

22   Dumbacher et al. (1993).

23   Pawley (2007).

24   Hale (1972:385–6).

25   Zepeda (2001).

26   Ameka (2006).

27   Haas (1984:69), cited in Ameka (2006:101).

28   Even in countries like Australia or the Netherlands where descriptive grammars are acceptable doctoral topics, a corresponding recognition does not extend to dictionaries or annotated text collections – the other parts of the Boasian trilogy – although in other language subjects (particularly the study of classical languages) this has long been recognized as a possible doctoral dissertation.

29   See Newman (1998) for some figures showing the neglect of most of the world's languages in doctoral linguistics dissertations submitted between January 1997 and January 1998.

30   Lorimer (1935–8:lxii).

31   Pawley (1993:123).

32   Himmelmann (1998, 2006).

33   Hyman (2007).

34   See Evans and Sasse (2007) for a more detailed statement of this position.

35   See Craig (2001).

36   Rhodes et al. (2006).
37   Murray (1977).
38   Maggie Tukumba, in the preface to Evans et al. (2004).
39   See for example http://paradisec.org.au, www.mpi.nl/world/ISLE/overview/overview.html, and www.ldc.upenn.edu./exploration/expl2000/papers/aristar/aristar2.pdf, as well as the DoBeS site mentioned above.
40   See Gippert (2006) for a clearly demonstrated cautionary tale of the gobbledygook that can be produced by multiple font migrations.
41   See www.rosettaproject.org for more information.
42   Although our extraterrestrial or future scholar will be left with the strange impression that thousands of different peoples all believed in the story told in Genesis, which is used as a parallel text – sadly the Rosetta Project does not attempt to portray the cultural diversity that these many languages represent.
43   With proper management, however, the costs of long-term archival preservation are much smaller than those of accessing and ingesting the data: a recent JISC study (UK, May 2008) showed that the costs were 35 percent for accessioning, 42 percent for ingestion, but only 23 percent for long-term preservation and archiving, and that the cumulative costs for long-term preservation level off to an ever smaller proportion through time (Beagrie et al. 2008).

Epilogue: Sitting in the Dust, Standing in the Sky

1   In yet another demonstration of how tenuous this knowledge is, Tim Mamitba died unexpectedly as I was revising the final draft of this epilogue. Lean, active, and seemingly in the prime of life (see figure 1.1) his premature death is typical of the epidemic of health problems afflicting young and middle-aged people in indigenous communities.
2   The classic illustration of this proposition comes from mathematics. Mathematicians studied prime numbers for over two thousand years, often voicing pride in the fact that they had no apparent use or economic value. The development of safe encryption devices over the Web – without which safe Internet financial transactions would be impossible – suddenly transformed prime-number theory from "pure" science to a field of immense economic value. Examples like this show how short-sighted it is for governments – my own country, Australia, being a particularly benighted example – to judge research by its immediate economic value.
3   Garde (in press).
4   See Hale (1971).

References

Adelaar, Alexander. 1989. Les langues austronésiennes et la place du Malagasy dans leur ensemble. *Archipel* 38:25–52.

Adelaar, Alexander. 1997. Grammar notes on Siraya, an extinct Formosan language. *Oceanic Linguistics* 36/2:362–97.

Adelaar, Alexander. In press a. The amalgamation of Malagasy. In *Festschrift for Andy Pawley*, ed. J. Bowden and Nikolaus Himmelmann. Canberra: Pacific Linguistics.

Adelaar, Alexander. In press b. Towards an integrated theory about the Indonesian migrations to Madagascar. In *Ancient Human Migrations: A Multidisciplinary Approach*, ed. Ilia Peiros, P. Peregrine, and M. Feldman. Salt Lake City: University of Utah Press, pp. 149–72.

Adelaar, Alexander, and Nikolaus Himmelmann. 2005. *The Austronesian Languages of Asia and Madagascar*. London: Routledge.

Adelaar, Willem. 2006. Threatened languages in Hispanic South America. In *Language Diversity Endangered*, ed. M. Brenzinger. Berlin: Mouton de Gruyter, pp. 9–28.

Aikhenvald, Alexandra Y. 2002. *Language Contact in Amazonia*. Oxford: Oxford University Press.

Aikhenvald, Alexandra Y. 2004. *Evidentiality*. Oxford: Oxford University Press.

Alesina, Alberto, Reza Baqir, and William Easterly. 1999. Public goods and ethnic divisions. *The Quarterly Journal of Economics* 114/4:1243–84.

Alexidze, Zaza, and Betty Blair. 2003. The Albanian script: the process – how its secrets were revealed. *Azerbaijan International* 11/3:44–51. Available online at www.azer.com/aiweb/categories/magazine/ai113_folder/113_articles/113_zaza_secrets_revealed.html, accessed November 11, 2008.

Alexidze, Zaza, and Jean-Pierre Mahé. 1997. Découverte d'un texte albanien: une langue ancienne du Caucase retrouvée. *Comptes-rendus de l'Académie des Inscriptions* 1997:517–32.

Allen, S. 1956. Zero and Panini. *Indian Linguistics* 16:106–13.

Álvarez Nazario, Manuel. 1996. *Arqueología Lingüística: Estudios Modernos Dirigidos al Rescate y Reconstrucción del Arahuaco Taíno*. San Juan: Editorial de la Universidad de Puerto Rico.

Ameka, F. 2006. Real descriptions: reflections on native speaker and non-native speaker descriptions of a language. In *Catching Language: The Standing Challenge of Grammar-Writing*, ed. F. Ameka, A. Dench, and N. Evans. Berlin: Mouton de Gruyter, pp. 69–112.

Amery, Robert. 2000. *Warrabarna Kaurna! Reclaiming an Australian Language*. Lisse: Swets & Zeitlinger.

Arvigo, Rosita, and Michael Balick. 1993. *Rainforest Remedies: One Hundred Healing Herbs of Belize.* Twin Lakes: Lotus Press.

Ashnin, F. D., V. M. Alpatov, and D. M. Nasilov. 2002. *Repressirovannaja Tjurkologija.* Moscow: Vostochnaja Literatura.

Auden, W. H. 1966. Anthem for St Cecilia's Day (for Benjamin Britten). In *Collected Shorter Poems 1927–1957.* New York: Random House.

Baker, Brett. 2007. Ethnobiological classification and the environment in Northern Australia. In *Mental States*, ed. Andrea C. Schalley and Drew Khlentzos. Amsterdam: John Benjamins, pp. 239–65.

Bakker, Peter. 1997. *A Language of Our Own: The Genesis of Michif, the Mixed Cree–French Language of the Canadian Métis.* New York: Oxford University Press.

Balick, Michael J., and Paul A. Cox. 1996. *Plants, People and Culture: The Science of Ethnobotany.* New York: W. H. Freeman.

Barwick, Linda, Bruce Birch, and J. Williams. 2005. *Jurtbirrk: Love Songs of North Western Arnhem Land.* Booklet accompanying CD of the same title. Batchelor, NT: Batchelor Press.

Barwick, Linda, Bruce Birch, and Nicholas Evans. 2007. Iwaidja Jurtbirrk songs: bringing language and music together. *Australian Aboriginal Studies* 2:6–34.

Barwick, Linda, and Nicholas Thieberger (eds). 2006. *Sustainable Data from Digital Fieldwork: Proceedings of the Conference Held at the University of Sydney, 4–6 December 2006.* Sydney: Sydney University Press.

Bauman, Richard. 1989. Folklore. In *International Encyclopaedia of Communication*, ed. Eric Barnouw. Oxford: Oxford University Press, pp. 171–81.

Beagrie, Neil, Julia Chruszcz, and Brian Lavoie. 2008. Keeping research data safe: a cost model and guidance for UK universities. Available online at www.jisc.ac.uk/publications/publications/keepingresearchdatasafe.aspx, accessed November 10, 2008.

Becker, Alton. 1995. *Beyond Translation.* Ann Arbor: University of Michigan Press.

Bellwood, Peter, and Colin Renfrew (eds). 2002. *Examining the Farming/Language Dispersal Hypothesis.* Cambridge: McDonald Institute for Archaeological Research.

Bellwood, Peter, and Eusebio Dizon. 2005. The Batanes archaeological project and the "Out of Taiwan" hypothesis for Austronesian dispersal. *Journal of Austronesian Studies* 1/1:1–31.

Bellwood, Peter, James Fox, and Darrell Tryon (eds). 1995. *The Austronesians: Historical and Comparative Perspectives.* Canberra: Department of Anthropology, RSPAS, Australian National University.

Berlin, Brent. 1992. *Ethnobiological Classification.* Princeton: Princeton University Press.

Berman, R. A., and D. I. Slobin (eds). 1994. *Relating Events in Narrative: A Crosslinguistic Developmental Study.* Hillsdale, NJ: Lawrence Erlbaum.

Bernard, H. Russell. 1992. Preserving language diversity. *Human Organization* 51/1:82–9.

Berndt, Ronald M. 1976. *Love Songs of Arnhem Land.* West Melbourne, VIC: T. Nelson.

Berndt, Ronald M., and Catherine H. Berndt. 1951. *Sexual Behavior in Western Arnhem Land.* New York: Viking Publications.

Birch, Bruce. 2006. *Erre, Mengerrdji, Urningangk: Three Languages from the Alligator Rivers Region of North Western Arnhem Land, Northern Territory, Australia.* Jabiru: Gundjeihmi Aboriginal Corporation.

Bird, Steven, and Gary Simons. 2003. Seven dimensions of portability for language documentation and description. *Language* 79/3:557–82.

Birket-Smith, Kaj, and Frederica De Laguna. 1976 [1938]. *The Eyak Indians of the Copper River Delta, Alaska.* Copenhagen: Levin & Munksgaard.

Blench, Roger. 2006. Endangered languages in West Africa. In *Language Diversity Endangered*, ed. M. Brenzinger. Berlin: Mouton de Gruyter, pp. 140–62.

Bloom, Harold. 2001. *How to Read and Why*. New York: Scribner.

Blust, Robert. 1999. Subgrouping, circularity and extinction: some issues in Austronesian comparative linguistics. In *Selected Papers from the Eighth International Conference on Austronesian Linguistics*, ed. E. Zeitoun and P. J. K. Li. Taipei: Academia Sinica, pp. 31–94.

Boas, Franz. 1911. Introduction. *Handbook of American Indian Languages: Part 1*. Washington: Smithsonian Institution, Bureau of American Ethnology, Bulletin 40.

Boevé, Marco. 2003. Arammba grammar essentials. Unpublished manuscript.

Bon, Ottaviano. 1996. *The Sultan's Seraglio: An Intimate Portrait of Life at the Ottoman Court: From the Seventeenth-Century Edition of John (i.e. Robert) Withers*. Introduced and annotated by Godfrey Goodwin. London: Sage.

Bonfante, Larissa. 1990. Etruscan. In *Reading the Past: Ancient Writing from Cuneiform to the Alphabet*, ed. J. T. Hooker. Berkeley: University of California Press, pp. 321–78.

Borges, Jorge Luis. 1972. *Selected Poems 1923–1967*. Edited with an introduction and notes by Norman Thomas di Giovanni. London: Allen Lane.

Borshchev, V. B. 2001. *Za Jazykom (Dagestan, Tuva, Abxazija): Dnevniki Lingvistichskix Ekspediticij*. Moscow: Azbukovnik.

Bowerman, Melissa. 2007. The tale of "tight fit": how a semantic category grew up. PowerPoint presentation for talk at "Language and Space" workshop. Lille, May 9, 2007.

Bowerman, Melissa, and Soonja Choi. 2001. Shaping meanings for language: universal and language-specific in the acquisition of spatial semantic categories. In *Language Acquisition and Conceptual Development*, ed. Melissa Bowerman and Stephen Levinson. Cambridge: Cambridge University Press, pp. 475–511.

Bowerman, Melissa, and Soonja Choi. 2003. Space under construction: language-specific spatial categorization in first language acquisition. In *Language in Mind: Advances in the Study of Language and Thought*, ed. Dedre Gentner and Susan Goldin-Meadow. Cambridge, MA: MIT Press, pp. 387–428.

Bowerman, Melissa, and Stephen Levinson. 2001. *Language Acquisition and Conceptual Development*. Cambridge: Cambridge University Press.

Bradley, David, and Maya Bradley. 2002. *Language Maintenance for Endangered Languages: An Active Approach*. London: Curzon Press.

Breen, Gavan, and Robert Pensalfini. 1999. A language with no syllable onsets. *Linguistic Inquiry* 30:1–25.

Brenzinger, Matthias (ed.). 2006a. *Language Diversity Endangered*. Berlin and New York: Mouton de Gruyter.

Brenzinger, Matthias. 2006b. Language endangerment in Southern and Eastern Africa. In *Language Diversity Endangered*, ed. M. Brenzinger. Berlin: Mouton de Gruyter, pp. 179–204.

Brown, Penelope. 2001. Learning to talk about motion UP and DOWN in Tzeltal: is there a language-specific bias for verb learning? In *Language Acquisition and Conceptual Development*, ed. Melissa Bowerman and Stephen C. Levinson. Cambridge: Cambridge University Press, pp. 512–43.

Campbell, Lyle. 1997. *American Indian Languages: The Historical Linguistics of Native America*. New York and Oxford: Oxford University Press.

Campbell, Lyle. 1999. *Historical Linguistics: An Introduction*. Cambridge, MA: MIT Press.

Campbell, Lyle, and Terrence Kaufman. 1976. A linguistic look at the Olmecs. *American Antiquity* 41:80–9.

Cann, Rebecca. 2000. Talking trees tell tales. *Nature* 405(29/6/00):1008–9.

Cardona, George. 2000. Panini. In *History of the Language Sciences: Handbücher zur Sprach- und Kommunikations-wissenschaft, Band 18.1*, ed. S. Auroux, E. F. K. Koerner, H. Niederehe, and K. Versteegh. Berlin: Walter de Gruyter, pp. 113–24.

Chadwick, John B. 1967. *The Decipherment of Linear B*, 2nd edn. Cambridge: Cambridge University Press.

Chafe, Wallace, and Johanna Nichols. 1986. *Evidentiality: The Linguistic Coding of Epistemology.* Norwood, NJ: Ablex.

Chaloupka, George. 1993. *Journey in Time: The World's Longest Continuing Art Tradition: The 50,000 Year Story of the Australian Aboriginal Rock Art of Arnhem Land.* Sydney: Reed.

Choi, S. 2006. Influence of language-specific input on spatial cognition: categories of containment. *First Language* 26/2:207–32.

Coe, Michael D. 1999. *Breaking the Maya Code*, revised edn. New York: Thames & Hudson.

Collard, I. F., and R. A. Foley. 2002. Latitudinal patterns and environmental determinants of recent human cultural diversity: do humans follow biogeographical rules? *Evolutionary Ecology Research* 5:517–27.

Collins, James. 1998. Our ideologies and theirs. In *Language Ideologies: Practice and Theory*, ed. B. B. Schieffelin, K. Woolard, and P. Kroskrity. New York: Oxford University Press, pp. 256–70.

Comrie, Bernard. 2005. Endangered numeral systems. In *Bedrohte Vielfalt: Aspekte des Sprach(en)tods* [*Endangered Diversity: Aspects of Language Death*], ed. Jan Wohlgemuth and Tyko Dirksmeyer. Berlin: Weissensee Verlag, pp. 203–30.

Connell, Bruce. 2006. Endangered languages in Central Africa. In *Language Diversity Endangered*, ed. M. Brenzinger. Berlin: Mouton de Gruyter, pp. 163–78.

Cook, Richard. 2007. *Tangut (Xīxià) Orthography and Unicode.* Available online at http://unicode.org/~rscook/Xixia/, accessed May 13, 2008.

Coulmas, Florian. 1989. *The Writing Systems of the World.* Oxford: Blackwell.

Coulmas, Florian. 1996. *The Blackwell Encyclopaedia of Writing Systems.* Oxford: Blackwell.

Cox, Paul, and Michael J. Balick. 1994. The ethnobotanical approach to drug discovery. *Scientific American* June 1994:82–7.

Craig, Colette. 2001. Encounters at the brink: linguistic fieldwork among speakers of endangered languages. In *Lectures on Endangered Languages*, ed. O. Sakiyama. Kyoto: ELPR, pp. 285–314.

Crowley, Terry. 1982. *The Paamese Language of Vanuatu.* Canberra: Pacific Linguistics.

Crowley, Terry. 1996. Inalienable possession in Paamese grammar. In *The Grammar of Inalienability*, ed. Hilary Chappell and William B. McGregor. Berlin: Mouton de Gruyter, pp. 383–432.

Crowley, Terry. 1997. *An Introduction to Historical Linguistics.* Oxford: Oxford University Press.

Crowley, Terry. 2000. The language situation in Vanuatu. *Current Issues in Language Planning* 1/1:47–132.

Crowley, Terry. 2006. *Naman: A Vanishing Language of Malakula (Vanuatu).* Canberra: Pacific Linguistics.

Crowley, Terry. 2007. *Field Linguistics: A Beginner's Guide.* Melbourne: Oxford University Press.

Crystal, David. 2000. *Language Death.* Cambridge and New York: Cambridge University Press.

Cummings, William. 2002. *Making Blood White: Historical Transformations in Early Modern Makassar.* Honolulu: University of Hawaii Press.

Dalby, Andrew. 2003. *Language in Danger: The Loss of Linguistic Diversity and the Threat to Our Future.* New York: Columbia University Press.

Darnell, Regna. 1990. *Edward Sapir: Linguist, Anthropologist, Humanist.* Berkeley, CA: University of California Press.

Darwin, Charles. 1859. *On the Origin of Species by Means of Natural Selection, or the Preservation of Favoured Races in the Struggle for Life.* London: John Murray.

Dauenhauer, Richard. 1980. *Glacier Bay Concerto.* Anchorage: Alaska Pacific University Press.

Davies, W. V. 1990. Egyptian hieroglyphs. In *Reading the Past: Ancient Writing from Cuneiform to the Alphabet*, ed. J. T. Hooker. London: British Museum Press, pp. 75–135.

De Lancey, Scott. 2001. The mirative and evidentiality. *Journal of Pragmatics* 33:369–82.

Dennett, Daniel C. 1995. *Darwin's Dangerous Idea: Evolution and the Meanings of Life*. New York: Simon & Schuster.

De Saussure, Ferdinand. 1979. *Cours de Linguistique Générale*. Critical edition prepared by Tullio de Mauro. Paris: Payot. Translated into English by Wade Baskin. 1959. *Course in General Linguistics*. New York: McGraw-Hill.

Diamond, Jared. 1991. Interview techniques in ethnobiology. In *Man and a Half: Essays in Pacific Anthropology and Ethnobiology in Honour of Ralph Bulmer*, ed. A. M. Pawley. Auckland: The Polynesian Society, pp. 83–6.

Dibble, Charles. 1982. Sahagún's *Historia*. In *Florentine Codex: General History of the Things of New Spain: Part 1, Introductions and Indices*, ed. Arthur J. O. Anderson and Charles E. Dibble. Salt Lake City: University of Utah Press, pp. 9–23.

Dixon, R. M. W. 1971. A method of semantic description. In *Semantics: An Interdisciplinary Reader*, ed. D. D. Steinberg and L. A. Jakobovits. Cambridge: Cambridge University Press, pp. 436–71.

Dixon, R. M. W. 1984. *Searching for Aboriginal Languages: Memoirs of a Fieldworker*. Brisbane: University of Queensland Press.

Dixon, R. M. W. 1997. *The Rise and Fall of Languages*. Cambridge: Cambridge University Press.

Dixon, R. M. W. 2006. Acceptance speech for 2006 Leonard Bloomfield award. LSA Meeting, Albuquerque, New Mexico. January 2006.

Dixon, Roland Burrage. 1974. *Maidu Texts*. New York: AMS Press.

Dobrin, Lise. In press. From linguistic elicitation to eliciting the linguist: lessons in community empowerment from Melanesia. *Language*.

Dolgopolsky, Aron. 1988. The Indo-European homeland and lexical contacts of proto-Indo-European with other languages. *Mediterranean Language Review* 3:7–31.

Dorian, Nancy. 1998. Western language ideologies and small-language prospects. In *Endangered Languages: Current Issues and Future Prospects*, ed. L. A. Grenoble and L. J. Whaley. Cambridge: Cambridge University Press, pp. 3–21.

Dryer, Matthew. 2005. Appendix. In *The World Atlas of Language Structures*, ed. Martin Haspelmath, Matthew S. Dryer, David Gil, and Bernard Comrie. Oxford: Oxford University Press, pp. 584–644.

Dumbacher, J. P., B. M. Beehler, T. F. Spande, H. M. Garraffo, and J. W. Daly. 1993. Pitohui: how toxic and to whom? *Science* 259:582–3.

Dumézil, Georges. 1931. *La Langue des Oubykhs*. Paris: Collection Linguistique publiée par la Société de Linguistique de Paris.

Dumézil, Georges. 1962. *Documents Anatoliens sur les Langues et les Traditions du Caucase, Vol. 2: Textes Oubykhs*. Paris: Institut d'Ethnologie.

Dunnell, Ruth W. 1996. *The Great State of White and High*. Honolulu: University of Hawaii Press.

Dunning, Alistair. 2000. Recounting digital tales: Chaucer scholarship and the Canterbury Tales Project. Available online at http://ahds.ac.uk/ictguides/otherResources/otherResource.jsp?otherResourceId=61, accessed November 10, 2008.

Ehret, Christopher. 1995. Reconstructing proto-Afroasiatic vocabulary (vowels, tone, consonants and vocabulary). In *UC Publications in Linguistics 16*. Berkeley, CA: University of California Press.

Ehret, Christopher. 1998. *An African Classical Age*. Charlottesville: University Press of Virginia.

Ehret, Christopher. 2000. Language and history. In *African Languages: An Introduction*, ed. Bernd Heine and Derek Nurse. Cambridge: Cambridge University Press, pp. 272–97.

Ehret, Christopher, S. O. Y. Keita, Paul Newman, and Peter Bellwood. 2003. The origins of Afroasiatic. *Science* 306/5702:1680.

Enfield, Nick J. (ed.). 2002. *Ethnosyntax: Explorations in Grammar and Culture*. Oxford: Oxford University Press.

Enfield, Nick J., Asifa Majid, and Miriam van Staden (eds). 2006. Cross-linguistic categorisation of the body: introduction. *Language Sciences* (March 1, 2006) 28/2–3:137–47.

Enfield, N. J., and Steven C. Levinson. 2006. *Roots of Human Sociality*. Oxford and New York: Berg.

England, Nora. 1998. Mayan efforts toward language preservation. In *Endangered Languages: Current Issues and Future Prospects*, ed. L. A. Grenoble and L. J. Whaley. Cambridge: Cambridge University Press, pp. 99–116.

England, Nora. 2007. The influence of Mayan-speaking linguists on the state of Mayan linguistics. *Linguistische Berichte, Sonderheft* 14:93–112.

Ergang, Robert R. 1931. *Herder and the Foundations of German Nationalism*. New York: Colorado University Press.

Essene, Frank. 1945. Culture element distributions: XXI. Round Valley. *UC-Anthropological Records* 8/1:1–97.

Ethnologue. 2005. *Languages of the World*, 15th edn. Dallas, TX: SIL International.

Evans, Nicholas. 1992a. Multiple semiotic systems, hyperpolysemy, and the reconstruction of semantic change in Australian languages. In *Diachrony within Synchrony*, ed. G. Kellerman and M. Morrissey. Bern: Peter Lang Verlag, pp. 475–508.

Evans, Nicholas. 1992b. Macassan loanwords in Top End languages. *Australian Journal of Linguistics* 12:45–91.

Evans, Nicholas. 1994. Kayardild. In *Semantic and Lexical Universals*, ed. C. Goddard and A. Wierzbicka. Amsterdam: John Benjamins, pp. 203–28.

Evans, Nicholas. 1995a. *A Grammar of Kayardild*. Berlin: Mouton de Gruyter.

Evans, Nicholas. 1995b. Multiple case in Kayardild: anti-iconicity and the diachronic filter. In *Double Case: Agreement by Suffixaufnahme*, ed. F. Plank. Oxford: Oxford University Press, pp. 396–428.

Evans, Nicholas. 1997. Sign metonymies and the problem of flora–fauna polysemy in Australian linguistics. In *Boundary Rider: Essays in Honour of Geoffrey O'Grady*, ed. D. Tryon and M. Walsh. Canberra: Pacific Linguistics, pp. 133–53.

Evans, Nicholas. 1998. Iwaidja mutation and its origins. In *Case, Typology and Grammar: In Honor of Barry J. Blake*, ed. A. Siewierska and J. J. Song. Amsterdam: Mouton de Gruyter, pp. 115–49.

Evans, Nicholas. 2001. The last speaker is dead – long live the last speaker! In *Linguistic Fieldwork*, ed. P. Newman and M. Ratliff. New York: Cambridge University Press, pp. 250–81.

Evans, Nicholas. 2003a. *Bininj Gun-wok: A Pan-Dialectal Grammar of Mayali, Kunwinjku and Kune*, 2 vols. Canberra: Pacific Linguistics.

Evans, Nicholas. 2003b. Typologies of agreement: some problems from Kayardild. *Transactions of the Philological Society* 101/2:203–34.

Evans, Nicholas. 2003c. Context, culture and structuration in the languages of Australia. *Annual Review of Anthropology* 32:13–40.

Evans, Nicholas. 2004. Experiencer objects in Iwaidjan languages. In *Non-nominative Subjects – Volume 1*, ed. B. Peri and S. K. Venkata. Amsterdam and Philadelphia: John Benjamins Publishing Company, pp. 169–92.

Evans, Nicholas. 2006. Warramurrungunji undone: Australian languages into the 51st millennium. In *Language Diversity Endangered*, ed. M. Brenzinger. Berlin: Mouton de Gruyter, pp. 342–73.

Evans, Nicholas. 2007. Standing up your mind: remembering in Dalabon. In *The Semantics of Remembering and Forgetting*, ed. M. Amberber. Amsterdam: John Benjamins, pp. 67–95.

Evans, Nicholas, Francesca Merlan, and Maggie Tukumba. 2004. *A First Dictionary of Dalabon (Ngalkbon)*. Maningrida, NT: Maningrida Arts and Culture.

Evans, Nicholas, and Hans-Jürgen Sasse. 2007. Searching for meaning in the Library of Babel: some thoughts of a field semanticist. Available online at http://socialstudies.cartagena.es/index.php?option=com_content&task=view&id=53&Itemid=42, accessed October 15, 2008.

Evans, Nicholas, Joy Williams Malwagag, and Khaki Marrala. 2006. *Marrku Inkawart.* Jabiru: Iwaidja Inyman.

Fabb, Nigel. 1997. *Linguistics and Literature.* Oxford: Blackwell.

Faltz, Leonard. 1998. *The Navajo Verb: A Grammar for Students and Scholars.* Albuquerque: University of New Mexico Press.

Feil, D. 1987. *The Evolution of Highland Papua New Guinea Societies.* New York: Cambridge University Press.

Felger, Richard S., and Mary B. Moser. 1973. Eelgrass (Zostera marina L.) in the Gulf of California: discovery of its nutritional value by the Seri Indians. *Science* 181:355–6.

Felger, Richard S., and Mary B. Moser. 1985. *People of the Desert and Sea: Ethnobotany of the Seri Indians.* Tucson: University of Arizona.

Fellman, Jack. 1973. *Revival of a Classical Tongue: Elizer Ben Yehuda and the Modern Hebrew Language.* The Hague: Mouton.

Ficowski, Jerzy. 1956. *Pieśni Papuszy (Papušakre Gila): Wiersze v języku Cygańskim przełcżył, opracował, wstępem i objaśnieniami opatrzył Jerzy Ficowski.* Wrocław: Zakładu Im. Ossolińskich.

Finnegan, Ruth. 1992 [1977]. *Oral Poetry: Its Nature, Significance and Social Context.* Cambridge: Cambridge University Press.

Fishman, Joshua. 1982. Whorfianism of the third kind: ethnolinguistic diversity as a worldwide societal asset. *Language in Society* 11:1–14.

Fishman, Joshua. 2001. *Can Threatened Languages Be Saved? Reversing Language Shift Revisited: A 21ˢᵗ Century Perspective.* Clevedon: Multilingual Matters.

Flannery, Tim. 2005. *The Weather Makers: The History and Future Impact of Climate Change.* Melbourne: Text Publishing.

Fleck, David W. 2007. Evidentiality and double tense in Matses. *Language* 83/3:589–614.

Fodor, Jerry. 1985. Precis of "Modularity of mind." *Behavioral and Brain Sciences* 8:1–42.

Fonseca, Isabel. 1996. *Bury me Standing: the Gypsies and Their Journey.* New York: Vintage Books.

Forsyth, George H., and Kurt Weitzmann, with Ihor Ševčenko and Fred Anderegg. 1973. *The Monastery of Saint Catherine at Mount Sinai: The Church and Fortress of Justinian, Plates.* Ann Arbor: The University of Michigan Press.

Foster, Michael. 1989 [1974]. When words become deeds: an analysis of three Iroquois Longhouse speech events. In *Explorations in the Ethnography of Speaking*, ed. Richard Bauman and Joel Sherzer. Cambridge: Cambridge University Press, pp. 354–67.

Fox, James. 1988. *To Speak in Pairs: Essays on the Ritual Languages of Eastern Indonesia.* Cambridge: Cambridge University Press.

Franchetto, Bruna. 2006. Ethnography in language documentation. In *Essentials of Language Documentation*, ed. J. Gippert, N. P. Himmelmann, and U. Mosel. Berlin: Mouton de Gruyter, pp. 183–211.

Friedrich, Paul. 1986. *The Language Parallax: Linguistic Relativism and Poetic Indeterminacy.* Austin: University of Texas Press.

Frishberg, Nancy. 1972. Navajo object markers and the great chain of being. In *Syntax and Semantics, Vol. 1*, ed. J. Kimball. New York: Seminar Press, pp. 259–66.

García Vega, Alfonso, and Jorge Gasché. 2007. *Ñekɨro Lletarafue. El consejo de la chambira. Texto en lengua huitoto (dialecto buue) y traducción al castellano.* Iquitos: Instituto de investigacione de la Amazonía Peruana.

Garde, Murray. 2003. Social deixis in Bininj Gun-wok conversation. Unpublished PhD dissertation, University of Queensland.

Garde, Murray. 2008. Kun-dangwok: "clan lects" and Ausbau in western Arnhem Land. *International Journal of the Sociology of Language* 191:141–69.

Garde, Murray. In press. The language of fire: seasonality, resources and landscape burning on the Arnhem Land plateau. In *Wurrk: Managing Fire Regimes in Northern Australian Savannas – Culture, Ecology, Economy*, ed. Jeremy Russell-Smith, P. J. Whitehead, and P. Cooke. Darwin: CSIRO Publications.

Gentner, Dedre, and Susan Goldin-Meadow. 2003. *Language in Mind: Advances in the Study of Language and Thought*. Cambridge, MA: MIT Press.

Gerrand, Peter. 2007. Estimating language diversity on the Internet: a taxonomy to avoid pitfalls and paradoxes. *Journal of Computer-mediated Communication* 12/4, article 8. Available online at http://jcmc.indiana.edu/vol12/issue4/gerrand.html, accessed October 15, 2008.

Gewald, J. B. 1994. Review of Jan Vansina, *Paths in the Rainforests: Toward a History of Political Tradition in Equatorial Africa* (1990). In *Leidschrift* 10–12 (June):123–31.

Gippert, Jost. 1987. Old Armenian and Caucasian calendar systems [III]: the Albanian month names. *Annual of Armenian Linguistics* 9:35–46.

Gippert, Jost. 2006. Linguistic documentation and the encoding of textual materials. In *Essentials of Language Documentation*, ed. J. Gippert, N. P. Himmelmann, and U. Mosel. Berlin: Mouton de Gruyter, pp. 337–62.

Gippert, Jost, Nikolaus P. Himmelmann, and Ulrike Mosel (eds). 2006. *Essentials of Language Documentation*. Berlin: Mouton de Gruyter.

Gippert, Jost, and Wolfgang Schulze. 2007. Some remarks on the Caucasian Albanian palimpsests. *Iran and the Caucasus* 2:201–11.

Goddard, Cliff, and Anna Wierzbicka (eds). 2002. *Meaning and Universal Grammar – Theory and Empirical Findings*, 2 vols. Amsterdam and Philadelphia: John Benjamins.

Goddard, Ives. 1975. Algonquian, Wiyot, and Yurok: proving a distant genetic relationship. In *Linguistics and Anthropology: In Honor of C. F. Voegelin*, ed. M. D. Kinkade, K. L. Hale, and O. Werner. Lisse: The Peter de Ridder Press, pp. 249–62.

Goddard, Ives (ed.). 1996. *Handbook of North American Indians, Vol. 17: Languages*. Washington, DC: Smithsonian Institution.

Golla, Victor. 1996. The problem of Athabaskan expansion south of British Columbia: perspectives from comparative linguistics, ethnography and archaeology. Address to the 23rd Annual Meeting, Alaska Anthropological Association, Fairbanks, April 6.

Golla, Victor. 2000. Language history and communicative strategies in Aboriginal California and Oregon. In *Languages of the North Pacific Rim, Vol. 5*, ed. Osahito Miyaoka. Suita: Faculty of Informatics, Osaka Gakuin University, pp. 43–64.

Golla, Victor. 2005. The attractions of American Indian languages. Paper presented at the 79th Annual Meeting, Linguistic Society of America, Oakland, California, January 7, 2005.

Gong, Hwang-Cherng. 2003. Tangut. In *The Sino-Tibetan Languages*, ed. Graham Thurgood and Randy LaPolla. London: Routledge, pp. 602–20.

Goody, Esther (ed.). 1995. *Social Intelligence and Interaction: Expressions and Implications of the Social Bias in Human Intelligence*. Cambridge: Cambridge University Press.

Gordon, Raymond G., Jr (ed.). 2005. *Ethnologue: Languages of the World*, 15th edn. Dallas, TX: SIL International. Available online at www.ethnologue.com/, accessed October 15, 2008.

Gossen, Gary H. 1984. *Chamulas in the World of the Sun: Time and Space in a Maya Oral Tradition*. Prospect Heights, IL: Waveland Press.

Gotzon Garate. 1998. *7173 Atsotitzak – Refranes – Proverbes – Proverbia*. Bilbao: Esaera Zaharrak.

Gray, Edward. 1999. *New World Babel: Languages and Nations in Early America*. Princeton, NJ: Princeton University Press.

Gray, Edward G. 2000. Missionary linguistics and the description of "exotic" languages. In *History of the Language Sciences: Handbücher zur Sprach- und Kommunikations-wissenschaft, Band 18.1*, ed. S. Auroux, E. F. K. Koerner, H. Niederehe, and K. Versteegh. Berlin: Walter de Gruyter, pp. 929–37.

Green, Rebecca. 2004. Gurr-goni, a minority language in a multilingual community: surviving into the 21st century. In *Proceedings of the Seventh FEL Conference, Broome, Western Australia, 22–24 September 2003*, ed. J. Blythe and R. McKenna-Brown. Bath: Foundation for Endangered Languages, pp. 127–34.

Greenberg, Joseph. 1966. *The Languages of Africa*. Bloomington: Indiana University Press.

Greenberg, Joseph H., Charles E. Osgood and James J. Jenkins. 1963. Memorandum concerning language universals. In *Universals of Language*, ed. Joseph H. Greenberg. Cambridge, MA: MIT Press, pp. xv–xxvii.

Grenoble, Lenore A., and Lindsay Whaley. 1998. *Endangered Languages: Current Issues and Future Prospects*. Cambridge: Cambridge University Press.

Grenoble, Lenore A., and Lindsay Whaley. 2006. *Saving Languages: An Introduction to Language Revitalization*. Cambridge: Cambridge University Press.

Grimes, Barbara (ed.). 1992. *Ethnologue: Languages of the World*, 12th edn. Dallas, TX: Summer Institute of Linguistics. Available online at www.ethnologue.com/, accessed October 15, 2008.

Grimshaw, B. 1912. *Guinea Gold*. London: Mills and Boon.

Güldemann, Tom. 2006. Changing profile when encroaching on hunter-gatherer territory: towards a history of the Khoe-Kwadi family in Southern Africa. Talk given at workshop on the linguistics of hunter-gatherers, Max Planck Institute for Evolutionary Anthropology, Leipzig, August 2006.

Güldemann, Tom, Alena Witzlack-Makarevich, Martina Ernszt, and Sven Siegmund. 2008. A text documentation of N|uu. Poster presented at Max Planck Institute for Evolutionary Anthropology, Leipzig, February 2008.

Gumperz, John, and Stephen C. Levinson (eds). 1996. *Rethinking Linguistic Relativity*. Cambridge: Cambridge University Press.

Haas, Mary. 1958. Algonkian-Ritwan: the end of a controversy. *International Journal of American Linguistics* 24:159–73.

Haas, Mary. 1966. Wiyot-Yurok-Algonkian and the problems of comparative Algonkian. *International Journal of American Linguistics* 32:101–7.

Haas, Mary. 1984. Lessons from American Indian linguistics. In *New Directions in Linguistics and Semiotics*, ed. J. E. Copeland. Houston: Rice University Studies, pp. 68–72.

Haas, William (ed.). 1969. *Alphabets for English*. Manchester: Manchester University Press.

Haffenden, John (ed.). 1985. *Novelists in Interview*. London: Methuen.

Hagège, C. 2000. *Halte à la Mort des Langues*. Paris, Editions Odile Jacob.

Hale, Ken. 1971. A note on a Walbiri tradition of antonymy. In *Semantics: A Reader*, ed. D. Steinberg and L. Jakobovits (eds). Cambridge: Cambridge University Press, pp. 472–82.

Hale, Ken. 1972. Some questions about anthropological linguistics: the role of native knowledge. In *Reinventing Anthropology*, ed. D. H. Hymes. New York: Pantheon Books, pp. 382–97.

Hale, Ken. 1973a. Deep-surface canonical disparities in relation to analysis and change: an Australian example. In *Current Trends in Linguistics 87: Linguistics in Oceania*, ed. T. A. Sebeok. The Hague: Mouton, pp. 401–58.

Hale, Ken. 1973b. A note on subject–object inversion in Navajo. In *Issues in Linguistics*, ed. B. Kachru et al. Urbana: University of Illinois Press.

Hale, Ken. 1998. On endangered languages and the importance of linguistic diversity. In *Endangered Languages: Current Issues and Future Prospects*, ed. L. A. Grenoble and L. J. Whaley. Cambridge: Cambridge University Press, pp. 192–216.

Hale, Ken, and David Nash. 1997. Damin and Lardil phonotactics. In *Boundary Rider: Essays in Honour of Geoffrey O'Grady*, ed. D. Tryon and M. Walsh. Canberra: Pacific Linguistics, pp. 247–59.

Halicarnassus, Dionysius of. 1914. *Roman Antiquities*, translated by E. Cary. Loeb Classical Library.

Hardman, Martha. 1981. *The Aymara Language in Its Social and Cultural Context.* Gainesville: University Presses of Florida.

Hardman, Martha. 1986. Data-source marking in the Jaqi languages. In *Evidentiality: The Linguistic Coding of Epistemology*, ed. W. Chafe and J. Nichols. Norwood, NJ: Ablex, pp. 113–36.

Hargreaves, David. 2005. Agency and intentional action in Kathmandu Newar. *Himalayan Linguistics* 5:1–48.

Harmon, D. 1996. Losing species, losing languages: connections between biological and linguistic diversity. *Southwest Journal of Linguistics* 15:89–108.

Harmon, D. 2002. *In Light of Our Differences: How Diversity in Nature and Cultures Makes Us Human.* Washington, DC: Smithsonian Institute Press.

Harmon, D., and L. Maffi. 2002. Are linguistic and biological diversity linked? *Conservation Biology in Practice* 3:26–27.

Harris, Alice. 2002. *Endoclitics and the Origins of Udi Morphosyntax.* Oxford: Oxford University Press.

Harrison, David. 2007. *When Languages Die: The Extinction of the World's Languages and the Erosion of Human Knowledge.* Cambridge: Cambridge University Press.

Harry, Anna N., and Michael E. Krauss. 1982. *In Honor of Eyak: The Art of Anna Nelson Harry.* Fairbanks, AK: Alaska Native Language Center, University of Alaska.

Haspelmath, Martin. 1993. *A Grammar of Lezgian.* Berlin and New York: Mouton de Gruyter.

Haspelmath, Martin, Matthew S. Dryer, David Gil, and Bernard Comrie (eds). 2005. *The World Atlas of Linguistic Structures.* Oxford: Oxford University Press.

Hassan, F. 1981. *Demographic archaeology.* New York: Academic Press.

Haudricourt, André. 1954. De l'origine des tons en vietnamien. *Journal Asiatique* 242:69–82.

Haudricourt, André, Jean-Claude Rivierre, Françoise Rivierre, C. Moyse Faurie, and Jacqueline de la Fontinelle. 1979. *Les Langues Mélanésiennes de Nouvelle Calédonie.* Nouméa: Bureau Psychopédagogique.

Haviland, John. 1993. Anchoring, iconicity and orientation in Guugu Yimithirr pointing gestures. *Journal of Linguistic Anthropology* 3/1:3–45.

Haviland, John. 2006. Documenting lexical knowledge. In *Essentials of Language Documentation*, ed. J. Gippert, N. P. Himmelmann, and U. Mosel. Berlin: Mouton de Gruyter, pp. 129–62.

Hayward, Richard. 2000. Afroasiatic languages. In *African Languages: An Introduction*, ed. Bernd Heine and Derek Nurse. Cambridge: Cambridge University Press, pp. 74–98.

Henderson, James E. 1995. *Phonology and Grammar of Yele, Papua New Guinea.* Canberra: Pacific Linguistics.

Hercus, Luise. 2008. Listening to the last speakers. In *Encountering Aboriginal Languages: Studies in the History of Australian Linguistics*, ed. William B. McGregor. Canberra: Pacific Linguistics, pp. 163–78.

Herder, Johann Gottfried. 1877. *Sämmtliche Werke*, vol. 17. Berlin: Weidmann.

Hergé. 1959. *The Secret of the Unicorn*, translated by Leslie Lonsdale-Cooper and Michael Turner. Boston, Toronto, and London: Little, Brown & Company. [French original 1946: *Le Secret de la Licorne*. Tournai: Editions Casterman.]

Hill, Archibald. 1952. Review of *Maya Hieroglyphic Writing*. Introduction by J. Eric S. Thompson. *International Journal of American Linguistics* 18/3:184–6.

Hill, Jane. 2001. Dating the break-up of Southern Uto-Aztecan. In *Avances y Balances de Lenguas Yutoaztecas: Homenaje a Wick R. Miller*, ed. J. L. M. Zamarrón and J. H. Hill. Mexico City: Instituto Nacional de Antropología e Historia, pp. 345–58.

Hill, Kenneth C., Emory Sekaquaptewa, Mary Black, and Ekkehart Malotki (eds). 1997. *Hopi Dictionary / Hopìikwa Lalàytutuveni*. Tucson: University of Arizona Press.

Himmelmann, Nikolaus. 1998. Documentary and descriptive linguistics. *Linguistics* 36:161–95.

Himmelmann, Nikolaus. 2006. Language documentation: what is it and what is it good for? In *Essentials of Language Documentation*, ed. J. Gippert, N. P. Himmelmann, and U. Mosel. Berlin: Mouton de Gruyter, pp. 1–30.

Hinton, Leanne. 1994. *Flutes of Fire: Essays on Californian Indian Languages*. Berkeley, CA: Heyday Books.

Hinton, Leanne, and Kenneth Hale. 2001. *The Green Book of Language Revitalization in Practice*. London: Academic Press.

Houston, Stephen D., and David Stuart. 1989. The *way* glyph: evidence for "co-essences" among the Classic Maya. *Research Reports on Ancient Maya Writing 30*. Washington: Center for Maya Research, pp. 1–16.

Humboldt, Wilhelm von. [1903–36]. *Gesammelte Schriften*, ed. Albert Leitzmann. Berlin: Behr.

Humboldt, Wilhelm von. 1999. *On Language: On the Diversity of Human Language Construction and Its Influence on the Mental Development of the Human Species*, ed. Michael Losonsky, translated by Peter Heath. Cambridge: Cambridge University Press.

Hurles, M. E., B. C. Sykes, M. A. Joblin, and P. Forster. 2005. The dual origin of the Malagasy in Island Southeast Asia and East Africa: evidence from maternal and paternal lineages. *American Journal of Human Genetics* 76:894–901.

Hyman, Larry. 2001. Fieldwork as a state of mind. In *Linguistic fieldwork*, ed. P. Newman and M. Ratliff. New York: Cambridge University Press, pp. 15–33.

Hyman, Larry. 2007. Elicitation as experimental phonology: Thlantlang Lai tonology. In *Experimental Approaches to Phonology*, ed. J. J. Solé, P. S. Beddor, and M. Ohala. Oxford: Oxford University Press.

Hymes, Dell. 1981. *"In Vain I Tried to Tell You": Essays in Native North American Ethnopoetics*. Philadelphia: University of Pennsylvania Press.

Imai, Mutsumi, and Derdre Gentner. 1997. A crosslinguistic study of early word meaning: universal ontology and linguistic influence. *Cognition* 62:169–200.

Imai, Mutsumi, and Reiko Mazuka. 2003. Reevaluating linguistic relativity: language-specific categories and the role of universal ontological knowledge in the construal of individuation. In *Language in Mind: Advances in the Study of Language and Thought*, ed. Dedre Gentner and Susan Goldin-Meadow. Cambridge, MA: MIT Press, pp. 429–64.

Jackson, J. 1983. *The Fish People: Linguistic Exogamy and Tukanoan Identity in Northwest Amazonia*. New York: Cambridge University Press.

Jakobson, Roman. 1987a. *Language in Literature*, ed. Krystyna Pomorska and Stephen Rudy. Cambridge, MA: Belknap Press.

Jakobson, Roman. 1987b. Subliminal verbal patterning in poetry. In *Language in Literature*, ed. Krystyna Pomorska and Stephen Rudy. Cambridge, MA: Belknap Press, pp. 250–61.

Jakobson, Roman. 1992 [1959]. On linguistic aspects of translation. In *Theories of Translation: An Anthology of Essays from Dryden to Derrida*, ed. Rainer Schulte and John Biguenet. Chicago and London: University of Chicago Press, pp. 144–51. Originally in Reuben A. Brower (ed.). *On Translation*. Cambridge: Harvard University Press.

Jankowsky, Kurt. 1972. *The Neogrammarians*. The Hague: Mouton.

Jankowsky, Kurt. 1995. Early historical and comparative studies in Scandinavia, the Low Countries and German-speaking Lands. In *Concise History of the Language Sciences: From the Sumerians to the Cognitivists*, ed. E. F. K. Koerner and R. E. Asher. Oxford: Elsevier Science, pp. 179–82.

Jena, Leonhard Schultze. 1944. *Popol Vuh: Das heilige Buch der Quiché-Indianer von Guatemala*. Stuttgart and Berlin: W. Kohlhammer.

Jespersen, Otto. 1924. *The Philosophy of Grammar*. London: Allen & Unwin.

Jocks, Christopher. 1998. Living words and cartoon translations: longhouse "texts" and the limitations of English. In *Endangered Languages: Current Issues and Future Prospects*, ed. L. A. Grenoble and L. J. Whaley. Cambridge: Cambridge University Press, pp. 217–33.

Jones, Sir William. 1786. The Sanscrit language. Address to the Asiatick Society of Bengal.

Joos, Martin (ed.). 1957. *Readings in Linguistics*. New York: American Council of Learned Societies.

Joseph, Brian D. 2006. The historical and cultural dimensions in grammar formation: the case of Modern Greek. In *Catching Language: The Standing Challenge of Grammar-Writing*, ed. F. Ameka, A. Dench, and N. Evans. Berlin: Mouton de Gruyter, pp. 549–64.

Jukes, Anthony. 2006. Makassarese (basa Mangkasara'): a description of an Austronesian language of South Sulawesi. Unpublished PhD dissertation, University of Melbourne.

Jungraithmayr, Herrmann. 1975. Der Imperfektivstamm im Migama. *Folia Orientalia* 16:85–100.

Justeson, John S., and Terrence Kaufman. 1993. Epi-Olmec writing. *Science* 259:1703–11.

Justeson, John S. and Terrence Kaufman. 1997. A newly discovered column in the hieroglyphic text on La Mojarra Stela 1: a test of the Epi-Olmec decipherment. *Science* 277/5323:207.

Kari, James. 1990. *Ahtna Athabaskan Dictionary*. Fairbanks, AK: Alaska Native Language Center, University of Alaska.

Kari, James. 2007. *Dena'ina Topical Dictionary*. Fairbanks, AK: Alaska Native Language Center, University of Alaska.

Karlsson, Fred. 2007. Constraints on multiple center-embedding of clauses. *Journal of Linguistics* 43:365–92.

Karttunen, Frances. 1995. From courtyard to the seat of government: the career of Antonio Valeriano, Nahua colleague of Bernardino de Sahagún. *Amerindia, revue d'ethnolinguistique amérindienne* 19/20, special issue: *La découverte des langages et des écritures d'Amérique*, pp. 113–20.

Kaufman, Terrence. 1973. *Gypsy wanderings and linguistic borrowing*. Unpublished manuscript.

Kaufman, Terrence, and John Justeson. 2001. Epi-Olmec hieroglyphic writing and texts. Available online at www.albany.edu/anthro/maldp/papers.htm, accessed October 15, 2008.

Kawano, Kenji. 1990. *Warriors: Navajo Code Talkers*. With foreword by Carl Gorman, code-talker, and introduction by Benis M. Frank, USMC. Flagstaff, AZ: Northland Publishing Company.

Keen, I. 1994. *Knowledge and Power in an Aboriginal Religion*. Oxford: Clarendon Press.

Keller, Rudi. 1994. *On Language Change: The Invisible Hand in Language*. London: Routledge.

Keller, Rudi. 1998. *A Theory of Linguistic Signs*. Oxford: Oxford University Press.

Kibrik, E. Aleksandr. 2006. Collective field work: advantages or disadvantages? *Studies in Language* 30/2:253–7.

Kiparsky, Paul. 1995. Paninian linguistics. In *Concise History of the Language Sciences: From the Sumerians to the Cognitivists*, ed. E. F. K. Koerner and R. E. Asher. Oxford: Elsevier Science, pp. 59–65.

Kirch, Patrick V., and Roger C. Green. 2001. *Hawaiki, Ancestral Polynesia: An Essay in Historical Reconstruction*. Cambridge: Cambridge University Press.

Kita, Sotaro, and Aslı Özyürek. 2003. What does cross-linguistic variation in semantic coordination of speech and gesture reveal? Evidence for an interface representation of spatial thinking and speaking. *Journal of Memory and Language* 48:16–32.

Kivisild, T., S. Rootsi, M. Metspalu et al. 2003. The genetic heritage of the earliest settlers persists both in Indian Tribal and caste populations. *American Journal of Human Genetics* 72:313–32.

Kotorova, Elizaveta. 2003. Ket lexical peculiarities and their presentation in a bilingual dictionary. *Sprachtypologie und Universalienforschung* 56/1–2:137–44.

Krauss, Michael E. 1969. On the classification in the Athapaskan, Eyak, and Tlingit verb. *International Journal of American Linguistics Supplement* 35/4:49–83.

Krauss, Michael E. 1992. The world's languages in crisis. *Language* 68:4–10.

Krauss, Michael E. 2006a. A history of Eyak language documentation and study: Fredericæ de Laguna in Memoriam. *Arctic Anthropology* 43/2:172–218.

Krauss, Michael E. 2006b. Classification and terminology for degrees of language endangerment. In *Language Diversity Endangered*, ed. M. Brenzinger. Berlin: Mouton de Gruyter, pp. 1–8.

Kroeber, A. L. 1963 [1939]. *Cultural and Natural Areas of Native North America*. Berkeley, CA: University of California Press. Originally in *California Publications: American Archaeology and Ethnology* 38.

Kroskrity, Paul V. 1998. Arizona Tewa Kiva speech as a manifestation of a dominant language ideology. In *Language Ideologies: Practice and Theory*, ed. B. B. Schieffelin, K. Woolard, and P. V. Kroskrity. New York: Oxford University Press, pp. 103–22.

Kulick, D. 1992. *Language Shift and Cultural Reproduction*. Cambridge: Cambridge University Press.

Labov, William. 1994. *Principles of Linguistic Change*. Oxford and Cambridge, MA: Blackwell.

Ladefoged, Peter. 1992. Another view of endangered languages. *Language* 68:809–11.

Laird, Carobeth. 1975. *Encounter with an Angry God*. Banning, CA: Malki Museum Press.

Landaburu, Jon. 2007. La modalisation du savoir en langue andoke (Amazonie Colombienne). In *Enonciation médiatisée et modalité épistémique*, ed. Z. Guéntcheva and J. Landaburu. Leuven: Peeters, pp. 23–48.

Lansky, Aaron. 2004. *Outwitting History*. New York: Algonquin Books.

Laughren, Mary. 2001. When every speaker counts: documenting Australia's indigenous languages. All Saints Day public lecture, University of Queensland. Available online at www.cccs.uq. edu.au/index.html?page=16423&pid=, accessed October 15, 2008.

Laycock, Don. 1982. Linguistic diversity in Melanesia: a tentative explanation. In *Gava': Studies in Austronesian Languages and Cultures Dedicated to Hans Kähler*, ed. R. Carle, M. Heinschke, P. Pink, C. Rost, and K. Stadtlander. Berlin: Reimer, pp. 31–7.

Lee, R. B., and I. DeVore (eds). 1968. *Man the Hunter*. Chicago: Aldine.

Leibniz, G. W. 1887. *Die philosophischen Schriften*, vol. 3, ed. C. I. Gerhardt. Berlin: Weidmann.

Leonard, William Eller (trans.). 1957. *Lucretius: On the Nature of Things*. New York: Dutton.

Levelt, W. J. M. 1989. *Speaking: From Intention to Articulation*. Cambridge, MA: MIT Press.

Levinson, Stephen C. 2003. *Space in Language and Cognition*. Cambridge: Cambridge University Press.

Lewis, David. 1984. Putnam's paradox. *Australasian Journal of Philosophy* 62:221–36.

Lieberman, Philip, and Robert McCarthy. 1999. Tracking the evolution of language and speech: comparing vocal tracts to identify speech capabilities. *Penn Museum* 49:15–20.

Lockhart, James (ed./trans.) 1993. *We People Here: Nahuatl Accounts of the Conquest of Mexico*. Berkeley, CA: University of California Press.

Lord, Albert B. 2000. *The Singer of Tales*, 2nd edn, ed. Stephen Mitchell and Gregory Nagy. Cambridge, MA: Harvard University Press.

Lorimer, David L. R. 1935–8. *The Burushaski Language, I: Introduction and Grammar; II: Texts and Translation; III: Vocabularies and Index*. Oslo: Instituttet for Sammenlignende Kulturforskning.

Loughnane, Robyn. In prep. A grammar of Oksapmin. PhD dissertation, University of Melbourne.

Lucy, John. 1992a. *Language Diversity and Thought: A Reformulation of the Linguistic Relativity Hypothesis*. Cambridge: Cambridge University Press.

Lucy, John. 1992b. *Grammatical Categories and Cognition: A Case Study of the Linguistic Relativity Hypothesis.* Cambridge: Cambridge University Press.

Lucy, John, and Suzanne Gaskins. 2001. Grammatical categories and the development of classification preferences: a comparative approach. In *Language Acquisition and Conceptual Development,* ed. Melissa Bowerman and Stephen C. Levinson. Cambridge: Cambridge University Press, pp. 257–83.

Lynch, John, Malcolm Ross, and Terry Crowley. 2002. *The Oceanic Languages.* Richmond, Surrey: Curzon.

Lynch, John, and Terry Crowley. 2001. *Languages of Vanuatu: A New Survey and Bibliography.* Canberra: Pacific Linguistics.

Maddieson, Ian, and Stephen Levinson. In prep. The phonemes and phonetics of Yélî-Dnye.

Maffi, Luisa (ed.). 2001. *On Biocultural Diversity: Linking Language, Knowledge, and the Environment.* Washington, DC: Smithsonian Institute Press.

Maffi, Luisa. 2005. Linguistic, cultural and biological diversity. *Annual Review of Anthropology* 34:599–617.

Majid, Asifa, Melissa Bowerman, Sotaro Kita, Daniel B. M. Haun, and Stephen C. Levinson. 2004. Can language restructure cognition? The case for space. *Trends in Cognitive Sciences* 8:108–14.

Majnep, I. S., and R. N. H. Bulmer. 1977. *Birds of My Kalam Country.* Auckland: University of Auckland Press.

Majnep, I. S., and R. N. H. Bulmer. 2007. *Animals the Ancestors Hunted: An Account of the Wild Mammals of the Kalam Area, Papua New Guinea.* Adelaide: Crawford.

Malotki, Ekkehart. 1983. *Hopi Time: A Linguistic Analysis of the Temporal Concepts in the Hopi Language.* Berlin: Mouton.

Mandelbaum, David G. (ed.). 1949. *Selected Writings of Edward Sapir.* Berkeley, CA: University of California Press.

Manne, Lisa L. 2003. Nothing has yet lasted forever: current and threatened levels of biological and cultural diversity. *Evolutionary Ecology Research* 5:517–27.

Martin, Laura. 1986. "Eskimo words for snow": a case study in the genesis and decay of an anthropological example. *American Anthropologist,* new series, 88/2 (June):418–23.

Matras, Yaron. 2002. *Romani: A Linguistic Introduction.* Cambridge: Cambridge University Press.

Maud, Ralph. 2000. *Transmission Difficulties: Franz Boas and Tsimshian Mythology.* Burnaby, BC: Talonbooks.

Mauro, Paolo. 1995. Corruption and growth. *Quarterly Journal of Economics* 110/2:681–712.

McConvell, Patrick. 1985. The origin of subsections in Northern Australia. *Oceania* 56:1–33.

McConvell, Patrick, and Michael Smith. 2003. Millers and mullers: the archaeo-linguistic stratigraphy of technological change in holocene Australia. In *Language Contacts in Prehistory: Studies in Stratigraphy,* ed. H. Andersen. Amsterdam: John Benjamins, pp. 177–200.

McDonough, L., S. Choi, and J. Mandler. 2003. Understanding spatial relations: flexible infants, lexical adults. *Cognitive Psychology* 46:229–59.

McKenna Brown, R. 2002. Preface. *Proceedings of the Sixth FEL Conference, Endangered Languages and Their Literatures. Antigua, Guatemala, 8–10 August 2002.* Bath: Foundation for Endangered Languages, pp. 1–4.

McKnight, David. 1999. *People, Countries and the Rainbow Serpent.* Oxford: Oxford University Press.

McLendon, Sally. 2003. Evidentials in Eastern Pomo with a comparative survey of the category in other Pomoan languages. In *Studies in Evidentiality,* ed. A. J. Aikhenvald and R. M. W. Dixon. Amsterdam: John Benjamins, pp. 101–29.

McNeill, D., and S. Duncan. 2000. Growth points in thinking-for-speaking. In *Language and Gesture,* ed. D. McNeill. Cambridge: Cambridge University Press, pp. 141–61.

McWhorter, John H. 2001. *The Power of Babel: A Natural History of Language.* New York: Times Books / Henry Holt.

Messineo, Cristina. 2003. *Lengua Toba (Guaycurú): Aspectos Gramaticales y Discursivos.* Munich: Lincom.

Miles, Mike. 2000. Signing in the seraglio: mutes, dwarfs and gestures at the Ottoman court 1500–1700. *Disability & Society* 15/1:115–34.

Militarev, Alexander. 2002. The prehistory of a dispersal: the proto-Afrasian (Afroasiatic) farming lexicon. In *Examining the Farming / Language Dispersal Hypothesis*, ed. P. Bellwood and C. Renfrew. McDonald Institute Monographs, Cambridge: McDonald Institute for Archaeological Research, pp. 135–50.

Miller, Amanda. 2003. *The Phonetics and Phonology of Gutturals: A Case Study from Ju|'hoansi.* Outstanding Dissertations in Linguistics Series, ed. Laurence Horn. New York: Routledge.

Miller, Wick. 1984. The classification of the Uto-Aztecan languages based on lexical evidence. *International Journal of American Linguistics* 50:1–24.

Miracle, A., and J. D. Yapita. 1981. Time and space in Aymara. In *The Aymara Language in Its Social and Cultural Context*, ed. M. Hardman. Gainesville: University Presses of Florida, pp. 33–56.

Mithun, Marianne. 1984. The evolution of noun incorporation. *Language* 60/4:847–95.

Mithun, Marianne. 1998. The significance of diversity in language endangerment and preservation. In *Endangered Languages: Current Issues and Future Prospects*, ed. L. A. Grenoble and L. J. Whaley. Cambridge: Cambridge University Press, pp. 163–91.

Mithun, Marianne. 2001. Who shapes the record: the speaker and the linguist. In *Linguistic Fieldwork*, ed. P. Newman and M. Ratliff. New York: Cambridge University Press, pp. 34–54.

Mithun, Marianne. 2007. Linguistics in the face of language endangerment. In *Language Endangerment and Endangered Languages: Linguistics and Anthropological Studies with Special Emphasis on the Languages and Cultures of the Andean-Amazonian Border area*, ed. W. L. Wetzels. Leiden: Research School of Asian, African and Amerindian Studies, pp. 15–34.

Moore, Denny. 2006. Endangered languages of Lowland Tropical South America. In *Language Diversity Endangered*, ed. M. Brenzinger. Berlin: Mouton de Gruyter, pp. 29–58.

Moore, J. L., L. Manne, T. M. Brooks et al. 2002. The distribution of biological and cultural diversity in Africa. *Proceedings of the Royal Society, London B* 269:1645–53.

Moore, Leslie C. 2004. Second language acquisition and use in the Mandara Mountains. In *Africa Meets Europe: Language Contact in West Africa*, ed. G. Echu and S. Gyasi Oben. New York: Nova Science, pp. 131–48.

Moratto, Michael J. 1984. *California Archaeology.* Orlando: Academic Press, Inc.

Morey, Stephen. 2005. *The Tai Languages of Assam – a Grammar and Texts.* Canberra: Pacific Linguistics, Research School of Pacific and Asian Studies.

Morpurgo Davies, Anna. 1998. *History of Linguistics, Volume IV: Nineteenth Century Linguistics*, ed. Giulio Lepschy. London: Longman.

Mosel, Ulrike. 2006. Grammatography: the art and craft of writing grammars. In *Catching Language: The Standing Challenge of Grammar-writing*, ed. F. Ameka, A. Dench, and N. Evans. Berlin: Mouton de Gruyter, pp. 41–68.

Munn, Nancy. 1973. *Walbiri Iconography: Graphic Representations and Cultural Symbolism in a Central Australian Society.* Ithaca: Cornell University Press.

Murray, Alexander. 1998. *Sir William Jones 1746–1794: A Commemoration.* Oxford: Oxford University Press.

Murray, Elizabeth. 1977. *Caught in the Web of Words: James Murray and the Oxford English Dictionary.* New Haven and London: Yale University Press.

Nakagawa, Hiroshi. 2006. Aspects of the phonetic and phonological structure of the G|ui language. Unpublished PhD dissertation, University of the Witwatersrand, Johannesburg.

Nettle, Daniel. 1998. Explaining global patterns of language diversity. *Journal of Anthropological Archaeology* 17:354–74.

Nettle, Daniel. 1999. *Linguistic Diversity*. Oxford: Oxford University Press.

Nettle, Daniel, and Suzanne Romaine. 2000. *Vanishing Voices: The Extinction of the World's Languages*. New York: Oxford University Press.

Nevermann, Hans. 1934. *Admiralitäts-Inseln*. In *Ergebnisse der Südsee-Expedition 1908–1910*, ed. G. Thilenus, vol. 2 A3. Hamburg: Friederichsen, De Gruyter & Co.

Newman, Paul. 1977. The formation of imperfective verb stem in Chadic. *Afrika und Übersee* 60:178–91.

Newman, Paul. 1998. "We has seen the enemy and it is us": the endangered languages issue as a hopeless cause. *Studies in the Linguistic Sciences* 28/2:11–20.

Newman, Paul, and M. Ratliff (eds). 2001. *Linguistic Fieldwork*. New York: Cambridge University Press.

Nichols, Johanna. 1996. The comparative method as heuristic. In *The Comparative Method Reviewed: Regularity and Irregularity in Language Change*, ed. Mark Durie and Malcolm Ross. New York and Oxford: Oxford University Press, pp. 39–71.

Nordlinger, R., and L. Sadler. 2004. Nominal tense in crosslinguistic perspective. *Language* 80:776–806.

Norman, Jerry. 1988. *Chinese*. Cambridge: Cambridge University Press.

Núñez, R., and E. Sweetser. 2006. With the future behind them: convergent evidence from Aymara language and gesture in the crosslinguistic comparison of spatial construals of time. *Cognitive Science* 30/3:401–50.

Ortega y Gasset, José. 1957. *Man and People* [*El Hombre y la Gente*], translated by Willard R. Trask. New York: Norton.

Ortega y Gasset, José. 1983 [1937]. Miseria y esplendor de la traducción. *La Nación* (Buenos Aires), May–June 1937. Reprinted in José Ortega y Gasset. 1983. *Obras Completas: Tomo V (1933–1941)*. Madrid: Aleanza Editorial, Revista de Occidente, pp. 429–48.

Ortega y Gasset, José. 1992. The misery and the splendor of translation, translated by Elizabeth Gamble Miller. In *Theories of Translation: An Anthology of Essays from Dryden to Derrida*, ed. Rainer Schulte and John Biguenet. Chicago and London: University of Chicago Press.

Ostler, Nicholas. 2005. *Empires of the Word: A Language History of the World*. London: Harper Collins.

Osumi, Midori. 1996. Body parts in Tinrin. In *The Grammar of Inalienability*, ed. H. Chappell and W. B. McGregor. Berlin: Mouton de Gruyter, pp. 433–62.

Papafragou, A., C. Massey, and L. Gleitman. 2002. Shake, rattle, 'n' roll: the representation of motion in language and cognition. *Cognition* 84:189–219.

Parry, Milman. 1928. *L'Epithète Traditionelle dans Homère: Essai sur un Problème de Style Homérique*. Paris: Société d'éditions "Les belles lettres."

Parry, Milman. 1930. Studies in the epic technique of oral verse-making, vol. 1: Homer and the Homeric style. *Harvard Studies in Classical Philology* 41:73–147.

Parry, Thomas. 1955. *A History of Welsh Literature* [*Hanes Llenyddiaeth Gymraeg*], translated by H. Idris Bell. Oxford: Clarendon Press.

Parry, Thomas (ed.). 1962. *The Oxford Book of Welsh Verse*. Oxford: Oxford University Press.

Paul, Doris A. 1973. *The Navajo Code Talkers*. Philadelphia: Dorance.

Pawley, Andrew. 1993. A language that defies description by ordinary means. In *The Role of Theory in Language Description*, ed. W. Foley. Berlin: Mouton de Gruyter, pp. 87–129.

Pawley, Andrew. 2007. Kalam's knowledge lives on. *Papua New Guinea Post Courier*, October 29, 2007.

Pedersen, Holger. 1962 [1931]. *The Discovery of Language: Linguistic Science in the Nineteenth Century*. Bloomington: Indiana University Press.

Pinker, Steven. 1994. *The Language Instinct: The New Science of Language and Mind*. London: Allen Lane.

Pinker, S., and P. Bloom. 1990. Natural language and natural selection. *Behavioral and Brain Sciences* 13:707–26.

Pulgram, E. 1958. *The Tongues of Italy*. Cambridge: Harvard University Press.

Pullum, Geoffrey. 1991. *The Great Eskimo Vocabulary Hoax and Other Irreverent Essays on the Study of Language*. Chicago: Chicago University Press.

Pullum, Geoffrey, and William Ladusaw. 1996. *Phonetic Symbol Guide*. Chicago: University of Chicago Press.

Quine, W. V. O. 1960. *Word and Object*. Cambridge, MA: MIT Press.

Quine, W. V. O. 1969. *Ontological Relativity, and Other Essays*. New York: Columbia University Press.

Rankin, Robert. 2000. On Siouan chronology. Seminar presented at University of Melbourne, Department of Linguistics & Applied Linguistics.

Rau, Wilhelm. 1977. *Bhartṛharis Vākyapadīya*. Wiesbaden: Franz Steiner.

Reesink, Ger. 1987. *Structures and Their Functions in Usan: A Papuan Language of Papua New Guinea*. Amsterdam and Philadelphia: J. Benjamins Pub. Co.

Rhodes, Richard A., Lenore A. Grenoble, Anna Berge, and Paula Radetzky. 2006. Adequacy of documentation: a preliminary report to the CELP. Draft presented at the 2007 meeting of the CELP at the LSA, Anaheim, CA.

Ribenboim, Paulo. 1988. *The Book of Prime Number Records*. New York: Springer-Verlag.

Rilly, Claude. 2005. The linguistic position of Meroitic. *ARKAMANI (Sudan Journal of Archaeology and Anthropology)*. Available online at www.arkamani.org/arkamani-library/meroitic/rilly.htm, accessed November 10, 2008.

Rivierre, Jean-Claude, and Sabine Ehrhart, with the collaboration of Raymond Diéla. 2006. *Le Bwatoo et les Dialectes de la Région de Koné (Nouvelle-Calédonie)*. Langues et Cultures du Pacifique 17. Paris, Leuven, and Dudley: Peeters.

Robb, John. 1993. A social prehistory of European languages. *Antiquity* 67:747–60.

Robins, R. H. 1979. *A Short History of Linguistics*, 2nd edn. London: Longman.

Roe, W. R. 1917. *Peeps into the Deaf World*. Derby: Bemrose.

Rogers, Henry. 2005. *Writing Systems: A Linguistic Approach*. Oxford: Blackwell Publishing.

Ross, Malcolm D., Andrew Pawley, and Meredith Osmond (eds). 1998. *The Lexicon of Proto-Oceanic: Volume 1, Material Culture*. Canberra: Australian National University.

Ross, Malcolm D., Andrew Pawley, and Meredith Osmond (eds). 2003. *The Lexicon of Proto-Oceanic: Volume 2, the Physical Environment*. Canberra: Australian National University.

Rowan, Kirsty. 2006. Meroitic – an Afroasiatic language? *SOAS Working Papers in Linguistics* 14:169–206.

Rumsey, Alan. 2001. Tom Yaya Kange: a metrical narrative genre from the New Guinea Highlands. *Journal of Linguistic Anthropology* 11/2:193–239.

Rumsey, Alan. 2006. Verbal art, politics and personal style in the New Guinea Highlands and beyond. In *Language, Culture, and the Individual: A Tribute to Paul Friedrich*, ed. C. O'Neil., M. Scoggin, and K. Tuite. Munich: Lincom, pp. 319–46.

Sahagún, Fray Bernardino de. 1950–82. *Florentine Codex: General History of the Things of New Spain*. Translated from the Aztec into English by A. J. O. Anderson and C. E. Dibble in 13 parts. Salt Lake City: University of Utah Press.

Sapir, Edward. 1921. *Language: An Introduction to the Study of Speech*. New York: Harcourt, Brace and World.

Sapir, Edward. 1924. The grammarian and his language. *American Mercury* 1 (1924):149–55. Reprinted in D. G. Mandelbaum (ed.). 1949. *Selected Writings of Edward Sapir*. Berkeley, CA: University of California Press, pp. 149–55.

Sapir, Edward. 1929. *The Status of Linguistics as a Science*. In *Selected Writings of Edward Sapir*, ed. D. G. Mandelbaum. Berkeley, CA: University of California Press, pp. 160–6.

Sapir, Edward. 1949a [1916]. Abnormal types of speech in Nootka. *Canada, Geological Survey, Memoir 62, Anthropological Series No. 5*, pp. 1–21. Reprinted in D. G. Mandelbaum (ed.). 1949. *Selected Writings of Edward Sapir*. Berkeley, CA: University of California Press, pp. 206–12.

Sapir, Edward. 1949b [1916]. Time perspective in Aboriginal American culture: a study in method. Memoir 90 Anthropological Series No. 13, Canada Department of Mines, Geological Survey. Ottawa: Government Printing Bureau. Reprinted in D. G. Mandelbaum (ed.). 1949. *Selected Writings of Edward Sapir*. Berkeley, CA: University of California Press, pp. 389–462.

Sapir, Edward. 1949 [1929]. The status of linguistics as a science. *Language* 5:207–14. Reprinted in D. G. Mandelbaum (ed.). 1949. *Selected Writings of Edward Sapir*. Berkeley, CA: University of California Press, pp. 160–6.

Sapir, Edward. 1964. Conceptual categories in primitive languages. In *Language in Culture and Society: A Reader in Linguistics and Anthropology*, ed. Dell Hymes. New York: Harper Row, p. 128.

Saxe, Geoffrey, and Indigo Esmonde. 2005. Studying cognition in flux: a historical treatment of Fu in the shifting structure of Oksapmin mathematics. *Mind, Culture and Activity* 12/3–4:171–225.

Schulze, Wolfgang. 1982. *Die Sprache der Uden in Nordazerbaidžan*. Wiesbaden: Harrassowitz.

Schulze, Wolfgang. 2001. *The Udi Gospels: Annotated Text, Etymological Index, Lemmatized Concordance*. Munich: Lincom.

Schulze, Wolfgang. 2003. Caucasian Albanian (Aluan): the language of the "Caucasian Albanian" palimpsest from Mt. Sinai and the "Caucasian Albanian" inscriptions. Available online at www.lrz-muenchen.de/~wschulze/Cauc_alb.htm, accessed October 15, 2008.

Schulze, Wolfgang. 2005. Towards a history of Udi. *International Journal of Diachronic Linguistics* 1:55–91.

Semur, Serge, with the collaboration of Nossor Doungouss, Oumar Hamit et al. 1983. *Essai de Classification des Verbes Migaama (Baro-Guera, Tchad)*. Sarh: Centre d'Etudes Linguistiques.

Senghas, A., Sotaro Kita, and Aslı Özyürek. 2004. Children creating core properties of language: evidence from an emerging sign language in Nicaragua. *Science* 303/5691:1779–82.

Sherzer, Joel, and Anthony Woodbury. 1987. *Native American Discourse*. Cambridge: Cambridge University Press.

Shipley, William. 1991. *The Maidu Indian Myths and Stories of Han'ibyjim*. Berkeley, CA: Heyday Books.

Simons, Gary F. 2006. Ensuring that digital data last: the priority of archival form over working form and presentation form. *SIL Electronic Working Papers 2006-003*, March 2006. Available online at www.sil.org/silewp/abstract.asp?ref=2006-003, accessed October 15, 2008.

Sims-Williams, Patrick. 2006. *Ancient Celtic Place-names in Europe and Asia Minor*. Oxford: Publications of the Philological Society.

Singer, Isaac Bashevis. 1976. Yiddish, the language of exile. In *Next Year in Jerusalem: Portraits of the Jew in the Twentieth Century*, ed. D. Villiers. New York: Viking Press.

Slobin, Dan. 1996. From "thought and language" to "thinking for speaking." In *Rethinking Linguistic Relativity*, ed. J. J. Gumperz and S. C. Levinson. Cambridge: Cambridge University Press, pp. 70–96.

Slobin, Dan. 2000. Verbalized events: a dynamic approach to linguistic relativity and determinism. In *Evidence for Linguistic Relativity*, ed. S. Niemeier and R. Dirven. Amsterdam: John Benjamins, pp. 107–38.

Slobin, Dan. 2003. Language and thought online. In *Language in Mind: Advances in the Study of Language and Thought*, ed. Dedre Gentner and Susan Goldin-Meadow. Cambridge, MA: MIT Press, pp. 157–91.

Snyder, Gary. 1990. *The Practice of the Wild.* San Francisco: North Point Press.

Sofowora, Abayomi. 1982. *Medicinal Plants and Traditional Medicine in Africa.* Chichester: John Wiley.

Staal, Frits. 1988. *Universals: Studies in Indian Logic and Linguistics.* Chicago: University of Chicago Press.

Staller, John, Robert Tykot, and Bruce Benz (eds). 2006. *Histories of Maize: Multidisciplinary Approaches to the Prehistory, Linguistics, Biogeography, Domestication and Evolution of Maize.* Burlington, MA: Academic Press.

Stein, Gertrude. 1973. *How to Write.* New York: Dover Publications.

Steiner, George. 1975. *After Babel: Aspects of Language and Translation.* Oxford: Oxford University Press.

Steinthal, Heymann. 1861. *Charakteristik der hauptsachlichsten Typen des Sprachbaues.* Berlin: Dümmler.

Stepp, J. R., S. Cervone, H. Castaneda et al. 2004. Development of a GIS for global biocultural diversity. In *Policy Matters*, ed. Borrini-Feyerabend et al., 13:267–71.

Stockwell, Robert P., Dale E. Elliott, and Marian C. Bean. 1977. *Workbook in Syntactic Theory and Analysis.* Englewood Cliffs, NJ: Prentice-Hall Inc.

Suarez, Jorge A. 1983. *The Meso-American Languages.* Cambridge: Cambridge University Press.

Sutton, Peter. 1978. Wik: Aboriginal society, territory and language at Cape Keerweer, Cape York Peninsula, Australia. Unpublished PhD dissertation, University of Queensland.

Talmy, Len. 1972. Semantic structures in English and Atsugewi. Unpublished PhD dissertation, University of California, Berkeley.

Talmy, Len. 1985. Lexicalization patterns: semantic structure in lexical forms. In *Language Typology and Syntactic Description, Vol. 3: Grammatical Categories and the Lexicon*, ed. T. Shopen. Cambridge: Cambridge University Press, pp. 57–149.

Talmy, Len. 2000. *Towards a cognitive semantics*, 2 vols. Cambridge, MA: MIT Press.

Tate, Henry Wellington. 1993. *The Porcupine Hunter and Other Stories: The Original Tsimshian Texts of Henry Tate*, ed. Ralph Maud. Vancouver, BC: Talon Books.

Tedlock, Dennis. 1983. *The Spoken Word and the Work of Interpretation.* Philadelphia: University of Pennsylvania Press.

Tedlock, Dennis. 1996. *Popol Vuh: The Mayan Book of the Dawn of Life*, revised edn. New York: Simon & Schuster.

Thomas, Dylan. 1988. *Collected poems 1934–1953*, ed. Walford Davies and Ralph Maud. London: J. M. Dent & Sons.

Thurston, W. R. 1987. *Processes of Change in the Languages of North-western New Britain.* Canberra: Pacific Linguistics, pp. xx–xx.

Thurston, W. R. 1992. Sociolinguistic typology and other factors effecting change in north-western New Britain, Papua New Guinea. In *Culture Change, Language Change: Case Studies from Melanesia*, ed. T. Dutton, Pacific Linguistics, pp. 123–39.

Tomasello, Michael. 1999a. The human adaptation for culture. *Annual Review of Anthropology* 28:509–29.

Tomasello, Michael. 1999b. *The Cultural Origins of Human Cognition.* Cambridge: Cambridge University Press.

Topping, Donald M., Pedro M. Ogo, and Bernadita C. Dungca. 1975. *Chamorro–English Dictionary.* Honolulu: University of Hawaii Press.

Torr, Geordie. 2000. *Pythons of Australia: A Natural History.* Sydney: University of New South Wales Press.

Traill, A. 1985. *Phonetic and Phonological Studies of !Xóõ Bushman.* Helmut Buske Verlag: Hamburg.

Traill, A., and H. Nakagawa. 2000. A historical !Xoo-/Gui contact zone: linguistic and other relations. In *The Current State of Khoesan Language Studies in Botswana*, ed. H. Batibo and J. Tsonope. Gaborone: IRD, pp. 1–17.

Trigger, David. 1987. Languages, linguistic groups and status relations at Doomadgee, an Aboriginal settlement in north-west Queensland, Australia. *Oceania* 57/3:217–38.

Tryon, Darrell. 1995. *Comparative Austronesian Dictionary: An Introduction to Austronesian Studies*. Berlin: Mouton de Gruyter.

Tsunoda, Tasaku. 2005. *Language Endangerment and Language Revitalisation*. Berlin: Mouton de Gruyter.

Urness, Carol (ed.). 1967. *A Naturalist in Russia*. Minneapolis: University Press.

Vajda, Edward. 2008. A Siberian link with Na-Dene languages: Dene-Yeniseic Symposium, Fairbanks, Alaska, February 2008.

Vajda, Edward, and David S. Anderson (eds). 2003. *Studia Yeniseica in Honor of Heinrich Werner*. Special issue of *Sprachtypologie und Universalien-Forschung* 56/1–2.

Vansina, Jan. 1990. *Paths in the Rainforest: Toward a History of Political Tradition in Equatorial Africa*. Madison: University of Wisconsin Press.

Vygotsky, Lev. 1962. *Thought and Language*, edited and translated by Eugenia Hanfmann and Gertrude Vakar. Cambridge, MA: MIT Press. Originally published in 1934 as *Myshlenie i rech': Psikhologicheskie issledovanija*. Moscow and Leningrad: Gosudarstvennoe Social'no-Ekonomicheskoe Izdatel'stvo.

Watters, David. 2006. Notes on Kusunda grammar: a language isolate of Nepal. *Himalayan Linguistics Archive* 3:1–182.

WCMC (World Conversation Monitoring Centre). 1992. Biodiversity data sourcebook. Cambridge: World Conservation Press.

Webb, L. J. 1969. Australian plants and chemical research. In *The Last of Lands*, ed. L. J. Webb, D. Whitelock, and J. Le Gay Brereton. Brisbane: Jacaranda Press.

Whorf, Benjamin Lee. 1956. *Language, Thought and Reality*. Cambridge, MA: MIT Press.

Wichmann, Søren. 1995. *The Relationship among the Mixe-Zoquean Languages of Mexico*. Salt Lake City: University of Utah Press.

Wierzbicka, Anna. 1992. *Language, Culture and Cognition*. Oxford: Oxford University Press.

Wilkins, David, P. 1993. Linguistic evidence in support of a holistic approach to traditional ecological knowledge. In *Traditional Ecological Knowledge*, ed. N. Williams and G. Baines. Canberra: CRES, pp. 71–93.

Williams, Francis. 1936. *Papuans of the Trans-Fly*. Oxford: Clarendon Press.

Williams, Gwyn. 1992. *An Introduction to Welsh Literature*. Cardiff: University of Wales Press.

Williams, Herbert W. 1971. *A Dictionary of the Maori Language*. Wellington: A. R. Shearer, Govt. Printer.

Williams, N. and G. Baines (eds). 1993. *Traditional Ecological Knowledge*. Canberra: CRES.

Witherspoon, Gary. 1977. *Language and Art in the Navajo Universe*. Ann Arbor: The University of Michigan Press.

Witzel, Michael. 2005. Central Asian roots and acculturation in South Asia. In *Linguistics, Archaeology and the Human Past: Occasional Papers No. 1*, ed. Toshiki Osada. Kyoto: Research Institute for Humanity and Nature, pp. 87–211.

Woodbury, Anthony C. 1993. A defense of the proposition, "When a language dies, a culture dies." Proceedings of the first annual symposium about language and society – Austin (SALSA). *Texas Linguistic Forum* 33:101–29.

Woodbury, Anthony. 1998. Documenting rhetorical, aesthetic and expressive loss in language shift. In *Endangered Languages: Current Issues and Future Prospects*, ed. L. A. Grenoble and L. J. Whaley. Cambridge: Cambridge University Press, pp. 234–60.

Wright, J. C. 1999. Old wives' tales in "Therīgāthā": a review article. *Bulletin of the School of Oriental and African Studies* 62/3:519–28.

Yeats, W. B. 1983. *The Poems*, ed. Richard J. Finneran. London: MacMillan.

Zavala, Roberto. 2000. *Inversion and Other Topics in the Grammar of Olutec (Mixean)*. Unpublished PhD dissertation, University of Oregon at Eugene.

Zepeda, Ofelia. 2001. Linguistics research at home: making it our own, for our own. Paper read at Second International Conference on Endangered Languages, Kyoto.

Zeshan, Ulrike. 2002. Sign language in Turkey: the story of a hidden language. *Turkic Languages* 6/2:229–74.

Websites

Online Bantu dictionary: www.cbold.ddl.ish-lyon.cnrs.fr/

The Romani language – an interactive journey: www.llc.manchester.ac.uk/Research/Projects/romani

Schulze's description of Udi grammar: www.lrz-muenchen.de/~wschulze/Uog.html

Kusunda materials: www.people.fas.harvard.edu/~witzel/kusunda.htm

Berliner Klassik Project: http://berliner-klassik.de

Project for the Documentation of the Languages of Mesoamerica: www.albany.edu/anthro/maldp

Dokumentation Bedrohter Sprachen (Documentation of Endangered Languages): www.mpi.nl/DOBES/

Paradisec: http://paradisec.org.au/

Rosetta Project: www.rosettaproject.org

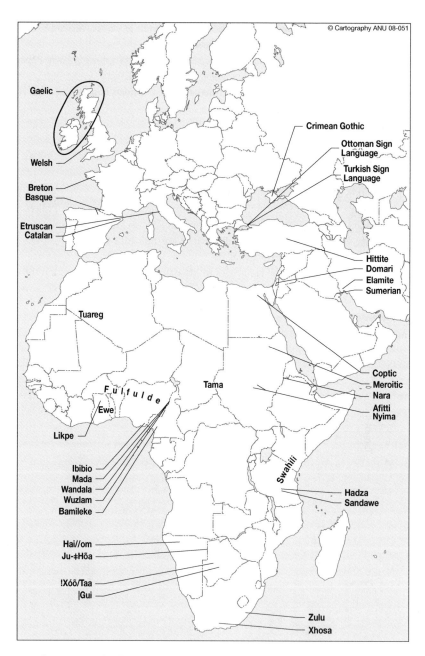

© Cartography ANU 08-051

Gaelic

Crimean Gothic

Ottoman Sign
Language

Turkish Sign
Language

Welsh

Breton
Basque

Etruscan
Catalan

Hittite
Domari
Elamite
Sumerian

Tuareg

F u l f u l d e

Tama

Coptic
Meroitic
Nara
Afitti
Nyima

Ewe

Likpe

Swahili

Ibibio
Mada
Wandala
Wuzlam
Bamileke

Hadza
Sandawe

Hai//om
Ju-‡Hõa

!Xóõ/Taa
|Gui

Zulu
Xhosa

Languages of Europe and Africa: Location Map

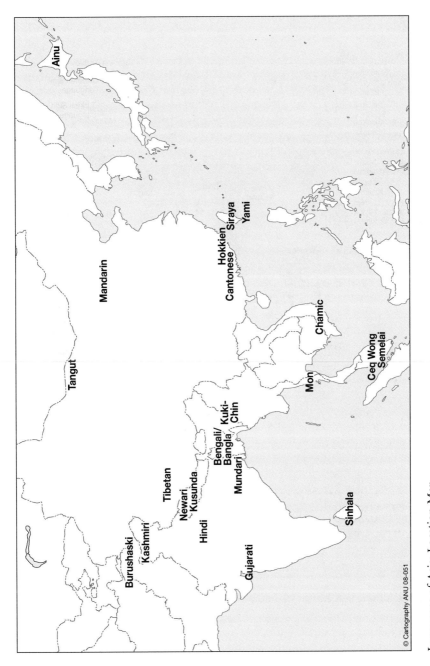

Languages of Asia: Location Map

© Cartography ANU 08-051

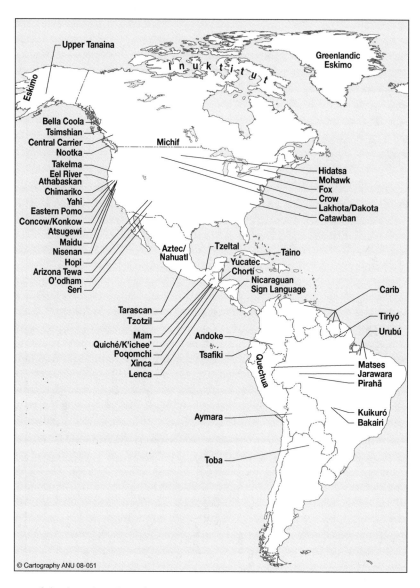

Languages of the Americas: Location Map

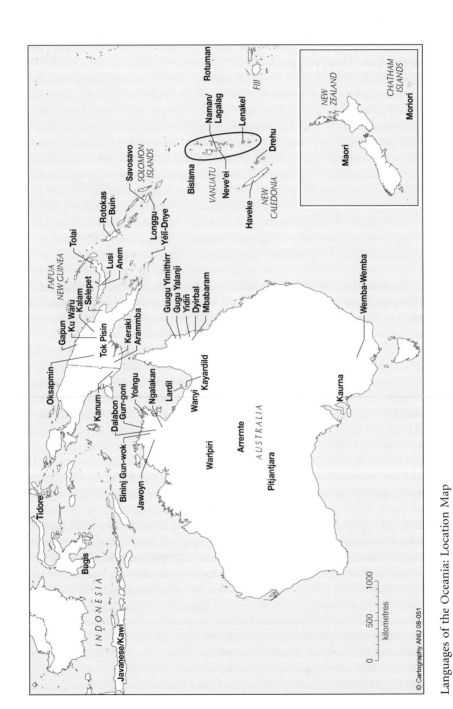

Languages of the Oceania: Location Map

© Cartography ANU 08-051

Index of Languages and Language Families

Note that English is not indexed (except for distinct regional varieties), since it is referred to on nearly every page. Proto-languages (e.g. proto-Uto-Aztecan) are indexed by the family name (e.g. Uto-Aztecan). Page numbers in italics indicate that the language is shown on a map on the relevant page, and n after a page number that it is referred to in the notes.

Index

Page numbers in *italics* indicate an illustration. Where there are two identical numbers and one is italic, there is both textual information and a picture.